Shelley
AND HIS AUDIENCES

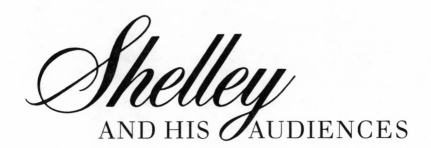

Shelley
AND HIS AUDIENCES

STEPHEN C. BEHRENDT

UNIVERSITY OF NEBRASKA PRESS

LINCOLN AND LONDON

Acknowledgments for the use of previously published material appear on
page x.

Copyright © 1989 by the University of Nebraska Press
All rights reserved
Manufactured in the United States of America

The paper in this book meets the minimum requirements of American
National Standard for Information Sciences—Permanence of Paper for
Printed Library Materials, ANSI Z39.48-1984.

Library of Congress Cataloging-in-Publication Data

Behrendt, Stephen C., 1947–
    Shelley and his audiences / Stephen C. Behrendt.
        p.   cm.
    Bibliography: p.
    Includes index.
    ISBN 0-8032-1208-9 (alk. paper)
        1.. Shelley, Percy Bysshe, 1792–1822—Criticism and interpretation.
    2. Shelley, Percy Bysshe, 1792–1822—Political and social views.
    3. Authors and readers—Great Britain—History—19th century.
    4. Politics and literature—Great Britain—History—19th century.
    5. Reader-response criticism. I. Title.
    PR5442.R36B44   1989
821'.7—dc19   88-31621
                                                                  CIP

For Patricia Flanagan Behrendt

CONTENTS

PREFACE

Especially when writing about an artist like Shelley, whose life and works have been sources of both stimulation and controversy for nearly two centuries, one always reaches the final pages with a keen awareness that the work has not been completed. One can only hope that it has been well begun and fairly pursued. That is my hope here. Shelley scholarship has proven not to be immune to the urge, common among literary enthusiasts, to sentimentalize or to beatify the author under consideration, and many well-intentioned students of Shelley's work object to any suggestion that seems to place the poet in any but the most attractive light, however dim that nonconforming light may be. I have tried to avoid that impulse here and to present Shelley as his words and his actions seem to me to reveal him. At the same time, however, I have become increasingly convinced that the sometimes unstable and always enthusiastic Shelley was one of the most generous and liberal-minded writers and thinkers of his age. I consider it particularly instructive to observe that though Shelley was routinely vilified in his lifetime by reviewers and political ax-grinders, there is virtually no indication that those who actually knew the man felt for him anything but the warmest regard.

I have tried to capture some sense of the human side of Shelley in this study in accordance with my thesis that he was a careful and deliberate stylist who consistently tried to adapt forms, formats, and rhetorical strategies to the variously conceived audiences he addressed. I have focused in particular detail upon Shelley's prose, which has all too often been underestimated, when it has not been either misrepresented or simply ignored. I have considered both Shelley's public prose (his published essays and the prefaces to his poems, as well as draft material for works that remained unpublished during his lifetime) and his private prose (his letters and notes). Although I examine some of Shelley's poetry—especially his most overtly political poems—my primary interest has been his remarkably consistent approach to his audiences and the equally consistent nature of his central themes, his intellectual and political preoccupations, and his portrayals of himself.

I am grateful to the National Endowment for the Humanities and to the American Council of Learned Societies for providing me with a summer stipend and a research fellowship, respectively. Their support came at crucial moments in my work and afforded me the valuable blocks of time for writing that enabled me to complete my manuscript. I am grateful as well to the Research Council of the University of Nebraska–Lincoln for its support of my research; in particular, this backing enabled me to undertake the detailed study of Shelley's manuscripts in the Bodleian Library and the British Library that significantly shaped the argument of this book. I thank also the chancellor and the vice chancellor for academic affairs of the University of Nebraska–Lincoln for the Layman grant that provided me with a reduced teaching load during the final semester of my research and writing.

My thanks go to the staff of the Bodleian Library in Oxford, and to Bruce Barker-Benfield in particular, for their assistance with my work and their prompt and helpful responses to my queries. The Bodleian Library has kindly granted me permission to quote from its Shelley manuscripts. I thank, too, the editors of *Genre* for allowing me to elaborate here upon material from an article I published in that journal in 1981. Finally, I thank Oxford University Press for allowing me to quote liberally from its editions of Shelley's works and letters and for allowing me likewise to draw upon material from my introduction to *Zastrozzi* and *St. Irvyne*, from Oxford's World Classics series.

Among the many colleagues who have been generous with their time and advice, I thank especially Donald H. Reiman, who has read and reread the manuscript with great care and sensitivity, answered queries, offered invaluable advice on matters both general and particular, and been consistently supportive. Within my department, I thank Moira Ferguson and Susan Rosowski, both of whom have generously read chapters and offered good advice, and Frederick M. Link, who in his role as chair has consistently supported my work with advice, funds, and a teaching schedule that greatly facilitated my work on this project.

Finally, and as always, I thank my wife, Patricia Flanagan Behrendt, who has been ever my best audience and most perceptive reader. The unfailing critical insight she brought to her readings of these pages as they evolved, and the invaluable suggestions she offered, have made this a better book. Her loving support has been both a comfort and an inspiration in my work. Though it is perhaps a small return for her large investment, I dedicate this book to her, with gratitude and with love.

ABBREVIATIONS

Works *Shelley: Poetical Works*, ed. Thomas Hutchinson, corrected by G. M. Matthews. Oxford: Oxford University Press, 1971.

I&P *The Complete Works of Percy Bysshe Shelley*, ed. Roger Ingpen and Walter E. Peck. 10 vols. London: Ernest Benn, 1926–28 (the Julian edition).

PP *Shelley's Poetry and Prose*, ed. Donald H. Reiman and Sharon B. Powers. New York: Norton, 1977.

Letters *The Letters of Percy Bysshe Shelley*, ed. Frederick L. Jones. 2 vols. Oxford: Clarendon Press, 1964.

SC *Shelley and His Circle, 1773–1822*, ed. Kenneth Neill Cameron and Donald H. Reiman. 8 vols. Cambridge, Mass.: Harvard University Press, 1961–86.

A Note on Transcriptions of Manuscript Materials

Legible deletions and cancellations are placed in square brackets: [ ]. Deletions or cancellations that occur within these bracketed passages are indicated by slashes: / /. Tentative, suggested readings of obscured or hard-to-decipher words or passages are preceded and followed by question marks: ?word?. The angle brackets that appear in quotations from *Shelley and His Circle, 1773–1822* are reproduced from that book.

You will make your hearer more excited and more
attentive, and full of active participation, if
you keep him alert by words addressed to himself.

LONGINUS, *On the Sublime*

Introduction

SHELLEY AND AUDIENCE

More than any other Romantic poet, more even than Byron, Percy
Bysshe Shelley evokes a remarkable ambivalence among his critics.
We expect Byron to shift his ground frequently; we know from the outset that his masterful irony may mislead us into confusing what he
appears to be saying with what he is actually saying. The case is different with Shelley, whose astonishing literary versatility and earnestness
of tone occasionally distract us from his considerable practical skill at
manipulating particular predetermined audiences. Too often Shelley
has been portrayed as an impulsive and self-indulgent writer who neither cared nor understood very much about his readers. A close reading of his works, however, and especially of his private and public
prose, reveals an author acutely sensitive to the advantages of defining
his audiences carefully and addressing them in an appropriate fashion.
    Animated by a sincere sense of personal honor and professing a
thoroughgoing commitment to the good of others, Shelley cast himself
both privately and publicly in the role of prophet and liberator. He
aspired to be both an active legislator of ethical and spiritual ideals
and a force in the movement for political reform in England. Shelley
set out to influence, to persuade, and to coerce his readers, both by
carefully controlling the linguistic, political, and intellectual contexts
of his writings and by deliberately manipulating the moral and imaginative attitudes and responses of his audiences.
    Recent critical studies by Richard Cronin, William Keach, and

1

others have called attention to Shelley's awareness that the inherent indeterminacy of language impedes authorial efforts to employ it in determinate fashion.[1] Poststructuralist criticism in particular has pointed out how language often conceals and obscures even when it is employed ostensibly to communicate and clarify. We are left with a troubling sense of the fragility and instability of language and with a view of both creative and critical activities as at least potentially destabilizing. Shelley's interest in language and linguistic theory, his particular admiration for David Hume's writings, and his fondness for the skeptical debate as a rhetorical strategy indicate his appreciation of the destabilizing potential of language carefully used. But he must certainly also have been aware of a different phenomenon that occurs frequently in later eighteenth-century literature and art: multistability.

Multistability enables images, words, or other constructs to alternate between, usually, two different schemata or significations. The most familiar multistable image is the two-dimensional picture that alternately discloses an urn and two face-to-face profiles. The spectator's mind shifts back and forth between the images, acknowledging first one, then the other, with the degree of relative separateness of these two acts of cognition increased in proportion to the complexity of the multistable images.[2] The phenomenon abounds in later eighteenth-century visual art, and in English literature it appears most prominently in *Tristram Shandy*. The attraction and delight of the multistable image is that in both concealing and revealing something that is present all the time it conveys multiple messages simultaneously so that the artist or author who employs the device communicates at once on more than one level. The extent to which Shelley's works, especially his prose, attempt to address different audiences or to convey different messages within the same work suggests the relevance of the concept of multistability to his writing.

Shelley's first works were executed in "popular" forms, most notably the Gothic romance and the dream-vision; he subsequently explored a dazzling array of genres, styles, and rhetorical strategies. He was unwilling to devote himself exclusively to the popular style that Mary Shelley and Leigh Hunt often urged upon him if that effort were to come at the expense of greater and more ambitious undertakings. But his deliberate manipulation of genre, style, and language in *The Cenci*, the exoteric political poems of 1819, *Swellfoot the Tyrant*, and *Peter Bell the Third*, among others, indicates his willingness—indeed his enthusiasm—simultaneously to address and capture both a general, "popular" audience and the limited circle of the SUNETOI,[3] the "ideal" readers for whom *Prometheus Unbound* and *Epipsychidion* were intended.

The concept of multistability bears on Shelley's view of himself as prophet as well, for it suggests how the prophet glimpses the future in the shadows it casts upon the present, apprehending what is actually, visibly present though the majority fail to see it. Prophecy is a matter not of "fortune telling" or superstitious divining but of absolute clarity and accuracy of vision. This view of prophecy and the prophet's role has links with the melioristic postmillennialist tradition that regarded the American and French revolutions as indicators of the steady march of progress that integrated Providence with natural law.[4] Common to both millennialist and millenarian thought is the concept of the prophet as interpreter of the immanent significance of signs and events of which the majority are at best only dimly aware.

Shelley's prophets can do little to hasten the millennium's arrival, but they can prepare the way for it by transmitting their vision to the people. The inauguration of the New World requires mass action; the new Eden will have to be founded, not merely found. Hence the missionary zeal that characterizes much of Shelley's prose is no mere self-serving exercise in egotism. He requires from his audience more than mere recognition or even praise, more than the public notice the disappointed visionary of Coleridge's "Kubla Khan" craves: he wants *action*, a public response that will make him proud to be the author. For Shelley, prophecy should elevate and transform not oneself but the collective audience, as *Prometheus Unbound* makes clear, and in this it shares important links with epic art. When the real apocalypse occurs the prophet is so subsumed into the audience—or the audience into the prophet—that apparent distinctions between them become irrelevant. Prophets succeed best when they render themselves unnecessary to their awakened audiences.

Shelley also engages his audiences by exploring parallels between himself, his literary predecessors and contemporaries and, most important, martyred prophetic forebears such as Socrates and especially Jesus Christ. One of the most powerful aspects of the Western Christian religious experience is the conviction that one is "imitating" Christ. The extent to which Shelley invoked the paradigm of Christ's mortal experience and its implications for him as a radical moral, social, and political prophet is directly proportional to the extent to which he saw himself (or tried to have others see him) retracing Christ's steps. Shelley's deliberate exploitation of these parallels develops a complex analog to Christ's experience in the Wilderness as Milton presents it in *Paradise Regained*: an exercise in individuation and the attaining of a sustaining self-knowledge, an expansion of consciousness, and a "growing into" a role one comes at last to believe has been prepared for one.[5]

Shelley was from the first a performer, determined both to entertain and to instruct his audiences. His scheme to enlist and "liberate" his youngest sister Hellen in December 1811 after his father had effectively disowned him following his expulsion from Oxford prefigures later experiences, from his liberation (by elopement and marriage) of Harriet Westbrook in 1811 to his participation in the *Liberal* some ten years later. Shelley was also a recruiter, striving to assemble from a variety of audiences a fiercely loyal army of disciples who would become the vanguard of the new order of peace, pacifism, and spiritual and moral brotherhood under his careful tutelage.

Shelley was acutely conscious of the delicate relationship between artist and audience. Walter J. Ong has written that the writer's audience is always a fiction.[6] The corollary is that the writer who creates that fictional audience also becomes something of a fiction as well, as do the transactions the author envisions taking place between him or herself and the imagined audience. According to Gerald Prince, any work of fiction (which I shall broaden here to include any written work) has three varieties of reader: (1) the *actual* reader, a real person who holds and reads the text; (2) the *virtual* reader, upon whom the author deliberately "bestows certain qualities, faculties, and inclinations according to his opinion of men in general (or in particular) and according to the obligations he feels should be respected"; and (3) the *ideal* reader, who "would understand perfectly and would approve entirely the least of his words, the most subtle of his intentions."[7] This latter reader suggests "the more select classes of poetical readers" Shelley addresses in *Prometheus Unbound,* and it is instructive to recall that Shelley professed to believe that few readers would fully appreciate that work. In an ideal world, all "actual" readers would also be "ideal" readers. But Shelley was not living in an ideal world, and he knew it.

Shelley stands at an important transitional point in the history of English author-audience relations, which changed drastically late in the eighteenth century with the decline of the patronage system and the rise of the largely self-supporting author addressing a rapidly expanding and diversifying reading public served by an equally rapidly diversifying print media. In this more modern arrangement, profound social, cultural, and intellectual differences often separate writers and readers. Liberal English authors writing between 1817 and 1822—the most productive years of Shelley's career—found increasingly that their commitment to the public cause was vitiated by the seeming dissolution of any clearly definable homogeneous reading public into a daunting multiplicity of potential publics.[8] Since literary activity in these circumstances tended to become at once "both impersonal and privatized,"[9] these writers frequently were left without any clear view of who their actual readers might be and with a disheartening sense of the scarcity of ideal readers. They were left, in other words, with audiences of virtual readers whom they needed in large measure to invent.

Most of Shelley's prose, and much of his poetry, addresses such virtual audiences, which Shelley takes care to shape in particular ways, dictating the terms upon which their relationship will exist. Ong's claim that author and reader form a compact in which the reader is required to play the role assigned by the author comes remarkably close to Shelley's view. Shelley attempts to regulate both the terms and the manner of discourse, recognizing that controlling the ground rules affords him the greatest power and flexibility while limiting his audiences' options for any but positive, cooperative responses. He requires that his readers be willing to participate actively in an intellectual dialogue of which he will supply both the principal ingredients and the rhetorical and intellectual framework. The dialogic form of this intellectual program is explicitly represented in Plato's dialogues, which reveal, as Jerome McGann has observed, that "truth must be understood in relation to one's social investments" and that real knowledge is a function of "a personal and a social interchange" that transpires within an actual community.[10]

Although Shelley became increasingly interested in ambiguity and multistability as facets of the imaginative use of language, his prose reflects his practical belief in language's potential for effecting tangible action in the public sphere. He held a classical conception of language and audience, envisioning the power of language on the world. This view differs considerably from that held by most poststructuralist critics and even some reader-response critics, who regard language less as an active force than as a series of signs to be deciphered.[11] The classical tradition held that the enormous influence of language on human behavior required the rhetorician to master its techniques and exercise ethical control over them. Shelley appreciated this view, but it would be grossly simplistic to assume that his complex writings can be reduced to a mere formulaic matrix of intention and device.

We cannot fully "know" either any author's exact intentions or the precise way her or his text functioned in delivering the formal articulation of those intentions *to an actual audience of readers*. Any act of formal written communication involves innumerable variables, some of which the author controls (or seeks to control), some of which are controlled (or determined) by the audience, and still others which are beyond the direct control of author or audience and impose conditions of their own on the transaction between author and audience. These variables influence the text's composition, its presentation in a physical format, the way it is read and internalized in its own time, and the way it is transformed, transmuted, and—not infrequently—misread or misrepresented by subsequent audiences who bring to it their own experiential frameworks, many of which are irrelevant to the work. Since any text is necessarily susceptible to external factors that affect its reception, active readers such as Shelley desires ought ideally to bring to their reading not just a literal understanding of the determinate meanings of the words but also "a whole body of cultural assumptions, practical knowledge, awareness of literary conventions, [and] readiness to think and feel."[12] This personal and societal "ideological overcoding" preconditions the innately dynamic acts of reading and interpreting. Like Wolfgang Iser, who argues that the literary text involves its readers by forcing them simultaneously to create and to puncture, modify, or reformulate illusions about "meaning," Umberto Eco regards every reader's experience of a text as both an interpretation and a performance of that text.[13] But reading with particular expectations which we attempt to make the text bear out is akin to placing blinders both on our cart-horse and on ourselves as well. We may get where we are going and we may see the road directly before us as we go, but we will miss so much of the surroundings that we will have no sense of the countryside through which we have traveled or of the geographical or other conditions that determined the size, shape, and general direction of that road.

The literary and cultural "countryside" through which Shelley's works pass is highly complex. The volatile nature of the Regency period in which most of Shelley's works were composed would have impressed on any public artist the need for judiciousness in public utterances. *Judicious* is a word one is seldom tempted to apply to Shelley, yet it is not inappropriate. I hope to demonstrate that a great deal of what has been judged rash and impulsive in Shelley's public performances was in fact a result of deliberate calculation (and in some cases miscalculation). Shelley consistently attempted to reconcile form and content with ideological intent based on his conception of the audience he was addressing, a point whose relevance to the letters is noted by Donald H. Reiman (*SC*, V, 436).

Shelley's real and assumed relation to his audiences has only recently begun to receive the attention it requires. It is almost a commonplace of Shelley scholarship to point out the extent to which his poetic evolved, a corpus of verse continually discovering, exploring, and abandoning new forms in which to embody the poet's visions. Shelley does not "use up" particular poetic forms as Milton does, stretching them to their aesthetic and generic limits. Rather, his work is characterized by a continual movement from one form to another in an attempt to discover the particular advantages and disadvantages of each. If Shelley is perpetually in search of audiences, he is also in search of vehicles and voices. The increasing attraction to classicism that led him to Italy (and to his notes on sculpture), for instance, is reflected with increasing clarity in Shelley's later poems, both in their forms and in the subjects and genres he chose. However we regard the satiric intent of *Swellfoot the Tyrant*, for instance, we need to consider the genre of the piece and its relation to classical comedy. We should entertain similar considerations about *Epipsychidion*, *Adonais*, and *Hellas*.

The prose prefaces to Shelley's poems are occasionally discussed briefly along with the poems they accompany, and more sustained prose performances like *A Defence of Poetry* receive frequent comment. But less frequently discussed prose essays, particularly the published and/or virtually complete formal essays, whose audiences are reasonably clear, display Shelley's considerable skill at audience manipulation.

Any study of an author's search for an audience must also consider that author's search for an appropriate language and rhetoric. The diversity among Shelley's intended audiences helps to explain the corresponding diversity among the styles, structures, and "voices" of his works in prose and poetry. But we must remember that Shelley died a young man. To speak of his "later" writing is to employ a misleading comparative and to suggest a terminus in a career characterized at all points by restlessness and relentless forward motion. The line Edward Trelawny attributed to Shelley years later is relevant, I believe, to Shelley's development as a writer: "I always go on until I am stopped, and I never am stopped." [14] Despite the presence in the Shelley canon of acknowledged masterpieces, Shelley's work was still evolving at the time of his death.

I shall argue that as a skilled rhetorician Shelley routinely and deliberately attempted to manipulate his audiences into positions favorable to him and his designs. I shall trace the main lines of Shelley's apparent conceptions of author-audience relations in the abstract and, more important, in the specific terms in which he assumed they concerned himself as poet and essayist, prophet and patriot. And I shall consider the consequences of those conceptions and assumptions for both the form and the content of his works and for his cultivation of characteristic rhetorical and thematic features like the skeptical debate, the *imitatio Christi*, the repudiation of vengeance, the appeal for the reader's charity, and the personal and patriotic imperative that drives socially and politically committed prophecy.

Because Shelley's private writings reflect many of the postures and preoccupations of the public works, often more candidly, I shall begin by examining the unfavorable record of his treatment of Harriet Shelley in 1814, when he abandoned her and eloped to France with Mary Wollstonecraft Godwin. Most critics and biographers understandably feel that Shelley treated his wife shabbily in this affair. But their generally harsh judgments tend to discount the young ages of the principal actors in this tragic drama, the economic and emotional pressures that had come to plague their unfortunate marriage, and Shelley's own terrible recognition—as he subsequently related it to Thomas Medwin and others—of the insufficiency of his original motive for marrying Harriet Westbrook in the first place. Too, their censure often ignores the financial settlements Shelley made in his wife's favor and the continuing sincere concern for her well-being evidenced in his subsequent words and actions. Typically, they also miss the significance of Shelley's attempt to strip away the emotional considerations from this human dilemma so that the ethical principles at its core might be examined dispassionately on intellectual grounds. Shelley's behavior, especially as his own words reveal it, sheds important and instructive light on the way he draws distinctions, chooses courses of action, and manipulates his audiences throughout his career in matters of broader and more public significance.

In his awkward and distressed letter to his wife of 14 July 1814, Shelley tries to locate the discussion within the context of principle:

> I repeat (& believe me, for I am sincere) that my attachment to you is unimpaired: I conceive that it has acquired even a deeper & more lasting character, that is now less exposed than ever to the fluctuations of phantasy or caprice. Our connection was not one of passion & impulse. Friendship was its basis, & on this basis it has enlarged & strengthened. It is no reproach to me that you never filled my heart with an all-sufficing passion—perhaps, you are even yourself a stranger to these impulses, which one day may be awakened by some nobler & worthier than me, and may you find a lover as passionate and faithful, as I shall ever be a friend affectionate & sincere! (*Letters*, I, 389–90)

Shelley's rationalizations reveal his obsessive drive to explain his actions, particularly to one he claims to hold in strong regard. Shelley may have married Harriet for the wrong reasons: enthusiasm at having apparently molded his most perfect disciple to date, elation at liberating his young bride from a repressive father's establishment, perhaps simply impulsive behavior. They had, however, attempted to build a relationship, and it is an injustice to both to claim that Bysshe merely tired of Harriet and so dropped her. In his letter Shelley invents a virtual reader in the person of his wife and then endeavors both to alter and to control the terms of their discourse, inventing also a version of himself whose principled motivation excuses him from accusations of callousness, although what he represents as principled behavior may justifiably be called self-deception.

Shelley's letter of 4 October 1814 to Thomas Jefferson Hogg clarifies the situation. Having for more than two years devoted himself "to the single purpose of cultivating Harriet," he had discovered upon a two-month separation from her in the spring of 1814 that his "rash & heartless union with Harriet" had been a "calamity": "I felt as if a dead & living body had been linked together in loathsome & horrible communion. It was no longer possible to practise self deception: I believed that one revolting duty yet remained, to continue to deceive my wife" (*Letters*, I, 402). Shelley fails to mention that he had met and fallen in love with Mary Godwin. Nevertheless, the conflicting impulses toward emotional honesty and concern for another's feelings expressed in this letter appear genuine, despite Shelley's exaggerations to Hogg, whose approval he is soliciting. But words like *heartless, duty,* and *deceive* indicate how Shelley had unilaterally reconceptualized the relationship. Ironically, eight years later Shelley employed strikingly similar language in voicing to John Gisborne a similar concern about his and Mary's estrangement: "I only feel the want of those who can feel, and understand me. Whether from proximity and the continuity of domestic intercourse, Mary does not. The necessity of concealing from her thoughts that would pain her, necessitates this, perhaps" (*Letters*, II, 435; 18 June 1822). Here is only one instance of the remarkable and generally overlooked continuity that characterizes both the sentiments of the letters Shelley wrote throughout his life and the terminology and rhetorical strategies through which he communicated them to his various correspondents.

In his letter to his wife Shelley moves from a declaration of continued attachment, underscored by the parenthetical declaration of sincerity, into an intellectual definition of love largely platonic in character. This definition of his current feeling for his wife leads naturally to a definition of what their relationship *was not*. It "was not one of passion & impulse," a curious declaration in light of the circumstances of their marriage. If not "passion & impulse," then what? Friendship, Shelley declares. It is a word for a deep and enduring relationship that Shelley does not normally use lightly.

For example, Shelley had suggested that his college *friend* Hogg should join the Shelleys in what would have been both an intellectual and a sexual triangle. This suggestion—previewed in 1810 in Shelley's plans for himself, his sister Elizabeth, and Hogg and subsequently resuscitated with Mary Shelley—implies a most unconventional notion of friendship: a communal arrangement extending not merely to the material possessions but to the bodies and minds of the participants. Of course, the conception was not without foundation in idealized classical notions of friendships that are not gender-specific. As happened frequently when Shelley's ideals collided with their practical applications, the scheme yielded very mixed results. Although he may have advocated this plan to his wife and Hogg early in his first marriage, when it appeared to have borne fruit (figuratively) at the end of

October 1811 Shelley was too outraged to be pleased. Upon learning that his friend had proven false—that he had attempted behind Shelley's back and apparently against Harriet Shelley's wishes to seduce her—he wrote bitterly to Hogg: "You have been led either by false reasoning, or as I conjecture more probable, *real* feeling, into a great & terrible mistake; . . . to me it appears in all it's [sic] features disgusting & horrid—. Do not suppose that I mean by thus fairly stating what I think of the late unexpected disclosure [that Hogg had been making advances to Harriet against her will] to assume on the strength of my apparent purity the character of a dictator, a lecturer..far otherwise I expect to derive more instruction than I may be adequate to give" (*SC*, III, 35; 6 November 1811). This letter that attempts to be both expansive and abrupt contains contradictory currents like those in Shelley's earlier letter to his wife.

Again Shelley presumes to correct what he represents as his correspondent's misunderstanding, which he suggests lowers the other—at least temporarily—in his regard. Then comes the magnanimous gesture, couched in an assertion of friendship: "To discuss is the privilegde [sic] of a friend, and a friend I am yet willing nay, *eager*, to be to you; tho you have forgotten for once that you had promised to be mine" (*SC*, III, 35). The shrill tone of this letter hints at the nature of his relationship with Hogg. Even Hogg's condescending Tory attitude and his tendency to suppress, alter, and falsely interpret evidence to protect himself and sentimentalize his dead friend did not prevent him from indicating in his memoir of Shelley the depth of their friendship from the first days of their acquaintance.[15] Hogg's rash decision to participate in Shelley's expulsion from Oxford stood as an initial, classical pledge of fidelity that could not have failed to impress Shelley; indeed the determination with which the two young men continued their friendship in open defiance of their fathers' strictures cemented their relationship as oppressed revolutionaries, though Hogg's subsequent recantation in the purely practical interest of becoming a lawyer contrasts with the direction Shelley took.

Shelley's letter to Hogg is an audacious and sophisticated attempt to manipulate his reader under the guise of calm, dispassionate argument. Though he is both physically and rhetorically at the center of the matter, Shelley attempts to eschew the role of wounded husband, casting himself—significantly—as the betrayed friend and counselor. Like that to Harriet Shelley in 1814, this letter assumes an exalted moral and ethical tone which it purports to reject: in citing "my apparent purity" but saying he will make no attempt to take advantage of it, Shelley does just that, bringing the notion into the discussion where it is not easily gotten rid of. Shelley offers to forgive, though in neither case is there any suggestion that he intends to forget. Rather, he will forgive while remembering, thus reinforcing his calculated posture of moral superiority.

But the most important connection between these two letters involves Shelley's use of the terms *friend* and *friendship*. In the full blush of his enthusiasm for Elizabeth Hitchener in 1811 he promotes her into his sacred company of disciples, dubbing her "my dear friend" (*Letters*, I, 153; 19 October 1811) and "Sister of my soul" (*Letters*, I, 152; 16 October 1811). Shelley closes the latter "With I hope your *eternal* love your Percy Shelley—" (*Letters*, I, 152). This *eternal* love, which Shelley's underscoring distinguishes from that other, temporal connection of "passion & impulse"—physical, sexual love—is also invoked when Shelley signs himself to Hogg, in May 1811, as "Yr. eternal friend" (*SC*, II, 771; 8 May 1811). During this period Shelley more frequently signed his letters to Hogg with some variation on "affectionate."

The *eternal* designation, particularly when it is linked with "friend," occurs most often in letters in which Shelley wishes his reader to share in the heightened intellectual passion that has resulted from writing about especially exciting or stressful topics. One naturally responds differently to a letter signed "your eternal friend" than to one subscribed "yours truly" or simply "good-bye." Like Coleridge, whose closings often function in the same way, Shelley deliberately employed the manipulative power of such phrases. When he signs himself to Hogg as "Yours most affectionately most unalterably" (*Letters*, I, 176; ca. 12 November 1811), "Ever your friend" (*SC*, III, 48; 13 November 1811), and "Your real true sincere frnd [sic]" (*SC*, III, 58; 17–18 November 1811) in letters written shortly after his bitter letter of 6 November, the censure implied in the brusque subscription to that letter, which reads simply and with disarming imperfection, "Your's" (*SC*, III, 36), becomes clear. The manipulative force of invocations of eternality figured in Shelley's correspondence throughout his life. His subscriptions in letters written in 1822 to close friends Edward and Jane Williams, Horace Smith, John Gisborne, and Claire Clairmont, though unquestionably formulaic, typically include some variation on "ever": "Yours ever affectionately," "Yours affectionately and ever," "Ever most faithfully yours" (*Letters*, II, 384, 405, 410). To others, such as Byron and Trelawny, he heightened the effect by adding an imperative: "Believe me, my dear Lord B.[,] Your's [sic] very faithfully" (*Letters*, II, 417).

That the rupture with Hogg was painful for Shelley is further indicated by other rhetorical phenomena. On 12 November, Shelley partially reinstates his fallen angel, hinting that Hogg may have seen the error of his ways and repented. Yet Shelley is unwilling to create a situation in which "you will again be tempted to what you now regard with horror" (*Letters*, I, 175), perhaps because he fears more for himself than for Hogg. A wounded pride heals more slowly than a wounded body. So Shelley forbade Hogg their society in a letter calculated to increase Hogg's remorse by making him feel keenly the pain his treachery had inflicted upon his friends:

> Certainly no desire for Harriets happiness or that of any other human being excepting *yourself* has been the cause of all our present misery. . . . Having committed one mistake will you rush into others more dismayingly terrible, rather than rationally endeavor to obviate the evil consequences of the past? Will you so?—Then are you *not* him whom I love, whom I deem not only retrievable—but capable of exciting the emulation of millions—. . . Oh how I have loved you. I was even ashamed to tell you how! & now to leave you *forever* . . . . . . no not forever . . Night comes . . . Death comes . . Cold, calm death almost I would it were tomorrow there is another life . . . . . are you not to be the first there. . . . Assuredly, dearest dearest friend reason wi⟨th⟩ me . . I am like a child in weakness..your letters came directly after dinner. how could any one read them unmoved . . . How cd. I forbear wishing that Death wd. yawn. Adieu. follow us not . . Dare to be good. Dare to be virtuous . . Seize once more what once thou didst relinquish never, never again to resign it. (*SC*, III, 41–42; 7–8 November 1811)

In the initial anguish of separation, his emotions perhaps colored by the homoerotic aspects of their relationship,[16] Shelley frames his reading of Hogg's betrayal as an irreversible act in the mortal world in language that might be drawn from his own Gothic romances. The histrionics, the declarations of love side by side with death-wishes, and the incongruous pedestrian details that interrupt the violently passionate flow of thought all suggest a dangerous emotional imbalance. Shelley's verbal self-flagellation is only partly self-indulgence, however: the melodramatic demonstration of his own misery is calculated ultimately to maintain his control over the situation and to spur Hogg's repentance and rehabilitation.

Hogg, of course, was not merely a passive reader willing to do as he was told. Nor does Shelley conceive of any of his audiences in such terms, for to do so would be to deprive them of the opportunities to think, to judge, to choose courses of action, and thereby to improve themselves. But since the role the author assigns to the reader seldom coincides with that reader's actual role or status in real life,[17] Shelley routinely employs rhetorical and intellectual ploys designed to persuade or coerce his readers to accept the former almost in defiance of the reality of the latter. One of his favorite strategies, both in his letters and in his formal public prose, is to set up a rhetorical context of genteel civility—of polite and proper decorum—that places the reader in danger of appearing uncivil, ungracious, and rude if she or he fails to respond to Shelley's polite and charitable tone by also adopting it.

Shelley's strategy with Hogg appears largely to have succeeded, for Hogg was eventually readmitted to the tight circle and a reconciliation effected. In the 10 November letter, however, Shelley muses on leaving Hogg "forever" and qualifies that finality only by invoking the vagueness of "another life." Particularly in light of the death-wishes with which the letter's conclusion fairly bristles, Shelley's hints make particularly ominous the only slightly veiled invitation to Hogg to join him in a suicide pact as a renewed pledge of eternal fidelity: only through his own death could Hogg "be the first there." Shelley plays a dangerous game here with the Narcissus theme. Had Hogg taken this letter at its apparent face value and responded to Shelley's apparent despondency by taking his own life, would Shelley have joined him? Of course not: even as he laments it, he reinforces the finality of physical separation: "To think of our again meeting were *impossible*" (*SC*, III, 67; 9–10 December 1811). The emotional displays Shelley stages in his letters to Hogg during this period reflect, I believe, both his insight into Hogg's impressionable personality and his confidence in his own ability to say exactly what is required to produce the desired response.

With a clearer sense of Shelley's rhetorical maneuvering, let us return to the 1814 letter to Harriet Shelley, which also contains the suggestion of self-destruction. Thanking her for her charitable understanding of Shelley's situation vis-à-vis Mary Godwin, he wrote, "My spirit turned to you for consolation & it found it. . . . This is perhaps the greatest among the many blessings which I have received, & still am destined to receive at your hands. I loathed the very light of day, & looked upon my own being with deep & unutterable abhorrence. I lived Mary too consented to survive. I lived in the hope of consolation and happiness from you & I have not been deceived" (*Letters*, I, 389; 14 July 1814). From this letter one might almost be uncertain who had left whom. Shelley is again manipulative: he invokes pity for the writer's suffering, making it appear practically unmerited; mythologizes the situation by reference to martyrdom; and represents the recipient's situation as one from which she may learn a lesson in charity and humanity—perhaps even humility. Finally, he suggests that the writer has learned from the experience and therefore *thanks* the recipient—either directly or indirectly—for providing him with that opportunity.

Shelley offered a revealing early working definition of *friendship* in a letter to his "dearest friend" Elizabeth Hitchener detailing Hogg's misconduct. After chastising Hogg for seizing "this passion of animal love," Shelley describes the noble alternative: "How much worthier of a rational being is *friendship* which tho it wants none of the impassionateness which some have characterized as the inseperable [sic] of the other, yet retains judgement, which is not blind tho it may chance to see something like perfections in its object, which retains it's [sic] sensibility but whose sensibility is celestial & intellectual unallied to the groveling passions of the Earth" (*Letters*, I, 208; 15 December 1811). This abstract, idealistic definition helps to clarify Shelley's letter to his wife, for it describes the mutually fulfilling marriage of the minds he means when he writes that "friendship was its basis." Significantly, that letter is addressed to "My dearest friend," a superlative salutation that is quickly replaced by cold impersonality in the letters that follow. The next extant letter, dated 13 August, begins "My dearest Harriet," the appellation of *friend* apparently having become inappropriate (*Letters*, I, 391). With the letter of 14 September the demotion proceeds as Shelley's wife is merely "My dear Harriet" in this and the letter of two days later (*Letters*, I, 394–95). The next letter begins ominously: "You abruptly closed all communication with me" (*Letters*, I, 396). This letter and those that follow in the next month open without the courtesy of a salutation.

When, like Hogg in 1811–12, his wife gave signs of behaving more as Shelley desired, of playing the role he had assigned her, Shelley began to demonstrate positive reinforcement. Mary Shelley's journal notes that on 11 October "a good-humoured letter from Harriet" arrived. Is it coincidence that Shelley tentatively reinstated his wife, albeit at reduced rank, beginning a letter on the next day with "My dear Harriet" (*Letters*, I, 406; 12 October 1814)? I think not. First impressions are powerful. A letter that begins abruptly *in medias res*, without a pro forma salutation, is both unsettling and belittling, and if Harriet had been startled by the harsh abruptness of Shelley's letters of late September, his reversion to "My dear Harriet," which he repeats in his next letter (25 October), must have been of some comfort, however small.

I dreamed that Milton's spirit rose, and took
  From life's green tree his Uranian lute;
And from his touch sweet thunder flowed, and shook
All human things built in contempt of man—
And sanguine thrones and impious altars quaked,
Prisons and citadels.

SHELLEY, "Milton's Spirit"

Chapter One

SHELLEY AS PUBLIC WRITER

The Revolt of Islam and the Hermit of Marlow Pamphlets

I will begin this study in the middle of Shelley's career by considering his preface to *The Revolt of Islam*.[1] *The Revolt* comes after Shelley's first poetic efforts had failed to bring him fame, fortune, or even acceptance, but before the eventual rupture with England that is frequently (and mistakenly, I believe) regarded as a pessimistic, even cynical dismissal of the causes of the very people he had envisioned himself leading into a millennial age of benevolence and love. It dates from the period of his Hermit of Marlow pamphlets, the prose essays he designed likewise to perform particular functions in his scheme for England's liberation. The preface illustrates the nature of Shelley's Wordsworthianism near the end of its ascendancy in his work and thought. Unlike the sprawling and frequently inartistic poem, the carefully structured preface deftly manipulates its readers' sensibilities through the author's assured handling of allusion, implication, logic, and persuasion.

In the fullest consideration to date of Shelley and his audiences, Michael Scrivener notes the strong echoes of both Wordsworth and Rousseau in preface and poem alike and stresses Shelley's strategy—learned, undoubtedly, from the Preface to *Lyrical Ballads*—of disfranchising the critics from the compact between artist and audience.[2] By late 1817 Shelley had already incurred the censure of a surfeit of critics—reviewers, Oxford authorities, fathers and father figures, and a grieving first wife. Not surprisingly he wished to take his case directly to his virtual readers who, presumably, would have no critical axes to grind and would be unprejudiced regarding his reputation. He claims to have attempted in his poem a telepathic communication with these readers that aims less at passing ideas to the logical mind than at generating emotions in the feeling heart, an approach whose resemblance to that of sentimentalism is not surprising in an author who began by writing Gothic novels.

But what is most interesting in this extraordinarily long preface is the sophistication with which Shelley manipulates his reader into particular intellectual positions in relation to which he then defines himself. Shelley's self-protective preface enables him to seem to assume responsibility for the poem's weaknesses and failures while in fact shifting that burden onto the shoulders of others.

> The Poem which I now present to the world is an attempt from which I scarcely dare to expect success, and in which a writer of established fame might fail without disgrace. It is an experiment on the temper of the public mind, as to how far a thirst for a happier condition of moral and political society survives, among the enlightened and refined, the tempests which have shaken the age in which we live. I have sought to enlist the harmony of metrical language, the ethereal combinations of the fancy, the rapid and subtle transitions of human passion, all those elements which essentially compose a Poem, in the cause of a liberal and comprehensive morality; and in the view of kindling within the bosoms of my readers a virtuous enthusiasm for those doctrines of liberty and justice, that faith and hope in something good, which neither violence nor misrepresentation nor prejudice can ever totally extinguish among mankind. (*Works*, 32)

Shelley's very first sentence raises the umbrella of his defense: by professing virtually no expectation of success he ensures that any praise, however slight, will provide greater credit than he had anticipated. Moreover, Shelley's claim that even an established writer might fail "without disgrace" in such an attempt lends him hypothetical parity with that elite. That Shelley's phrase is "a writer"—not "writers"— of established fame indicates by use of the singular that he probably meant Byron, not only for the logical public reason of Byron's great fame but for the more private reason that Shelley had for at least a year been trying to get Byron to attempt an epic on the French Revolution. Since Shelley's and Byron's works frequently function as opposing sides in a public skeptical debate conducted in the forum of the press, Shelley's public suggestion is probably intended to press Byron to take up the challenge. Although Shelley's enthusiasm for setting

Byron to the task of writing "an epic of hope" on the French Revolution may have been tempered by anxiety that Byron would actually do so "and thereby condemn *Laon and Cythna* to obscurity,"[3] Shelley had little cause for concern, for in the summer of 1817 Byron was busy publishing *Manfred* and working on *Childe Harold* IV. Shelley's deliberate flattery of Byron in this period, however, is analogous to manipulations that he attempted with other friends and correspondents whose responses and activities he wished to supervise. The self-sacrificing posture Shelley assumes in the preface is entirely consistent with those he strikes in the letters to Hogg and Harriet Shelley: making his own "humble" effort to assist humanity in its liberation, Shelley stands prepared to defer to the superior efforts of "our greatest contemporary Poets."

Shelley's second sentence places the burden for the poem's success or failure squarely upon the reader. In calling his poem "an experiment," as Wordsworth had called the *Lyrical Ballads*, Shelley implies that his poem is entitled to a more generous, charitable reading than might be accorded a more polished poem executed in a more conventional fashion. But Shelley's caveat also insinuates that hostility to the poem would be synonymous with hostility to its intellectual content and therefore to humanity generally. Those who will savage the poem, Shelley implies, are those in whom "no thirst for a happier condition of moral and political society survives." Shelley thus renders his critics impotent by creating a rhetorical situation in which any act of condemnation on their part is defined in advance as an act of self-condemnation as well.

In the Advertisement to the *Lyrical Ballads*, Wordsworth had written

> It is desirable that . . . readers, for their own sakes, should not suffer the solitary word Poetry, a word of very disputed meaning, to stand in the way of their gratification; but that, while they are perusing this book, they should ask themselves if it contains a natural delineation of human passions, human characters, and human incidents; and if the answer be favourable to the author's wishes, that they should consent to be pleased in spite of that most dreadful enemy to our pleasures, our own pre-established codes of decision.[4]

The first sentence of Shelley's second paragraph reveals how similar to Wordsworth's are his motives: "For this purpose I have chosen a story of human passion in its most universal character, diversified with moving and romantic adventures, and appealing, in contempt of all artificial opinions or institutions, to the common sympathies of the human breast" (*Works*, 32). Like Wordsworth, Shelley invites his readers to accept him as an equal desiring to communicate an interesting story without critical or political interference. The appeal to "human passion" and to "the human breast," with its deliberate echoes of the Advertisement, proceeds from the tenets of sentimentalism, lending emotion ("passion") precedence over strict rationality even as it recalls the democratizing impulse of Wordsworth's "one human Heart." Moreover, Shelley's leveling appeal for a universal readership—indeed a classless one—rests on a notion of universal equality that he tends to idealize even when it is clear to him that such absolute equality is neither practical nor feasible.

Invoking the precedent of *Lyrical Ballads* was deliberate, of course. Shelley would have been aware that *Lyrical Ballads* had initially met with an unenthusiastic reception, though by 1817 its importance was recognized. Thus if Shelley appears initially defensive, it may be because he is already counting on a similar long-term vindication. Wordsworth's attack on the Augustan poets and his advocacy of the ordinary in his poems, as stated in the Advertisement and subsequently elaborated in his Preface, was originally regarded by some as a lame excuse for questionable poetic talent. But in the radical subject matter and approach of most of his poems Wordsworth had enfranchised the very figures the authorities of the revolutionary age regarded with mingled contempt and horror. These were the people the elite wanted kept *out* of art, partly from fear that their presence might encourage the few literate members of the lower classes to stimulate a desire for literacy among their peers. Their attitude reflected the fear of mass incursions upon one of the few real bastions of the elite: literacy itself. Many of the reading members of the upper classes believed that extending literacy to the "lower ranks" "would breed all sorts of disorder and debauchery."[5] An audience that could read the *Lyrical Ballads* might (and did) read Thomas Paine's *Rights of Man* or *Age of Reason* and other "seditious" (that is, radical) material, to the detriment of the elite and the advantage of the social levelers.

Finally, the opening of Shelley's preface announces one of his favorite objectives: uniting the characteristics of the sublime idiom ("the harmony of metrical language, the ethereal combinations of the fancy, the rapid and subtle transitions of human passion") with a decidedly practical, temporal purpose. He cites as his primary object "the cause of a liberal and comprehensive morality." That this is no mere abstract philosophical poem, however, is made clear not only by Shelley's emphasis on the universality of human emotion but also, and more importantly, by his second expressed object: the "kindling within the bosoms of my readers a virtuous enthusiasm" for liberty and justice. Shelley's poem aims at a raising of consciousness among its readers intended to lead from private contemplation to direct public action.

Shelley's claim that innate impulses toward liberty and justice are in-eradicable even by the machinery of the greatest oppression reflects the poet's belief in humanity's natural nobility. Like Rousseau and William Blake before him, Shelley believed that humanity had fallen victim to its own "mind-forged manacles," its essential dignity becoming both concealed and crippled by a self-generated and self-perpetuating institutional corruption. Shelley shared with Blake an intellectual and political quest for the dismantling—the uncovering—of the natural man hidden within the repressive robes of human institutions.

Shelley's meliorism was significantly colored by a belief that humanity's task was less to put on new moral, political, and intellectual clothing than to remove the old and to go naked, a position frequently reflected in his metaphors of clothing and nakedness. And yet, as a writer unwilling to disclose his own subversive intentions too explicitly, Shelley occasionally assumed a verbal disguise: "I have simply clothed my thoughts in what appeared to me the most obvious and appropriate language" (*Works*, 34). As is already apparent, though, the appropriate and effective language is *not* so immediately obvious, nor the composing process so simple, as Shelley would have us believe. Shelley aims to disarm by assuming an apparently unpretentious manner, knowing that even radical reformers must make small concessions for the sake of large gains, clothing themselves physically and semantically until the nakedness they advocate is regarded not as deviant but natural.

In a more strictly political context Shelley writes:

> The French Revolution may be considered as one of those manifestations of a general state of feeling among civilised mankind produced by a defect of correspondence between the knowledge existing in society and the improvement or gradual abolition of political institutions. . . . If the Revolution had been in every respect prosperous, then misrule and superstition would lose half their claims to our abhorrence, as fetters which the captive can unlock with the slightest motion of his fingers, and which do not eat with poisonous rust into the soul. (*Works*, 33)

"Misrule and superstition" are broadly synonymous with "political institutions," which mantle the natural individual and are epitomized here in the fetters that suffering humanity might presumably remove with ease if the Revolution could be internalized and perfected. That the rust is poisonous indicates that, as in the case of the crippled Oedipus or Byron's prisoner of Chillon, the acquired debilities outlast the fetters: even breaking its present chains may not fully return humanity to its natural pristine innocence and nobility. That the fetters leave permanent scars may, in fact, account for the apparent contradiction in Shelley's first sentence between the "improvement" and the "gradual abolition" of political institutions.

That contradiction is only seeming, though, not real. Steeped as he was in Godwinian thought, Shelley undoubtedly regarded these terms as nearly synonymous, not mutually exclusive. The greatest improvement that might be made in human institutions would, according to the dicta of Godwinian anarchism, be their total abolition. The spectacular failure of such immediate institutional disrobing in the denouement of the French Revolution and Napoleon's subsequent donning of the robe and crown of emperor led both William Godwin (in the 1790s) and Shelley (two decades later) to adopt a doctrine of gradualism: at no time was the desirability of gradual—rather than precipitous—alteration in the power structure far from Shelley's mind. Indeed, his disavowal of violent change is clear from even relatively minor alterations in the draft of his preface. For instance, echoing Milton's description of the "noble and puissant nation rousing herself like a strong man after sleep" (*Areopagitica*), Shelley originally wrote in the second paragraph that his poem illustrated "the awakening of an immense nation from their slavery and degradation to a true sense of dignity and freedom; the dethronement of their oppressors." He subsequently inserted into the draft qualifying adjectives to emphasize the essentially nonviolent nature of the moral and intellectual transformation he envisions: "dignity" becomes "*moral* dignity" and "dethronement" "*bloodless* dethronement" (Bodleian MS Shelley d. 3, fol. 2 verso; my italics), as they stand in the printed version of the preface.

Shelley also follows Wordsworth's lead in portraying himself within the context of his discussion of the poet as prophet and patriot, both of which roles involve a substantial mediatorial function. Early in the preface, for instance, Shelley reminds us that should his poem fail it cannot be the fault of its subject matter: "If the lofty passions with which it has been my scope to distinguish this story shall not excite in the reader a generous impulse, an ardent thirst for excellence, an interest profound and strong such as belongs to no meaner desires, let not the failure be imputed to a natural unfitness for human sympathy in these sublime and animating themes" (*Works*, 32–33). Where, then, would the blame lie? "It is the business of the Poet to communicate to others the pleasure and the enthusiasm arising out of those images and feelings in the vivid presence of which within his own mind consists at once his inspiration and his reward" (*Works*, 33). Presumably, then, any misfire must be charged to the poet. Yet Shelley has already placed primary responsibility for the poem's success or failure upon the audience. If it is "the business of the poet *to communicate*" his pleasure and enthusiasm, then he obviously requires a cooperative reader.

Shelley is careful, here and elsewhere, to defend himself in advance against charges of poor or ineffective writing by invoking the leading literary figures as both superiors and peers. In writing "I do not presume to enter into competition with our greatest contemporary Poets" (*Works*, 34), Shelley invokes their presence nonetheless. His shift to the plural (unlike the pointed singular in the preface's first sentence) enfolds both Byron and Wordsworth and leaves the door open for the reader to include any other favorite as well. Knowing that critical readers are at least as prone to evaluating and ranking as to equating and leveling, Shelley expects his readers to measure *The Revolt of Islam* against other poems of the age. Consequently, he takes pains to specify the lines along which comparative analysis is to proceed. Hence the long paragraph in which the poet presents his credentials as a sophisticated student of the world: he has seen much, experienced much, and thus presumably knows much, both in nature and in the arts and artifacts of human endeavor. Yet, as he disarmingly tells us at the end of this heroic catalog, "the experience and the feelings to which I refer do not in themselves constitute men Poets, but only prepares them to be the auditors of those who are" (*Works*, 35). Indeed, Shelley's catalog of preparatory experience applies to his audience ("auditors") as much as it does to him. His circuitous compliment to his readers (another rhetorical strategy he uses repeatedly) is yet another attempt to establish with his audience a sense of community and shared endeavor. The real qualification of a poet, though, is his ability to act as mediator, to become a conduit between his own vision and the sensibilities of his fellow men, to awaken in others "sensations like those which animate my own bosom."

In claiming to be unsure whether he possesses such a power, Shelley publicly takes the posture of self-effacing openness he had assumed privately in July 1814 with Harriet Shelley, suggesting that he takes his audience very seriously and is willing—even anxious—to learn from its responses: "With an acquiescent and contented spirit, *I expect to be taught* by the effect which I shall produce upon those whom I now address" (*Works*, 35; my italics). In this, he appears to follow up on a suggestion made at the beginning of the "credentials" paragraph concerning the poet's education: "No education, indeed, can entitle to this appellation [of poet] a dull and unobservant mind, or one, though neither dull nor unobservant, in which the channels of communication between thought and expression have been obstructed or closed. How far it is my fortune to belong to either of the latter classes I cannot know. I aspire to be something better" (*Works*, 34). These seem odd words from the poet who had received considerable reinforcement during his summer with Byron in 1816 and consistent praise and encouragement from Leigh Hunt, Mary Shelley, and others.

Like other explanatory prefaces (such as those employed by Wordsworth, Coleridge, Byron, Keats, Southey, Hunt, and others), Shelley's preface is an exercise in "special pleading" in which the poet attempts to maneuver the reader into reading and evaluating the text as the author directs. It is an "act of disburdenment" designed to instruct the reader in the ways in which Shelley has recast both personal and universal experience within literature.[6] An important feature of this genre of prefaces is the invocation of literary tradition to legitimize and sanctify what one has done. Apropos of his claim not to be competing with his contemporaries, Shelley notes that his writing, like that of all ages, bears an inevitable relationship with other writings of the period, a point he will make with greater force in the preface to *Prometheus Unbound*. Writers are at all times the products of their ages, which force upon them certain similarities of thought and expression: "This is an influence which neither the meanest scribbler nor the sublimest genius of any era can escape" (*Works*, 35). Shelley modestly fails to indicate among which class of writer he includes himself, but he introduces the predecessors by whose standard he wishes to be evaluated and in whose company he wants the reader to number him. It is an exalted company that transcends the limits of nationality, time, and philosophical orientation. By repeatedly invoking Homer, Shakespeare, and Milton—as well as Spenser by adopting his stanza—Shelley aligns himself with the tradition of epic poets and prophets, presumably to sanction his claim that "in this as in every other respect I have written fearlessly" (*Works*, 35) and by extension ranking himself with exponents of freethinking at all times.

Asserting that "poetry, and the art which professes to regulate and limit its power, cannot subsist together," Shelley again entrusts himself to the charity and goodwill of his audience:

> I have sought therefore to write, as I believe that Homer, Shakespeare, and Milton, wrote, with an utter disregard of anonymous censure. I am certain that calumny and misrepresentation, though it may move me to compassion, cannot disturb my peace. I shall understand the expressive silence of those sagacious enemies who dare not trust themselves to speak. I shall endeavour to extract, from the midst of insult and contempt and maledictions, those admonitions which may tend to correct whatever imperfections such censurers may discover in this my first serious appeal to the Public. . . . Should the Public judge that my composition is worthless, I shall indeed bow before the tribunal from which Milton received his crown of immortality; and shall seek to gather, if I live, strength from that defeat, which may nerve me to some

new enterprise of thought which may *not* be worthless. (*Works*, 36)

Thus congratulated for possessing greater perspicacity than the critical establishment and for judging rightly in the case of Milton and, more recently, of Wordsworth, and thus prepared for yet another literary gift offered by an author who cares sincerely about them and values their honest opinions, the readers are invited to read on and to judge independently. Shelley offers as proof of his own earnest sincerity his promise to take serious responses seriously, to learn from the honest criticism of his audience, his partners in creation. All this comes after the paragraph in which, in discussing his choice of the Spenserian stanza, Shelley has with calculated "frankness" admitted to his reader that in some cases "I have completely failed" in versification, even to the extent of having apparently inadvertently left "an alexandrine in the middle of a stanza." This latter flaw, however, Shelley requests "the reader to consider as an erratum." I think it not unreasonable to suspect that Shelley may have intended here a not-so-covert allusion to the act of charity that informs the old adage "to err is human, to forgive divine." To such lofty heights does the author want his audience to feel elevated as he prepares their minds *and their hearts* for his poem's subversive message.

His claim in the preface's second paragraph that his poem is "narrative, not didactic" (*Works*, 32), suggests that Shelley is again following Wordsworth (and Aristotle) in suggesting that the narrative, or plot, should move the reader and that the *process* of reading is central to his design: "I would only awaken the feelings, so that the reader should see the beauty of true virtue, and be incited to those inquiries which have led to my moral and political creed, *and that of some of the sublimest intellects in the world*" (*Works*, 32; my italics). In his brief summary of its contents, Shelley observes that his poem portrays "the growth and progress of individual mind aspiring after excellence, and devoted to the love of mankind" (*Works*, 32). In his manuscript draft (Bodleian MS Shelley d. 3, fol. 2 verso) Shelley wrote "the growth and progress of [an] individual Mind." The initial letter of "mind" appears to be a capital: it is larger than the lower-case letters, though slightly smaller than most of the other capitals near it. More important is the cancellation—either as he was writing or, less likely, later—of "an," a change that helps to reveal Shelley's intention not to specify any particular exemplary figure but rather to indicate mind in general—the collective mind of humanity freeing itself from institutionalized tutelage and reverting to elemental impulses of love and social integration. This suggestion is borne out by Shelley's comment in a letter to a publisher (probably Longman and Co.) that *Laon and Cythna* illustrates a "Revolution" such as might be supposed to be produced "by the influence of individual genius, & out of general knowledge" (*Letters*, I, 564; 13 October 1817), in which the two final noun phrases are similarly devoid of articles.

P. M. S. Dawson objects that Shelley seems to be distinguishing here between a private, correct vision shared by the two protagonists and the muddled, unenlightened view of the general public which combines to crush the incipient revolution. But *individual* genius (or individual anything) rarely sustains revolutions of whatever dimensions and frequently has to settle for the private solace of a moral victory as the executioner's ax falls. Dawson reasonably claims that Shelley has composed a poem on the way visionary revolutionaries should conduct a revolution *that they are aware is doomed to failure.*[7] That their efforts are doomed does not diminish the fundamental integrity of their course, nor does it deter them. They are, quite simply, playing to an unresponsive audience, and they know it. They can choose to abandon their revolution, reenter the collective moral and intellectual torpor of the majority, and thereby surrender to the oppressors in the self-serving interest of their own physical well-being. Or they can pursue their painful course (which, not by mere coincidence, is analogous to the Passion of Christ), secure in the knowledge that they have acted according to their principles and hopeful that their example may serve as stimulus or paradigm in some future upsurge of social and intellectual consciousness.

Inherent in millennialist thought is the recognition that whenever any social unit sinks to its nadir—morally, intellectually, or politically—its potential for both dangerous and constructive action reaches is zenith. Laon and Cythna, and by extension Shelley as their author, represent the "innate integrative function" that activates the images of apocalypse produced at moments of cultural crisis. This partly unconscious life-affirming "voice of human nature" becomes loudest "when integrity is most deeply threatened, when the conflicting forces in men and society are most at odds and the need of synthesis most acute."[8] To compose a poem whose protagonists pursue to its bitter end what they recognize to be a failed cause is to preserve the ideal of community for some more enlightened audience to realize in the temporal world. The ultimately responsive internal audience in *Prometheus Unbound*—the entire universe of Act IV—accepts and fulfills the charge which the internal audience in *The Revolt of Islam*—the destroyers of Laon and Cythna—rejects. The epic struggle that consumes *The Revolt*'s exemplary protagonists points to a *potential* universal army of visionaries among the poem's readers. This potential is always present in Shelley's work; the sparks (like those at the end of the "Ode to the West Wind") require only a bit of receptive tinder to feed the flames— if not of the apocalypse that ushers in the new world, then of the purgatory that burns away the impurities of the old. Shelley engineers his preface so as at once to link himself with "the sublimest intellects in the world" and to invite his readers to join this visionary community.

Shelley intended his poem not for radical activists like the followers of William Cobbett or Thomas Wooler but for an audience composed primarily of leisure-class liberals.[9] Since he made careful plans for providing influential political leaders with copies of *A Proposal for Putting Reform to the Vote throughout the Kingdom* (as Wordsworth had done with *Lyrical Ballads*), to instruct them in both the benevolent and the practical aspects of their roles as leaders, and since his letter of 12 November 1817 to Charles Ollier indicates a clear plan for publishing *An Address to the People on the Death of the Princess Charlotte*, it is particularly important for us better to understand Shelley's conception of this, his longest poem, and his plans for it as a vehicle for manipulating public action. In this, we are well guided by Donald H. Reiman's detailed discussion in *Shelley and His Circle*, volume V, of the poem's composition and publication history, as well as by Shelley's own comments, the first of which, concerning the unaltered *Laon and Cythna*, was addressed to Byron. In a pair of private statements that seem strikingly at variance with his public posture in the preface, Shelley tells Byron, "It is in the style & for the same object as Queen Mab but, interwoven with a story of human passion & composed with more attention to the refinement & accuracy of language, & the connection of its parts" (*SC*, V, 291; 24 September 1817). But the style is not that of *Queen Mab*, nor is the language quite what Shelley seems to suggest. Characteristically, Shelley seems bent on having it both ways; while stressing the care and deliberation applied to the language of a piece, he will at practically the same moment affect nonchalance toward it, as he does late in the preface: "I would willingly have sent it [the poem] forth to the world with that perfection which long labour and revision is said to bestow. But I found that, if I should gain something in exactness by this method, I might lose much of the newness and energy of imagery and language as it flowed fresh from my mind" (*Works*, 36).

This self-protective attitude toward the poem's language resembles that which Shelley often adopts (as do authors of other defensive, apologetic prefaces such as Keats's to *Endymion*) as well toward a work's reception by public and critics alike. Continuing to Byron, Shelley states with unusual frankness his view of himself and his relation to his audiences:

> It *is* to be *published* . . . & for this simple reason, that I am careless of the consequences as they regard myself. I only feel persecution bitterly, because I bitterly [mistake] lament the depravity & mistake of those who persecute. As to me, I can but die, I can but be torn to pieces, or devoted to infamy most

undeserved, & whether this is inflicted by the necessity of nature & circumstances, or thro a principle pregnant, as I believe,
with important benefit to mankind is an alternative to which I
cannot be indifferent. (*SC*, V, 291)

Shelley's final sentence—with both the implicit allusion to the Passion
of Christ and the explicit reference to Actaeon that will recur powerfully in *Adonais*—is both intellectually and syntactically difficult. He
seems to be considering whether the persecution the poem could cause
him might not in fact result from a curious mutation of the principle
of intellectual beauty, in a process of intellectual natural selection that
includes the destruction even of the good and the well-intentioned as
part of an overall "master plan" leading finally and inevitably toward
human amelioration (*SC*, V, 295).

Another letter introducing the unaltered *Laon and Cythna* to a
potential publisher tells us still more. Though he was submitting only
"the first 4 sheets," Shelley had obviously finished the poem, which he
describes briefly in the letter. His description differs somewhat from
the summary he included in the preface, particularly in its direct reference to the French Revolution (of which Shelley says the revolution
in his poem is the *beau ideal*). Like the preface, the letter stresses
community in the poet's desire "to speak to the common & elementary
emotions of the human heart" (*Letters*, I, 563). It also adopts a posture
of uncertainty about the poem's merits, which is only in part a literary
convention. Shelley introduces the matter with the characteristic self-
deprecation intended to disarm: "My private friends have expressed to
me a very high & therefore I do not doubt a very erroneous judgement
of my work. However of this I can determine neither way. I have resolved to give it a fair chance, & my wish therefore is first, to know
whether you would purchase *my* interest in the copyright, an arrangement which if there be any truth in the opinions of my friends Lord
Byron & Mr. Leigh Hunt of my powers cannot be disadvantageous to
you" (*Letters*, I, 564). Shelley handles suspension here by mentioning
his "private friends" as admirers, then humbling himself, next offering
the publisher the opportunity to get in on a good thing, and only then
dropping the names of Byron and Hunt.

If this letter was indeed written to Longman and Co.,[10] it miscarried in its purpose, for it was Charles Ollier who finally undertook the
distribution of *Laon and Cythna* in its altered form as *The Revolt of
Islam*. Significantly, however, Shelley had also engaged as co-publisher
the firm of Sherwood, Neely, and Jones, the strongly liberal, antigov-
ernment publisher that had published Southey's *Wat Tyler* (to his mor-
tification) in February 1817. Indeed, in his 11 December response to
Ollier's threats to withdraw as publisher of *Laon and Cythna*, Shelley

asserts that "Sherwood & Neely wished to be the principal publishers" (*SC*, V, 349). We need not examine each of Shelley's letters to Ollier on the subject of the poem; they are characterized by vacillation between affected indifference and an obviously burning desire that his poem reach a substantial readership. Already on 3 December 1817 he writes: "I should be glad to hear any news that is authentic & that would mark the feeling of people public or private respecting the Poem—I am tolerably indifferent as to whether it be good or bad—" (*Letters*, I, 571).

Shortly after posting this comment Shelley learned that he was in danger of finding himself left speechless by virtue of Ollier's plan to defer to the objections of his printer, Buchanan McMillan, and to withdraw as publisher. Even in the heat of his indignant response, Shelley frames his case so as to place the burden of guilt squarely upon Ollier:

> You must be aware of the great injury that you prepare for me. . . . I beseech you to reconsider the matter, for your sake [& for n] no less than for my own. Assume the high & the secure ground of courage. The people who visit your shop, & the wretched bigot who gave his worthless custom to some other bookseller, are not the public. The public respects talent, & a large portion of them are already undecieved with regard to the prejudices which my book attacks. You would lose some customers but you would gain others. Your trade would be diverted into a channel more consistent with your own principles. (*SC*, V, 347–48)

This is a venerable merchandising technique, of course: convince the buyer of the inestimable value *to that buyer* of the product being offered. Shelley argues that Ollier's withdrawal from the agreement at this point would be foolish, counterproductive, and certainly not in his best interest as a businessman.

More important, however, Shelley appeals directly to Ollier's sense of fair play: having made a gentleman's agreement to publish the poem, Ollier is chastised for his unwillingness to discharge with dignity and propriety the obligations to which he had committed himself. Shelley reinforces his arguments on both these counts by warning Ollier that withdrawing now will constitute a sign of weakness (not to mention inexcusably bad manners) and will encourage the already powerful opponents of the hard-pressed friends of liberty and liberal opinion:

> To withdraw your names entirely would be to inflict on me a bitter & undeserved injury. . . . I hope that you will be influenced to *fulfil your engagement with me*, & proceed with the

publication, *as justice to me* & indeed a well understood estimate of your own interest & character, demand. . . . I have the
fairest chance of the public approaching my work with un-
biassed & unperverted feelings—the fruit of reputation, (&
you know for *what purposes* [Shelley's italics] I value it) is
within my reach—it is for you, now you have been once named
as publisher *& have me in your power*, to blast all this & to hold
up my literary [inserted] character in the eye of mankind, as
that of a proscribed & rejected outcast.—*And no evil that I
have ever done you*, but in return for a preference, which although you falsely [inserted] now, esteem injurious to you, was
[conferred &] solicited by Hunt & conferred by me, as a source
& a proof of nothing but kind intentions. (*SC*, V, 349–50; my
italics)

Shelley's strategy is transparent but shrewd. Basing his argument on
moral obligation and intellectual fairness, he effectively negates the
practical legal considerations that had understandably alarmed Ollier.
He casts Ollier as the villain, holding in his hand the fate of a thoroughly benevolent aspiring author who only coincidentally happens to
be writing what Ollier's printer labels impious blasphemy. At this time
habeas corpus had been suspended (as it had been since 4 March
1817), William Cobbett had fled to America, and Thomas Wooler and
William Hone were on trial for their radical publishing activities. Shelley's admonition that Ollier opt for the "high and secure ground of
courage" must have struck him with a sense either of remarkable na-
ïveté or of still more remarkable gall.

Still, Shelley was so determined to be heard that after Ollier informed him more precisely what was deemed objectionable he altered
his poem to meet many, though not all, the objections. These changes
made, Shelley pressed more adamantly for distribution and aggressive
advertising of the poem. Less than two weeks later, for instance, he
writes, "I wish, on publication, copies to be sent to all the principal
Reviews" (*SC*, V, 369; 22 December 1817), and he subsequently reminds Ollier repeatedly to publicize the work energetically: "Keep it
well advertised" (*SC*, V, 445; 11 January 1818); "don't relax in the advertising" (*Letters*, I, 594; 22 January 1818); "You ought to continue to
advertise the poem vigorously" (*SC*, V, 476; 25 January 1818). The
wave of enthusiasm and frustration crests in his note to Ollier of 16
January: "Can't you *make* the Booksellers subscribe [for] more of the
Poem?" (*Letters*, I, 593).

It appears, however, that Shelley soon faced facts; he seems not to
have mentioned his poem to Ollier again until his flat declaration

seven months later that "my own book of course acquires little attention" (*Letters*, II, 31; 16 August 1818). Yet Shelley did not give up on
the poem. As late as early 1821, he inquired whether Ollier held out
any hope for a second edition, for which Shelley declares his readiness
to make "many corrections" in the text, including "one part which will
be wholly remodelled" (*Letters*, II, 263; 16 February 1821).

I have examined this, the longest of Shelley's prefaces, at length
partly because its composition late in 1817 places it in an interesting
position within the evolution of Shelley's art. It is in many ways an
aesthetic manifesto, the principles of which are developed and articulated again in the greater poetry and prose that followed *The Revolt of
Islam*. But since art and politics so often proceed hand in hand with
Shelley, it is also a political manifesto, voicing Shelley's notions about
the artist's public, political function in raising the audience's consciousness. The preface reveals Shelley's view late in 1817 of the "liberating effects of the imaginative process" and of poetry's role as "the
instrument of corrective enlightenment"[11] in an intellectual and imaginative revolution in which he invites his reader to enlist and participate. That Shelley places himself in a line of artists that includes
Homer, Spenser, Shakespeare, and Milton indicates his view of himself as an epic prophet, a view reflected by the size and structure of
The Revolt. And his inclusion of Shakespeare in this list (as he includes
Wordsworth by allusion) suggests Shelley's sense of the more "human"
(or humane) prophecy to which he aspires, a prophecy committed to
"all human kind" (*Works*, 531).

Another reason for beginning here emerges from another letter to
Ollier:

> I inclose you what I have written of a pamphlet on the subject
> of our conversation the other evening. I wish it to be sent to
> press without an hours delay—I dont think the whole will
> make a pamphlet larger or so large as my last; but the printer
> can go on with this & send me a proof & the rest of the Mss.
> shall be sent before evening. If you should have any objections
> to publish it you can state them as soon as the whole is printed
> before the title goes to press: tho' I dont think that you will as
> the subject tho treated boldly is treated delicately. (*Letters*, I,
> 566; 12 November 1817)

The new pamphlet was *An Address to the People on the Death of the
Princess Charlotte*; the previous one had been *A Proposal for Putting
Reform to the Vote throughout the Kingdom*. The *Proposal* preceded
Shelley's poem, and *An Address* followed it. They form a revealing
frame around that work, demonstrating that Shelley's idealism existed

together with a surprising astuteness about practical matters of reform politics.

Shelley's reasonable proposal was intended to suggest a middle ground between the radical reformers and the more moderate factions. The call for a meeting at the Crown and Anchor Tavern is sensible enough; the 2 March 1817 issue of Hunt's *Examiner* reports such a meeting as having transpired at the Freemason Tavern. Shelley's choice of location is significant. A bastion of liberalism, the Crown and Anchor had been the site of Charles James Fox's birthday party in 1798, at which the eleventh Duke of Norfolk (Sir Bysshe Shelley's patron) had toasted "our sovereign's health: 'the majesty of the people'" (*SC*, VI, 541–42). It was at the Crown and Anchor, too, that William Hazlitt had repeated his lectures on the living poets in the spring of 1817. Godwin had attended some of these lectures, and his journal indicates that among the members of the diverse and predominantly liberal audiences at these sessions were the Lambs, the Basil Montagus, and the radical publisher William Hone.

Although there is much that is overtly radical about Shelley's pamphlet and its suggestions, it is interesting to observe how Shelley strategically adjusts both tone and position in the essay on the basis of his assessment of his audience. We need only look at the differences among beginning, middle, and conclusion to see how pronounced these shifts really are. After a two-sentence, formulaic opening paragraph, Shelley launches his proposal with one of the favorite devices of his political poems: the "negative definition"—the definition that operates by delineating what the term being defined is *not*. England furnishes the converse of a properly represented nation, and Shelley remarks on the madness of this state of affairs: "An hospital for lunatics is the only theatre where we can conceive so mournful a comedy to be exhibited as this mighty nation now exhibits: a single person bullying and swindling a thousand of his comrades out of all they possessed in the world, and then trampling and spitting upon them, though he were the most contemptible and degraded of mankind, and they had strength in their arms and courage in their hearts" (I&P, VI, 63). It seems at first that Shelley will maintain this aggressive tone, for his fourth paragraph opens with what is often taken to be wry irony: "Servitude is sometimes voluntary. Perhaps the People choose to be enslaved; perhaps it is their will to be degraded and ignorant and famished; perhaps custom is their only God, and they its fanatic worshippers will shiver in frost and waste in famine rather than deny that idol" (I&P, VI 63). I believe Shelley is chillingly serious here. Hierarchical power structures such as those upon which received religions, governments, and sociopolitical institutions in the West rest typically encourage and perpetuate the destructive self-denigration of those on the lower end of the scale. As Shelley sees it, those at the bottom oppress themselves. Conditioned by the demeaning status quo, they grow accustomed to the faulty notion, pressed upon them from above, that they are inherently inferior. Consequently, they complacently consent to their slavery as unfortunate but inevitable. But for Shelley, self-contempt is as great an evil as self-adoration. Indeed, William Keach makes this point about *The Revolt of Islam*, writing that throughout that poem "political oppression is imaged reflexively, suggesting that to an important degree it is, at least passively, self-imposed."[12] Shelley alters the tone of his essay almost immediately, however, significantly modulating the stridency of his language. The middle of the essay, which presents Shelley's plan for determining and accomplishing the will of the people, is both moderate and reasoned in tone.

Shelley postpones until the conclusion any extensive explanation of his own position on the matter, a position that contains some surprises for those who instinctively class Shelley with the forces of liberal extremism. Indeed, the concluding section of the essay is an impassioned argument for *gradualism*, which recalls both Godwin's views and the speeches of Sir Francis Burdett and Thomas Brand to "the Friends of Public Order, Retrenchment, and Reform" reported by the *Examiner* on 2 March 1817: "The securest method of arriving at such beneficial innovations, is to proceed gradually and with caution; or in the place of that order and freedom which the Friends of Reform assert to be violated now, anarchy and despotism will follow. . . . The consequences of the immediate extension of the elective franchise to every male adult, would be to place power in the hands of men who have been rendered brutal and torpid and ferocious by ages of slavery" (I&P, VI, 68). In short, since the male portion of the populace is largely unprepared for the rights and responsibilities of the franchise, it should be denied them, at least for the moment, while the way is prepared by more sophisticated—and presumably less volatile—reformers. Although Shelley was deeply committed to women's rights, as his actions and writings repeatedly demonstrate, his essay entertains no suggestion of fully enfranchising women. Very likely he appreciated the impracticality of including a gesture so inflammatory as to doom any other proposal for reform to which it might be attached. He was, after all, writing for a male audience, as his list of persons to whom copies should be sent indicates. Probably he simply suppressed out of practical expediency any overt advocacy of the early feminist agenda of women like Mary Wollstonecraft or the supporters of the abolitionist movement.[13]

The shifts in tone in *A Proposal* move the essay from the deliberately strong and contentious language of the opening to the intellectual and semantic moderation of the conclusion. Since Shelley devotes most of the essay to proposing a mechanism for promulgating, not the radical changes he wants himself, but rather what may be determined to be the general will of the people for gradual reform,[14] what could be more appropriate than a moderate tone, from the bluster of the opening, which reflects the discontent and barely repressed rage of the people, to the reasoned words of the conclusion, with its rueful acceptance of the plain fact that not everyone is ready to have his hand placed on the tiller? In short, form reinforces content.

Shelley's gradualism is a considered position, of course. He had read the authors whose ideas informed the American and French revolutions, just as he had studied metaphysics in an attempt to understand the extrapolitical bases of revolution. Shelley's early political writings advocate reform through indirect means: education, discussion, public meetings and philanthropic associations rather than direct action (*SC*, VI, 948). In this course he seconds Godwin's counsel: "Infuse just views of society into a certain number of the liberally educated and reflecting members; give to the people guides and instructors; and the business is done. This however is not to be done but in a gradual manner."[15] Ultimately, for Shelley as for Godwin, the reform of individuals and of institutions must proceed concurrently. But that reform must *begin* at the level of the individual.

One other point is important here: the author's projected relationship with his audience. One ploy used more than once is the suggestion that he is only a hesitant participant in the discussion. He would rather defer to others, if others there were to take the lead:

> It is the object of the Reformers to restore the People to a sovereignty thus held in their contempt. It is my object, *or I would be silent now. . . .* If it shall prove that I have in any degree afforded a hint to men, who have earned and established their popularity by personal sacrifices and intellectual eminence *such as I have not the presumption to rival. . . .* The statement [of my own views] is indeed quite foreign to the merits of the Proposal in itself, and *I should have suppressed it* until called upon to subscribe such a requisition as I have suggested. (I&P, VI, 63, 66–67, my italics)

Shelley's assumed humility is calculated to reduce the resistance he expects his plan to generate. So, too, is his decision to attribute his proposal to "the Hermit of Marlow." To put his own name to his proposal would have been to condemn it immediately. The relative anonymity assured by the pseudonym (even though Southey, for one, recognized Shelley as the author[16]) also invites a fairer reading, as does his plan for circulating copies to select readers. Designating himself a "hermit," though, reflects the extent to which Shelley already early in 1817 viewed himself as both recluse and outcast. Rousseau is not Shelley's only predecessor in this matter, but the example of that social reformer could not have been far from the poet's thoughts.

The phrasing of the passage just cited also demonstrates Shelley's shrewdness in presenting himself to his audience as a well-meaning outsider, modest and probably harmless, and thus defusing in advance the threat he knows the essay will pose to the reader. This accomplished, he then numbers himself with that audience, partly by flattery ("men, who have earned") and partly by the subterfuge of envisioning himself as a co-signer of such a proposal as the one he has authored. Shelley deliberately addresses his essay to those who possess the power, those who can adjust the status quo from within. Had he by 1817 read Coleridge's statement in *Conciones ad Populum* (1795) that "we . . . should plead *for* the Oppressed, not *to* them"?[17] The *Proposal* certainly seems to share Coleridge's sentiments. Shelley had in any case in 1816 read Coleridge's *Statesman's Manual*, in which he would have encountered the explicit distinction Coleridge draws between "a promiscuous audience" (defined in the *Conciones* as those whose minds are insusceptible of reasoning) and "men of *clerkly* [i.e., learned] acquirements, of whatever profession."[18]

An Address to the People on the Death of the Princess Charlotte, which involves different—though related—issues, was apparently composed rapidly, if we take at face value Shelley's comment to Ollier that the pamphlet stemmed from "the subject of our conversation the other evening" (*Letters*, I, 566; 12 November 1817). When he wrote Ollier on the morning of 12 November, Shelley had not yet completed the *Address*, whose length he is still only estimating, although he apparently finished the essay later in the day.[19] Aside from this single letter, however, Shelley never again mentions the essay. Why? Shelley normally worries his publishers over the advertising of his works, as for instance when he wrote Ollier in February about the *Proposal*: "Do not advertise sparingly: & get as many booksellers as you can to take copies on their own account" (*Letters*, I, 533). Yet Shelley's only extant remarks to Ollier on *An Address* concern production arrangements and Shelley's assertion that the pamphlet is safe to print, that "the subject tho treated boldly is treated delicately" (*Letters*, I, 566). Considering the skill with which the *Address* is written, Shelley's lack of further comment is curious.

Perhaps Shelley saw the need for caution, for despite his claims, his subject is not treated delicately, but rather with remarkable daring. It interweaves the death of Princess Charlotte with the executions of three Derbyshire rebels—Jeremiah Brandreth, Isaac Ludlam, and William Turner—in what becomes an apocalyptic essay on the death and potential resurrection of English liberty. The seeming indelicacy of Shelley's approach is apparent from the first, for barely two sentences into the essay we encounter the dead princess yoked in simile with "the clay with which she is about to mingle . . . a putrid corpse, who but a few days since was full of life and hope" (I&P, VI, 73). After this abrupt, stark, and brutal beginning clearly intended to shock the reader, Shelley observes in the second paragraph that the sad event of the princess's death is made uncommon only by her royal status, for the death of young women is common. Perhaps recalling Godwin's *Essay on Sepulchres* (1809), Shelley next lauds public rituals of mourning over the deaths of the world's notables, from the Athenians to the present. Among these luminaries he numbers Milton, Voltaire, Rousseau, and the French Republic, expanding his focus at the end of this third paragraph from individuals to entire societies and thereby repoliticizing his essay. The fourth paragraph stresses the linkage between universal mourning and universal calamity that transcends national, social, or ideological distinctions. It also injects a Wordsworthian note in its image of "those fertilizing streams of sympathy": universal mourning is an exercise in community, an activity that renovates and invigorates society by helping to "maintain that connexion between one man and another, and all men considered as a whole, which is the bond of social life" (paragraph 3). This principle of sympathy figures prominently in the writings of one of Shelley's favorite authors, David Hume, who had designated it as "the chief source of moral distinctions," an agent of "the communication of passions," whose locus is not the rational mind but the matrix of human feelings.[20] Hence its immediate relevance to Shelley's conception of the socially integrative stimulus provided by the several deaths and calamities his address details.

The fifth paragraph introduces the Derbyshire rebels even as it dismisses Princess Charlotte temporarily. Shelley damns her subtly with very faint praise, pointing to her singular lack of accomplishment in any field, unlike Mary Wollstonecraft, of whom he must have been thinking, and whose death was a "real" loss to liberty, variously defined. Having diminished the princess's distinction, Shelley suggests that we disregard what we have just read: "Let us speak no evil of the dead." If the lesson is apposite to the dead princess, then it is doubly relevant to the executed rebels whom the government was continuing to vilify, and Shelley moves from this common denominator to a delineation of the relative innocence of the rebels and the culpability of their executioners. Shelley's description of the rebels' final moments merely echoes the graphic account that had appeared in the *Examiner*. During this period issue after issue of the periodical press—regardless of political orientation—was filled with detailed accounts of all manner of crimes and trials, which the public read with great relish. Adopting a highly dramatic, graphic narrative at this point in his essay is Shelley's way of heightening sympathy, of drawing his audience more effectively into the pathos of the joint experience of Brandreth, Ludlam, and Turner. Reinforcing his essay with the conventions of early mass journalism strengthens Shelley's bond with his reader.

The readers who unconsciously begin to associate Shelley's essay at this point with the sort of detailed crime-reporting they are accustomed to find, say, in the *Examiner*, are seduced into accepting the spurious objectivity of journalistic writing. Their appetites for sensationalism now whetted, they should be more receptive to Shelley's loaded sentence in the seventh paragraph: "The events which led to the death of those unfortunate men are a public calamity" (I&P, VI, 77). Since public calamities are occasions for universal mourning, their causes are—or ought to be—the objects of universal revulsion. So even though Shelley deplores the violence the rebels had employed in pursuing their goals, he decries with far stronger voice "the circumstances of which it [their death] is the characteristic and the consequence" (I&P, VI, 77). At this point Shelley's argument turns economic, reading in the abortive Derby uprising the inevitable consequence of the oppression of the masses caused by the economic crises stemming from the extravagances of the wealthy. The result of these excesses for the workingman has been "that the day labourer gains no more now by working sixteen hours a day than he gained before by working eight" (I&P, VI, 78). As the economic inequality becomes ever more oppressive and the gulf between the wealthy and the poor more painfully apparent, the available options narrow to those Shelley here suggests: "Our alternatives are a despotism, a revolution, or reform" (I&P, VI, 80). As he had written in the preceding paragraph, "I put the thing in its simplest and most intelligible shape" (I&P, VI, 78).

The penultimate paragraph returns to the executions of the Derbyshire rebels and to their dying accusations of government collusion in their crimes. Shelley repeats what other printed accounts had reported of the denouement: the "sudden frenzy" of the crowd when the executions were performed. At the crisis, he implies, the masses had recognized their common bond with those executed, hence the common revulsion. But Shelley caps his account by disclosing what is most genuinely revolting about the affair. It is not so much the executions themselves that disgrace England, he argues, for executions are the common gifts of tyrants at all times. Rather, "it is a national calamity, that we endure men to rule over us, who sanction for whatever ends a conspiracy which is to arrive at its purpose through such a frightful pouring forth of human blood and agony" (I&P, VI, 81). The "conspiracies" had been revealed by Turner's dying accusation that "this is all Oliver and the Government." That Oliver, a government spy, and presumably other government agents as well had infiltrated the Derbyshire opposition and had actively encouraged the fatal rebellion had increasingly become public knowledge. The government's involvement in such vicious forms of entrapment infuriated Shelley: when such conspiracies are hatched in repeated determined efforts "to trample upon our rights and liberties for ever" (I&P, VI, 81), they are doubly insidious.

It is in the final paragraph of the *Address*, however, that the full virtuosity of Shelley's performance emerges. Princess Charlotte is metamorphosed into Liberty, borne to her grave after her murder by humanity. The princess had died of "natural causes," but the deaths of the Derbyshire rebels are all unnatural. In killing them, mankind—through its "representatives," the government—kills Liberty. Hence the greater tragedy of liberticide is that it is always preventable. As universal mourning is an exercise in community, so is universal complicity in the death of any individual. The apocalypse foreshadowed in the conclusion is a future event not necessarily assured by present circumstances, however. As does *The Mask of Anarchy* two years later, this essay concludes with the image of the Phantom arising from the ruins of human institutions, but that resurrection is only potential, not assured.

Scrivener remarks of the "curious" nature of the final paragraph, which is half sentimental, half apocalyptic, that "the prose changes abruptly to an allegorical mode in which tyranny is a spiritual force present everywhere in society. . . . The imagery and rhetoric are republican, not moderate. It is typical that as Shelley's language becomes more 'poetic' and allegorical, the politics seem more radical." [21] We can go further: in passages like the last paragraph of the *Address*, as Shelley moves to the most direct forms of address ("Mourn then People of England") he turns to shorter sentences, often cast in the imperative, and to such rhetorical devices as cadences and formulaic repetitions, all of which reflect familiar conventions of the literature of the masses, including popular hymns and the Bible. They also resemble the prose style of Hunt and Hazlitt in their more heated essays in the *Examiner* and the blunter, "pungent, vigorous paragraphs" of William Cobbett in the *Political Register,* a model many sought in vain to imitate. [22] The discourse of the *Address* differs significantly from that of *A Proposal,* indicating that Shelley could with equal facility take the other position Coleridge had indicated in the *Conciones,* addressing not the political leadership but what he perceived to be "the people" themselves.

The function of Shelley's epigraph ("We Pity the Plumage, but

Forget The Dying bird"), derived from Paine's *Rights of Man*, has generally been insufficiently understood. Egalitarian liberty is inherently incompatible with hereditary monarchy's titles and strata. Although Liberty is both mourned and anticipated here as titular sovereign, the real sovereign is the people, a point implicit as well in *A Proposal*. The princess is but plumage, a superfluous royal decoration. The execution of the Derbyshire rebels is an act of violence against the people, but it is facilitated by the people's inaction. In not resisting tyranny the people subscribe to and reinforce it: acts of omission are as culpable as acts of commission. Hence the final paragraph of *An Address* bears a latent image of the essay's readers as attendants at their own collective funeral. Nevertheless, those who have slaughtered Liberty have the concomitant power to revive Liberty if they so choose. The phoenixlike Phantom's resurrection must be the people's as well.

The considerable variety of voices, stylistic features, and rhetorical devices Shelley employs in *An Address* suggest not a disordered rhetorical patchwork quilt but the heterogeneity associated with literature of prophecy. That we hear echoes of real funeral rites in an essay that reads in places like a police thriller, or that a frankly sentimental discourse on the pathos of young mothers dying in childbirth is linked to a scathing attack on the public debt, evidences Shelley's attempt to touch and to unite the hearts and minds of a widely diversified audience. His attack on the establishment is more direct than in the other Marlow pamphlet because he addresses an audience whose fellow sufferers had been terminally disfranchised by that establishment at Derby. Hence Shelley directed his address *"to the People,"* not to the upper or even the middle class. The measured, speculative idealism of the *Proposal* with which he had begun 1817 gives way here to the indignation of the prophet raging against the establishment in the common cause of mankind. This is no longer the deferential Shelley who reinforces the reader's ego and humbles himself but a commanding voice characterized by the final paragraph's resounding imperatives. No longer is there reticence—Shelley speaking only because no one else is doing so—but the impassioned but shrewd argument of a strong voice demanding to be heard and to be obeyed in some public fashion.

This pamphlet marks an important transition in Shelley's assumptions about himself and his audience. He had just completed his longest poem to date, the yet-unaltered *Laon and Cythna*, an epic contribution to what he regarded as the vanguard of the new order among humanity. That his optimism should carry over into the assured, assertive form of *An Address* is, therefore, not surprising. That he attached his own name to the poem but not to the pamphlets that bracket that poem in time suggests the extent to which he was aware of distinctions among the audiences he was addressing in 1817. It is not necessarily a compromise to conceal one's identity temporarily or to adapt oneself to the abilities and expectations of one's audience (as Shelley observed of Christ in his "Essay on Christianity," much of which seems to date from the final quarter of 1817[23]). Rather, it is practical politics. Shelley clearly proposes to let the essays speak for themselves while he lets his long poem speak for *him*.

Something is wrong with the disciplines of knowledge.

JEROME MCGANN, *Social Values and Poetic Acts*

Chapter Two

THE EARLY WORKS

Critical response to Shelley's earliest works has never been particularly friendly, especially when comparisons are made with the later works. It is, therefore, occasionally surprising to discover in these often rough early works themes we typically associate with the later Shelley. Although Shelley's skill as a writer increased throughout his career— sometimes with spectacular leaps forward—at no point, not even in the very early works, is he ever entirely insensitive to the particular characteristics of the audiences he set out to address. Consequently, his assumptions about these virtual audiences bear heavily upon Shelley's decisions about form and content.

The Gothic Romances and Early Poems

Zastrozzi and *St. Irvyne* reveal their young author writing with one eye fixed upon his potential audience, eager to begin promulgating an antinomian doctrine of insubordination to authority, renunciation of revenge, and indulgence in antimatrimonial free love[1] under the guise of sexual and psychological thrillers calculated to satisfy the popular appetite for such titillation. The "Novels & Romances" he tells James Tisdall he is reading in January 1809[2] probably included not only various of the cheap Minerva Press thrillers but also sentimental novels and more substantial Gothic fiction. He must have appreciated the psychological astuteness of Anne Radcliffe's *Mysteries of Udolpho* (1794) and *The Italian* (1797), the latter of which Thomas Medwin reports particularly appealed to him, and Rosa Matilda's (Charlotte Dacre's) long *Zofloya, or, The Moor: A Romance of the Fifteenth Century* (1806), which "enchanted him."[3] To this list might be added Matthew G. ("Monk") Lewis's *The Monk* (1796) and Godwin's novels, *Caleb Williams* (1794) and *St. Leon* (1799) in particular.

The violent, perverse, scheming villains of the Gothic tradition are seldom without connections to Christian typological representations of the "subtile" Serpent that disrupts the serenity of Eden in an orgy of duplicity and deceit made possible by that most delicate trigger to human gullibility: pride. Indeed the Gothic tradition replays with almost infinite variations the myths both of the temptation and Fall and of the perilous experience in the postlapsarian Wilderness. The fruit consumed in Eden turns poisonous, withering humanity's world into one of suffering and death rather than opening it into the bloom of divine infinity Satan had promised. So, too, do both real and metaphorical poisons operate in Gothic fiction. The poison by which Wolfstein frees himself and Megalena from the bandit chief Cavigni in *St. Irvyne*, for instance, effectively poisons their relationship and brings the shadowy Ginotti, who had witnessed the crime, into the picture to dog Wolfstein's steps much as the misbegotten Creature does Victor Frankenstein's a few years later in Mary Shelley's novel. The dark and threatening natural environments of Gothic fiction, the frequent storms, the multiple violent deaths, the decaying and collapsing castles with their perpetually twisting passageways and secret chambers—all bespeak a world in decline, an ominous world that everywhere threatens its inhabitants, none of whom, it seems, can ever entirely be trusted to be what she or he appears.

Shelley often appears to step in as morally judicious narrator to help his reader recognize the evil that lurks behind the seductive facades. But even this assistance has its subversive purpose. In a particularly nasty scene in *Zastrozzi* in which the murder of Matilda's rival Julia is arranged, Zastrozzi delivers a heretical argument against the orthodox Christian doctrine of the soul's immortality (I&P, V, 47–48). Lest we be tempted to blame Shelley for Zastrozzi's heresies, though, as Dr. Johnson chastised Milton for Satan's, Shelley's narrator brackets Zastrozzi's opinions with expressions of dismay and cautions to the reader. These narratorial admonitions, couched in the language of moral disapprobation, would seem to reinforce the reader's own moral security, satisfying the need to counsel and reassure the reader by distancing and thus insulating the narrator (and presumably the author) from Zastrozzi's heresies. Despite this rhetorical insulation in the surface of the narrative, however, his words are not to be avoided, for in permitting the rhetorically forceful Zastrozzi to speak at length Shelley conveys his radical message in words that easily overshadow his narrator's weak and unremarkable language. Thus while the narrator is apparently sincere, within the text's narrative conventions, the author is deliberately and subversively ironic. Indeed, Shelley seduces his readers here as he will do throughout his career. Entrapping the readers through the apparent form or technique of a work, he saturates them with subversions of various sorts, forcing them into active thought and judgment rather than mere passive observation. This strategy reflects Shelley's lifelong fondness for the skeptical debate, the rhetorical mode in which each side argues so effectively that the other is demolished, leaving the audience to construct a third, more tenable position.

It is no coincidence that Zastrozzi's view of religion ("false, foolish, and vulgar prejudices") so nearly approximates Shelley's own in 1810, nor that when Ginotti recounts his own history in chapter X of *St. Irvyne*, it sounds curiously like Shelley's, right down to his age at the time when he "dived into the depths of metaphysical speculations" (I&P, V, 181): like Shelley, he is seventeen, just beginning to learn that there is more to heaven and earth than is dreamed of in his nature-based philosophy. Like Zastrozzi, Ginotti faced a crucial decision: he stood at seventeen at much the same crossroads as had his Faustian predecessors, having to choose, essentially, between a bond with humanity (represented in acceptance of natural, bodily mortality) and a breach with it in the form of the opening abyss of speculative science (represented by the elixir). The former is selfless, the latter selfish; the first is social and integrative, leading to the fullness of shared human experience, the latter self-centered and isolating, leading to the physical and psychological horrors of alienation experienced by moral and social deviants like Cain, the Wandering Jew, and Victor Frankenstein. Like so much of Shelley's writing, both these novels are profoundly autobiographical, either of real external incidents or, as is more often the case, of internal psychological crises.

Both *Zastrozzi* and *St. Irvyne* provide multiple object lessons about vengeance, for Shelley the epitome of alienation and self-centeredness. Zastrozzi is most malicious in his manipulation of others in his pursuit of revenge, but his physical immensity, which Shelley stresses repeatedly, symbolizes his spiritual immensity. Like Satan, Zastrozzi has been corrupted from within, poisoned by an ego grown out of all bounds of reason; as self-appointed avenger he resembles the cruel and retributive God of the Old Testament whom Shelley rejected. Nevertheless, this dark giant's noble bearing as he faces death is strangely compelling, especially when contrasted to that of Matilda, who by the end has repented and assumed the conventional visual trappings of innocence. Even in apparent defeat his obduracy is more powerful than Matilda's conformity, and in this he prefigures in flawed form the perfect hero of *Prometheus Unbound.* Shelley's ambivalent conclusion poses a problem for the reader not unlike that posed by the denouement of *Moll Flanders,* which leaves the reader with troubling, unresolved questions about real and false repentance (i.e., remorse and reformation as opposed to fear and conformity), about hypocrisy (means, ends, and rewards in capitalistic society), and about the nature of laws and justice. Shelley wants his readers to examine the assumptions that govern their customary responses to typological fiction and to determine whose is finally the greater sin, Matilda's or Zastrozzi's. Matilda is, after all, still the immediate cause of Julia's death, both in intent (when she frees Zastrozzi supposedly to kill her) and in fact (when she ultimately both kills and mutilates her in Venice).

Zastrozzi and Ginotti follow the Faustian pattern that recurs later in Byron's *Manfred* (1817), with resoluteness of purpose being weighed against apparent error of motivation. Shelley's point is not that Zastrozzi is reprehensible but that he has fallen through a weakness of human character, essentially the traditional tragic flaw of hubris. To color him entirely black would be to render him a farcical figure, a two-dimensional, cardboard Gothic silhouette. To empower him with the ability to choose—however wrongly—and to obey an inner necessity—however misguided—is to invest him with the properties of tragedy. The Gothic universe is, in fact, a tragic one,[4] and Zastrozzi is a tragic hero whose ancestry reaches back to the great fallen figures of Aeschylus and, more recently, Milton, complex characters engaged in momentous psychological struggles. The fatal sin of pride here takes the form of an irrational and inhumane dedication to vengeance against one's perceived enemies without care for the cost to the innocent. There is a creeping moral and intellectual horror in *Zastrozzi,* an internal erosion that the author wishes his readers to perceive.

Zastrozzi embodies the potential for good, as Wolfstein and to a lesser extent Ginotti do in *St. Irvyne.* In *Queen Mab* (1812–13), Ianthe's surpassing virtue is rewarded by the dream-vision the Fairy spirit confers upon her. Embedded within the text of that poem is Shelley's most pressing, most persistent message: "Learn to make others happy" (*QM,* II, 65; *PP,* 23). Indeed, in dedicating herself to the task of enlightening her fellow humanity, the Spirit of Ianthe indicates she has learned her lesson well: she will become a prophetess,

> "For, when the power of imparting joy
> Is equal to the will, the human soul
>   Requires no other Heaven."
>   (*QM,* III, 11–13; *PP,* 28)

The "For" is important, for it establishes causality: the melioristic socializing impulse consistently informs the actions (and the writings) of the Shelleyan prophet. It is precisely in this respect that Zastrozzi is a failure, for the power (and the will) to impart joy has given place in him to the joy of imparting pain—benevolence has become sadism, poisoning the "milk of human kindness" and making a Hell of Heaven. Convinced that "Heaven" is a fiction of vulgar religious superstition, an intellectual carrot or a psychological club depending upon the purpose for which it is invoked (in both cases, ultimately, to coerce into conformity with the wishes of another), Shelley argues explicitly in *Queen Mab* and implicitly in both *Zastrozzi* and *St. Irvyne* for a secular heaven, a recreation of paradise on earth within the universe of human society.

After writing Tisdall from Field Place that "in this Solitude I have no Employment, except writing Novels & Letters" (*Letters*, I, 3; 26 March 1809), on 7 May 1809 Shelley wrote to offer Longman "a Romance, of which I have already written a large portion" (*Letters*, I, 4). That we cannot be sure whether the novel was *Zastrozzi* or one of "several novels which never got into print"[5] is a further indication of how much Shelley was writing. When Timothy Shelley introduced his son to Henry Slatter, Oxford's leading bookseller, in the fall of 1810, he supposedly remarked that "my son here has a literary turn; he is already an author, and do pray indulge him in his printing freaks."[6] It seems unlikely that Shelley took his early writing as lightly as either his father or his modern critics, and a reevaluation is in order. Had Shelley continued to write in this vein, he might have attained considerable eminence (or notoriety) as a novelist, for the advances in style and overall sophistication from *Zastrozzi* to *St. Irvyne* are striking. Shelley had internalized the essence of the Gothic novel form, and the conventions of such formulaic fiction fill both novels and echo through the works of his later years.

Stylistically, *Zastrozzi* and *St. Irvyne* are very different. The short, breathless paragraphs and crisp sentences of the former give place to complex periodicity in the latter: "It was at this dark and silent hour, that Wolfstein, unheeding the surrounding objects,—objects which might have touched with awe, or heightened to devotion, any other breast,—wandered alone—pensively he wandered—dark images for futurity possessed his soul: he shuddered when he reflected upon what had passed; nor was his present situation calculated to satisfy a mind eagerly panting for liberty and independence" (I&P, V, 114). The abrupt beginning of *Zastrozzi*, with Verezzi's unexplained dilemma thrust suddenly upon the reader in a sequence of rapidly moving paragraphs, is markedly different from the slow, involuted paragraph that opens *St. Irvyne*, where visual as well as verbal density complicates the reader's task. In *St. Irvyne*, no matter how fast the plot may move, the language in which it is expressed forces the reader to slow down, to internalize the text. In many places the diction and syntax are strongly poetic, emphasizing internal repetitions, rhythms, and cadences. Indeed, Shelley even inserts several poems into the narrative.

There is also a greater and more sophisticated use of metaphor in *St. Irvyne*, particularly in attention positions at the beginnings or conclusions of chapters. At the end of the first chapter, for instance, Shelley writes of Wolfstein: "He longed again to try his fortune; he longed to re-enter that world which he had never tried but once, and that indeed for a short time; sufficiently long, however, to blast his blooming hopes, and to graft on the stock, which otherwise might have produced virtue, the fatal seeds of vice" (p. 124). Like Zastrozzi, Wolfstein (who is related to the powerful dark figure of Karl Moor from Schiller's *The Robbers* [1781], a play that likewise features a robber band and whose influence had motivated Wordsworth and Coleridge, among many others, to compose dramas[7]) is another figure whose potential for good has been misdirected, both by circumstance and by choice.

The characters in *St. Irvyne* frequently speak in the conventional stilted and highly artificial diction of the Gothic romance tradition. Its artificiality is heightened by its strong contrast with the narrator's sensuous, often almost incantatory language, a contrast much less apparent in *Zastrozzi*, where the tale and its teller are less clearly differentiated. Finally, natural settings are handled differently in *St. Irvyne*. Instead of relying on the verbal shorthand of formulaic moonlit scenes and thunderstorms as in *Zastrozzi*, Shelley paints lusher, more particularized landscapes, which his characters consciously muse upon or react to.

Both novels contain obvious invitations to the reader to participate actively in the process of creation. In *Zastrozzi*, for instance, after Matilda is first interrogated by the Inquisition, she is led to a cell, where, the narrator tells us, "Matilda's situation is better conceived than described" (I&P, V, 95). Likewise, after Wolfstein and Megalena escape the robber band in *St. Irvyne*, they repair to a friendly inn, where the narrator remarks of their amorous evening that "it is sufficient to conceive what cannot be so well described" (I&P, V, 132). Such comments, a stock device of later eighteenth-century fiction—perhaps epitomized in Tristram Shandy's genial invitation to the reader to use the blank page provided in the text for her or his own portrait of the widow Wadman—are very much a part of Romantic notions of reader participation. In another context, for instance, when words fail Shelley at a crucial point in his "Hymn to Intellectual Beauty," the poet turns that apparent failure into a rhetorical climax, implicitly inviting the reader to leap from the inadequacies of language to the fullness of pure idea:

even now

I call the phantoms of a thousand hours
Each from his voiceless grave: they have in visioned bowers
  Of studious zeal or love's delight
  Outwatched with me the envious night—
They know that never joy illumed my brow
  Unlinked with the hope that thou wouldst free
  This world from its dark slavery,
  That thou—O awful LOVELINESS,
Wouldst give *whate'er these words cannot express.*

(PP, 95; my italics)

Other such invitations abound, as for instance in the narrator's frequent addresses to the reader in the Eloise sections: "Reflect on *this*, ye libertines, and, in the full career of the lasciviousness which has unfitted your souls for enjoying the *slightest* real happiness here or hereafter, tremble! Tremble! I say; for the day of retribution will arrive" (I&P, V, 176). The Eloise sections provide a number of curiosities, not the least of which is the apparent absence of the fifth and sixth chapters, which one might expect to supply an explicit transition from the Wolfstein-Megalena story line. Sometimes regarded as "a deliberate ploy to intensify the reader's consternation,"[8] these two "missing" chapters may simply have been left unwritten as Shelley composed, intending to fill them in later, much as he often left gaps marked only by dashes in early drafts of his poems. But Shelley's generally underestimated sense of humor tempts us to see in these chapters a joke on the reader in the manner of Mackenzie in *The Man of Feeling* (which novel begins with chapter 11) or Sterne in *Tristram Shandy* (which omits two chapters that are inserted in the middle of a subsequent chapter). Still, chapter 7 of *St. Irvyne* contains enough information to enable the reader to fill the gap Shelley has left. Perhaps Shelley simply misnumbered his chapters and in his hasty and careless submission of the manuscript to its publisher failed to renumber them, just as he failed to correct other anomalies in the text. But the "missing" chapter 7 in *Zastrozzi*—although there is no perceptible gap in the narrative between chapters 6 and 8—makes one suspect that Shelley's unconventional numbering may have been deliberate.

Finally, in these early works Shelley plants the seeds of liberal and humanitarian ideas that would reach their fruition in later, greater works: notions of the necessity for selfless love and integration, of the poisonous nature of selfish revenge as a motive for human activity, of liberty in opposition to the tyranny of custom and received ideas. Hence in *Zastrozzi* Matilda exclaims in a frenzy of despairing passion, " 'Where, then, is the boasted mercy of God, . . . if he suffer his creatures to endure such agony as this? or where his wisdom, if he implant in the heart passions furious—uncontrollable—as mine, doomed to destroy their happiness?'" (I&P, V, 52). Once again, though the narrator frames her outburst with the verbal semblance of disapprobation, the author presses upon the reader the skeptical view of God as a supposedly benevolent deity who in fact dooms his human creations by demanding that they conform to his impossible expectations. Even Megalena, herself a villainess of considerable proportions, becomes both a vehicle and an occasion for a narratorial outburst in *St. Irvyne* that clearly reflects the author's deepest sympathies at this early point: "Still, though veiled beneath the most artful dissimulation, did the fair Megalena pant ardently for liberty—for, oh! liberty is sweet, sweeter even than all the other pleasures of life, to full satiety, without it" (I&P, V, 119). In *St. Irvyne*, too, the identifiably Shelleyan Fitzeustace presents a very Shelleyan view of marriage as "an human institution, and incapable of furnishing that bond of union by which alone can intellect be conjoined; I regard it as a chain, which, although it keeps the body bound, still leaves the soul unfettered" (I&P, V, 197). Presumably "that bond of union" is the idealized friendship we have already considered. One can only wonder what Harriet Westbrook Shelley might later have made of these lines.

His biographers have attributed to Shelley an "almost feverish" interest in "a quick, schoolboy fame."[9] But immediate fame is usually only an immediate goal, a door opening upon some projected future of public activity. If Shelley desired quick fame, it was because he planned to write more and so wanted to cultivate an audience. At the time he was composing his Gothic romances his primary interest was not money, as is clear from his letter to Longman and Company offering a work that was probably *Zastrozzi:* "My object in writing it was not *pecuniary,* as I am independent, being the heir of a gentleman of large fortune in the County of Sussex, & prosecuting my studies as an *Oppidan* at Eton; . . . Should it produce any pecuniary advantages, so much the better for me, I do not expect it" (*Letters,* I, 4–5; 7 May 1809). The reference to his father's estate is only one instance among many of Shelley's attempts to pressure a prospective publisher.

He played a similar game with his reader. Although he attributed the authorship of *Zastrozzi* to "P.B.S.," for instance, when *St. Irvyne* appeared the still anonymous (or nearly so) author presented his more substantial credentials as "a Gentleman of the University of Oxford" (I&P, V, 3, 107). He also made clear his plan to purchase good reviews of *Zastrozzi* in a letter to Edward Fergus Graham:

> Robinson [*Zastrozzi*'s publisher] will take no trouble about the reviewers, let every thing proper be done about the venal vil-

lains & I will settle with you when we meet at Easter. . . . *Pouch* the reviewers—10£ will be sufficient I should suppose, & that I can with the greatest ease repay when we meet at Passion Week. Send the reviews in which Zastrozzi is mentioned to Field Place, the British review is the hardest, let that be pouched well—My note of hand if for any larger sum is quite at your service, as it is of consequence in fiction to establish your na[me] as high as you can in literary lists—(*Letters*, I, 5–6; 1 April 1810)

Shelley already understands audiences well enough to recognize the importance of a great show to the success of a literary endeavor. That publishers and potential publishers are also audiences for whom an author must perform is clear from Shelley's suggestion in the same letter that he, Graham, and probably Harriet Grove and one or more of her brothers should "go in a posse to booksellers in Mr. Groves [sic] barouche & four—shew them we are no grub street gareteers" (*Letters*, I, 6).

Shelley apparently conceived of *St. Irvyne* as a "three-decker" aimed at circulating libraries: "As to the method of publishing it, I think as it is a thing which almost *mechanically* sells to circulating libraries, &c. I would wish it to be published on my *own* account" (*Letters*, I, 20; 14 November 1810). When Joseph Stockdale advertised the novel, Shelley wrote approvingly that the advertisement was "likely to excite curiosity" (*Letters*, I, 24; 18 December 1810) and in the same letter offered Stockdale his latest effort in prose fiction. His description of the new work indicates the direction Shelley's work was beginning to take: "I have in preparation a Novel; it is principally constructed to convey metaphysical & political opinions by way of conversation; it shall be sent to you as soon as completed, but it shall receive more correction than I trouble myself to give to wild Romance & Poetry.—" (*Letters*, I, 25). Interestingly, Shelley distinguishes between the work represented by *Zastrozzi* and *St. Irvyne*, both of which are identified on their title pages as "Romances," and this new work, to which he gives the more substantial name of "Novel." [10]

It would be interesting to know for certain whether he was referring to the never-seen *Hubert Cauvin*, which he describes to Elizabeth Hitchener some twelve months later as "a tale in which I design to exhibit the cause of the failure of the French Revolution, and the state of morals and opinions in France during the latter years of its monarchy" (*Letters*, I, 218; 2 January 1812). Shelley's description to Stockdale seems consistent with what he later tells Hitchener about his deliberate exclusion from *Hubert Cauvin* of "the sexual passion" that had figured so largely in the two Gothic romances and his inclusion of "some of the leading passions of the human mind." That he tells her he has completed about two hundred pages of the tale suggests the two may be the same. The lapse of a full year between the letter to Stockdale and that to Hitchener, even granting Stockdale's apparent lack of interest, seems at variance with the speed with which Shelley often composed. Perhaps *Hubert Cauvin* was very tough going, given the method of presentation outlined to Stockdale. Perhaps Shelley was simply busy with other matters.

By late 1810 Shelley's interest in the Gothic romance formula was already diminishing. Moreover, he was growing dissatisfied with Stockdale.[11] He was apparently uncertain where to turn, though he mentions Wilkie and Robinson, who had published *Zastrozzi*, as a possible publisher for Hogg's *Leonora*, then in progress.[12] Shelley's letter to Hogg two days after the offer to Stockdale is interesting for the poet's outburst against his father and his agents, all of whom Shelley sees as laboring under the "error" of "Xtianity." Shelley assures Hogg that "booksellers possess more power than we are aware of, in impeding the sale of any book whose opinions are displeasing to them," suggests Wilkie and Robinson (significantly adding, "he publishes Godwin's works"), and recommends that if all else fails Hogg should publish the novel himself (that is, privately). The increasingly disjointed and convoluted discussion culminates in a passionate outburst:

> Oh! I burn with impatience for the moment of Xtianity's dissolution, it has injured me; I swear on the altar of perjured love to revenge myself on the hated cause of the effect which *even now* I can scarcely help deploring.—Indeed I think it is to the benefit of society to destroy the opinions which *can* annihilate the dearest of its ties.—Inconv[en]iences would now result from my *owning* the novel which I have in preparation for the press. I give out therefore that 1 will publish no more; every one here, but the select few who enter into its schemes believe my assertion—I will stab the wretch in secret.—Let us hope that the wound which we inflict tho' the dagger be conceald [sic], will rankle in the heart of our adversary. (*Letters*, I, 27–28; 20 December 1810)[13]

Shelley proposes a sort of intellectual guerrilla warfare fought in the press, in which the instruments of the oppressors might be turned against themselves. Despite his campaign in the romances against the passion for vengeance, Shelley is not reluctant to reveal his own feverish desire to be revenged on the "Xtians" whom he perceives to have injured him.

But why does Shelley say it would be inconvenient to own his authorship of the novel then in preparation? Partly, he wishes not to jeopardize the fiction he is promulgating about having renounced writing. But if he was going to write apparently harmless things, thereby seeming to return to moral and social conformity, why appear to renounce writing? Clearly he has no intention of writing anything harmless. When he later returns to the topic of his novel in a letter to Hogg, he asserts that "*Mine* is not printable, it is as bad as [?la Necessite] [*The Necessity of Atheism*] & would certainly be prosecuted" (*SC*, II, 785; 14 May 1811).

Shelley did not break entirely with Stockdale, though their relationship deteriorated in the aftermath of the investigation of Hogg. He wrote a brief, polite note to Stockdale in April 1811, for instance, inquiring about the sales of *St. Irvyne*. Apparently Stockdale's reply was long in reaching Shelley at Cwm Elan, for his reply to the publisher is dated 1 August. In it, Shelley seems genuinely surprised by what must have been disappointing news, probably put to him by Stockdale as admonishing him for the carelessness with which he had completed and revised (or not revised) *St. Irvyne:* "I am aware of the imprudence of publishing a book so ill-digested as St. Irvyne, but are there no expectations on the profits of it's sale?" (*Letters*, I, 130).[14] Apparently Shelley's instructions to Graham to "get as many copies sold as you can as I want the business out of Stockdales hand" (*Letters*, I, 52; 17 February 1811) had proved unsuccessful.

The eighteen months or so leading up to Shelley's expulsion from Oxford must have been extraordinarily productive, for he seems to have been engaged in a variety of literary projects. In addition to the romances, completed and unfinished, he and Medwin were busy with *The Wandering Jew*, and with his sister Elizabeth he was producing the much-indebted *Original Poetry of Victor and Cazire*, which would be followed at Oxford by his collaboration with Hogg, the *Posthumous Fragments of Margaret Nicholson*. He was also composing in the Esdaile Notebook poems of substantially higher quality—though still rough—than those in either of the collaborative volumes. He mentions having a tragedy to offer the manager of Covent Garden, as well as a farce "which my friend is composing" (*Letters*, I, 14; ?10 August 1810). Who was the friend? Was it Elizabeth? Was the term merely a ruse, with Shelley himself being the "friend," as was the case in 1822, when in the letter to Jane and Edward Williams in which he enclosed "The serpent is shut out from Paradise" he attributed that poem to "my friend" (*Letters*, II, 384; 26 January 1822)? Since neither the tragedy nor the farce is known to have survived (if they ever existed) we must be content with Shelley's protestations to Graham about "how anxiously I desire its [the farce's] acceptance" and his hope to secure an overture for the piece from Joseph Woelff, Graham's music tutor (*Letters*, I, 16, 14).

Added to all this activity is Shelley's practice of engaging promi- nent strangers in correspondence, writing under assumed names (and, presumably, assumed styles) in a sort of "intellectual ambush"[15] de- signed to entrap various correspondents in shrewd argument with a youth they would otherwise very likely ignore. This early chicanery further illustrates Shelley's recognition of the practical necessity of ad- dressing audiences in suitable fashion. Shelley apparently conducted much, if not all, of this clandestine correspondence from Graham's London address, and though he seems to have assumed many identi- ties, his favorite pseudonym was "Reverend Merton" (a jest on Merton College?), which may be the "Revd. Charles Meyton" Shelley men- tions as the addressee of a letter that might be delivered to Graham's address (*Letters*, I, 52; 17 February 1811). Shelley had few reservations about sending copies of his work to others, using them to introduce himself to those he wished to know (or to have know him). Godwin is a good example. The practice continued throughout Shelley's career, taking perhaps its most ambitious form in 1817, in the poet's directions for distributing his Marlow pamphlet on reform. Though Shelley's name does not appear on the title page, *The Necessity of Atheism* was undoubtedly both noticed and regarded (probably with considerable horror) by some very shocked clergy, for Shelley closes his brief 17 February letter to Graham with the revelation that "All the Bishops have the Atheism" (*Letters*, I, 52).

We have already seen how strongly Shelley felt about proper ad- vertising. When his most ambitious incendiary device to date, *The Ne- cessity of Atheism*, was akindling at Oxford, Shelley wrote to Graham in London: "I send you *a book*. You must be particularly intent about it. Cut out the title page & advertise it in 8 famous papers, & in the Globe advertise the *Adverstiment* [sic] in the 3rd page. I wish you to be particularly quick about it" (*Letters*, I, 51–52; 14 February 1811). The instructions are countermanded almost immediately, however, as Shelley writes only three days later to inform Graham not to advertise "the Atheism" as it is not yet published because Shelley and Hogg are worried about the political consequences of apparent heresy (*Letters*, I, 52; 17 February 1811). Shelley was typically in a rush to get his words into print and, more important, to get them noticed, a fact that underlies his plans for the political poems of 1819, some of which— like *The Mask of Anarchy*—he submitted directly to a periodical pub- lisher such as Leigh Hunt for immediate publication,[16] others of which he planned to gather together in a propagandistic volume whose vari- ous excesses, from all appearance, might have alarmed even so radical a publisher as Richard Carlile. Shelley's sense of the impressionability of his audience was keen enough by 1811 to suggest to him and Hogg that the Margaret Nicholson poems might attract greater attention by being printed in the gaudy Gothic type and expensive binding in which they subsequently appeared and that the implicit sexual indulgence of the "Epithalamium" in that volume would "make it sell like wildfire" (*SC*, II, 646; 30 November 1810). Shelley was not even averse to attacking his own work in print (just as, in 1815, he would apparently review *Queen Mab* in the *Theological Inquirer*), if Frederick L. Jones is correct in concluding from Shelley's remark that "I shall possibly send you the abuse today, but I am afraid that they will not insert it" that he had written an abusive review of the poems as a means of generating controversy and hence sales.[17]

Finally, Shelley understood the power of a strategically dropped name or title. To Stockdale he had written, "Do you find that the public are captivated by the title page of St. Irvyne?" (*Letters*, I, 40; 11 February 1811). On two possible points only might the title page have "captivated" a potential reader: the reference in the subtitle to "The Rosicrucian," which reference Shelley had felt called upon to explain to Stockdale in an earlier letter (*Letters*, I, 21; 19 November 1810), or the citation of the author as "A Gentleman of the University of Oxford." Less than a month after his 11 February inquiry to Stockdale, Shelley was advertising *A Poetical Essay on the Existing State of Things*, authored "by a Gentleman of the University of Oxford."[18] Shelley's title suggests the Godwin both of *Political Justice* and of *Caleb Williams*, whose original 1794 title page gave the full title as *Things as They Are; or, the Adventures of Caleb Williams*. Shelley's poem was designed, according to the advertisement in the *Oxford Herald* of 2 March 1811, "For assisting to maintain in Prison Mr. Peter Finnerty, Imprisoned for a Libel." Hence the poem constituted an explicit public gesture that would place him in visible opposition to the political establishment just as "the Atheism" had vis-à-vis the religious.

Finnerty, an Irish journalist, had on 7 February 1811 been sentenced to eighteen months' imprisonment for his protests against the conduct of English military policies. That his case was taken up by Sir Francis Burdett, the popular leader of the reform movement and a particular favorite of Shelley at the time, helps explain Shelley's own interest in the matter, including his subscription in Oxford to a sympathetic fund for Finnerty.[19] Shelley undoubtedly suspected that Finnerty's difficulties arose at least in part from his nationality. More important, the *Examiner*'s advocacy of Finnerty had apparently suggested to Shelley still another vehicle for disseminating his views. Hence his interesting letter to Leigh Hunt, on the occasion of the acquittal of Leigh and John Hunt at the conclusion of their libel trial, which had also involved criticizing in print an issue of military policy, flogging.

This letter, written from Oxford on 2 March 1811 (*Letters*, I, 54–

55), the day Shelley signed himself to the subscription fund for Finnerty, displays Shelley's considerable rhetorical skill. From a distance of nearly two centuries, and with the hindsight that allows us to place the letter within its proper context, Shelley's plan seems transparent. To Hunt, however, having just escaped the talons of the law, the letter undoubtedly came as one of the many congratulatory expressions the brothers received from liberal reformers and advocates of a free press. Shelley begins with congratulations and flattery, dubbing Hunt "one of the most fearless enlighteners of the public mind at the present time," and passes quickly to an invitation to the publisher to involve himself with a scheme to organize the reform movement. As he would again from Ireland in 1812 and from Marlow in 1817, Shelley suggests "a *meeting* of . . . enlightened unprejudiced members of the community" to form "a methodical society which should be organized so as to resist the coalition of the enemies of liberty which at present renders any expression of opinion on matters of policy dangerous to individuals." Hunt is presumably to infer that he and Finnerty are two examples of such endangered freethinkers, but Shelley undoubtedly adds himself silently to this company. *The Necessity of Atheism* had been printed and was in the hands of "All the Bishops"; the "Poetical Essay" was apparently completed and either at or on its way to the printer, for the advertisement would appear in the *Herald* on this same day. Perhaps Shelley foresaw some of the difficulties these endeavors might cause him, for his letter to Hunt implies that Shelley wishes to establish what modern psychology might call a support system. Although the letter enlists that support ostensibly in the cause of reform—the liberal freethinkers presumably would gain strength from their perceived numbers—it also hints at the cultivation of a receptive and sympathetic audience, and hence at a mechanism for positive reinforcement. Articulated in the semblance of moderate discourse, Shelley's letter still exudes this missionary zeal. Of course, the missionary's task is considerably simplified when the zealots are already converts, in which case the leader becomes less a missionary than a general marshaling the forces. That Shelley looked to Hunt for an entrée to a sympathetic audience (Hunt's readers) is scarcely more surprising than is his decision later in 1811 to go to Ireland (where else would he find—so he must have reasoned—a more naturally, universally sympathetic and receptive audience?).

Shelley's final paragraph engages in both name-dropping and an implied promise of future favors if Hunt responds positively: "My father is in parliament, and on attaining 21 I shall, in all probability, fill his vacant seat. On account of the responsibility to which my residence at this University subjects me, I of course, dare not publicly to avow all that I think, but the time will come when I hope that my every endeavour, insufficient as this may be, will be directed to the advancement of liberty" (55). Support me now, in other words; encourage me in my efforts now, and when I come into my own I will remember (and reward) you. The paragraph clearly establishes four points: (1) Shelley fully expects to be his father's full heir; though he foresees a potential brouhaha over "the Atheism," he mistakenly considers himself fully equal to the task of mollifying his father. (2) He is apparently still maintaining the appearance of having given up writing, presumably trusting the form of the title pages of *St. Irvyne, The Necessity of Atheism,* and the "Poetical Essay" to perpetuate the ruse. (3) He has committed himself fully to what he here calls "the advancement of liberty" and what he later refers to more generally as "bettering the condition of human kind" (*Letters;* I, 255; 14 February 1812, to Elizabeth Hitchener). (4) He is already aware of the benefits that derive from assuming a posture of humility in presenting the brashest proposals ("insufficient as this may be" is an open invitation to the reader to reassure the writer).

This letter, replete with its suggestion of a methodical society to improve humanity's lot by establishing "rational liberty" (presumably unlike the conspiratorial antinomian procedures of the Illuminists Shelley suggests as precedent[20]) provides important evidence about this transitional stage in Shelley's development. The young author has apparently ended the major Gothic phase of his fiction writing and has begun to move in the direction of metaphysical and more explicitly sociopolitical fiction. He has likewise culminated his attempts to engage various figures of the political, philosophical, and religious establishment in correspondence by loosing on the world his (and Hogg's) radical pamphlet on atheism. At the same time, he has taken the very public step of signing his name to the Finnerty subscription in Oxford and of likewise signing his name to a letter of introduction and invitation addressed to one of the more active liberal/reform publishers, though Hunt seems not to have responded. Finally, invoking the presumed clout of his position as "a Gentleman of the University of Oxford," he has authored an apparently explicit poem of some length on current affairs.

The poems from the Esdaile Notebook span the entirety of Shelley's early writing career. He divided these poems into two groups, apparently regarding those composed before mid-1811 as "younger poems" and those from then to the end of 1812 as "later ones."[21] Since Kenneth Cameron has detailed the history of the Esdaile Notebook poems, we need only observe a few points about them that relate directly to the matter of Shelley and his audiences.

The poems appear to have figured in a wide-ranging publishing plan that also included a surprising subject. He remarked to Elizabeth Hitchener that "I have often thought that the moral sayings of Jesus Christ might be very useful if selected from the mystery and immorality which surrounds them—it is a little work I have in contemplation" (*Letters*, I, 265; 27 February 1812). Shelley hoped to employ essential Christianity (as epitomized in the person and practice of Christ, with whom he was already beginning to feel he had something in common as a radical social and philosophical reformer) as a weapon against dogmatic, orthodox religion. He had apparently offered this collection of sayings in the fall of 1812 to the London publisher and bookseller Thomas Hookham, with whom he had begun to deal; the letters of late 1812 attest to the movement of parcels of manuscripts and printed works from Shelley to Hookham and of ordered books from Hookham to Shelley. Apparently Hookham was interested in the collection but not sufficiently so to publish it himself, for on 17 December Shelley inquires "would not Daniel I. Eaton publish them?—Could the question be asked him in any manner?" (*Letters*, I, 340). Like Shelley's tragedy, his "friend's" farce, and apparently several novels (*Hubert Cauvin* among them), the "Biblical Extracts" have not survived, depriving us of potentially useful insight into what Shelley regarded as the exemplary "moral sayings" of Christ, together—undoubtedly—with Shelley's commentary on those sayings.

Shelley nevertheless had a clear sense of how this projected volume was to appear: "I think that the type & size of Godwin's Essay on Sepulcher[s] [1809] would be a good model for The Biblical Extracts. At all events I would wish them to be sent to the press. If you cannot have access to Eaton 250 copies would suffice. Small Christmas or *Easter offerings* of a neat little book have frequently a surprising effect" (*Letters*, I, 348; 2 January 1813). That Shelley is thinking of a book physically resembling Godwin's essay reveals his desire to link himself with that established philosopher and his readership. It also demonstrates his sense of marketing strategy, his awareness that potential buyers do indeed judge a book, if not by its cover then at least by its general physical appearance. Shelley plants two significant suggestions: if Hookham sees to the publication himself Shelley will be satisfied with a mere 250 copies, though he implies that Eaton would produce a much larger press run; and Shelley's underscored words give Hookham a perceptible shove, suggesting that though Hookham has already missed the Christmas trade he may yet be in time for the Easter trade if he hurries. Shelley thus promotes his own interests under the guise of an action presumably beneficial to Hookham.

Shelley's correspondence with Hookham apparently gave him hope as well for other enterprises that had begun to take shape in the aftermath of his sojourn to Ireland. In the letter of 17 December, Shelley opens a new door and asks a pointed question about audience: "I am also preparing a Volume of Minor Poems. Respecting whose publication I shall request your judgement both as publisher & friend. A very obvious question would be.—Will they sell or not?" (*Letters*, I, 340). Shelley had reason to be apprehensive. Not only do the poems leave much to be desired aesthetically, their content subjects poet, printer, and bookseller to real risks. Shelley admits as much on 2 January but rationalizes by claiming that the poems are accurate records of spiritual and imaginative autobiography: "My Poems will I fear little stand the criticism even of friendship.—Some of the later ones have the merit of conveying a meaning in every word, and these all are faithful pictures of my feelings at the time of writing them, but they are in a great measure abrupt & obscure. All breathing hatred to government & religion, but I think not too openly for publication" (*Letters*, I, 348). This passage, in which Shelley tries at once to announce his radical design and to reassure Hookham, reflects that curious sense of "truth in packaging" that characterizes so many of Shelley's statements—both private and public—about himself and his work. But it also puts Hookham in a difficult position. It implies that Shelley has learned from his previous experience and that he can now prepare a manuscript sufficiently moderate in content and tone to be published safely. More important, it makes clear that any criticism of the poems will constitute not just an uncharitable response but behavior unbecoming a friend. Shelley thus heads off any negative response on Hookham's part, rendering him unable gracefully to criticize the poet either in his public capacity as a publisher or in his private one as a friend.

The Esdaile Notebook poems reflect distinctions Shelley drew among the various types of poems and prose pieces he wrote. Set off from those works in the sublime, esoteric medium—and from works in a middle style, like *Julian and Maddalo, The Cenci,* and the Gothic romances—is another class which he later characterized to Leigh Hunt as "exoteric."[22] The *Oxford English Dictionary* defines *exoteric,* as it relates to philosophical doctrines, treatises, and modes of speech, as "designed for or suitable to the generality of disciples; communicated to outsiders, intelligible to the public." All these fit very well the audience Shelley sought at this time to address. These would be poems not only for the disciples—the zealots already enlisted in the army of radical reform—but also for outsiders, the general public that might be receptive to the missionary zeal of the young Shelley who, emulating Jesus, envisioned a public career of conversion. Jesus Christ would remind Pilate, of course, that "My kingdom is not of this world" (John 18:36, 37). Shelley, too, as *Prometheus Unbound* later demonstrates, is thinking of a spiritual kingdom, but in these early years, when reform seemed genuinely attainable, that kingdom presumably could be both prefigured and instituted in the temporal world of human affairs. Like Blake and other postmillennialists, Shelley would have Jerusalem built "in Englands green & pleasant Land."[23]

Shelley's exoteric writings in general indicate their author's keen awareness of both the hortatory purpose for which he wrote and the restrictions imposed on him by the limited sophistication of his intended audiences. The ardently republican poems of the Esdaile Notebook, for instance, are immediately and overtly topical, frequently invoking clear references to the manifestations and effects of British tyranny and oppression. Like the political poems of 1819, they are "poems of exhortation, of vituperation and of fundamental political analysis, designed for the popular reader,"[24] deliberately employing common language, plain allegories, and generally familiar, simple poetic structures. "A Tale of Society as it is: from facts 1811," which may be the "Poetical Essay on the Existing State of Things" discussed earlier, demonstrates that Shelley was as adept at taking up popular verse forms as he was at duplicating the Gothic romance formula. The opening of this melodramatic tale identifies its subject, who resembles the remarkable vagrant widows of Wordsworth's *An Evening Walk* and "The Female Vagrant" and recalls as well the general style of popular social parables by Southey and Coleridge:

> She was an Aged Woman. & the years
> Which she had numbered on her toilsome way
> Had bowed her natural powers to decay[.]
> She was an Aged Woman yet the ray
> Which faintly glimmered thro['] the starting tears
> Pressed from their beds by silent misery
> Hath soul[']s imperishable energy[.]
> She was a cripple, & incapable
> To add one mite to golden luxury
> And therefore did her spirit clearly feel
> That Poverty the crime of tainting stain
> Would merge her in its depths never to rise again [.]
>
> (*SC*, IV, 950)

This largely conventional, pathos-laden narrative form was by 1811 an established vehicle for protesting social injustices and advancing radical means of redressing these ills. In works of this sort both style and content deflect the overt burden of didacticism from the poet, suggesting that the poet is somehow merely an objective observer recording human suffering—that the radical views expressed spring from the hearts and mouths of the oppressed figures whose plight the poems ostensibly record. Shelley's bowed, crippled old woman is a stock character drawn from the pool of victims of an uncaring political, social, and religious establishment that anticipates the more overtly violated victims Shelley treats in such later works as *An Address to the People on the Death of the Princess Charlotte* and *The Mask of Anarchy.*

There are significant stylistic anticipations of the 1819 political poems in Esdaile Notebook poems "The Crisis" and "To Liberty." "The Crisis" might have been composed anytime between 1809 and the time of the Notebook's compilation, yet its "stark directness" suggests that it is one of the "later" rather than the "early" poems.[25] The poem begins with a catalog of the wrongs under which humanity languishes and culminates with a potential glimmer of hope:

> When we see Despots prosper in their weakness
> When we see Falshood triumph in it's folly
> When we see Evil Tyranny, Corruption
> > Grin, grow & fatten
>
> When Virtue toileth thro a world of sorrow
> When Freedom dwelleth in the deepest dungeon
> When Truth in chains & infamy bewaileth
> > Oer a worlds ruin
>
> When Monarhs laugh upon their thrones securely
> Mocking the woes which are to them a treasure
> Hear the deep curse, & quench the Mothers hunger
> > In her child's murder
>
> Then may we hope the consummating hour
> Dreadfully, sweetly, swiftly is arriving
> When light from Darkness, peace from desolation
> > Bursts unresisted
>
> Then mid the gloom of doubt & fear & anguish
> The votaries of virtue may raise their eyes to Heaven
> And confident watch till the renovating day star
> > Gild the horizon[.]
> > > (*SC*, IV, 928–29)

This poem offers a good example of the negative or inverted definition Shelley frequently employs, both in poems in the sublime, esoteric mode (like *Prometheus Unbound*) and in those in the exoteric (like *The Mask of Anarchy*). Wolfgang Iser has observed that such a construction forces its readers to fill in the blanks, to resolve the disjunction between their expectations and the text itself by supplying the material the author has left unstated: "What is said only appears to take on significance as a reference to what is not said; it is the implications and not the statements that give shape and weight to the meaning. But as the unsaid comes to life in the reader's imagination, so the said 'expands' to take on greater significance than might have been supposed."[26] In other words, the horror of the situation described in the first three stanzas is heightened for the readers, who measure the description against their standard of normalcy: the pejorative sense of the lines is thus both defined and enhanced by the external norm of moderate, "civil" behavior the reader brings to the text. The conspicuous absence from the poem of any such balancing norm further heightens the effect of the words that describe "what is." Here and elsewhere Shelley's negative definitions pursue a double purpose: to alert and to incite and motivate.

"The Crisis" introduces in its first four lines the oppressors, followed by their victims, Virtue, Freedom, and Truth. Last of the oppressors to appear is the Monarch, whom Shelley sets specifically against the Mother in a way that recalls Blake's treatment in early poems such as *Tiriel* and *America* of the dominating patriarch-monarch who sacrifices his wife (the "mother country"). In a poem whose major characters are, for the most part, allegorical personifications, Shelley's employment of these two specifically human characters, Monarch and Mother, sets up the point he will make again later in his career: that the cruel class system figurehead—the monarch— is implicitly antagonistic to the egalitarianism of the companionate family represented in the nurturant figure of the mother.[27] His gross villainy, his insatiable appetite for the lives of his children-subjects, is clear from another of the notebook poems, "The Monarch's Funeral: An Anticipation":[28]

> —Yes, 'tis a scene of wondrous awe
> To see a coffined Monarch lay
> That the wide graves insatiate maw
> Be glutted with a regal prey!
>
> Who *now* shall public councils guide?
> Who rack the poor on gold to dine
> Who waste the means of regal pride
> For which a million wretches pine?
> (*SC*, IV, 957–58)

The monarch's is the domination of power over blind obedience, that of the lawgiver who tolerates neither question nor resistance to his dictates; the mother's is the rule of love and nurturance, traditionally submissive and thus both subject to and dependent upon the will (and the whim) of the male. He is a disciplinarian, maintaining a mechanistic order by negative reinforcement of behavioral choices of which he disapproves; she is the supportive nurturer, promoting an organic order by positive reinforcement of integrative behavior. In a word (and it is perhaps too simplistic a formulation), she is civilization and a social contract of mutually beneficial rights and privileges; he is barbarity and a predatory, unprincipled social cannibalism held in place neither by ethics nor by love but simply by force.

Shelley's Esdaile Notebook poems cannot be satisfactorily evaluated as a coherent formal group because they were never published. It is uncertain, for instance, whether the order of the poems in the notebook corresponds to the overall design of the collection as Shelley envisioned it, though Cameron's study of Shelley's line-count numbers suggests that it may.[29] Had the collection actually been printed, formal features like physical design or any introductory remarks by the poet could have given us a clearer sense of just what Shelley intended. As it is, the poems are best regarded as good indicators of Shelley's ideas and of his skill (or lack of skill) as a poet during this early, formative period. His comments about the nature of his poems as antiestablishment documents certainly say a good deal. That Shelley's public ambitions both as writer and as social activist underlie his efforts in poetry and prose alike is, I believe, highly significant, not just for the present study but for any balanced assessment of Shelley's work generally. In "The Crisis" Shelley appears to allow "the votaries of virtue" to pierce "the gloom of doubt & fear & anguish," but he does so only in a qualified sense, for the "may" in line 13 of that poem is a conditional as well as an invocative imperative: "then may we" translates both as "then perhaps we shall" and as "then may it be" (i.e., "let this be"). Things will have to change, and Shelley expects to play a major part in effecting those changes.

Shelley's Irish Campaign

Shelley's Irish enterprise is perhaps best approached initially through the poet's own words. Writing to Elizabeth Hitchener late in January 1812, Shelley makes clear that his plans include a veritable barrage of literary heavy artillery:

> All is prepared. I have been busily engaged in an address to the Irish which will be printed as Paine's works were, and pasted on the walls of Dublin: my Poems will be printed there, Hubert [Cauvin], and the Essays—. . . .

> My address to the Irish . . . is intended to familiarize to uneducated apprehensions ideas of liberty, benevolence *peace* and toleration. It is *secretly* intended also as a preliminary to other pamphlets to shake Catholicism at its basis, and to induce

59

Quakerish and Socinian principle[s] of politics without object-
ing to the Christian Religion, which would do no good to the
vulgar just now, and cast an odium over the other principles
which are advanced. My Volume of Poetry will be I fear an
inferior production, it will be only valuable to philosophical
and reflecting minds who love to trace the early state of human
feelings and opinions, who can make allowances for some bad
versification. (*Letters*, I, 238–39; 26 January 1812)

The "Volume of Poetry" must be the Esdaile Notebook poems, the
projected companion volume to *Queen Mab*. Though Shelley properly
regarded his poetry as the weakest part of his writing at this point, he
characteristically implies that any reader who objects to his well-
intentioned poetry is being both uncharitable and intolerant because
he has modestly acknowledged the deficiencies of his verses but has
published them for the benefit of others.

Other revealing suggestions lie in these lines. The reference to
Paine, for instance, involves Shelley's plans for the "Biblical Extracts"
he hoped Daniel I. Eaton might publish, for Eaton was tried and sentenced in the spring of 1812 for publishing the third part of Paine's
radical attack on orthodox religion in *The Age of Reason*. The trial was
begun on 6 March 1812, some six weeks after the letter just quoted, so
it is perhaps not surprising that Shelley should have been contemplat-
ing involving Eaton in his plan for undermining received opinion, both
as possible publisher and (later) as ostensible subject for *A Letter to
Lord Ellenborough*. Of course, these plans evolved as Shelley followed
the developments in Eaton's trial, which was reported prominently in
the *Examiner*. But the importance of the Paine reference in his letter is
that it verifies that Shelley knew not only Paine's works but also the
manner in which they had been and continued to be circulated and
that he was already familiar—probably from firsthand experience—
with the radical material Eaton had been publishing. At the same time
he was courting the restrained, rhetorically chilly Godwin, Shelley was
also warming his hands at Paine's fire.

Catalogs of works both projected and completed occur regularly in
Shelley's letters during this period and reflect a coordinated design
involving a variety of audiences and what seems at first a considerable
variety of topics. In them, however, we perceive the already established
Shelleyan foci: achievement of social and intellectual integration
through personal and social liberty, renunciation of self-interested
vengeance as motive, and rejection of received orthodox thought generally—whether religious, political, social, or aesthetic. He is now
pondering both general and particular "proposals for instituting associations for bettering the condition of human kind": "*I* even I, weak

young poor as I am will attempt to organize them. The society of peace and love! Oh! that I [may] be a successful apostle of this only true religion, the religion of philanthropy—" (*Letters*, I, 255; 14 February 1812). Consciously loaded words like *apostle* and *religion* in this letter indicate Shelley's evangelistic attitude toward his perceived mission.

Shelley's statement of his objective in addressing the Irish likewise reflects his "religious" fervor:

> I seek your confidence, not that I may betray it, but that I may teach you to be happy, and wise, and good. . . .
>
> No pleasure is so great to me than that which I should feel if my advice could make men of any professions of faith, wiser, better, and happier. . . .
>
> I have told you what I think upon this subject [of temperance and gradualism in change], because I wish to produce in your minds an awe and caution necessary, before the happy state of which I have spoken can be introduced. This cautious awe, is very different from the prudential fear, which leads you to consider yourself as the first object, as on the contrary it is full of that warm and ardent love for others that burns in your hearts, O Irishmen! and from which I have fondly hoped to light a flame that may illumine and invigorate the world.
>
> (I&P, V, 218–19, 216, 235)

The final passage links Shelley's professedly beneficent motive with his audience's best interests in its advocacy of selfless social integration and interaction, for excessive self-involvement directs the purgative and apocalyptic flames inward only, leading to spectacular but pointless self-immolation. Redirecting those flames outward into society, where subsequent similar redirections fan the fire still further serves the greatest, most beneficial purpose.

In disparaging his early poems in his 26 January letter, Shelley sounds a theme that recurs often in his comments about his work. Although his remark serves as self-defense against potential criticism, it also reveals that Shelley sees his works both as directives and as gifts to his audiences.[30] In a pair of letters aimed at increasing the favor and seriousness with which Shelley hoped Godwin would view him, Shelley explains:

> You regard early authorship detrimental to the cause of general happiness. I confess this has not been my opinion even when I bestowed deep, and I hope disinterested thought upon the subject: If any man would determine sincerely and cautiously at *every* period of his life to publish books which should

contain the real state of his feelings and opinions, I am willing
to suppose that this portraiture of his mind would be worth
many metaphysical disquisitions; and one whose mind is
strongly imbued with an ardent desire of communicating plea-
surable sensations is of all others the least likely to publish any
feelings or opinions but such as should excite the reader to
discipline in some sort his mind into the same state as that of
the writer. . . .

I hope that the motives which induce me to publish thus early
in life do not arise from any desire of distinguishing myself,
any more than is consistent with, and subordinate to useful-
ness.

(*Letters*, I, 242–43, 259; ?26 January, 24 February 1812)

In each case Shelley's self-effacing claims preface discussion of
projects currently in hand; in the first it is *An Address to the Irish People*,
in the latter, his Irish campaign generally. He had already declared his
motive to Godwin: "No sooner had I formed the principles which I now
profess, than I was anxious to disseminate their benefits. . . . My Plan
is that of resolving to lose no opportunity to disseminate truth and
happiness" (*Letters*, I, 228–29; 10 January 1812). Shelley says he
"formed" the principles: it is an audacious claim to make to Godwin,
who might have expected the acknowledgment of influence conveyed
by a verb like *absorbed* or *digested*. In the same letter Shelley attempts,
through a mixture of fact and fiction, to credit Godwin's considerable
effect on his career:

It is now a period of more than two years since first I saw your
inestimable book on "Political Justice"; it opened to my mind
fresh & more extensive views, it materially influenced my
character, and I rose from its perusal a wiser and a better
man.—I was no longer the votary of Romance; till then I had
existed in an ideal world; now I found that in this universe of
ours was enough to excite the interest of the heart, enough to
employ the discussions of Reason. I beheld in short that I had
duties to perform. (*Letters*, I, 227–28)

In this, his first letter to Godwin, Shelley adopts a deliberate dignity of
tone that reflects the "Godwinian style" of discourse, in which sentiments are considered and expressed as impersonal and objective facts
according to the universal principles of reason.[31] Shelley's letter, which
conceals even as it invites and discloses, demonstrates his skill at following literary models and suiting the shape and substance of his discourse to his envisioned audience.

Shelley's rhetorical coolness was not achieved without effort, however. Even when writing to the frosty Godwin he can scarcely conceal the ardor for "the cause of virtue liberty and happiness," which he declares to Elizabeth Hitchener (*Letters*, I, 246; 29 January 1812). When Shelley was indulging his passion for reforming the world, at moments when he was relatively free of the financial, political, and emotional entanglements that often plagued him, his enthusiasm was boundless. It must have been infectious, too, if we may judge from his relations with Harriet Westbrook (at least initially), with Hogg (who was clearly an early co-enthusiast in a number of schemes), and, later, with Mary Wollstonecraft Godwin, Leigh Hunt, and Byron. Indeed, Shelley seems to have counted on his demonstrated success with his earliest disciples to buoy him in his efforts to produce similar results with his Irish audiences.

I shall begin with *An Address to the Irish People*, the style of which Shelley explained in some detail to his correspondents:

> It consists of the benevolent and tolerant deductions of Philosophy *reduced into the simplest language,* and such as those who by their uneducated poverty are most susceptible of evil impressions from Catholicism may clearly comprehend. (*Letters*, I, 243; ?26 January 1812, to Godwin; my italics)

> I have wilfully *vulgarized the language* of this pamphlet in order to reduce the remarks it contains *to the taste and comprehension* of the Irish peasantry who have been too long brutalized by vice and ignorance. . . . I have another pamphlet [*Proposals for an Association of Philanthropists*] in the press earnestly recommending *to a different class,* the institution of a Philanthropic Society. (*Letters*, I, 258–59; 24 February 1812, to Godwin; my italics)

> The "Address" was principally designed to operate on the Irish *mob*. Can they be in a worse state that at present? Intemperance and hard labour have reduced them to machines. The oyster that is washed and driven at the mercy of the tides appears to me an animal of almost equal elevation in the scale of intellectual being.—Is it impossible to awaken a moral sense in the breasts of these who appear so unfitted for the high destination of their nature? Might not an *unadorned* display of moral truth, *suited* to their comprehensions produce the best effects[?] . . . The poor of Dublin are assuredly the meanest & most miserable of all.—In their narrow streets thousands seem huddled together—one mass of animated filth! With what *eagerness* do such scenes as these inspire me, *how self confident* too, do I feel in my assumption to teach the lessons of virtue

to those who grind their fellow beings into worse than anni-
hilation. (*Letters*, I, 267–68; 8 March 1812, to Godwin; Shelley italicized "mob"; the other italics are mine)

This last letter is, the quoted passage notwithstanding, the one in
which Shelley ruefully acknowledges to Godwin that he had erred in
his attempts to rectify matters in Ireland, and to that painful acknowledgment I shall turn presently.

Shelley distinguishes in the 8 March letter between the miserable
Irish peasantry, whom he hopes to assist, and the possessors of power,
whom he hopes to educate. Something of the elitist aristocrat shows
through in these passages, and Shelley never did entirely rid himself
of the revulsion toward the lowest members of the social scale that was
part of the ethical baggage of the class system of which he was a ben-
eficiary; his subsequent remarks to his correspondents in the spring of
1818 about the Italians—particularly the women—reflect the same
cultural elitism. His egalitarian ideals notwithstanding, he could be
callous, as in his choice of an *oyster* as the simile for the Irish mob's
intellectual state and his broad characterization of the unfortunate
poor as "one mass of animated filth." By the time he wrote Godwin in
March, Shelley had recognized the futility of the course he had been
pursuing. Having failed to build an adequate self-defensive mechanism into his Address, and having strutted his enthusiasm in his previous letters, Shelley now found it necessary to humble himself before
Godwin. Rather than lose face entirely, he first describes the abject
wretchedness of the Irish commoners and the insensibility to which
their oppression has reduced them, which he intimates is the real
cause of their unresponsiveness. They have not been merely unresponsive but uncharitable in rejecting the gift in which Shelley claims to
have made concessions both of philosophy and of language to make it
attractive and comprehensible. Shelley softens the blow to his ego by
characterizing the Irish rejection as a demonstration both of bad manners and of intellectual incompetence. Moreover, here (and again later
in his career) he apparently separates, at least in his own mind and
language, these people for whom he holds a scarcely veiled contempt
and their abstract class identity as a rhetorical construct.

More important is the matter of "vulgarizing" the language. The
debate among linguistic theorists during Shelley's lifetime about the
status of "refined" and "vulgar" language was as much political as
linguistic. Olivia Smith explains succinctly: "The political and social
effectiveness of ideas about language derived from the presupposition
that language revealed the mind. To speak the vulgar language demonstrated that one belonged to the vulgar class; that is, that one was
morally and intellectually unfit to participate in the culture. Only the

refined language was capable of expressing intellectual ideas and worthy sentiments, while the vulgar language was limited to the expression of the sensations and the passions."[32] The logical consequence of this two-tiered conception of language was the widely held belief that speakers of the vulgar language were hindered by a preoccupation with the immediate present, excessively concerned with material objects, and dominated by the passions. Only those who spoke the refined language were assumed to be properly moral, ethical, rational, "civilized," and capable of abstract thinking. Furthermore, only these were deemed worthy of possessing political power or influence. By 1812 the sharp distinctions between refined and vulgar language had begun to blur, however, helped along by the change in the author-audience relations embodied in the radical writings of such authors as Thomas Spence, Daniel Isaac Eaton (again), John Horne Tooke, and William Cobbett. Shelley was himself vitally interested in this question and read widely and carefully among the major theorists of his time, digesting and incorporating many of their theories into the speculations on language so evident among his works.[33]

In this light, Shelley's comment about "vulgarizing" the language of his *Address* assumes added significance. The terminology recurs publicly in the preface to *Julian and Maddalo* (1818–19) and, more significantly, in the *Essay on Christianity*, in which he implicitly links his own manipulation of language with that practiced by others—most notably Jesus Christ, to whom Shelley had earlier likened himself:

> Jesus Christ did what every other reformer who has produced any considerable effect on the world has done. He accommodated his doctrines to the prepossessions of those whom he addressed. He used a language for this view sufficiently familiar to our comprehensions. . . . Let not this practice be considered as an unworthy artifice. . . . All reformers have been compelled to practice this misrepresentation of their own true feelings and opinions. . . . In fact, truth cannot be communicated until it is perceived. The interests therefore of truth required that an orator should so far as possible produce in his hearers that state of mind in which alone his exhortations could fairly be contemplated and examined. (I&P, VI, 242–43)

It is a most perceptive formulation, but it places the prophet-orator in an impossible situation. To articulate his vision he must compromise and misrepresent it by "deliberately vulgarizing" the language through which he presents it to his audience. Yet to reject this compromise is to risk cutting himself off from his audience by addressing them in an essentially foreign (that is, unfamiliar) language.

In the same essay Shelley identifies precisely the advantage gained by such an intellectual and semantic compromise: "Thus like a skilful orator (see Cicero de Oratore), he secures the prejudices of his auditors, and induces them by his professions of sympathy with their feelings to enter with a willing mind into the exposition of his own" (I&P, VI, 242). It is startlingly instructive to discover that in his manuscript draft of this passage Shelley originally wrote not "induces" but, more tellingly, "seduces" (Bodleian MS Shelley e. 4, fol. 23 recto). Shelley's original verb most accurately captures his conception of the situation, though one can understand why he altered his language away from such an overt statement. The orator's compromise is a subterfuge, a seduction via a nonconfrontational attitude, for "you cannot alter a man's opinion by beating or burning, but by persuading him that what you think is right, and this can only be done by fair words and reason. It is ridiculous to call a man a heretic because he thinks differently from you, he might as well call you one" (I&P, V, 221). Overcoming unreasoning (and hence both unfriendly and uncharitable) resistance from the audience is the messianic prophet/patriot's first priority, and Shelley counsels creating between speaker and audience a semblance of familiarity—in this case semantic or idiomatic familiarity—to defuse hostility and eliminate thoughtless, "knee-jerk" rejections of his advice. Timing is all-important in group dynamics: "Nothing can be more rash and thoughtless than to shew in ourselves singular instances of any particular doctrine, before the general mass of the people are so convinced by the reasons of the doctrine, that it will be no longer singular" (I&P, V, 236). Rather than defiantly articulating a nonconformist position and thereby activating the audience's enmity, the successful orator (whether Jesus or Shelley) first engineers such empathy with the audience that when the radical position is finally articulated it seems neither radical nor heretical but the just and elegant embodiment of views the audience has been seduced into believing it has held all along.

In practice, Shelley normally preserves the distinctions between himself and his audiences even while claiming through his language to overcome them. Indeed, the opening of *An Address to the Irish People* sets out overtly to capitalize on one such difference by stressing that Shelley has already overcome it himself in the interests of his humanitarian aims:

> Fellow men,—I am not an Irishman, yet I can feel for you. I hope there are none among you who will read this address with prejudice or levity, because it is made by an Englishman, indeed, I believe there are not. The Irish are a brave nation. They have a heart of liberty in their breasts, but they are much mistaken if they fancy that a stranger cannot have as warm a

one. Those are my brothers and my countrymen, who are unfortunate. I should like to know what there is in a man being
an Englishman, a Spaniard, or a Frenchman, that makes him
worse or better than he really is. (I&P, V, 215)

Shelley's opening gambit is interesting for several reasons. First,
he makes it clear that his pamphlet is not just the transcription of a
public speech but also a prose essay designed to be read. Second, he
immediately introduces the Shelley-Christ parallel that is so vital to
his subsequent public stance, both in his explicit reference to his brotherhood with the unfortunate (recalling Christ's admonishments about
"these, the least of my brethren," Matt. 25:34–46) and in the implicit
image of the visionary spiritual and political leader who has "descended" so as to redeem a nation. Third, his list of nationalities is
interesting. In 1812 Shelley regarded the French Revolution as an exemplar—albeit a failed one—of the most spectacular outburst of liberty in rebellion against tyranny and oppression.[34] His low opinion of
England is founded upon official English efforts to suppress republican
insurrections both in America and in France and upon its unscrupulous treatment of Ireland. Spain, of course, was a Catholic country that
had risen against outside oppressors. Even Wordsworth had decried
the shameful treatment of Spain by French invaders and English liberators alike in his essay on the Convention of Cintra (1809), lamenting the paradox of the supposedly freedom-loving English siding
against the forces of liberty.

Shelley sets out to turn both the customary English contempt for
the Irish and the justifiable Irish hatred for the contemptuous English
to his advantage through a flattering appeal to *Irish* pride, *Irish* bravery,
Irish love of liberty—values he claims to share. As an Englishman
speaking to Irishmen, Shelley hopes to gain points by explicitly repudiating the "prepossessions" he attributes to his intemperate countrymen:

> I address you then, as my brothers and fellow men, for I should
> wish to see the Irishman who, if England was persecuted as
> Ireland is, who, if France was persecuted as Ireland is, who, if
> any set of men that helped to do a public service were pre-
> vented from enjoying its benefits as Irishmen are—I should
> like to see the man, I say, who would see these misfortunes,
> and not attempt to succour the sufferers when he could, just
> that I might tell him that he was no Irishman, but some bas-
> tard mongrel bred up in a court, or some coward fool who was
> a democrat to all above him, and an aristocrat to all below him.
> I think there are few true Irishmen who would not be ashamed
> of such a character, still fewer who possess it. (I&P, V, 215)

Shelley tailors both diction and syntax carefully here, introducing into the language of refined discussion the passion and intemperance that characterize the vulgar language. But he also makes it clear from the start that his argument is ultimately not merely concerned with national politics but with human (and humanitarian) behavior generally. Hence he raises the issue of national distinction so as to dismiss it. The injustice being done in Ireland (and elsewhere) stems not from national antipathies but from the fact that its perpetrators are *evil and immoral men*, a designation that has absolutely nothing to do with nation or race. Hence Shelley asserts that when Englishmen revile their Irish brothers "it is not because these men are Englishmen . . . , but because they wish to get money, and titles, and power" (I&P, V, 215).

Shelley's *Address* has been called a "manifesto of his new faith" in the inevitability of millennial reform.[35] The essay implies a trust in the slow, inexorable workings of time: change might be hastened if men's minds could be made more pliant, more receptive to well-meaning suggestions like Shelley's, but lasting improvement requires a gradual process rather than an abrupt, possibly bloody shift in the power structure. Hence Shelley everywhere counsels moderation, a tempering of the Irishman's "honourable warmth" at his oppression (I&P, V, 216): "Be warm in your cause, yet rational, and charitable, and tolerant— never let the oppressor grind you into justifying his conduct by imitating his meanness" (I&P, V, 226). Shelley proposes psychological warfare against the oppressors. Although he has not yet advanced so far as to advocate passive resistance as he would in *The Mask of Anarchy*, he already sees the need to avoid lowering oneself to the opponent's base level.

Shelley was, I believe, cognizant of the potential dangers involved in his use of what I have termed the negative definition, chief among which is the possibility that his exertions may arouse in his audience not a reforming spirit but a destructive, revengeful rage. Though Shelley uses the device repeatedly in *An Address* to impress upon his audience the extent of their oppression, he tries in advance to mollify those who would object to so inflammatory a technique, inserting several caveats that serve a double purpose. A single example will suffice: "It will be said, that my design is to make you dissatisfied with your present condition, and that I wish to raise a Rebellion. But how stupid and sottish must those men be, who think that violence and uneasiness of mind have any thing to do with forwarding the views of peace, harmony, and happiness. They should know that nothing was so well-fitted to produce slavery, tyranny, and vice, as the violence which is attributed to the friends of liberty, and which the real friends of liberty are the only persons who disdain" (I&P, V, 234).

The first function of this cautionary passage is to anticipate and defuse criticism. Shelley turns this potential criticism against those who would utter it: those alarmist critics who accuse him of fomenting rebellion merely exhibit their own thick-headed impercipience and insensitivity to humanitarian intentions, leaguing themselves thereby with the oppressors.

The second function is revealed in the final sentence, which echoes Shelley's earlier reference to "*true* Irishmen." Shelley again reduces a complex difference of perception and perspective to a matter of language. "Friends of liberty" may be real friends or false friends, genuine egalitarians or subtle and reactionary dissemblers. The oppressive establishment typically attributes acts of radical resistance to what it contemptuously terms "friends of liberty," but the truest friends of liberty are those who, like Shelley, counsel moderation and gradualism in the service of dissent and reform. Shelley advises his audience, for instance, "In no case employ violence, the way to liberty and happiness is never to transgress the rules of virtue and justice. . . . However ill others may act, this will be no excuse for you if you follow their example; it ought rather to warn you from pursuing so bad a method" (I&P, V, 224). This advice notwithstanding, here and elsewhere in the essay it is apparent that Shelley has not entirely reconciled the roles of warmaker and peacemaker, millenarian and gradualist. Such ambivalences are the essay's greatest weaknesses. Like both the Gothic romances and the Esdaile Notebook poems, *An Address to the Irish People* may be most valuable to us today as an indicator both of Shelley's thoughts at the time and of his efforts at manipulating his audience in yet another literary mode.

Shelley's essay reflects Godwin's influence both in its moderation and in its advocacy of cultivation of mind:

> You can in no measure more effectually forward the cause of reform than by employing your leisure time in reasoning, or the cultivation of your minds. Think and talk, and discuss. . . .
>
> In the interval, that public or private duties and necessary labours allow, husband your time so, that you may do to others and yourselves the most real good. To improve your own minds is to join these two views: conversation and reading are the principal and chief methods of awakening the mind to knowledge and goodness. (I&P, V, 224, 237)

The reading and discussing Shelley recommends would have required considerably more than minimal literacy, as is evident in his comment to Elizabeth Hitchener that "at all events I *will* have a debating society & see what will grow out of that" (*Letters*, I, 255; 14 February 1812).

Indeed, to read and discuss even the *Address* would have required some sophistication. And yet if the "Postscript" Shelley appended to the *Address* once he arrived in Ireland seems to acknowledge that he reassessed the matter, that reassessment merely hardened his resolve to go on as he had begun. His comments on the relationship of style and content, written in retrospect, still point to an unrealistic view of the audience: "I have published the above address (written in England) *in the cheapest possible form,* and have taken pains that the remarks which it contains, should be intelligible to *the most uneducated minds....* In doing so, I have but *translated my thoughts into another language;* and, as language is only useful as it communicates ideas, I shall think my style so far good, as it is successful as a means to bring about the end which I desire, on any occasion, to accomplish" (I&P, V, 246–47; my italics). Shelley appears, however, not to have altered his main text from the form in which he had carried it to Ireland. Perhaps his own education and the amount of time he had devoted to the *Address* made it seem to him much simpler than it was. But his subsequent frustrated comments about the essay's reception (or lack thereof) reveals that he had grossly miscalculated. Having in his enthusiasm invented an ideal Irish audience even before leaving England (where the *Address* was written), it is not surprising that he was unable to assess his actual audience with any real discrimination. Shelley was not alone in this misperception, however, for most English politicians brought to Irish affairs a similar ignorance.[36]

An Address also reveals the influence of Thomas Paine, in whose works Shelley had read widely, not only in the libertarian sentiments but also in the flamboyant imagery, the rousing cadences and the blunt, staccato phrasing in which they are expressed: "Government is an evil, it is only the thoughtlessness and vices of men that make it a necessary evil. When all men are good and wise, Government will of itself decay, so long as men continue foolish and vicious, so long will Government, even such a Government as that of England, continue necessary in order to prevent the crimes of bad men" (I&P, V, 232). Shelley makes a related observation in *Proposals for an Association of Philanthropists,*[37] his formal invitation to other liberal freethinkers to join him in the revitalization of society through enlightened philanthropy, first in Ireland (and, by implication, in England) and ultimately throughout the world (I&P, V, 257). Having observed firsthand the abject and unstable condition of the Irish masses by the time he composed the *Proposals,* Shelley recognized more clearly the danger of suddenly placing power in the hands of an ill-educated mob unprepared to employ it intelligently and judiciously.

Shelley's observations on this point reveal another deliberate persuasive strategy. *An Address* was ostensibly intended to sensitize the mass of Catholic poor to their oppressed condition, whereas Shelley's *Proposals* were intended for "the professional classes," from whose number he hoped to generate another set of disciples,[38] and whom he therefore wished to avoid alarming unnecessarily. He employs a startling image:

> The aristocracy of Ireland (for much as I may disapprove other distinctions than those of virtue and talent, I consider it useless, hasty, and violent, not *for the present* to acquiesce in their continuance.) The aristocracy of Ireland suck the veins of its inhabitants and consume the blood in England. I mean not to deny the unhappy truth, that there is much misery and vice in the world. I mean to say that Ireland shares largely of both.— *England has made her poor;* and the poverty of a rich nation will make its people very desperate and wicked. (I&P, V, 255; my italics)

Rather than driving his point home, Shelley quickly shifts gears in much the same way he had in *An Address*, making it clear that these vampires are in fact English and that they could scarcely be *true* Irishmen, whatever their nationality. The analogy is historically accurate for the consequences of the Act of Union, which had institutionalized at the national level a self-serving, self-centered parasitism. Shelley implies that the "professional classes"—merchants, doctors, lawyers, and others, who were also natural enemies of the landed aristocracy—need not fear for their security from any of his plans. Rather, they should calm their fears and recognize that Shelley is not threatening them at all but is offering them the opportunity to become the vanguard for humanitarian social change and thereby to earn the respect and gratitude of the masses and of posterity. It is much the same approach Thomas Carlyle would take in *Past and Present* (1843) in addressing the "Captains of Industry."

Shelley pursues this strategy of reassurance elsewhere in the essay, most notably in his disclaimer about any subversive intent. Correctly anticipating that the government would be among those groups or institutions that would feel most threatened, Shelley shrewdly states that "nothing would be farther from the views of associated philanthropists than attempting to subvert establishments forcibly, or even hastily" (I&P, V, 258). Shelley does not disavow a subversive *purpose*, but only the notion of forcible or hasty subversion. Depending on the orientation of the audience, and the way one chooses to interpret the rhetorical emphases, the message can be read two ways. The ambiguous rhetoric insulates Shelley even as it advocates the very subversion it seems to disavow.

Predictably, Shelley's essay contains several of his negative definitions, both at the outset, where he defines the role of philanthropy in terms of what it is not, and later in an attack on Malthusian principles prefaced by yet another inverted description of the state of the poor and oppressed (I&P, V, 253, 266). The essay's opening suggests the connection between the negative definition as a rhetorical device and the humanitarian ideals of Shelley's writing generally. The first three paragraphs turn on the principle of philanthropy defined as love and concern *"for a people"* (I&P, V, 253):

> Man cannot make occasions, but he may seize those that offer. None are more interesting to Philanthropy, than those which excite the benevolent passions, that generalize and expand private into public feelings, and make the hearts of individuals vibrate not merely for themselves, their families, and their friends, but for posterity, *for a people;* till their country becomes the world, and their family the sensitive creation. . . . [The philanthropist is] accustomed to place individuals at a distance from self; for in proportion as he is absorbed in public feeling, so will a consideration of his proper benefit be generalized. In proportion as he feels with, or for a nation or a world, so will man consider himself less as that centre, to which we are but too prone to believe that every line of human concern does, or ought to converge. (I&P, V, 253)

Shelley's philanthropy is grounded in the same selfless service to the interests of the human community that informs the conclusion of the "Hymn to Intellectual Beauty," whose narrator learns that the key to the universe, so to speak, is "to fear himself, and love all human kind" (*Works*, 531). This moral code leads directly through the essay on love to its fullest prose articulation in *A Defence of Poetry:* "The great secret of morals is love; or a going out of our own nature, and an identification of ourselves with the beautiful which exists in thought, action, or person, not our own. A man, to be greatly good, must imagine intensely and comprehensively; he must put himself in the place of another and of many others; the pains and pleasures of his species must become his own" (I&P, VII, 118). Shelley's inclusion in this last statement of both the pleasure and the pains of one's fellow beings reveals a notion of sympathetic consciousness already implicit in early works like *An Address* and *Proposals*. Shelley hopes to invoke sympathy as a means of drawing his audiences nearer the experience of those whose misery he hopes to alleviate. In the *Proposals*, for instance, he sketches a picture of the Irish victims of parasitical English tyranny to press his more comfortably secure readers to exercise their imaginations, go out of themselves, learn about the life of the oppressed, and consequently respond to the imperative Shelley raises. What Jean-Paul Sartre writes of the reader's relation to author and text is particularly appropriate to the relation Shelley himself envisions: "reading is an exercise in generosity, and what the writer requires of the reader is not the application of an abstract freedom but the gift of his whole person, with his passions, his prepossessions, his sympathies, his sexual temperament, and his scale of values. . . . He also requires that they return [the] confidence which he has given them, that they recognize his creative freedom, and that they in return solicit it by a symmetrical and inverse appeal." [39] Reading Shelley is always an act of sharing and of mutual creation, as Shelley's prefaces make clear, and the extent to which author and reader alike discharge their obligations determines in large measure the success or failure of any work.

Shelley's stipulation that the association he proposes be entirely public and above ground repudiates any notion of a revolutionary secret society and announces his high social ideals: "I disclaim all connexion with insincerity and concealment. The latter implies the former, as much as the former stands in need of the latter. . . . I propose, therefore, that the association shall be established and conducted in the open face of day, with the utmost possible publicity" (I&P, V, 259). Not by mere coincidence would such a public display reflect *publicly* to the credit of its young organizer, both among the participants, who would perforce respect and appreciate his efforts in the philanthropic endeavor, and among its immediate and future beneficiaries, who could not but associate their improved state with the humanitarian prophet who had come to their country (or their *world*, to use Shelley's own conspicuous word) for their benefit.

Finally, the *Proposals* also project the posture of the self-effacing humanitarian we have encountered before. At the end of the essay, after he has delivered not only his proposals for Catholic emancipation and the repeal of the Act of Union but also capsule lectures on governmental prerogatives, the French Revolution, and Malthusian ethics, Shelley announces his willingness to benefit from the support and advice of others: "I invite to an Association of Philanthropy those of whatever ultimate expectations, who will employ the same means that I employ; let their designs differ as much as they may from mine, I shall rejoice at their co-operation; because if the ultimatum of my hopes be founded on the unity of truth, I shall then have auxiliaries in its cause, and if it be false I shall rejoice that means are not neglected for forwarding that which is true" (I&P, V, 267). In concluding, Shelley proclaims that his concerns are not merely national but universal and his purpose philosophical: the pursuit of truth by an association of enlightened thinkers and reformers, who, following Shelley's lead, may set in motion the wheels of genuine change. If his secondary purpose is to create a public discussion group as he had indicated to Elizabeth

Hitchener, then the closing section of the *Proposals* would seem geared to ensuring its initiation, for Shelley's declaration of openness to agreement and disagreement alike ought ideally to encourage the communication he attempts to facilitate by including at the conclusion of the text his Dublin address. Sadly, the *Proposals* elicited little if any response; even Hogg's suggestion that there was one meeting of such an association has been largely disproved.[40] Shelley had to try yet another only hazily defined audience.

A Letter to Lord Ellenborough

Discrepancies between Shelley's actual and his invented audiences are apparent as well in *A Letter to Lord Ellenborough*, written in response to the conviction of Daniel I. Eaton, the radical Deist journalist, for publishing the third part of Paine's *Age of Reason*. Eaton's trial had been "a travesty on justice" in which the issue of the trial—whether Eaton had actually been guilty of the "blasphemous and profane libel" his Tory accusers claimed—was entirely lost in a hysterical attack on Eaton's personal beliefs, among which the attorney general and Lord Chief Justice Ellenborough found his Deistical principles particularly horrifying.[41] In the little of his defense Lord Ellenborough actually permitted him to present, Eaton said that though the Jehovah of the old Testament was a cruel tyrant, Jesus was "an exceedingly virtuous, good man, but nothing supernatural or divine,"[42] a view similar to Shelley's. Eaton was active on several fronts, publishing militantly anti-Christian authors such as Paul d'Holbach and his own politically radical *Politics for the People; or, A Salmagundy for Swine*. Shelley had thought about Eaton as a potential publisher for his Biblical Extracts—which suggests something of the nature of the book he envisioned. A selection of the sayings of Jesus is one thing; published by a militant Deist like Eaton, it becomes something quite different, as Shelley certainly realized. He wanted Eaton as his publisher because he wanted access to the audience Eaton still commanded.

But Shelley would have been drawn to Eaton's defense for a much more personal reason that is directly relevant to our concerns here. As most discussions of the *Letter* note, its topic is only partially the injustice done to Eaton by an oppressive Establishment. Its larger topic is liberty—in this case freedom of expression, freedom of the press. Shelley had been expelled from Oxford for a not dissimilar offense, and he felt with some justification that he too had been the victim of vilification over irrelevant issues. His letter to Godwin of 11 June is revealing:

> What do you think of *Eaton's* trial & sentence. I mean not to insinuate that this poor bookseller has any characteristics in

common with Socrates or Jesus Christ, still the spirit which pillories & imprisons him, is the same which brought them to an untimely end. Still, even in this enlightened age, the moralist & reformer may expect coercion analogous to that used with the humble yet zealous imitator of their endeavours. I have thought of addressing the public on the subject, & indeed have begun an outline of the address. (*Letters*, I, 307–8; 11 June 1812)

Both in this letter to Godwin and in the finished *Letter*, Shelley places his own unhappy public experiences at Oxford and in Ireland in direct relationship to Eaton's and thus also to Socrates' and Christ's.

The autobiographical center of the *Letter* lies at virtually the numerical center:

> Persecution is the only name applicable to punishment inflicted on an individual in consequence of his opinions. . . . Socrates was poisoned because he dared to combat the degrading superstitions in which his countrymen were educated. . . . Jesus Christ was crucified because he attempted to supersede the ritual of Moses with regulations more moral and humane. . . . *Christianity* is now the established religion; he who attempts to disprove it must behold murderers and traitors take precedence of him in public opinion, tho', if his genius be equal to his courage, and assisted by a peculiar coalition of circumstances, future ages may exalt him to a divinity, and persecute others in his name, as he was persecuted in the name of his predecessor in the homage of the world. (I&P, V, 289–90)

These words have a very familiar ring, even so early in Shelley's writing. The references to Socrates and Christ as victims of culturally imposed superstitions (the very word Shelley applies to Christianity in the letters of 1810–12) reveal how completely Shelley has in mind his own particular experience. His final sentence here vacillates between the desire for vindication and the thirst for revenge. Still bitter at what *The Necessity of Atheism* had cost him and at Godwin's general disapproval of both the principles and the public pursual of his Irish campaign, Shelley complains that both Christianity and the institutions that profess to embrace it have inverted the moral imperative of its central figure in order to suppress any who, like Eaton (or Shelley), have dared to question or criticize the status quo. I find it hard to believe that Shelley actually wishes at any future date to be deified, vindicated, and revenged in quite the fashion his final sentence suggests, however, for that would impossibly corrupt and compromise the leading principle of benevolence. The issue is, rather, the proper reward for the seeker of truth:

> But I will demand, if that man is not rather entitled to the respect than the discountenance of society, who, by disputing a received doctrine, either proves its falsehood and inutility, thereby aiming at the abolition of what is false and useless, or giving to its adherents an opportunity of establishing its excellence and truth.—Surely this can be no crime. Surely the individual who devotes his time to fearless and unrestricted inquiry into the grand questions arising out of our moral nature, ought rather to receive the patronage, than encounter the vengeance, of an enlightened legislature. (I&P, V, 291)

At issue here is Shelley's conception of the prophet as patriot, sacrificing his or her own comfort and security in the interest of assisting the country generally. That such a noble ambition meets so often with resistance leads directly to John Stuart Mill's perception in *On Liberty* of the rapid spread in Western society of a nonthreatening "collective mediocrity," a slavish subjection of individuality to the crushing force of Custom which "is everywhere the standing hindrance to human advancement."[43] Writing in 1859, Mill asserts explicitly the point to which Shelley addressed himself, the invigorating effect upon society of responsible dissent: "In proportion to the development of his individuality, each person becomes more valuable to himself, and is therefore capable of being more valuable to others. . . . it is necessary further to show, that these developed human beings are of some use to the undeveloped—to point out to those who do not desire liberty, and would not avail themselves of it, that they may be in some intelligible manner rewarded for allowing other people to make use of it without hindrance."[44]

The radical dissenter performs a salutary public function in marshaling the forces on either side of the issue she or he has addressed. This notion, which is fundamental to Shelley's understanding of the intellectual and rhetorical function of the skeptical debate, is inextricably bound up with his view of the prophet's public role. Writing in response to Godwin's objections to both the *Address* and the *Proposals for an Association of Philanthropists*, Shelley remarks how "indescribably painful" it is for him to see the oppressed condition of the Irish, who have such great potential, "without attempting to *awaken* them from a state of lethargy so opposite" (*Letters*, I, 276; 18 March 1812; my italics). The trope of awakening recurs throughout Shelley's works, particularly in the strident rallying cries of the political poems of 1819. That the note is sounded already in the early (pre-1813) works indicates how consistently Shelley represented his career as a public ministry not unlike that of the martyred social, political, and moral activist Jesus Christ.

In his "Advertisement" to the *Letter* Shelley employs yet another rhetorical ruse: "I have waited patiently for these last four months, in the hopes, that some pen, fitter for the important task, would have spared me the perilous pleasure of becoming the champion of an innocent man" (I&P, V, 281). Since no writer of any stature has stepped forward in Eaton's defense, Shelley implies, he has taken up the task out of a sense of civic responsibility: someone needs to do it, and even if he cannot do it well, he is at least making an attempt. The linking of peril and pleasure reflects the climate of the intellectual sublime that informs Shelley's Gothic fiction. The choice of *spared* as the verb introducing this idea is likewise intriguing, for it suggests that Shelley already has a fair idea of the negative response his letter is likely to generate and that he is proceeding at least in part in anticipation of the egotistical satisfaction of annoying the conservative Establishment by again making himself obnoxious. This paradoxical combination of selflessness and self-advancement is characteristic of the martyr, whether political or religious, for "only the martyr can be sure of his unselfishness."[45] Yet to choose martyrdom is in many ways to make the most self-oriented public show one can make, increasing rather than decreasing one's visibility to contemporaries and posterity alike.

Either Shelley was deliberately hiding the truth (a possibility) or he was very much out of touch with the contemporary radical press during the four months of which his Advertisement speaks (a much more likely possibility). He was not the first writer to attack the injustice of Eaton's conviction: both Cobbett and Hunt had taken His Majesty's government soundly to task by the time Shelley's own *Letter* went to the printer. Whether Shelley may have meant to imply, in his Advertisement, that Hunt or Cobbett were writers of insufficient stature for the important task at hand seems to me another matter entirely. Even if he had seen or heard about the pieces by Cobbett and Hunt, Shelley would probably have retained his posture as the solitary voice for rhetorical purposes.

But such double—or perhaps more correctly, ambivalent—signaling to the audience takes its toll on Shelley's essay. In his better moments Shelley writes with real fire, with the impassioned prose cadences of Paine himself, and with a voice of protest that recalls figures as relatively diverse as Hunt, Cobbett, Burdett, and Byron.[46] In the essay's conclusion that rhetorical fire becomes more tangible in the final paragraph's apocalyptic imagery. But at other points his diction and syntax try even the most determined reader, as a single example indicates:

The test of truth is an undivided reliance on its inclusive powers;—the test of conscious falsehood is the variety of the forms
under which it presents itself, and its tendency towards employing whatever coercive means may be within its command,
in order to procure the admission of what is unsusceptible of
support from reason or persuasion. A dispassionate observer
would feel himself more powerfully interested in favor of a
man, who depending on the truth of his opinions, simply
stated his reasons for entertaining them, than in that of his
aggressor, who daringly avowing his unwillingness to answer
them by argument, proceeded to repress the activity and break
the spirit of their promulgator, by that torture and imprisonment whose infliction he could command. (I&P, V, 286)

Form and content are often at odds in word-heavy writing of this sort,
especially when it appears together in an essay with terse, incendiary
prose freighted with outrage and invective (see, for instance, the barrage of rhetorical questions in the essay's fourth paragraph).

Shelley knew, of course, that he was not writing for the same sort
of audience he had envisioned in Ireland; in the 18 March letter to
Godwin in which he speaks of his desire to awaken the oppressed he
also declares that he will no longer address himself to the illiterate.
Scrivener reasonably suggests that Shelley addressed the *Letter* to "the
intellectuals, the members of the leisure classes," and points out that
"the *Letter*'s diction, rhetorical techniques, and argumentative logic
are all designed to apply anarchist principles to a particular instance
of injustice in such a way that the readership will be moved in a libertarian direction."[47] But who is that readership? Shelley probably had a
vaguer conception of the audience for this essay than for anything he
had written previously. That Shelley seems to have had such an imperfect vision (or no vision at all) of his intended audience helps explain
both the occasional directionlessness of the argument and the absence
of a consistent rhetorical and stylistic pattern in the essay.

Shelley hoped to marshal the forces behind Eaton (and behind
reformers and dissenters generally) but more importantly to encourage
those forces to see the situation in broader terms, to regard Eaton's
persecution not as the disease itself but rather as a particular symptom
of the much more virulent disease of intolerant, mindless bigotry. At
stake is not merely freedom of the press (the right to publish, or to have
access to, a variety of views on any issue) but the principle of personal
liberty upon which the principle of freedom of the press is based. Shelley's *Letter* explores the implications of the apparently systematic judicial opposition to philosophy and the cultural bias against fearless
inquiry out of which such institutional opposition springs.[48]

This matter is far more complex than one might think who responded carelessly to the millennial tropes Shelley incorporates in the conclusion of the *Letter*, which not only recall those of *An Address to the Irish People* but also foreshadow those of the Princess Charlotte essay and the "Ode to the West Wind." The millennium is coming, Shelley argues, and it is pointless to deny that fact or to resist its necessity. But instead of the cataclysm envisioned by political and religious millenarians, Shelley advocates a gradual apocalypse that evolves from within. This important distinction has at least one very significant precedent in English social, political, and intellectual tradition.

The final paragraph of the *Letter* opens thus: "The time is rapidly approaching, I hope, that you, my Lord, may live to behold its arrival, that the Mahometan, the Jew, the Christian, the Deist, and the Atheist, will live together in one community, equally sharing the benefits which arise from its association, and united in the bonds of charity and brotherly love" (I&P, V, 294). This view of the peaceable kingdom of Revelation directly echoes *Proposals for an Association of Philanthropists*, where Shelley had said of his hopes for Catholic emancipation and enfranchisement that "it is a sign of benefits approaching, a prophet of good about to come. . . . It is the fore-ground of a picture, in the dimness of whose distance, I behold the lion lay down with the lamb, and the infant play with the basilisk. For it supposes the extermination of the eyeless monster bigotry. . . . I hear the teeth of the palsied bedlame [sic] Superstition chatter, and I see her descending to the grave!" (I&P, V, 254–55). Shelley's imagery of the millennial new Eden owes a good deal to Milton, whose *Areopagitica* stood as *the* English exemplar of a stirring defense of freedom of the press. Specifically, Shelley seems to draw his images from Milton's vision of the awakening English nation: "Methinks I see in my mind a noble and puissant nation rousing herself like a strong man after sleep, and shaking her invincible locks. Methinks I see her as an eagle muing her mighty youth, and kindling her undazzled eyes at the full midday beam; purging and unscaling her long-abused sight at the fountain itself of heavenly radiance."[49] Invoking Milton—and specifically the *Areopagitica*—in the context of the *Letter to Lord Ellenborough* is both appropriate and shrewd. It applies the precedent of the great blind poet and patriot (who was, as Shelley well knew, also a prolific prose essayist) to the libertarian principles the *Letter* enunciates even as it permits Shelley tacitly to add Milton's to the names of Socrates and Christ as principled freethinking geniuses who suffered neglect, oppression, or even death in their own times only to be vindicated by subsequent, more enlightened generations. Significantly, the *Letter* is the first major essay Shelley wrote after declaring to Godwin that he would henceforth "look to events in which it will be impossible that I can share, and make myself the cause of an effect which will take place ages after *I* shall have mouldered into dust" (*Letters*, I, 277; 18 March 1812).

It is not uncommon for public figures to set out after the fact to rewrite history to their own advantage, but it is unusual for an author not yet twenty to set out to do so in advance. That Shelley made the attempt indicates insecurity, even desperation. But it also reveals his insightful assessment of the growing power of the printed word and of what we now call the media. Like Mill later, Shelley saw the enormous power of the media for enforcing conformity, for concealing in the guise of public opinion the repressive designs of an elite power structure.[50] And like Mill, he feared what the twentieth century terms "stampeding," the engineering of mindless and compulsive mass conformity to suggestion. In stampeding, people submerge their individuality and join the mob, allowing others to do their thinking—and their choosing—for them.

Shelley's concern about this phenomenon in the England of 1812 is paradoxical, for we must ask whether Shelley was not himself participating in a calculated exercise in propaganda. If the *Letter* was addressed to kindred spirits—to a predetermined, sympathetic audience, however vaguely envisioned it may have been—then was he not advocating a similarly unthinking response? I suspect he was, although such a plea for intellectual safe harbor upon his return to England is understandable in light of the failure of his recent public activities. Not only had they not accomplished what Shelley had intended; they had apparently worked to the contrary. The printer's subsequent destruction of all but fifty copies of the *Letter* and Hookham's refusal to publish it with his imprint undoubtedly compounded Shelley's frustrations. Nevertheless, as he would do again with his 1817 Marlow proposals for reform, Shelley sent copies to readers he regarded as sympathetic, including Godwin, Sir Francis Burdett, Lord Stanhope, and his Irish friend Mrs. Catherine Nugent. One senses in all this activity two related—and in some ways very moving—impulses: first, the desire to keep the pot boiling by acting as a public conscience, and, second, the almost desperate desire for acknowledgment, for encouragement, for praise. That this second desire went largely unfulfilled says much about Shelley's apparent withdrawal from this sort of public activity in 1813 and his concurrent interest in the hands-on community activism in which he became engaged at Tremadoc.

"Learn to make others happy."

SHELLEY, *Queen Mab*

Chapter Three
BACK IN ENGLAND
1812–1817

I hear that a bookseller of the name of Clarke has published a
poem which I wrote in my early youth, called Queen Mab. I
have not seen it for years, but inasmuch as I recollect it is vil-
lainous trash; & I dare say much better fitted to injure than to
serve the cause which it advocates.—In the name of poetry, &
as you are a bookseller (you observe the strength of these con-
jurations) pray give all manner of publicity to my disapprobation of this publication; in fact protest for me in an advertisement in the strongest terms. (*Letters*, II, 298; 11 June 1821)

Thus Shelley wrote to his publisher, Charles Ollier, from Pisa after
William Clarke's pirated edition of *Queen Mab* appeared in 1821. It is
worth considering at the outset of this chapter Shelley's intentions in
his letter to Ollier and those of 22 June to the *Examiner* and the *Morning Chronicle* apparently repudiating his poem. The carefully constructed duplicate letters for the press must be seen whole:

Sir,
    Having heard that a poem, entitled 'Queen Mab', has been
surreptitiously published in London, and that legal proceedings have been instituted against the publisher, I request the
favour of your insertion of the following explanation of the
affair as it relates to me.
    A poem, entitled 'Queen Mab', was written by me at the age

of eighteen, I dare say in a sufficiently intemperate spirit—but even then was not intended for publication, and a few copies only were struck off, to be distributed among my personal friends. I have not seen this production for several years; I doubt not but that it is perfectly worthless in point of literary composition; and that in all that concerns moral and political speculation, as well as in the subtler discriminations of metaphysical and religious doctrine, it is still more crude and immature. I am a devoted enemy to religious, political, and domestic oppression; and I regret this publication, not so much from literary vanity, as because I fear it is better fitted to injure than to serve the cause of freedom. I have directed my solicitor to apply to Chancery for an injunction to restrain the sale; but after the precedent of Mr. Southey's 'Wat Tyler' (a poem, written, I believe, at the same age, and with the same unreflecting enthusiasm), with little hope of success.

Whilst I exonerate myself from all share in having divulged opinions hostile to existing sanctions, under the form, whatever it may be, which they assume in this poem, it is scarcely necessary for me to protest against this system of inculcating the truth of Christianity and the excellence of Monarchy however true or however excellent they may be, by such equivocal arguments as confiscation, and imprisonment, and invective, and slander, and the insolent violation of the most sacred ties of nature and society.

> Sir, I am,
>
> Your obliged and obedient servant,
> Percy B. Shelley
> (*Letters*, II, 304–5; 22 June 1821)

Shelley apparently sent the two formal letters to Ollier, with instructions to pass one copy to Hunt "for the twopenny post" (*Letters*, II, 305). Shelley's letter satisfies the letter of the law in repudiating *Queen Mab* even as it advertises the poem to the curious reader. These letters and the preceding one to Ollier would seem to relieve Shelley of legal responsibility for Clarke's pirated edition and also for his own 1813 edition, which was never actually sold. But let us consider some of the ruses contained in Shelley's formal letter.

First, Shelley was not eighteen when he wrote *Queen Mab*: he was twenty. But the earlier age better squares with the "intemperate spirit" he says characterizes the poem. By the time he completed the poem, though, he was no mere intemperate novice, no matter how impetuous he may have been. He had already completed and published a pair of novels, two volumes of admittedly questionable poetry, several political and philosophical pamphlets, and his *Letter to Lord Ellenborough*. And *Queen Mab* was no mere recapitulation but was, rather, all new material, composed after his return to England from his Irish enterprise.[1] It was a major effort at a long revolutionary sociopolitical poem, and for a first effort in the genre Shelley had good reason to remain proud of the poem, flawed though it unquestionably is.

The deliberate fiction about Shelley's age is followed by another. The poem was in fact originally intended for publication. Shelley had announced to Elizabeth Hitchener in December of 1811 his intention to compose a poem that was to be "by anticipation a picture of the manners, simplicity and delights of a perfect state of society; tho still earthly. . . . I only thought of it last night.—I design to accomplish it and publish." (*Letters*, I, 201; ?10 December 1811) Shelley's letters to Thomas Hookham, with whom he was dealing at this time, also make it clear that he expected Hookham to sell the poem. (*Letters*, I, 324, 350, 354; 18 August 1812, 26 January, 15 February 1813). When he sent Hookham the finished manuscript—before completing the notes—Shelley reasserted his intentions: "In spite of its various errors, I am determined to give it to the world. . . . If you do not dread the arm of the law, or any exasperation of public opinion against yourself, I wish that it should be printed & published immediately" (*Letters*, I, 361; March 1813).

Finally, there is Shelley's note to Hookham: "I expect no success.—Let only 250 Copies be printed. A small neat Quarto, on fine paper & so as to catch the aristocrats: They will not read it, but their sons & daughters may" (*Letters*, I, 361; March 1813). Shelley's strategy is to make the book attractive enough to sell, even if the readership he seeks is not the purchasers themselves—the wealthy but nonreading collectors of fine editions—but rather their more inquisitive offspring, whom Shelley might enlist in his army of young reformers.

Queen Mab was printed in an edition of 250, as Shelley had specified, with Shelley's name given as both author and printer. Since English law requires that the printer's name appear twice in any publication, on the first leaf and on the final page of text, the presence of Shelley's name as printer suggests that the actual printer was sufficiently concerned about prosecution to refuse to list his own name. Shelley apparently became cautious as well, for in the copies he distributed he cut away both the title page and the foot of the final page.[2] Writing to the Shelleys' Irish friend Catherine Nugent, Harriet Shelley intimates the danger: "'Queen Mab' is begun [apparently to be printed], tho' it must not be published under pain of death, because it is too much against every existing establishment. It is to be privately distributed to his friends, and some copies sent over to America. Do you [know] any one that would wish for so dangerous a gift?" (*Letters*,

I, 368n.; 21 May 1813). The "pain of death" is of course an exaggeration, but it suggests why Shelley must have decided not to risk open sale of his poem but rather to distribute it privately—as he had *The Necessity of Atheism*—in the hope of arousing interest and response.

Shelley's public protestations about the literary worthlessness of the poem and about the crudeness and immaturity of its political, metaphysical, and religious speculations nevertheless serve to publicize both the original and the pirated poems while also soliciting reassurance. The humble admission of the insufficiency of his efforts deprives the readers of the opportunity to call that deficiency to his attention: it would be rude to criticize a poem its author has already freely branded as juvenile, intemperate, and worthless. So the readers must read the poem and either agree, in which case Shelley has anticipated them and thus insulated himself from censure, or disagree, in which case the readers are forced to praise and reinforce what is admirable while no more than tacitly acknowledging the poem's imperfections. Moreover, Shelley links *Queen Mab* explicitly with Southey's *Wat Tyler*, ascribing to both a youthful impetuosity that returned to haunt the two poets in the subsequent publication of early poems. Like Wordsworth, Southey had abandoned his early republicanism for much more conservative ground. By 1821 Shelley was also convinced that Southey, with whom he had corresponded, had been responsible for some of the attacks on his own works (as we see in the preface to *Adonais*) and so would have enjoyed the irony of publicly linking their careers in these formal letters. It is name-dropping, to be sure, but it is also a reminder to the public about intellectual steadfastness, especially if we choose to understand from the previous sections of Shelley's letter than his repudiation applies more to his poem *as poem* than to the libertarian principles articulated therein.

Finally, Shelley closes his letter with a stirring defense of personal liberty articulated in terms of freedom of the press. He had already defended Eaton in the *Letter to Lord Ellenborough* and had taken up Carlile's cause in November 1819 in another letter to Hunt and the *Examiner*. Here in 1821 he lashes out at the Society for the Suppression of Vice, which had appropriated all but about fifty copies of the pirated *Queen Mab* (which had already been put into circulation) from Clarke's stock and had subsequently initiated a successful lawsuit against Clarke which resulted in a four-month sentence at Cold Bath Fields Prison. Shelley nowhere blames Clarke for republishing *Queen Mab*, which further suggests that Shelley was not displeased by that republication and that he gladly seized upon the persecution of Clarke as yet another occasion for an attack on the repressive system holding sway in England. The final section of his letter condemns the savageness of the official response to the poem (and its author) which Shelley sets out here to claim is really comparatively unimportant. That response he characterizes as out of proportion to the offense, as exceeding all limits of decency and typifying the paranoid frenzy with which the oppressors of liberty persecute the true "friends of liberty."

That the oppressors have resorted to force (confiscation and imprisonment), scarcely surprises Shelley, who has pointed out in his previous essays on freedom of expression that suppression is a typical response to dissenting views, be they hostile or simply honestly critical. Nor has Shelley forgotten the action of Lord Eldon and the English court system in depriving him of his children by Harriet, as the reference to "the insolent violation of the most sacred ties of nature and society" indicates. That the oppressors resort as well to *ad hominem* attacks, however, Shelley clearly regards as proof not only of their moral and ethical bankruptcy but also of their inordinate fear over the revelation of their own errors. Since the charges leveled against them are irrefutable, Shelley implies, they respond not to the charges but to their spokesman, defaming and slandering in an attempt to defuse the criticism, forgetting that the aggrieved are no mere rare, isolated individuals but a massive body, the lions rising after slumber to which Shelley appeals in *The Mask of Anarchy*. The conclusion of Shelley's letter implies that he and Clarke are being martyred by a crumbling power structure and that readers who find themselves oppressed by this same power structure are members of a persecuted sect whose day may yet arrive. Indeed, this is precisely the point of Shelley's long note (*Works*, 819–25) on the fate of Jesus at the hands not just of his pagan accusers and executioners but also of that orthodox Christianity which tyrannizes all who would emulate the humanitarian ideals of its founder, Jesus Christ. Asserting pointedly that "the common fate of all who desire to benefit humanity awaited him," Shelley distinguishes between the Son of God typically invoked by an atonement-oriented orthodoxy and the man Jesus who "stands in the foremost list of those true heroes who have died in the glorious martyrdom of liberty, and have braved torture, contempt, and poverty in the cause of suffering humanity" (*Works*, 820).

Some light is shed on this situation by a revealing letter to John Gisborne in which Shelley writes unguardedly about the matter:

> A droll circumstance has occurred. Queen Mab, a poem written by me when very young, in the most furious style, with long notes against Jesus Christ, & God the Father and the King & the Bishops & marriage & the Devil knows what, is just published by one of the low booksellers in the Strand, against my wish & consent, and all the people are at loggerheads about it. . . . You may imagine how much I am

amused.—For the sake of a dignified appearance however, & really because I wish to protest against all the bad poetry in it, I have given orders to say that it is all done against my desire.—and have directed an attorney to apply to Chancery for an injunction, which he will not get. (*Letters*, II, 300–301; 16 June 1821)

Shelley's certainty that the application for a Chancery injunction will fail indicates how knowledgeably he was going through the motions of seeming to retract and disavow *Queen Mab* without actually doing so and how much he was enjoying the irony of the situation.

Shelley's comments also illustrate why we need to be especially wary of measuring calculated, formal public statements (like the letters to the *Examiner* and the *Morning Chronicle*) by the same standards as unguarded private ones (like that to Gisborne).[3] They help us to appreciate that statements that might appear at first glance to be contradictory often prove upon closer inspection to be evidence of the subtle and sophisticated campaign of audience manipulation that is so much a part of Shelley's verbal artistry.

We might next consider a statement to a Mr. Waller, written in November 1817 in a presentation copy of the poem:[4]

The Author sends 'Queen Mab' to Mr. Waller, as Cardinal Wolsey was sent to Heaven, 'with all his imperfections on his head.' It was composed in early youth, & is full of those errors which belong to youth, as far as arrangement of imagery & language & a connected plan is concerned.—But it was a sincere overflowing of the heart & mind, & that at a period when they are most uncorrupted & pure. It is the Author's boast & it constitutes no small portion of his happiness that, after six years of added experience & reflection, the doctrines of equality & liberty & disinterestedness, & entire unbelief in religion of any sort, to which this Poem is devoted, have gained rather than lost that beauty & that grandeur which first determined him to devote his life to the investigation & inculcation of them—(*Letters*, I, 566–67; 22 November 1817).

Shelley's careful distinction in this letter between what he regards as *Queen Mab*'s poetic failings and what he still sees as the moral and intellectual ideals embodied there is important in light of his observation to Ollier in 1821 that he is happy that Clarke has removed from the pirated edition the original dedication to Harriet, "the only part of the business that could seriously have annoyed me" (*Letters*, II, 298). That Shelley continued to work with the original *Queen Mab*, revising it in at least two different versions (the copies at the British Museum and the Pforzheimer Library), incorporating some of its passages into *Alastor*, and recasting still other sections as *The Daemon of the World* (itself subsequently annotated for revision in at least two copies) suggests that he was determined to salvage as much as possible from the original wreck without sacrificing the principles it had voiced.[5]

The enthusiasm Shelley later professed to Mr. Waller for the sentiments in *Queen Mab* is no less than that with which he seems to have set about composing in the first place. Because Hookham was apparently his bookseller during this early period, Shelley kept him informed of the poem's progress throughout 1812. Hookham must have been rattled to receive in mid-August what Shelley called a "specimen" of some early passages of *Queen Mab*, together with the unsettling remark that "You will perceive that I have not attempted to temper my constitutional enthusiasm in that Poem. Indeed a Poem is safe, the iron-souled Attorney general would scarcely dare to attack 'genus irritabile vatum'" (*Letters*, I, 324; 18 August 1812).

Apparently Shelley developed some misgivings about the poem, though, particularly after he fully realized its nature when completed. Writing to Hogg, for instance, he combines arrogance and defensiveness:

> I have finished the rough sketch [apparently the first draft] of my Poem.—As I have not abated an iota of the infidelity or cosmopolicy of it [Hogg had apparently cautioned him on this score], sufficient will remain, exclusive of innumerable faults invisible to partial eyes to make it very unpopular. Like all egoists I shall console myself with what I may call if I please the suffrages of the chosen few who can think & feel, or those friends whose personal partialities may blind them to all defects.—I mean to subjoin copious philosophical notes. (*Letters*, I, 352–53; 7 February 1813)

Carl Woodring has remarked that when Shelley recast parts of *Queen Mab* as *The Daemon of the World* he had begun to conceive of poetry in a less didactic fashion and that by the end of 1814 he began to expect "to reach and modify fewer minds by either prose or poetry" and to refer disparagingly to what we might call the "average" reader with increasing frequency.[6] Actually, as this passage to Hogg indicates, that distinction was becoming clear even earlier. The shift is in part sincere, in part mere self-defensive rhetoric, but it is significant nevertheless. After his expulsion from Oxford and the failures both of literary efforts in poetry and prose and of on-the-scene political efforts, it is not surprising that Shelley should have objectified his need to withdraw from such crisis situations in remarks of this sort.

Shelley's subsequent caution may have stemmed from the direction his notes to the poem finally took, for those notes bore the brunt of the criticism when the pirated edition appeared in 1821. Almost from the beginning Shelley conceived of a heavily annotated poem, perhaps recalling his earlier favorite, Southey's *Thalaba the Destroyer*. Indeed, Shelley had *Thalaba* in mind in the poem itself (together with other models, from "the Greek Choruses" to Milton and Erasmus Darwin), as his letter to Hogg of 7 February 1813 acknowledges,[7] and he already knew the advantage of composing a poem whose stylistic similarities might lend it greater marketability. The young Shelley would ride Southey's coattails, as he would Radcliffe's, Hunt's, or Godwin's, if doing so would get him an audience. Relying on conventional literary devices to communicate an unorthodox message, as Shelley does in *Queen Mab*, is a standard tactic of subversive writing, whether propagandistic or not, and it is a tactic of which Shelley remained fond, as demonstrated in such later works as *Swellfoot the Tyrant* and "A New National Anthem." In the notes, however, which his letters indicate were composed after the poem was completed, Shelley adopted a directness he had not permitted himself in the verse: "The notes to Q. M. will be long & philosophical. I shall take that opportunity *which I judge to be a safe one* of propagating my principles, which I decline to do syllogistically in a poem. A poem very didactic is I think very stupid" (*Letters*, I, 350; 26 January 1813; my italics). If didacticism is "stupid" in poetry, it is apparently not so in philosophical prose, where directness and bluntness are presumably both appropriate and admirable. Shelley seems to have wished to reassure Hookham that the notes' volatility posed no danger: "The notes will be long philosophical, & Anti Christian.—*this will be unnoticed in a Note*" (*Letters*, I, 361; March 1813; my italics). Why would the anti-Christian sentiment be "unnoticed" in a note? Because no one reads notes? Because notes are read by a different sort of reader than the one who reads only the verse? Because the notes are placed separately in the text (Hookham printed them at the end)?

If Shelley meant to suggest that he could "hide" even his bluntest and most radically nonconformist ideas in the notes, we need only look at a copy of *Queen Mab* to appreciate his miscalculation. The finished copies included some 240 pages. The poem itself, together with the front matter, occupy the first 122 pages. The notes occupy pages 125 to 240 and are printed in the same typeface, with the same wide spacing, as the verses that precede them. The notes are not hidden, merely separated; they occupy nearly half the volume. Could their length have been the crucial factor in Shelley's decision not to publish the poem even in the limited edition he had contemplated? Something surely went awry, for Shelley's extant letters make no further mention of the poem until 1817, a fact surprising in itself because Shelley normally has something to say about the fate of his works, even if only a self-deprecating reference.

It may have gone unsold, but Shelley's poem did not go entirely unnoticed, although the author was almost certainly involved in the single contemporary notice of *Queen Mab*, the long extract-review that appeared in the *Theological Inquirer, or Polemical Magazine* from March through July 1815.[8] The review stresses the notes by pointedly claiming not to do so: "The copious and elegant notes to the poem, it is not within my design to call your attention to." A long review of this sort neatly gets around the difficulties involved in direct publication of *Queen Mab*: the contents of the poem are publicized without their having been formally published, and since the identity of the poem's author is carefully concealed, the author is thus shielded against prosecution. That the review, which quotes the poem extensively, appeared over a five-month period would have contributed further to keeping the otherwise unknown poem in the public's eye. None of Shelley's attempts to publicize and distribute his poem seem to have met with much success, though, for when the radical publisher Richard Carlile bought up the remainder of the original 250 copies in 1822 he found that only 70 had been disposed of.[9]

The publicizing of *Queen Mab* may have lain behind the publication later in 1813 of *A Vindication of Natural Diet*, whose title is followed by the words, "being one in a series of notes to Queen Mab, A Philosophical Poem." Although the essay is simply an expanded reprint of one of the longest notes in *Queen Mab*, its title page explicitly refers to that poem and probably was intended to function, like the subsequent 1815 review, as a means of generating reader interest in the poem. Or perhaps Shelley's great interest in vegetarianism impelled him to publish the essay separately as part of another crusade. Nevertheless, the explicit reference to the suppressed poem still smacks of shrewd marketing strategy.

The very magnitude of the "Notes" section of *Queen Mab* relates to another standard rhetorical strategy: the argument by testimony, by authority. Reiman observes that many of the notes are in fact "full essays" (as evidenced as well from Shelley's publication of two of them in separate issues), filled with supporting quotations from authors ranging from the classical to the contemporary and representing "a broad range of poets, philosophers, and historians."[10] Shelley's copious use of these diverse sources constitutes an implicit claim to authority, demonstrating not only the depth and breadth of his own reading but also the degree to which he had digested this wide-ranging reading and brought it to bear on his own formulations. His careful citation of his sources serves at least in part also to soften the radicalism of many of his arguments by linking them to the writings of more thoroughly established thinkers.

Finally, in that March letter accompanying the text of *Queen Mab* Shelley makes what would become a standard appeal to his reader—here in the person of Hookham—for constructive criticism: "I send you my Poem. To your remarks on its defects I shall listen & derive improvement. No duty on a friend is more imperious than an utter sincerity & unreservedness & criticism; none of which a candid mind can be the object with more inward complacency & satisfaction" (*Letters*, I, 361; March 1813). Shelley places Hookham in one of those uncomfortable positions I have already described. As usual on these occasions, Shelley's message points in different directions: he deliberately charges Hookham as a *friend* to be candid with him, despite having addressed him formally in the letter's superscription as "My dear Sir." As a bookseller, it is Hookham's business specifically to behave in business affairs *not* as a friend but rather as an objective and professional businessman. Hookham is trapped whichever way he turns, for Shelley's apparent protestation of his willingness to accept the sincere criticism of a friend renders it far more difficult for Hookham to respond to the poem in his professional capacity. By means of devices like these, aimed at keeping his reader or audience off balance almost from the first, Shelley consistently attempts to gain an initial advantage.

A similar strategy appears in the preface to *A Refutation of Deism*, written and published in 1814. Hogg says the work "was published in a legal sense, unquestionably; whether it was also published in a publisher's sense, and offered for sale, I know not, but I rather think, that it was: the preface informs us that it was intended it should be. I never heard that anybody bought a copy; the only copy I ever saw is that which my friend kindly sent to me. . . . I never heard it mentioned any farther than this, that two or three of the author's friends told me, that it had been sent as a present." With the denigration that characterizes so much of what he has to say about Shelley's writings, Hogg dismisses the *Refutation* as neither new nor important in content, though he does credit its "powerful, energetic, contentious style." Yet Hogg may be misrepresenting fact, for while he claims the piece was "composed and printed also, in a hurry," he notes that the volume was "handsomely, expensively, and very incorrectly printed, in octavo."[11]

Hogg's account minimizes clear indications of Shelley's care in the preparation and publication of this work. The *Refutation* also draws on the notes to *Queen Mab*, but that earlier material is elaborately reworked and expanded and the style made smoother and less noticeably tendentious. Furthermore, Shelley's copy from the error-filled first press impression (the copy in the British Library) contains a number of corrections which he made in the text and which were subsequently gathered in an errata list.[12] The way the volume was issued adds further weight to the argument that the dialogue was a more serious effort than Hogg admits. Hogg's suggestion about the relative luxury of the volume is borne out by the third and final paragraph of Shelley's preface: "The mode of printing this little work may appear too expensive, either for its merits or its length. However inimical this practice confessedly is, to the general diffusion of knowledge, yet it was adopted in this instance with a view of excluding the multitude from the abuse of a mode of reasoning, liable to misconstruction on account of its novelty" (I&P, VI, 25). This curious little paragraph, which seems to fly in the face of all of Shelley's egalitarian ideals, certainly requires a closer look.

First, and most obvious, is the declared intent of "excluding the multitude." This gesture owes something to the growing ambivalence in Shelley's attitudes toward what he increasingly considered the lower orders of readers. He signals his express intention of maintaining law and order—both religious and societal—by not making available to such readers sensitive material with which they might not be prepared to deal intelligently and which might therefore prove detrimental both to their own interests and to those of society generally. In other words, he makes a gesture in the direction of social responsibility, albeit an elitist one, which he observes is "confessedly" hostile to the otherwise noble design of spreading knowledge. Furthermore, the exclusion of this less fit audience becomes both a concession and a compliment to the included readers, who are both flattered by the gesture and subtly obligated to reciprocate in a spirit of charity and collegiality by demonstrating that they are worthy of that inclusion. This demonstration, presumably, is to take the form of comprehension and assent, for to object would be ungenerous, uncharitable. Shelley's self-effacing reference to "this little work" underscores the aura of inoffensiveness he wishes to establish before the reader gets to the dialogue itself. "Little" serves as both a qualitative and a quantitative term, for the work is not really "little": it runs some 101 pages in octavo, even though those hundred plus pages are set in an admittedly large typeface.

The second paragraph of Shelley's preface sounds a familiar note: "The Author endeavours to shew how much the cause of natural and revealed Religion has suffered from the mode of defence adopted by Theosophistical Christians. How far he will accomplish what he proposed to himself, in the composition of this Dialogue, the world will finally determine" (I&P, VI, 25). Shelley's success depends only partially on him, and more on his audience's willingness to exercise the charity and goodwill the author calls for. Taken in its entirety, this is in many ways a prototypical Shelleyan public preface. It sets up a frame for the work that follows, bracketing the body of the work with a caution to the reader to expect nothing miraculous but simply an honest and sincere effort to be of service to humanity undertaken in full knowledge that the effort might prove costly to its well-intentioned author. Hence we return to the gentle—but strategic—self-deprecation in the final paragraph, in which Shelley confesses the seeming presumption of presenting his modest effort to the discerning public in its present expensive form.[13] Addressing an audience that often judges books by their covers, he builds into his preface a disarming appeal to the very elitist value system he is elsewhere at pains to disapprove. It is first-rate rhetorical and intellectual seduction. The *Refutation* constitutes a remarkable exercise in duplicity (upon both the reader and the Establishment) that "not only circumvents government repression (by appearing to uphold the established order), but undermines orthodox thinking."[14] Shelley's apparently modest preface introduces a prototypical skeptical debate in which each side demolishes the other, leaving the reader who has been following the progress of the argument with little alternative but to reject both Deism and Christianity.

A Refutation of Deism was subsequently reprinted in corrected form in the *Theological Inquirer, or Polemical Magazine* from March through September 1815, making its appearance there contemporaneous with the long extract-review of *Queen Mab* and further suggesting Shelley's direct involvement in this clever exploitation of his work. Lending additional credence is the fact that following the text of *A Refutation* in the *Inquirer* is a letter signed by "Mary Anne" and taking issue with the work. Newman Ivey White remarks that "Mary Anne is not wholly convincing as a genuine antagonist,"[15] but she does function well as a surrogate discussant of the sort Shelley may have envisioned for the *Posthumous Fragments of Margaret Nicholson* when he told his correspondent and cohort Edward Fergus Graham that he would likely send him "the abuse" (the spurious letter to the editor criticizing the poems) shortly. If Shelley could not elicit actual responses, he stood ready to supply the deficiency himself and appears always to have delighted in doing so.

Shelley had now reached his twenty-second year. He had already written a great deal of poetry and prose, and whether or not it was in fact widely read, or even read at all, is in many ways beside the point, although it is interesting to consider how his career might have developed had any of these early works been a smashing success. What would have become of the crusading radical had he been, like Byron, blessed—or cursed—with an overnight best-seller? One looks at Harriet Shelley's accounts of the Shelleys distributing their pamphlets in

Ireland by stuffing them into passing baby carriages and the pockets of passers-by, and after the initial amusement of the scene passes, one is touched by such desperate measures. To be sure, youthful enthusiasm is frequently reduced to such measures, partly to salve the wounds of rejection and partly to demonstrate its own resiliency and ardor. But then there are poems like "Sonnet: To a Balloon Laden with Knowledge" and "Sonnet: On Launching some Bottles filled with Knowledge into the Bristol Channel," whose pathos is increased by our recognition that they surely refer to still other of Shelley's methods for disseminating his ideas to a public often hostile, more frequently simply indifferent. Indeed, the former poem, from the Esdaile Notebook and dating presumably from mid-1812, might be regarded as an appropriate emblem of Shelley not just at the time but for much of his life and beyond:

> Bright ball of flame that thro' the gloom of even
> Silently takest thine etherial way
> And with surpassing glory dimmst each ray
> Twinkling amid the dark blue Depths of Heaven;
> Unlike the Fire thou bearest, soon shall thou
> Fade like a meteor in surrounding gloom,
> Whilst that, unquenchable, is doomed to glow
> A watch light by the patriot's lonely tomb,
> A ray of courage to the opprest and poor,
> A spark, tho' gleaming on the hovel's hearth,
> Which thro' the tyrants' gilded domes shall roar,
> A beacon in the darkness of the Earth,
> A Sun which o'er the renovated scene
> Shall dart like Truth where Falsehood yet has been.[16]

The event celebrated here is likely factual, since the bottle launching in the other poem is verified by the letter to Lord Sidmouth, the home secretary, written in full steam by one Henry Drake, town clerk of Barnstaple, the town near the Devonshire village of Lynmouth to which the Shelleys had retired after their return from Ireland. Drake reports that Shelley had been seen dropping bottles into the sea and that one of these bottles having been obtained was found to contain "a seditious Paper," which turned out to be Shelley's broadside "The Devil's Walk," his variation on the better-known theme of the Prince Regent's follies authored by Southey and Coleridge. A second captured bottle yielded up to yet another of Sidmouth's operatives a copy of Shelley's Irish broadside *Declaration of Rights*.[17] It is moving to contemplate from a distance of nearly two centuries the increasingly predictable rebuffs to Shelley's exertion of both physical and intellectual energy in service to his "passion for reforming the world." One of the marvels of Shelley's career is the author's dogged persistence. He would tell Trelawny later, "I always go on until I am stopped, and I never am stopped."[18] Indeed, it would take the intervention of nature to finally stop him.

By mid-1814 other matters were more pressing, more momentous, for on 28 July he eloped to the Continent with Mary Wollstonecraft Godwin and her stepsister Claire Clairmont. The journal begun by Bysshe at the time and carried on by Mary resulted eventually in the *History of a Six Weeks' Tour*, which I shall consider briefly later. When the trio returned to England on 13 September, Shelley plunged back into his accustomed activities, both literary and economic. One poignant letter to Mary from early November reveals the extent to which the latter consumed both his time and his energies: "Thus it is—my letters are full of money, whilst my being overflows with unbounded love, & elevated thoughts. How little philosophy & affection consort with this turbid scene—this dark scheme of things finishing in unfruitful death. There are moments in your absence my own love when the bitterness with which I regret the irrevocable time wasted in unprofitable solitude & worldly cares is a most painful weight. You alone reconcile me to myself & to my beloved hopes" (*Letters*, I, 419; 4 November 1814). All was not so bleak as Shelley's outburst here suggests, though, for within a week the lovers were reunited, both with each other and with their circle of friends, and within this fragile peace Shelley soon undertook an effort in a genre new to him.

Mary Shelley's journal records that Shelley began a "critique" on 16 November, working earnestly "till half-past 3," and apparently finishing the piece the next day. The critique must have been Shelley's review of Hogg's odd novel, the *Memoirs of Prince Alexy Haimatoff*, the publication of which in the *Critical Review and Annals of Literature* for December 1814 she reported with some excitement upon their receiving their copy of the journal on 3 January 1815.[19] It would be interesting to know how Shelley's review came to appear in the *Critical Review*; the only previous connection had been that journal's publication in November 1810 of a decidedly unpleasant review of *Zastrozzi*, which it had branded an "execrable production" whose author "cannot be too severely reprobated."[20]

Shelley's ambitious review places Hogg's novel within the broad contexts of intellectual and artistic activity generally, exploring the fate of genius in a world apparently committed to mediocrity: "Mediocrity alone seems unvaryingly to escape rebuke and obloquy, it accommodates its attempts to the spirit of the age, which has produced it, and adopts with mimic effrontery the cant of the day and hour for which alone it lives" (I&P, VI, 176). Shelley's philosophical point here is colored, of course, by his surely deliberate use of Hogg as a stand-in for himself. Indeed, Shelley might as well be speaking of his own work as of Hogg's when he says "As a composition the book is far from faultless. Its abruptness and angularities do not appear to have received the slightest polish or correction. The author has written with fervour but has disdained to revise at leisure. These errors are the errors of youth and genius and the fervid impatience of sensibilities impetuously disburthening their fulness" (I&P, VI, 176–77). Shelley would in 1817 characterize his own performance in *Queen Mab* in much the same way to Mr. Waller.

The fate of genius, Shelley's essay makes clear, is too often made to hinge upon the artist's willingness to subject his or her vision to the dictates of the popular taste. Popular fame depends upon such conformity, and though genius may in an ideal world transcend such petty, material concerns, in the real world it goes often castigated—and still more often unnoticed—if it is unwilling thus to bend: "What does utter obscurity express? if the public do not advert even in censure to a performance, has that performance already received its commendation?" (I&P, VI, 175). The real dichotomy is not between fame and obscurity but between the radical independence of genius and the groveling subservience of vulgar pandering. Recognizing that prior fame or notoriety colors the audience's assessment of the artist's productions, Shelley ostensibly attempts to evaluate Hogg's novel objectively, on reasonable intellectual and aesthetic grounds, thereby helping launch its unknown author[21] on a productive career by a judiciously balanced review, rather than irresponsibly damning him because he has not yet attained the preeminence to make him impervious to rational criticism. Shelley grants Hogg a favor here that too few of his own critics would ever grant him, and in that sense Shelley's review stands as an interesting model of the "charitable" criticism he so often solicited from correspondents and readers.

As he had done in the *Refutation*, Shelley again draws distinctions among the literary audience, dividing them into "the ignorant" and "the enlightened," and noting that the former are typically characterized by their contempt for the latter. This state of affairs Shelley finds not at all remarkable, ascribing it to a fundamental flaw in human nature in its present unregenerate state: "the vulgar pride of folly, delights to triumph upon mind" (I&P, VI, 175). Inflated pride is incompatible with enlightened intellect, whose selflessness renders it insusceptible to baser passions. Shelley again sets up a "we-they" relationship, addressing himself to an audience he characterizes as sufficiently enlightened to appreciate his compliment. The editorial first-person plural serves Shelley well in this instance, allowing him to use standard critical terminology to extend a rhetorical arm around the reader's shoulder to draw him or her into the speaker's intimacy and confidence.

Shelley further exploits the rhetorical gesture by which he separates the sheep from the goats, first unleashing a direct attack:

> Is the suffrage of mankind the legitimate criterion of intellectual energy? Are complaints of aspirants to literary fame, to be considered as the honourable disappointment of neglected genius, or the sickly impatience of a dreamer miserably self-deceived? the most illustrious ornaments of the annals of the human race, have been stigmatised by the contempt and abhorrence of entire communities of man; but this injustice arose out of some temporary superstition, some partial interest, some national doctrine: a glorious redemption awaited their remembrance. (I&P, VI, 175)

Notice the curious shift in verb number in the second sentence: the complaining "aspirants" to literary fame diminish in the second half of the question to "*a* dreamer miserably self-deceived," which dreamer is almost certainly Shelley himself, slipping here in print in a periodical in which the slip could not be rectified by subsequent revision. The rest of this passage, and indeed all of the philosophical disquisition that precedes the specific discussion of Hogg's text, may reasonably be read as a covert statement of his conviction that time would vindicate him from the slings and arrows of outrageous contemporaries. Furthermore, Shelley's list of reasons for the public rejection of the enlightened includes some of his familiar self-referential terms: "some temporary *superstition*," for instance—the word he had for several years been associating with Christianity—or "some national doctrine," like the English position vis-à-vis Ireland, which Shelley understood to have prompted his harassment over the Irish affair. Nor does casting the "glorious redemption" of the spirits thus wronged into the past tense do much to disguise Shelley's contemplation of his own *future* remembrance and vindication.

The thrust of the opening argument is clear: the ignorant masses always misunderstand what is going on around them and either short-circuit or hopelessly misdirect and pervert the progressive exertions of the few enlightened reformers. Such had been the fate of the French Revolution, as Shelley had planned to demonstrate in *Hubert Cauvin* and as he would demonstrate in *The Revolt of Islam*, and of Socrates and Jesus Christ. Granting the impercipience of the ignorant multitude, Shelley perforce dismisses them from his essay and addresses his invented enlightened and sympathetic audience. The "ingenuous critic" must be aware of the powerful societal impulse toward uncomprehending nay-saying, Shelley continues ironically: "His labours are indeed, miserably worthless, if their objects may invariably be attained before their application" (I&P, VI, 175). There is little point in attacking a good new work, in other words, since misguided popular taste will itself provide a superabundance of negative response: "No excellencies, where prudish cant and dull regularity are absent, can preserve it from the contempt and abhorrence of the multitude" (I&P, VI, 176). To be of real service, then, the honest and objective critic must particularly emphasize and laud those "excellencies," which will otherwise go unremarked in the storm of popular abuse.

Shelley postpones until his fourth paragraph any first-person references; there his "we" encompasses by implication not just the editorial voice but also the assenting consciousness of the enlightened audience, fit though few. Shelley juxtaposes the attentive and appreciative "we" with "the vulgar" and "the unenlightened," reminding the readers again of the crucial distinction: "The vulgar observe no resemblances or discrepancies, but such as are gross and glaring. The science of mind to which history, poetry, and biography serve as the materials, consists in the discernment of shades and distinctions where the unenlightened discover nothing but a shapeless and unmeaning mass. *The faculty for this discernment distinguishes genius from dulness*" (I&P, VI, 176; my italics). In a manner reminiscent of Wordsworth's discussion of the poet and his proper audience, Shelley's last sentence attributes at least the potential—if not the actual presence—of genius not just to original artists but to their audiences and critics (the "we" of Shelley's review) as well.

On the whole, Shelley's assessment of Hogg's novel is remarkably balanced, considering that he was also in some sense reviewing his own works and their critical reception, as well as navigating the treacherous waters of reviewing the work of a close friend. Furthermore, by attributing the novel's imperfections sometimes to the author's apparent youth, sometimes to the unreadiness of society for the view articulated therein, and sometimes to the acknowledged inadequacies of the reviewer's trade, Shelley is able to cushion some sharp and particular criticisms in a relatively gentle, good-humored, and nonthreatening fashion. That he made these statements publicly, in the formal shape of a professional review, rather than simply passing them along to Hogg privately during a friendly conversation, indicates Shelley's already keen awareness of the press's power in shaping public taste. Finally, his use of the public forum provided by the *Critical Review* anticipates his use of the press in the years that would follow for the poetic debate in which he would engage Byron over a variety of issues.

One wonders what Hogg thought of Shelley's review. Whether he really grasped Shelley's intentions in the brief essay, and particularly in the opening sections, is uncertain, even granting their long acquaintance. What is certain is that on 3 January 1815 the arrival of the issue of the *Critical Review* bearing the essay was followed soon afterward by the arrival of the novelist himself. Mary's journal states simply, "Hogg comes. A very pleasant evening."[22] That Hogg appears on nearly a daily basis thereafter, and that Mary Shelley's letters to him in the period that follows become increasingly intimate and frequently address him as "Alexy," suggest that Hogg was anything but displeased by the review.[23]

Despite the complicated personal affairs that drained his time and energy during this period, Shelley had not neglected his poetry. In addition to recasting the less dangerous sections of *Queen Mab* as *The Daemon of the World*, he had prepared the other poems for the *Alastor* volume, which was printed in January 1816 and published the next month.[24] Mary Shelley's retrospective note to the title poem, which recounts (and exaggerates) various aspects of Shelley's physical suffering at the time of the poem's genesis, begins with an assertion that *Alastor* was by design a much more private and introverted production than anything that had preceded it:

> *Alastor* is written in a very different tone from *Queen Mab*. In the latter, Shelley poured out all the cherished speculations of his youth—all the irrepressible emotions of sympathy, censure, and hope, to which the present suffering [i.e., in 1839], and what he considers the proper destiny, of his fellow-creatures, gave birth. *Alastor*, on the contrary, contains an individual interest only. A very few years, with their attendant events, had checked the ardour of Shelley's hopes, though he still thought them well grounded, and that to advance their fulfilment was the noblest task man could achieve. (*Works*, 30)

The note goes on to claim that Shelley had decided to "turn his eyes inward" and focus on "the thoughts and emotions of his own soul" rather than following his procedure in *Queen Mab* and making "the whole universe the object and subject of his song" (*Works*, 30). Her assessment, however, is only partially accurate. That the poem is more overtly an examination of Shelley's own psyche than *Queen Mab* is immediately apparent, even without the autobiographical references, like that to the Poet's "thin hair" (line 471). But the note suggests that the disappointing response to his humanitarian efforts—both in person and in print—had prompted Shelley to shift course rather more than he actually did. Indeed, the suggestion is even more explicit in Mary Shelley's note to the poems of 1815: "Hitherto, he had chiefly aimed at extending his political doctrines, and attempted so to do by appeals in prose essays to the people, exhorting them to claim their rights; but he had now begun to feel that the time for action was not ripe in England, and that the pen was the only instrument wherewith to prepare the way for better things" (*Works*, 528). Writing some twenty-five years after the fact, she may simply be misremembering history rather than intentionally distorting it. Although Shelley's strategy in the volume involves a less overt appeal for immediate, popular action by the masses and a more moderate and highly polished style, he was still campaigning actively for ideological, ethical, and social reform.

Alastor; or the Spirit of Solitude: And Other Poems is a coherent and carefully structured representation of Shelley's views on the public role and function of the poet, with respect both to the dreams and ideals with which the volume begins and ends (*Alastor* and *The Daemon of the World*) and to the realities of the public world ("To Wordsworth," "Feelings of a Republican on the Fall of Bonaparte," and "Superstition"). Shelley's volume presents the reader with two conspicuous failures, Wordsworth and Napoleon, each of whom had initially represented great potential for good to his nation and each of whom had, in Shelley's eyes, ended by betraying the causes of political and intellectual liberty.[25] The poems on Napoleon and Wordsworth, like *The Daemon of the World*, reflect Shelley's conviction that the friend of humanity must be involved rather than detached or isolated. Napoleon's political fall, for instance, stems from his spiritual and imaginative fall. Like Satan, Napoleon had placed the general good of humanity second to his self-serving aspirations. Yet even Napoleon is not the paramount villain: like Wordsworth, Napoleon falls ultimately by succumbing to the crippling pressure of Custom:

> I know
> Too late, since thou and France are in the dust,
> That virtue owns a more eternal foe
> Than Force or Fraud: old Custom, legal Crime,
> And bloody Faith the foulest birth of Time.
> (*Works*, 527)

The ninth poem in Shelley's volume, "Superstition" (recast from *Queen Mab*, VI, 72–102), examines, under the banner of Shelley's familiar catchword, the real danger to humanity. The poem is "an anatomy" of the way the imaginative mind destroys itself by surrendering its liberty to embrace a stabilizing but self-reflexive image of its own creation.[26] When one commands the public influence of a Napoleon or a Wordsworth the perniciousness of this self-aggrandizing involution is compounded by the individual's ability to inflict the internalized error upon the mass of humanity. Like the poems in the magnificent *Prometheus Unbound* volume of 1820, the poems in the *Alastor* volume cast significant light upon one another, providing multiple contexts for the particular subjects of the individual poems. That the poem at the numerical center of the volume, "To Wordsworth," is so explicitly critical of the elder poet whom Shelley had so revered[27] suggests the extent to which Shelley feels compelled to alert his audience to the seductive potential of the statements of all public figures—even himself. The narrator in *Alastor*, who fails adequately to understand the Visionary because of his own conditioned Wordsworthianism, mirrors the public generally, who too often unthinkingly equate public position with reliability of opinion. The preface to *Alastor* is, it turns out, the preface to all the poems, and its position at the beginning of the volume ensures its applicability not just to the title poem to which it explicitly refers but also to all the poems that follow.

Like *Queen Mab*, the *Alastor* volume was prepared initially in some 250 copies. Most significantly, Shelley sent one copy to John Murray, Byron's publisher, inviting him to become the official publisher, undoubtedly hoping to gain access to Byron's already considerable audience. A "Byron connection" is evident elsewhere in the *Alastor* volume. The brief poem beginning "Oh! there are spirits of the air," for instance, seems to have puzzled a number of editors, from Mary Shelley—who regarded it as an address to Coleridge (*Works*, 527)—to others who see it as "an address by Shelley in a despondent mood to his own spirit."[28] Embedded in Canto II of *Childe Harold's Pilgrimage*, however, is a brief lyric inscribed "To Inez," which anticipates both in theme and in attitude not only Shelley's lyric but also *Alastor* itself. This suggests that before he actually met him in 1816 Shelley may have been beginning to envision himself as Byron's counterpart among the younger Romantics.[29] Attempting to enlist Byron's own publisher would thus be a logical move. Had Murray taken up the volume Shelley offered him, he might well have been expected to promote this young, aristocratic contemporary of Byron, with Shelley standing to gain most from the association.

Writing to Murray, Shelley is characteristically deferential in inviting the publisher's judgment about his work: "I should certainly prefer to sell the copyright. But I am aware that an Author cannot expect much encouragement for his first poetical production before the public shall have passed their judgment on its merits" (*Letters*, I, 439; 6 January 1816). His first poetical production? Shelley conveniently omits mention of *Queen Mab*, the *Original Poetry*, and the *Posthumous Fragments* in introducing himself as a hopeful neophyte. This is a reasonable omission, though, since none of these had actually appeared over his own name and since Southey was the only one of Murray's authors who knew Shelley at this point. Shelley's letter contrives the rules by which Murray is expected to play. Choosing not to disclose his previous publications, Shelley places Murray under a polite obligation to assess the work offered him purely on its own merits, regardless of any other knowledge he may have of the author.

Murray turned down Shelley's offer, however, and the volume was printed by Samuel Hamilton and published jointly by Baldwin, Craddock, and Joy, and by Carpenter and Son. Typically, Shelley sent off copies. The one he sent to Southey took with it a cover letter acknowledging Shelley's differences with the elder poet: "Regarding you with admiration as a poet, and with respect as a man, I send you, as an intimation of those sentiments, my first serious attempt to interest the best feelings of the human heart, believing that you have so much general charity as to forget, like me, how widely in moral and political opinions we disagree, and to attribute that difference to better motives than the multitude are disposed to allege as the cause of dissent from their institutions" (*Letters*, I, 462; 7 March 1816). Shelley's explicit appeal to Southey's "charity" is a striking attempt to exclude from Southey's judgment of the volume all that does not relate directly to an assessment of man and poet. Notice that Shelley cleverly asks Southey to forget, "*like me*," their differences, thereby obligating him to reciprocate with a similar gesture of magnanimity. Furthermore, note Shelley's slight shift away from the neophyte posture he had assumed in his unproductive letter to Murray: the *Alastor* volume is now regarded as his first *serious* attempt.

Despite his effort in this volume to interest "the best feelings of the human heart," Shelley failed to win the full, ungrudging approval of the reviewers, though several acknowledged that his abilities were considerable. Furthermore, the *Alastor* volume seemed to reach few readers and to inspire or activate still fewer. Hence by the end of 1816, writing to Hunt, Shelley apparently dismisses the volume casually, claiming "the oblivion which overtook my little attempt of Alastor I am ready to acknowledge was sufficiently merited in *itself*" (*Letters*, I, 517; 8 December 1816). But he did not give up entirely, as his correspondence with Charles Ollier in 1818 indicates. In a pair of letters in January dealing with the publication of *The Revolt of Islam*, Shelley still presses for publicizing the earlier volume: "The advertisements of the 'Revolt of Islam' ought to contain a notice of Alastor. . . . Alastor may be adv[ertise]d *with it*" (*SC*, V, 393, 445; 2,11 January 1818).

In her note to *Alastor* Mary Shelley remarks that "the poem ought rather to be considered didactic than narrative" (*Works*, 31), confirming the suggestion in the second paragraph of Shelley's preface that "the picture is not barren of instruction to actual men" (*Works*, 15). Shelley may have intended his preface to function in a manner analogous to that of Coleridge's preface to "Kubla Khan," as both introduction and preliminary (or subsequent) example, as an apparent explanation of the poem that embodies its very contradictions in what appears to be a straightforward address to the reader.[30] Certainly the preface is an integral part of the poem as a whole and cannot be discounted or overlooked.[31] Like Coleridge, Shelley does not introduce himself explicitly as author, but opts for a detached, third-person voice. Prefaces are inherently paradoxical creatures, normally written only after the completion of a work.[32] For the reader about to read (i.e., to "make" or perform) the text, however, the term is entirely appropriate. This is a distinction Shelley himself undoubtedly drew, for he consistently uses his prefaces skillfully to precondition his readers before launching them into the main text of a work.

The preface to *Alastor* is a good example of this careful control. Its binary structure reflects the division discussed therein between the psychological allegory (paragraph 1) and its application to reality (paragraph 2). The second paragraph, in which the world of "actual men" is considered, is the more rhetorically forceful, as are the poems on external, topical figures and events throughout the volume. Here Shelley attacks the visionary Poet's critics (and his own critics, to be sure) as accessories to the destruction of the Poet. Shelley's narrative invokes the story of Narcissus and Echo as partial context for the Poet's obsessive pursuit of his idealized alter ego, that "ideal prototype of everything excellent or lovely that we are capable of conceiving as belonging to the nature of man," that "soul within our soul" ("On Love," I&P, VI, 202). But the myth of Actaeon—which would resurface in *Adonais*—is here as well, handled in a subtle and intriguing fashion.

Shelley's Poet falls victim to the self-destructive pursuit of the prototype that engenders the hounds that tear him to pieces psychologically. The most violent phase of this destructive cycle occurs after the Poet is embraced by the "veiled maid" in his erotic dream. As the dream dissipates and the Poet returns to external consciousness, the universe he perceives is transformed as a result of the trauma induced by that failure of involuntary vision.[33] His "vacant brain" (line 191), activated by his "wan eyes" that "Gaze on the empty scene . . . vacantly" (lines 200–201) now perceives only "vacant woods" (line 195). "Nothing exists but as it is perceived," Shelley later writes in "On Life" (1819; I&P, VI, 194); the seeming change in external nature in *Alastor* from this point onward is an illusion produced by the Poet's altered state of consciousness. Furthermore, Shelley's visionary Actaeon also feeds the critics who perform the hounds' function literally and metaphorically. Unlike Actaeon, however, both the Poet and Shelley *choose* their course rather than blundering upon Diana. We need to distinguish Shelley from the Poet, however. For the Poet is indeed self-deluded, and the mark of his error is his isolation from his fellow mortals, a separation that renders him a superfluous man incapable of being of service to humanity.

For Shelley as author, however, isolation is not chosen but imposed by hostile audiences. Hence the persecutors come in for the strongest language of the preface, which sentences them to "a slow and poisonous decay": "They are morally dead. They are neither friends, nor lovers, nor fathers, nor citizens of the world, nor benefactors of their country" (*Works*, 15). If these are the characteristics of the unsympathetic, "those unforeseeing multitudes," then the qualities of the clearsighted benefactors of humanity must be the converse, and if we reverse Shelley's other terms we find that the description accords with the principal roles he had already attached to himself. His insistence upon the need for charity and generosity on his reader's part lends force to his final line: "Those who love not their fellow-beings live unfruitful lives, and prepare for their old age a miserable grave" (*Works*, 15).

Alastor documents the need for community among humanity and the terrible consequences for all parties of the failure to achieve such community. Both the self-isolating Poet and the well-meaning but traditionalist narrator, who bewails his loss without comprehending the significance of his history, bear witness to the tragedy of failed human communication, of unrecognized "sympathies with their kind." It is an error to regard the narrator as the poem's "true hero" on the grounds that only he initiates the "communitarian act of sharing" and "only he knits the fabric of an organic connectedness between people."[34] While he professes a humanitarian concern for the Poet, he also falls victim to error. The narrator's unquestioning satisfaction with the sufficiency of nature to humanity's needs leaves him unable fully to understand or appreciate the nature of the Poet's quest for the ideal: the gesture of community embedded in his meditations on the Poet's case is undermined by his own "prepossessions" (as Shelley would have called them), which leave him reacting to the wrong aspects of the Poet's experience, pitying rather than comprehending and judging his history. William Keach is nearer the truth in suggesting that the Poet may not be a separate entity at all but rather "the projection of a submerged impulse in the narrator's own mind," the narrator's "deeper self projected as spectral other," much as the veiled maiden functions vis-à-vis the Poet.[35] Shelley's poem dramatically documents the collision of two differently oriented sensibilities, a drama he complicates by the rhetorical device of having the story of the first both filtered through and narrated by the narrative persona of the second. Shelley is again invoking the artist's prerogative to distinguish between the authorial and the narrative audiences as a means of involving his readers in the creative process of evaluating, considering, and choosing.

Shelley's procedure in *Alastor* is best understood in light of the poet's "experiment with the skeptical and paradoxical manner of proceeding" in *A Refutation of Deism*.[36] Just as a careful reading of the

Refutation forces the reader to realize that neither of the positions advanced therein is finally tenable, so should a proper reading of *Alastor* produce a similar reaction to the stances adopted by the narrator and the Poet. If the Poet errs in rejecting his mortal peers to pursue his obsessive quest, the rest of the world errs along with the narrator who is its spokesman in taking the position that what is different is to be pitied, if not overtly condemned. Both elements, in other words, need to modify their presently irreconcilable, self-preserving positions if they are to be of any help to each other. Meanwhile, Shelley complicates matters by introducing in the preface an authorial (or pseudo-authorial) voice different from those in the poem proper. This voice, which is oratorical and increasingly strident, epitomizes the paradoxes upon which the entire poem turns. Preaching the doctrine of love and integration, the speaker concludes with harshly judgmental language for those who are perceived to be proceeding incorrectly. In disparaging and condemning these unregenerate individuals rather than extending to them the love and charity of community that revives and rejuvenates, and which he purports to advocate, the speaker reveals an inflexibility and intolerance greater even than that of Poet or narrator. The preface's two paragraphs encapsulate the structure of the skeptical debate that likewise governs the poem that follows. The preface is the key to understanding both the real tragedy and the didactic purpose of the poem.

Alastor is also a calculated response to Wordsworth, a reformulation of both the philosophy and the poetry of the poet whom Shelley had once so admired and whose fall from favor is commemorated in this volume by the poem at its center, "To Wordsworth." Much of the Poet's history may be seen to parallel the tale related in the elder poet's "Lines left upon a Seat in a Yew-Tree," the third poem (and the first by Wordsworth) in the 1798 *Lyrical Ballads*. Indeed, *Alastor* combines the sort of sad history Wordsworth's poem records with a Wordsworthian observer who narrates and interprets it for the reader, Shelley having formulated in two dramatic personae the psychological or intellectual division inherent in Wordsworth's "Lines."

Moreover, the opening of Shelley's preface immediately invokes the context of Wordsworth's Advertisement to the *Lyrical Ballads*. Shelley writes: "The poem entitled "Alastor," may be considered as allegorical of one of the most interesting situations of the human mind" (*Works*, 14). Wordsworth's first sentence is "It is the honourable characteristic of Poetry that its materials are to be found in every subject which can interest the human mind."[37] The similarity of phrasing and key terminology in these two sentences is too striking to be coincidental. Shelley intends his reader to recognize that the young poet is engaging the elder on the latter's own ground. His revisionist reading is designed to expose the inadequacies he has come to perceive in the Wordsworthian moral and aesthetic agenda. It is an audacious endeavor, a declaration of poetic independence and self-sufficiency which the works that follow would entirely justify.

Shelley professed a strong dislike of overt didacticism in poetry. But he early adopted the moral and humane goal of the sort of prophecy we see in Dante and Milton: "to 'awaken and enlarge' the minds of his readers to the understanding of man's condition as it is, *and as it might be*"[38] (my italics). Their didactic purpose already inherent in their prophetic nature, Shelley's long poems reveal their author's concern with "how to be didactic most tellingly."[39] In his best works, his objective is less to impose his own view upon his audience than to kindle in that audience its own capacity for vision. The preface to *Alastor* challenges the reader to evaluate not only the moral and ethical preconceptions embedded therein but also the behavior of the two characters. Within the autobiographical context of Shelley's works, it stands also as an accusation, an indictment of what Shelley perceived as the mindless bias against him over private matters which he considered irrelevant to any reasonable assessment of him either as man or as poet, much less as reformer of the world and friend of humanity.

A much slighter production is the *History of a Six Weeks' Tour* (1817), the revised and composed-to-order version of the journal apparently kept jointly by Shelley and Mary Godwin following their flight to the Continent on 28 July 1814. Although the *History* in its present form is substantially Mary Shelley's, internal evidence identifies its preface as Shelley's.[40] Shelley's three short, disarming paragraphs do their best to ensure a friendly reading, as the opening passage indicates:

> Nothing can be more unpresuming than this little volume. It contains the account of some desultory visits by a party of young people to scenes which are now so familiar to our countrymen, that few facts relating to them can be expected to have escaped the many more experienced and exact observers, who have sent their journals to the press. In fact, they have done little else than arrange the few materials which an imperfect journal, and two or three letters to their friends in England afforded. They regret, since their little History is to be offered to the public, that these materials were not more copious and complete. This is a just topic of censure to those who are less inclined to be amused than to condemn. (I&P, VI, 87)

The final sentence serves the familiar Shelleyan notice that to object to the nature or substance of what follows is to identify oneself with the latter, the humorless castigators of innocent efforts. After all, how can criticism be anything but *uncharitable* behavior, since the preface's first sentence makes any such response ignoble indeed?

This seemingly casual preface is in fact carefully constructed. Shelley takes pains to be inoffensive, even advertising the inadequacies of the text that will follow: it is too short, it deserved better notes than those that were kept; it is a heterodox mixture of journal entries, letters, and poetry; and in any event it records things the audience probably knows all about anyway. Given all this, one might wonder why this "little History is to be offered to the public." The remainder of the preface replies by citing the enthusiasm of youth for new scenes, new sensations, addressing not only the sympathetic young but also those who can still remember with delight the similar experiences of their own youth. Furthermore, it appeals to the reader's imagination, inviting her or him to participate with the authors in a shared experience else unknown.

Enthusiasm is the key term here, and Shelley emphasizes it in the second paragraph, in appealing to the generous reader to "forgive the imperfections of [the] narrative for the sympathy which the adventures and feelings which it recounts, and a curiosity respecting scenes already rendered interesting, and illustrious, may excite" (87). This appeal to the strength of enthusiasm in enabling the audience to overlook defects in the interest of appreciating the sentiment leads into the final brief paragraph: "The Poem, entitled 'Mont Blanc,' is written by the author of the two letters from Chamouni and Vevai. It was composed under the immediate impression of the deep and powerful feelings excited by the objects which it attempts to describe; and as an undisciplined overflowing of the soul, rests its claim to approbation on an attempt to imitate the untamable wildness and inaccessible solemnity from which those feelings sprang" (87–88). This passage clearly echoes Wordsworth's "spontaneous overflow of powerful feeling," though Shelley seems conveniently to have forgotten Wordsworth's qualifier about "recollected in tranquillity." In fact, Shelley aims not at the psychological and aesthetic distance Wordsworth achieves by recollecting in tranquillity but instead at the vibrant immediacy that results from composing while the powerful feeling is at full flood, a point he makes explicitly in his preface to *The Revolt of Islam*. Shelley is invoking the tradition of sentimentalism, in which what is seen or experienced is less important than the feelings it produces in the individual. He wants his reader to credit the author's sincerity in presenting a work still wet with the dew of its birth and not tamed and reworked into a more perfect, more "civilized" form. Roughness was, we recall, a quality in Milton's verse to which the Augustan critics had particularly objected and which the Romantics had come very much to admire.

Shelley's preface also invokes Byron, the "great Poet," who has subsequently observed the same scenes the *History* records but who has clothed them "with the freshness of a diviner nature" (87). Since the preface was written after Shelley had spent the summer of 1816 with Byron, I believe Shelley's reference here is more than mere polite deference to Byron. Shelley had brought back to England with him Byron's manuscript of Canto III of *Childe Harold's Pilgrimage*, which he was to deliver to John Murray—the same publisher he had attempted less than a year earlier to interest in his own *Alastor* volume. Shelley had much to gain with Murray from both a real and a perceived connection with Byron; it is not necessarily unkind to believe that Shelley had devised a practical scheme of riding Byron's coattails in his quest for access to an audience. Shelley surely knew Byron had informed Murray that the manuscript he carried back to England—and not the one borne by Scrope Davies—was the one to be used for printing purposes: they had undoubtedly discussed the matter before Byron wrote Murray to that effect on 9 October 1816 (*Letters*, I, 504n.). Shelley, however, could not have anticipated losing his seemingly trusted position as shepherd of Canto III to William Gifford, who ultimately saw to the proofreading chores. His exclusion may have left Shelley to suspect that he had presumed too much upon his new association with Byron, who, for all his subsequent contact with the Shelleys, seems never sufficiently to have accepted Shelley to be either very regular or very candid in his subsequent correspondence with him.[41]

The summer months spent in Switzerland with Byron had impressed upon Shelley the disadvantage of working without real fame and with only a counterproductive notoriety. The title page of the *History* identifies no authors, nor is their identity revealed in the contents. Perhaps Shelley simply wished not to intrude upon Mary's project. Perhaps he wished to avoid destining the little volume to the castigation and then oblivion even his surname on the title page would, he believed, ensure. Or perhaps his comment in a letter to Tom Moore should be taken at face value: "I ought to say that the Journal was written some years ago—the style of it is almost infantine, & it was published in the idea that the Author would never be recognized" (*Letters*, I, 583; 16 December 1817). Yet if we add to this remark what Mary Shelley said about the publication of the volume, another picture—hazier but more intriguing—begins to emerge. She wrote in the second volume of *Essays, Letters from Abroad, Translations and Fragments* (1840), that the *History* was "published many years ago by Shelley himself. The Journal is singular, from the circumstance that it was not written for publication, and was deemed too trivial for such by its author. Shelley caused it to be printed, and added to it his own letters, which contain some of the most beautiful descriptions ever written" (I&P, V, xiii).

Why did Shelley have the *History* printed? Was it simply a convenient means of getting something of his own into print? To some extent, yes: publication was a response to the simple craving for fame—even the dubious fame of being an unacknowledged author. There is, after all, a private pleasure in knowing that one is the author of an anonymous work which is being talked up, and something of this pleasure leaks out in Shelley's letter to Tom Moore. And Shelley would doubtless have found a good deal of satisfaction in publishing a work in which his own hand was not immediately identifiable, especially if that work should prove popular, not only because he would thus have managed to outmaneuver his detractors but also because by such a shift he might even have procured both the objective reading and the broader readership he always sought. Coupled with all these possibilities is Shelley's demonstrated interest in joint publication with his friends and disciples: the *Original Poetry* (with Elizabeth Shelley), "The Wandering Jew" (with Medwin), the *Posthumous Fragments* (with Hogg), and *The Necessity of Atheism* (at least in part with Hogg). A similar joint effort, with his wife this time at the center of the production, would not be surprising. Furthermore, such an enterprise might have provided Shelley with a graceful opportunity to exert some editorial influence (both in substantive content and in general "constructive criticism") on Mary's efforts toward publication. In this light the *History* may be regarded for both as a trial balloon for the more ambitious work, *Frankenstein*, which was already in preparation—to be published anonymously—and in which Shelley would be still more involved and for which he would again compose a preface. The letter to Moore provides some support for this latter supposition in its genial concluding intimation that Shelley was letting the Irish author in on a carefully guarded secret: "I ought to say that Mrs. Shelley, tho' sorry that her secret is discovered, is exceedingly delighted to hear that you have derived any amusement from our book.—Let me say in her defence that the Journal of the Six Weeks Tour was written before she was seventeen, & that she has another literary secret which I will in a short time ask you to *keep* in return for having *discovered* this" (*Letters*, I, 583). In a most Shelleyan flourish, the young correspondent introduces his reader, Moore, into the select circle of those to whom the secret of *Frankenstein*'s authorship is to be known. Furthermore, this gesture of intimacy is one of faith as well, as the reference to keeping the secret indicates. It seems that Shelley was virtually always at work pulling people's strings, engineering—or hoping to engineer—particular responses. It is a preoccupation that we may consider remarkable only if we overlook the degree to which manipulative processes underlie all of human behavior, both in word and in action. Shelley proves to be very much one of us, as he always believed himself to be.

Was it possible this mild-looking beardless boy
could be the veritable monster
at war with all the world?

TRELAWNY, *Records of Shelley, Byron,*
and the Author

Chapter Four

SKIRMISHING ON
SEVERAL FRONTS

1816–1819

By the middle of October 1817 Shelley had completed *Laon and
Cythna* in its original form and was dealing with Lackington, Allen
and Co., who were publishing his new wife's anonymous *Frankenstein*,
the proofs of which he was to correct. He was also advertising their
home at Marlow, the pressure to move to Italy having increased with
the Shelleys' mounting debts. Still Shelley continued to write in a variety of modes. One result was his "modern eclogue," *Rosalind and
Helen*, begun at Marlow presumably in October and completed at the
Bagni di Lucca in August of the following year. This curious work is
generally regarded as inferior to Shelley's other work, even "dreadful."[1] The circumstances of its composition help to explain its questionable merit. Begun as a gift to Mary Shelley and apparently completed largely at her and Ollier's insistence, the poem figuratively
contrasts the Shelleys' supposedly ideal relationship with that of
Mary's friend Isabella Baxter Booth and her husband. Booth apparently was a dominating man who disapproved of the Shelleys and
therefore forbade his wife their society, even though she and Mary had
been friends.[2]

Shelley appears to have had mixed feelings about *Rosalind and
Helen*. That he had to be prodded to complete the text, a substantial
number of whose pages had already been set by the printer, is suggested by his comment to Ollier: "The tone of your reproaches and the
printer's wonder operated as Muse on the occasion" (*Letters*, II, 31).
Typically, Shelly is mildly deprecating about his "little poem."[3] He tells

Peacock, for instance, that "its structure is slight & aery—its subject ideal" (*SC*, VI, 656). But his remark to Ollier—who was to publish the poem—is more illuminating: "You will observe that the fabric of the composition is light and unstudied—and that if it have little merit it has as much as it aspires to. I cannot expect that that prig the public will trouble itself to desert its cherished wines and drink a drop of dew so evanescent" (*Letters*, II, 31). That final sentence reflects neither apathy nor resignation at having completed a poor poem, but, rather, natural pride of authorship only partially dampened by the increasingly customary expectation of immediate—perhaps even permanent—public failure. Writing to Byron nearly a year after its publication in the spring of 1819, after having completed *Prometheus Unbound*, *The Cenci*, and the other remarkable works of 1819 and early 1820, Shelley still calls his eclogue "a mere extempore thing, and worth little, I believe" (*Letters*, II, 199; 26 May 1820).

Shelley's preface to *Rosalind and Helen* reflects some of this ambivalence and suggests an author less in control of the practical details of publication than do any of his other prefaces. Like most of the prefaces, this one includes direct instructions to the reader concerning not only the nature of the poem that is to follow but also the manner in which the reader is expected to respond to it:

> The story of *Rosalind and Helen* is, undoubtedly, not an attempt in the highest style of poetry. It is in no degree calculated to excite profound meditation; and if, by interesting the affections and amusing the imagination, it awakens a certain ideal melancholy favourable to the reception of more important impressions, it will produce in the reader all that the writer experienced in the composition. I resigned myself, as I wrote, to the impulse of the feelings which moulded the conception of the story; and this impulse determined the pauses of a measure, which only pretends to be regular inasmuch as it corresponds with, and expresses, the irregularity of the imaginations which inspired it. (*Works*, 167)

If we read this preface as I believe Shelley intended us to do, we can scarcely miss his invitation to participate in a highly subjective, almost telepathic reading experience, which once again invokes no less a precedent than Wordsworth.

Shelley's second sentence specifically invokes the affections and the imagination. In his Intimations Ode Wordsworth had lauded the redemptive power of

> those first affections,
> Those shadowy recollections,

Which, be they what they may,
Are yet the fountain light of all our day,
Are yet a master light of all our seeing.[4]

For the Hartleyan Wordsworth, the imagination, working in active concert with the affections, facilitates the alterations of consciousness we perceive in poems of transformation such as "I Wandered Lonely as a Cloud." Shelley asks of his reader not "profound meditation"— systematic and rational thought—but a thought-less responsiveness to suggestion, to intimation. He aims less at the transmission of a message than the recreation of a mood. Wordsworth had described the phenomenon in his preface to *Lyrical Ballads*, citing it as the prerequisite for successful poetic composition. If the poet requires such a procedure, Shelley implies, so does the reader, who participates with the poet—and without the interference of third parties—in the creation of the poem.

In describing the process of composition by which he had arrived at his poem's irregular form, Shelley does no more than reiterate what he had told Peacock: "The metre corresponds with the spirit of the poem, & varies with the flow of the feeling" (*SC*, VI, 656). It is not a new idea, but it is nevertheless a radical one to suggest that a poem's form may be dictated from within, that the connections among thought, language, and poetic style are more significant and vital than are generally appreciated.[5] In this light we can better appreciate the double function of the first sentence of Shelley's preface: not the depreciation of the poem it is customarily considered, the sentence is in fact a critical touchstone, a declaration not about the poem's quality but about its nature.

Shelley's poem has distinct ties not just with the tradition of pastoral romance but also with that of sentimental fiction generally. Mary Shelley's fondness for sentimental fiction may account for her high estimate of *Rosalind and Helen*. The same preference is apparent in the very favorable review in which Leigh Hunt pronounces the poem superior to *The Revolt of Islam* in that it contains "a still finer and more various, *as well as a more popular* style of poetry" (*Examiner*, 9 May 1819, 303; my italics). Hunt and Mary Shelley were not incorrect in recognizing that his more philosophical, esoteric poetry could not hope to achieve the widespread popular readership Shelley desired in the expanding literary market of the Regency. The typical reader was ill prepared for the rigors of *Alastor* or even *Queen Mab*; less difficult, sentimental works like *Rosalind and Helen* had at least some chance of reaching a broader and less sophisticated readership, and Shelley was right to reduce the difficulties for such readers. The other poems included in the volume ("Lines Written among the Euganean Hills,"

"Ozymandias," and "Hymn to Intellectual Beauty") are also relatively accessible. Although Shelley was understandably unwilling to devote himself exclusively to works in this more "popular" style at the expense of greater and more ambitious undertakings, his subsequent deliberate manipulation of genre, style, and language in works like *The Cenci*, the exoteric political poems of 1819, *Swellfoot the Tyrant*, and *Peter Bell the Third* indicates his willingness—indeed his enthusiastic effort—simultaneously to court both a general, popular audience and the limited circle of ideal readers for whom *Prometheus Unbound* and *Epipsychidion* were intended.

Shelley's own experience informs the fiction of his poem on two points especially. The latter part of the poem resembles the final section of *St. Irvyne*, with Lionel cast in the role of Shelleyan nonconformist that Fitzeustace performs there. Idealist and activist, Lionel is an undaunted enthusiast of the French Revolution whose imprisonment for voicing his radical beliefs is both a metaphor for Shelley's view of his own perceived persecution and an echo of the actual fates of dissenters like Horne Tooke, Daniel Isaac Eaton, and the Hunts. Likewise, Shelley's loss of custody of his children by chancery decision is reflected in the situation of Rosalind, who is deprived of her children by "a sallow lawyer, cruel and cold" because "she is adultrous, and doth hold / In secret that the Christian creed / is false" (*Works*, 175). Shelley's violent resentment of this judicial decision appears again and again in his works.

Just before this passage, Rosalind describes with the voice of Shelley's strong social conscience the most pernicious of poverty's effects:

> Thou knowest what a thing is Poverty
> Among the fallen on evil days:
> 'Tis Crime, and Fear, and Infamy,
> And houseless Want in frozen ways
> Wandering ungarmented, and Pain
> And, worse than all, that inward stain
> Foul Self-contempt, which drowns in sneers
> Youth's starlight smile, and makes its tears
> First like hot gall, then dry for ever!
> (*Works*, 175)

Poverty is the product of enforced inquality; it is injustice made visible and concrete to its victims, whose retaliation invariably follows the road taken by the grossly oppressed—violent, malicious destruction not just of the oppressive social structure but also, in the process, of their own moral and ethical constitution. This is why self-contempt is poverty's greatest scourge: it dehumanizes its victims, consuming from within the dignity that has been attacked from without. And without dignity the individual spirals downward from rage through bitterness to social and intellectual dysfunction. That such distress is not only present but immanent in the world the poem describes is an indication of Shelley's innovative use of the pastoral. Rather than resolving the tension between the pastoral ideal which the imagination projects and the destructive, mechanistic presence that continually threatens that ideal, as Stuart Curran observes, Shelley deliberately leaves the antagonism in place.[6] Even the pastoral world is not immune to Shelley's skepticism, nor to the obligation he places upon his reader to consider and to judge.

We need not go through the second paragraph of the preface, other than to remark that Shelley there once again shields himself from blame for potential objections. He declares that he does not know what other poems may be included in the volume, but he already qualifies "Lines from the Euganean Hills" (just in case Ollier happens to include the poem!) by remarking that though some readers might object to the poem's effusive opening, any such objections really ought in fairness to be laid at the doorstep not of the author but of an unidentified "dear friend" (presumably his wife), at whose request they were not erased (*Works*, 167).

Rosalind and Helen reveals in Shelley's work the pattern of following one of his "public 'visionary' poems" with a "more intimate, 'domestic' poem" in which the central theme is repeated from the first poem.[7] The pattern is apparent also among Shelley's prose works. Not only are themes carried over from essay to essay—or preface to preface—but so are images and strategies. Furthermore, Shelley's manuscripts reveal the presence of such a carryover even at the level of the composing process. For example, in Canto VI of *The Revolt of Islam* Shelley writes:

[XXXVI]

. . . What is the strong control
Which leads the heart the dizzy steep to climb,
Where far over the world those vapours roll,
Which blend two restless frames in one reposing soul?

XXXVII

It is the shadow which doth float unseen,
But not unfelt, o'er blind mortality,
Whose divine darkness fled not, from that green
And lone recess, where lapped in peace did lie
Our linked frames till, from the changing sky,
That night and still another day had fled;
And then I saw and felt.

(*Works*, 102)

The passage echoes and elaborates the language and imagery both of "Mont Blanc" and of the "Hymn to Intellectual Beauty":

> The awful shadow of some unseen Power
> Floats though unseen among us.
>
> *(Works,* 529)

The context of these two lines, carried over into *The Revolt*, is likewise appropriate to the elemental spirit of Intellectual Beauty that provides the hymn's poet with his powerful impulse toward both greater community and expanded humanity.

A good illustration of this carryover in Shelley's prose occurs in the *Essay on Christianity*, most of which seems to have been composed in 1817.[8] In his draft Shelley twice deletes a reference to the serpent. The manuscript reads as follows: "Pain has been inflicted, therefore pain should be inflicted in return. Retaliation [of injuries] is the only remedy [of] which can be applied to violence, because it teaches the injurer the true nature of his own conduct, & operates as a warning against its repetition. [Thus the serpent is avoided because its bite is mortal, & it lives securely in the recesses of the wilderness & hiss] Nor must the same [fashion] measure of calamity be returned as was received" (Bodleian MS Shelley e. 4, fol. 16v; see I&P, VI, 237). Shelley obviously hated to lose his excellent serpent figure, and so after crossing it out here, he tried it again only three pages later.[9] Taking "the extinction of the Persian Empire by Alexander of Macedon" as an example of the destructive effects of revenge, Shelley writes: "Was not the pretext of this latter system of spoliation derived immediately from the former? [The serpent is avoided & desly (deadly? despised?)] [All men] [All things make war upon the serpent because its bite is mortal, because it inflicts death upon the heel that tramples, it puts] Had revenge in this instance any other effect than to increase instead of diminishing the [sum] mass of malice & evil already existing in the world?" (Bodleian MS Shelley e. 4, ff.17v, 18r; see I&P, VI, 238). Shelley subsequently deleted this reference to the serpent as well, but it is interesting to note how the serpent's nature modulates from the first passage to the second. Initially, people avoid the serpent, leaving it to live shunned but secure in the wilderness, where it hisses. In the second passage, though, the serpent becomes the object of overt aggression, with people invading its personal space to destroy it because its venom is perceived to threaten the majority. Shelley increases the serpent's symbolic significance in the second passage, making it an emblem of the potentially lethal spirit of resistance that resides in the oppressed.

That the essay was composed at about the time of both "Mont Blanc" and the "Hymn" is indicated also by the carried-over language in the passage treating the "Power" surrounding us "which visits with its breath our silent chords, at will" (I&P, VI, 231). While Shelley's imagery recalls a myriad of Romantic eolian harps, including Coleridge's, it also recalls his own two poems. Similar echoes occur later in his speculations on the state that is to ensue after death: "This is Heaven, when pain and evil cease, and when the benignant principle unt[rammel]led and uncontrolled, visits in the fulness of its power the universal frame of things. Human life with all its unreal ills and transitory hopes is as a dream which departs before the dawn leaving no trace of its evanescent hues. All that it contains of pure or of divine visits the passive mind in some serenest mood. Most holy are the affections thro which our fellow-beings are rendered dear and venerable to the heart" (I&P, VI, 236).

Throughout his career Shelley consistently kept his deletions in mind for reuse. It is a natural enough procedure; hitting upon a strong image or a felicitous phrase, we instinctively want to preserve it, employing it where it may prove most effective. So if we must cancel that phrase or image, we naturally look for ways to build it into what follows. Shelley was no exception. In draft after draft, canceled words and phrases reappear quickly after being deleted. Shelley's sense of oratory was sharp and sophisticated: seldom are there elaborate, extensive corrections or substitutions; rather, most changes are grammatical and stylistic, as in the *Essay on Christianity*. In most of the manuscript drafts the prose flows as smoothly and compellingly as the argument. Indeed, many of the manuscripts of Shelley's prose essays are remarkably lightly revised, although we must be careful about what conclusions to draw from this evidence. We cannot be certain that the notebook drafts are actually first drafts; they may be intermediate compilations which Shelley planned to revise further. We do not have the manuscript drafts for the separate essays (like the *Address to the Irish People*) that were published during Shelley's lifetime and might indicate more clearly the extent of Shelley's revision of his prose in readying it for the printer. Manuscripts of essays like *A Philosophical View of Reform* or *A Proposal for Putting Reform to the Vote* (both published in Shelley's lifetime), however, exhibit signs of considerable revision. An extreme example is *A Defence of Poetry*, the heavily revised manuscripts of which have harried their editors for more than a century since that essay's first publication in 1840.[10] These manuscripts demonstrate not only the considerable haste with which Shelley could compose but also his care in revising a manuscript he obviously intended for publication.

It was some time before Shelley attained in poetry the consistent skill his early prose exhibits. The evidence of the manuscripts suggests that if composing verse was not inherently more difficult for Shelley than composing prose, it certainly was more painstaking. That he could compose verse rapidly is borne out by his completion of *The Cenci* in barely two months in 1819. He appears to have composed his prose even more rapidly, however, as is indicated both by his comment to Ollier about how quickly he had written the *Address to the People on the Death of the Princess Charlotte* and by Mary Shelley's remarks on the review of Hogg's *Prince Alexy*. Yet as William Keach notes, it is naive to assume that in reading Shelley we are merely "following the tracks of a compositional dash."[11] The characteristic breathless pace of poems like the "Ode to the West Wind" results from careful and deliberate manipulation of language and syntax. As his manuscripts everywhere reveal, though Shelley may have composed rapidly, he revised meticulously. We do well to recall, for instance, his original final line for the "Ode to the West Wind": "When Winter comes Spring lags not far behind" (Bodleian MS Shelley adds. e. 6, p. 137). That line, perhaps more than any other, testifies to the value of careful revision.

Shelley's revisions are important for the present study as indicators of his consistent concern with sharpening language and rhetorical structures alike as part of his effort to communicate most effectively while still exerting control over his audience's response both to the writing and to the roles in which Shelley presents himself. In a characteristic sputtering start to a paragraph in the *Essay on Christianity*, Shelley writes and cancels in a series of quick operations: "[God, the most venerable of names,] God. [The meaning of] The thoughts which the word, God, [is] [varies] [suggests various] suggests to the human mind are susceptible of as many variations as human minds themselves" (Bodleian MS Shelley e. 4, fol. 8v; see I&P, VI, 229). Once he gets the sentence started through this process of trial and error, Shelley cruises smoothly through the rest of the paragraph. A similar difficulty with the opening of a paragraph occurs later in the essay: "[The opposite] [This rule of c] [It is incumbent in every inquiry to adopt] The rule of criticism to be adopted in judging the life actions & words of a man who has acted any conspicuous part in the revolution of the world should not be narrow" (Bodleian MS Shelley e. 4, fol. 21v; see I&P, VI, 241). The revised sentence projects the figure of the artist as he wishes to be perceived, as a counterpart to temporal revolutionaries in general and to Christ in particular.

Another example of the carryover effect in Shelley's surface revisions occurs in the discussion of vengeance in history and the fate of Athens, where the sharpening and reclamation operations proceed simultaneously:

> [A] An Athenian soldier [of] in the Ionian army which had assembled for the purpose of vindicating the liberty of the

Asiatic Greeks, accidentally set fire to Sardis. The city [was] being composed of [in] combustible materials was burned to the ground. The Persians [King] [invaded Greece &] [to retaliate] [considered] believed that this circumstance of aggression made it their duty to retaliate on Athens. They assembled successive expeditions on the most extensive scale. Every nation of the East was united to ruin the Graecian [nations] states. Athens was [laid wa] [utterly destroyed] burned to the ground, the whole territory laid waste. (Bodleian MS Shelley e.4, fol. 17r; see I&P, VI, 237)

Finally, Shelley sometimes rescues a sentence by substantially recasting its core. Speaking of Jesus, Shelley observes:

We discover that he is the enemy of oppression & of falsehood, that he is the advocate of equal justice, that he is neither disposed to sanction bloodshed or deceit under whatsoever pretences their practise [sic] may be vindicated. [That he is this, the meekness & the majesty of his demeanour as well as the / connections / unbroken laws of his doctrines contribute to establish] We discover that he was a man of meek and majestic demeanour, calm in danger, of natural & simple thoughts & habits, beloved to adoration by his adherents, [was] unmoved & solemn & serene. (Bodleian MS Shelley e. 4, fol. 21r; see I&P, VI, 240–41)

The *Essay on Christianity* also demonstrates some of the strategies of audience manipulation I have already identified. One of the most important deletions occurs in what is generally called the "Introduction"; its importance stems not only from its content but also because the deleted sentence is never explicitly recast in the text but is diffused within the tone of the essay generally. Placed in its original context, Shelley's sentence reads thus:

It cannot be [discovered] precisely ascertained to what degree Jesus Christ accommodated his doctrines to the [persuasions] opinions of his auditors, or in what degree he really said all that he is related to have said. [In the picture which /is/ here attempted to be delineated of his system & his character the most liberal construction is carefully put on those circumstances which have been considered most equivocal.] He has left no [record] written record of himself [but a variety] & we are compelled to judge from the imperfect & obscure [histories] information which his biographers, persons certainly of very undisciplined & undiscriminating minds, have transmitted to posterity. (Bodleian MS Shelley e.4, fol. 20r–v; see I&P, VI, 240)

It is as if Shelley realized upon consideration that his second sentence was an instruction to himself, a statement of strategy for his own guidance in writing which was unnecessary for his reader. Indeed, to leave it in would have betrayed a certain smugness, an overanxiousness to be fair with Christ, likely to alienate the reader. The standard treatises on rhetoric, like Hugh Blair's popular *Lectures on Rhetoric and Belles Lettres*, stressed the need for factual accuracy and, more important, understatement in effective persuasion. Since these are qualities that Shelley's prose particularly exhibits, it is fair to speculate that his revisions generally reflect not just intuition but also a sound theoretical basis. Thus Shelley often deliberately softens his language to defuse negative response to his nonconformist views on Christ. For example: "It is not asserted that [some] no degree of human indignation ever hurried him beyond the limits which his calmer mood had placed to disapprobation against vice & folly. [But that the essential basis of char] [The only] Those deviations [which are from the] [documents] [historical documents] [also] from the history of his life are alone to be vindicated which [appea] represent his own essential character in contradiction with itself [which represent the mildest of men as a breathing maniac [?] avenge & persecution]" (Bodleian MS Shelley e. 4, ff. 21v–22r; see I&P, VI, 241). Rather than pursue this warm rhetoric, Shelley turned the argument of his paragraph in a less dangerous direction.

Donald Reiman suggests that Shelley possessed the same "tangential intellect" frequently attributed to Coleridge, a mental set in which the multiple relationships among the various aspects of his topic are so readily apparent to the author that he finds himself constantly "in danger of being led from his ostensible topic to one of its ramifications" (*SC*, VI, 958). In his manuscript drafts of *A Philosophical View of Reform*, Reiman observes, Shelley kept himself on course by relegating his tangential remarks to footnotes or by subsequently eliminating them altogether. Something of the sort appears to have been taking place as Shelley worked on the *Essay on Christianity*, dividing it into sections as he wrote. Hence instead of a fully articulated work, it is a fragment comprised of several false starts, a more formal beginning, and several related fragments. Shelley realized that he was not composing his essay "in a straight line," so to speak. The section usually designated as the "Introduction" was originally simply a new paragraph continuing the discussion of Jesus. But at some point Shelley went back and wrote in small letters in the blank space at the end of the previous paragraph, "To belong to some other part," and beneath that the notation, "Introduction." He then drew a line to set off the left edge of the new paragraph (Bodleian MS Shelley e. 4, fol. 2or; see I&P, VI, 240).

Why did Shelley compose this essay, the working document in which he explores not only an intellectual crux but also the practical matter of defining an audience and discovering the appropriate vehicle for addressing it? Given his "high philosophical purpose," what methods, what rhetorical strategies, and what modes of composition would be appropriate?[12] Shelley answered some of these questions as he composed, but another prose fragment, *The Moral Teaching of Jesus Christ*, may provide the clearest indication of Shelley's aim.[13] This fragment, perhaps related to his early plan for a collection of the sayings of Jesus, is probably another tangential discussion begun in the heat of composing the *Essay* and simply never developed any further. In it Shelley grafts Godwinian utopian anarchism onto the principles of Christ:

> The doctrines [of Christ] indeed, in my judgment, are excellent and strike at the root of moral evil. If acted upon, no political or religious institution could subsist a moment. Every man would be his own magistrate and priest; the change so long desired would have attained its consummation, and man exempt from the external evils of his own choice would be left to struggle with the physical evils which exist in spite of him. . . . —Doctrines of reform were never carried to so great a length as by Jesus Christ. The republic of Plato and the Political Justice of Godwin are probable and practical systems in the comparison. (I&P, VI, 255)

Shelley follows earlier writers such as Paine and Horne Tooke in claiming Christ for the reform movement, as Henry Hunt and John Cartwright would also do.[14] The idea is to make the radical author's opinions palatable, even stimulating, to the reader by making them appear to resemble Christ's. The corollary is clear: to reject Shelley is to reject Christ, while to embrace Christ is to embrace Shelley as well.

Shelley wrote most actively about Christ and Christianity and drew parallels between himself and Christ when he was most assiduous in public campaigns for liberating the oppressed. The Irish enterprise, for instance, was accompanied by Shelley's plan for the collection of biblical extracts that would reveal Jesus as the determined political activist Shelley envisioned, freed of the trappings of orthodox doctrine and superstition. In 1817 the Marlow pamphlets and poems were attended by the first and longest section of the *Essay on Christianity*.[15] The resurgence of Shelley's "passion for reforming the world" in the works of late 1819 that followed Peterloo seems to have included a return to the overt interest in Christ: the manuscripts suggest that both the final section of the *Essay on Christianity* and *The Moral Teaching of Jesus Christ* were composed at about this time.[16]

Shelley's recurrent explicit and implicit linking of himself with Christ suggests, as I have already noted, his growing conviction that the clear-headed, benevolent reformer is always sacrificed by the very oppressed whom he seeks to free from their "self-incurred tutelage."[17] Shelley made a very personal addition to his discussion of reputation. The insertion is italicized: "If a man borrows a certain sum from me, he is bound to repay that sum. Shall no more be required from the [robber] enemy who *destroys my reputation* or ravages my fields?" (Bodleian MS Shelley e. 4, ff. 16v–17r; see I&P, VI, 237). The last resort of the oppressor is the *ad hominem* attack, and Shelley's point here is that the proper redress for such attacks lies not in retaliation and revenge but in justice. Shelley's Christ rejected the sadistic pleasure of seeing his enemies suffer:[18] he could forgive both the crowd that demanded his death and Pilate who permitted it. Observing that Jesus "is neither disposed to sanction bloodshed or deceit under whatsoever pretences their practice may be vindicated" (I&P, VI, 240), Shelley describes the ripple effect of unchecked retaliation: "The great community of mankind had been subdivided into ten thousand communities each organized for the ruin of the other. Wheel within wheel the vast machine was instinct with the restless spirit of desolation. [It is human to err, it is human to desire that what these possess should be our own.] The most conspicuous instance of this [spirit, ed] is revenge" (Bodleian MS Shelley e. 4, fol. 16v; I&P, VI, 236–37). Interestingly, neither the canceled sentence (bracketed) nor its penciled replacement ("The most . . .") appears in the "final" version of the essay. Did Shelley perhaps consider it too radical a compromise of his beliefs to call (even ironically) the desire for revenge, retaliation, and atonement "human"—or even "natural"? His point, after all, is that though the desire for revenge may be understandable, it is nevertheless *un*natural, *in*human, and monstrous. Retaliation is not justice but vengeance: it demeans its author rather than vindicating or ennobling him or her, making one no better than the oppressor. The oppressors are masters of crowd control; like the Roman occupiers of Jerusalem who oversaw Christ's execution, they know how to incite the unreasoning masses into demanding what they themselves would dare not attempt without the popular mandate thus engineered. Shelley reasons properly that if the people can be manipulated by unscrupulous leaders into demanding the *wrong* things, then they ought to be equally susceptible to being manipulated by enlightened, reforming leaders into demanding (and, as in both America and France, securing) the *right* things.

With England apparently drawing ever nearer to revolution, Shelley argues not only for tolerance and the fair hearing of conscientious dissenters but also for repudiation of violent redress of perceived injustices. Alexander's destruction of the Persian empire in the culmination of a cycle of senseless blood-lust is cited as graphic proof of "the emptiness and folly of retaliation" (I&P, VI, 238). Shelley is moving toward a view of passive resistance which he articulates in 1819 in *The Mask of Anarchy*, that variety of psychological warfare in which shaming and reforming the conscience take precedence over destroying the body.

Another point needs to be made concerning the post-Enlightenment orientation of Shelley's thought in the *Essay on Christianity*. Already in 1812 he had written Hookham that he "certainly wish[ed] to have all Kants works" (*Letters*, I, 350), and despite Hogg's claim that he subsequently saw Kant's works "uncut, and unopened," Shelley had some knowledge of the German philosopher.[19] In an argument anticipating Shelley's by nearly thirty years, Kant had written in "What Is Enlightenment?" (1784):

> Through laziness and cowardice a large part of mankind, even after nature has freed them from alien guidance, gladly remain immature. It is because of laziness and cowardice that it is so easy for others to usurp the role of guardians. . . . After having made their domestic animals dumb and having carefully prevented these quiet creatures from daring to take any step beyond the lead-strings to which they have fastened them, these guardians then show them the danger which threatens them, should they attempt to walk alone. . . . It is difficult for the isolated individual to work himself out of the immaturity which has become almost natural for him. He has even become fond of it and for the time being is incapable of employing his own intelligence, because he has never been allowed to make the attempt. . . . But it is more nearly possible for a public to enlighten itself: this is even inescapable if only the public is given its freedom. For there will always be some people who think for themselves, even among the self-appointed guardians of the great mass who, after having thrown off the yoke of immaturity themselves, will spread about them the spirit of a reasonable estimate of their own value and the need for every man to think for himself. . . . All that is required for this enlightenment is *freedom*.[20]

The latter part of this passage might almost serve as a gloss on Shelley's plan for works such as the *Proposal for Putting Reform to the Vote*, designed expressly to mobilize the enlightened few in the cause of reform and freedom. Moreover, Kant's observation that the individual "has even become fond of" his or her immaturity prefigures Shelley's suggestion in his essay on the death of Princess Charlotte that perhaps humanity *chooses* its enslavement rather than risk the rigors of emotional, spiritual, or political independence.

The Diogenes passage in the "Equality of Mankind" section of Shelley's essay reiterates the message in terminology remarkably similar to Kant's:

> He [Diogenes] said, It is in the power of each individual to level the inequality which is the topic of the complaint of mankind. Let him be aware of his own worth and the station which he really occupies in the scale of moral beings. . . . Every man possesses the power in this respect, to legislate for himself. Let him be well aware of his own worth, and moral dignity. . . . With all those who are truly wise, there will be an entire community, not only of thoughts and feelings, but also of external possessions. . . . Before man can be free and equal and truly wise he must cast aside the chains of habit and superstition, he must strip sensuality of its pomp and selfishness of its excuses, and contemplate actions and objects as they really are. He will discover the wisdom of universal love. He will feel the meanness and the injustice of sacrificing the leisure and the liberty of his fellow-men to the indulgence of his physical appetites and becoming a party to their degradation by the consummation of his own. (I&P, VI, 244–46)

The key to enlightenment and humanity is the love—epitomized in Shelley's Christ and Prometheus and professed by the poet himself— that overcomes the distinctions and petty jealousies raised by self-centeredness and merges the individual into the classless human community.

Shelley's discussion of Jesus' public career (I&P, VI, 240–43) establishes him as a paradigm for humanitarian reformers generally. Even the most exemplary reformer requires an audience capable of comprehending what he presents to it; to succeed, the teacher must mold his own audience: "This practice of entire sincerity towards other men would avail to no good end, if they were incapable of practising it towards their own minds. In fact, truth cannot be communicated until it is perceived. The interests therefore of truth required that an orator should so far as possible produce in his hearers that state of mind in which alone his exhortations could fairly be contemplated and examined. Having produced this favourable disposition of mind Jesus Christ proceeds to qualify and finally to abrogate the system of the Jewish law" (I&P, VI, 243). Like Blake, Shelley realizes that error must be given tangible form before it can be recognized and repudiated in the sort of mental apocalypse Blake describes: "Error is Created[;] Truth is Eternal[.] Error or Creation will be Burned Up & then & not till then Truth or Eternity will appear[.] It is Burnt up the Moment Men cease to behold it[.]"²¹ In voicing his dissenting opinions, Jesus invites the destructive wrath of his opponents, thereby forcing them, through the sacrifice of his own life, into a public demonstration of their intolerance and inhumanity and ensuring by his martyrdom not merely the collapse of their system but also the stain of infamy attached throughout subsequent history to the killers of Jesus Christ. Though Jesus forgives them, history refuses to forget.

I would also stress Shelley's use of the word *orator* in the passage above (as well as earlier in the manuscript paragraph). His reference specifically to public speaking—as opposed to public writing—emphasizes the particular manipulative facility of the orator, whose presentation can naturally be endowed with greater animation and dramatic force than the writer's. All the ploys and pyrotechnics of rhetoric are justified when they are employed in the service of truth, of enlightenment. Shelley suggests that the effective orator produces in his or her hearers a state of mind in which the fairest hearing may be obtained. Shelley's next sentence reminds his readers that, having generated such a favorable group consciousness, Christ was able "in a strain of most daring and most impassioned speculation" to begin dismantling his audience's religious convictions: "He said—However new or strange my doctrines may appear to you, they are, in fact only the restoration and re-establishment of those original institutions and ancient customs of your own law and religion. The constitution of your faith and policy, altho perfect in their origin, have become corrupt and altered, and have fallen into decay. I profess to restore them to their pristine authority and splendour. 'Think not that I am come to destroy the law and the prophets. I am not come to destroy but to fulfil'" (I&P, VI, 242).²² Common to all members of the oppressed at moments of cultural crisis is the increasing fervency with which a vision of millennial reorientation is held. It is the vision of the last becoming first, of the meek inheriting the earth, promised by the Bible as future reward for present endurance. But when the crisis is greatest, the oppression felt to be most intolerable, the suffering masses tend to try to speed up the process and seize the promised reward. Calling attention to the prevailing inversion of spiritual (and social) values, Shelley's Christ aligns himself with the heroes of biblical prophecy, come to return things to their proper orientation. He is a revolutionary, but unlike historical predecessors such as the Persian leader or Alexander, Christ advocates not the retaliatory destruction of the oppressors but their redemption, their conversion and incorporation into the new community.

"Revolution" is, after all, an astronomer's term denoting a return to a place of origin or previous position, as in the earth's revolution about the sun. This is the sort of revolution at the forefront of which Shelley's Christ appears, and it is very much the sort which Shelley advocated. The French Revolution had failed—as, for the most part, the American Revolution had not—because the masses had proved inadequate to their new freedom, retaliating against their former oppressors in bloody vengeance rather than practicing the spirit of liberty, equality, and fraternity emblazoned on their own banners. Although Shelley becomes increasingly vocal in his support of insurrection and revolution elsewhere (in countries such as Greece, where the despotism is crushingly absolute), he continues to insist on moderation as the proper course for his own country,[23] believing that both general moral improvement and particular political reform are still possible in England if thoughtful and sympathetic reformers can be inspired to undertake the reconstruction. The object is not to create *ex nihilo* but to renovate what already exists, retaining elements of the old system but altering their relations to one another. Shelley sees this work, like his projects in Ireland and at Tremadoc, as a shared activity in which the leader becomes less leader than comrade, the group as a whole seeming to invent and complete its own revolution. The revolutionary Shelleyan prophet's success depends upon his or her ability to convince the audience that "genius is inspired recombination"[24] and that the prophet's proposals articulate the audience's own opinions, "what oft was *Thought*, but ne'er so well *Exprest*."[25]

The unfinished *Essay on Christianity* reveals much about the way Shelley attempted to work out—even as he composed—a variety of intellectual and rhetorical problems in trying to circumvent the instinctive resistance of conventional, conservative readers. The stimulus of daily contact with Byron in Switzerland during the summer of 1816 left its mark not only on the significantly improved poems that followed but also on this essay, which seems to mark an intellectual turning point for Shelley. Doctrines of benevolence and nonviolence he had previously conceived abstractly are now worked out in relation to practical, historical precedents. Furthermore, attaching those doctrines here to the person of Christ affords Shelley a way out of the stalemate his earlier blanket repudiation of Christianity had imposed upon him. More fully and concretely developing his image of the historical Christ as liberal reformer allows him to continue to reject the superstructure of orthodox religion while retaining its philosophical center.

Frankenstein, which was issued anonymously early in 1818, also originated in the summer of 1816. Although Shelley minimized his direct intervention in his wife's novel, and always referred to it afterward as entirely her work, Anne Mellor has demonstrated that Shelley's influence on the novel was considerable.[26] In addition to making technical corrections in the manuscript as his wife completed her chapters, Shelley frequently altered the narrative's style, introducing a more elevated, Latinate idiom that recasts Mary Shelley's sentimental but vigorous writing in an ornate and oratorical Ciceronian style to which readers have justifiably objected. Shelley also introduced some of his favorite philosophical, political, and aesthetic theories, regardless of the contradictions they created. Finally, he occasionally misrepresented his wife's text in his alterations, partly because he misread and partly because he wished to tilt the text toward his own thinking. As Betty T. Bennett implies, Shelley's editorial alterations seem to have been a well-meaning effort to anticipate and accommodate a primarily male audience accustomed to such a periphrastic manner.[27] Mary Shelley's unwillingness silently to defer to Shelley's emendations is indicated by the extensive revisions she undertook for the 1831 edition of the novel.[28] In any event, the full extent of Shelley's liberties with his wife's text, particularly in light of his anger when his own texts were altered or misprinted, reflects his occasional insensitivity to the women with whom he was on intimate terms.

The preface to the 1818 version of *Frankenstein* appears to be entirely Shelley's work, and the notable similarity of its preoccupations to those of the prefaces to his own works makes it relevant here. Shelley acts as ventriloquist, adopting the conventional first-person persona of the author discussing the work to follow. He immediately suggests that one of the novel's principal merits is that it "affords a point of view to the imagination for the delineating of human passions more comprehensive and commanding than any which the ordinary relations of interesting events can yield" (I&P, VI, 259). To this end, he writes, the treatment of "whatever moral tendencies exist in the sentiments or characters" is conscientiously directed toward "the exhibition of the amiableness of domestic affection, and the excellence of universal virtue" (259–60). Shelley invokes authorial liberty, however, in dissociating the author from the opinions spoken or implied in the novel, disclaiming any intentional philosophical prejudice and pointing out that the hero's convictions are not to be misconstrued as the author's.

In a formula to which he returns perhaps most conspicuously in his preface to *Prometheus Unbound*, Shelley invokes a series of models and precedents for what is attempted in *Frankenstein*:

> I have thus endeavoured to preserve the truth of the elementary principles of human nature, while I have not scrupled to innovate upon their combinations. The *Iliad*, the tragic poetry of Greece,—Shakespeare, in the *Tempest* and *Midsummer Night's Dream*,—and most especially Milton, in *Paradise Lost*,

conform to this rule; and the most humble novelist, who seeks to confer or receive amusement from his labours, may, without presumption, apply to prose fiction a licence, or rather a rule, from the adoption of which so many exquisite combinations of human feeling have resulted in the highest specimens of poetry. (259)

The point is simply to head off criticism by anticipating it, citing the giants of literature as precedents for the author's new attempts. This tactic not only legitimizes the author's practice—reminding the reader of the lineage of such innovations—but also applies to the novel the prestigious traditions of the epic and the drama. Invoking *Paradise Lost* is, of course, a natural gesture, considering not only the novel's title page but also its entire revisionist reading of both Milton's epic and the Bible. But the reference to Shakespeare is more interesting, for it invites the reader to see in the Creature another Caliban (and, in some respects, the good-natured Bottom). More important, it suggests ethical questions of freedom and tyranny involved in the manipulation of other creatures' wills by superior powers (Prospero, Oberon, Titania, Puck), whose motives and intentions are often questionable. Like the novel itself, which proceeds to the Creature's own words through a series of narrative frames, Shelley's preface inscribes both an intellectual and a literary-historical frame around what will follow, suggesting to the alert reader the parameters for interpretation.

Having expressed this considerable ambition, Shelley softens his tone and concludes with a capsule history of the novel's composition which includes the characteristic gesture of deferral to Byron. Explaining the ghost-story contest, he writes, "Two other friends (a tale from the pen of one of whom would be far more acceptable to the public than any thing I can ever hope to produce) and myself agreed to write each a story" (260). That parenthetical statement reveals much about Shelley's self-image during 1817, when he felt so acutely the differences between himself and the spectacularly popular Byron. Clearly, it frustrated Shelley to work so hard at literary and nonliterary schemes only to be attacked for his efforts, while Byron's seemingly careless, cavalier behavior and writing endeared him to the very public he seemed to disdain. As we shall see, this remained a sore point.

Shelley's flurry of literary activity as 1817 became 1818 included, presumably in January following the novel's appearance, a review of *Frankenstein*, which he may have intended for the *Examiner* but which did not appear until Medwin published it in the *Athenaeum* for 10 November 1832. The review is interesting for the formal distance Shelley creates between himself and his subject, even to the point of noting that "some points of subordinate interest" would seem to mark the novel as its author's first (I&P, VI, 263). His rereading of Godwin's novels in connection with his review of his father-in-law's *Mandeville* (which unpublished review had grown out of an exchange of letters between the two authors in December 1817) doubtlessly informs the comparison of Frankenstein's encounter with his Creature on the sea of ice and the confrontation of Caleb Williams and Falkland (264).

Not surprisingly, Shelley's review emphasizes the theme that had recently occupied him in the *Essay on Christianity*: the pernicious effects of vengeance. He argues that the Creature's crimes are not the result of some inexplicable propensity to evil but rather the inevitable consequence of socially engineered behavior modification:

> In this the direct moral of the book consists; and it is perhaps the most important, and of the most universal application, of any moral that can be enforced by example. Treat a person ill, and he will become wicked. Requite affection with scorn;—let one being be selected, for whatever cause, as the refuse of his kind—divide him, a social being, from society, and you impose upon him the irresistible obligations—malevolence and self-ishness. It is thus that, too often in society, those who are best qualified to be its benefactors and its ornaments are branded by some accident with scorn, and changed, by neglect and solitude of heart, into a scourge and a curse. (264)

Shelley notes that the Creature's "original goodness was gradually turned into inextinguishable misanthropy and *revenge* (264; my italics). How much of himself did Shelley glimpse in the Creature and his fate? How much of the Actaeon myth informs Frankenstein's promethean debacle? Shelley's reference to the Creature's misanthropy and revenge as "inextinguishable" reflects his conception of the largely irreversible nature of the lust for revenge and hints at his own efforts to resist any such undesirable response to his own besieged situation.

During the winter of 1817–18 Shelley also composed formal reviews of Godwin's *Mandeville* (December 1817) and Thomas Love Peacock's *Rhododaphne* (February 1818). The latter enthusiastically places Peacock's poem in a context of Greek classicism without revealing much about Shelley beyond his taste and erudition at the time. Presumably also intended for the *Examiner*, this brief review remained unpublished until 1879–80.[29] The review of *Mandeville* has a more interesting history. Writing to Godwin on 1 December 1817 Shelley announces the novel's arrival at Marlow; on the seventh he has finished the novel and includes two enthusiastic paragraphs in another letter to Godwin (*Letters*, I, 573–74). Godwin's delight moved him to insert Shelley's praise, slightly modified, in the 9 December *Morning Chronicle* and to send Shelley a "long & interesting" letter (*Letters*, I, 576).

Responding, Shelley informs Godwin of his own subsequent decision to expand his comments in a full, formal review of the novel for the *Examiner*. Before looking further at Shelley's letter to Godwin, it may be useful to consider his review, which appeared in the *Examiner* on 28 December 1817.

Despite his general preference for *Caleb Williams*, Shelley observes that "'Mandeville' yields in interest and importance to none of the productions of the Author." The novel's greatest achievement, he claims, is its exploration of "the varieties of human character, the depth and complexity of human motive, those sources of the union of strength and weakness, those useful occasions for pleading in favour of universal kindness and toleration" (I&P, VI, 221). Nor does Shelley ignore Godwin's style, remarking on the rich and sweetly eloquent language, the less obtrusive emphasis on moral speculation in comparison to the earlier novels, and the sense of irresistible force that drives the narrative forward.

That Shelley's concerns extend beyond *Mandeville* is immediately apparent. Calling on his readers to join him in a brief overview of Godwin's previous work as prelude to the present consideration, Shelley dubs him "one of the most illustrious examples of intellectual power of the present age" and declares that Godwin has "exhibited that variety and universality of talent which distinguishes him who is destined to inherit lasting renown, from the possessors of temporary celebrity" (219). If we take into account Shelley's pride in the variety and universality of his own works—many of which he claimed (at least to Godwin) were strongly influenced by Godwin—then we may wish to look more carefully at the beginning of the review's fourth paragraph: "It may be said with truth, that Godwin has been treated unjustly by those of his countrymen, upon whose favour temporary distinction depends. If he had devoted his high accomplishments to flatter the selfishness of the rich, or enforced those doctrines on which the powerful depend for power, they would no doubt have rewarded him with their countenance, and he might have been more fortunate in that sunshine than Mr. Malthus or Dr. Paley. But the difference would still have been as wide as that which must for ever divide notoriety from fame," (219–20).

Shelley then proceeds to an attack that expands upon "To Wordsworth," citing the elder poet as an example of the recantation of liberal principles and consequent servility to and dependence upon the prevailing power structure. Shelley found such a surrender particularly appalling in a poet who had seemed to him originally to possess so much grandeur of mind and heart, so great a potential for benefiting humanity. His condemnation of Wordsworth is a condemnation of the popular, uneducated, unenlightened taste that rejects (or seduces) the few luminaries, the true heroes of the age, much as the crowds reject and attack Victor Frankenstein's poor new Adam, forcing them into either humiliating capitulation or violent revenge. The implied pairing of Shelley with Godwin in the review as exemplars of tireless resistance to all such intellectual and political surrender is inescapable. That the visionaries do not "sell out" under this societal pressure testifies, of course, to the tenacity of their vision, but their perseverence also highlights the ethical bankruptcy of the public system that forces upon them the deprivation that attends such steadfastness. Shelley deplored the public neglect of Godwin after the initial success of *Caleb Williams* in 1794 and the ignominious financial dependence to which Godwin had by 1817 been reduced.

In his 11 December letter, Shelley's expressions of appreciation over Godwin's approval of his estimate of *Mandeville* are generous— almost aggressively so. Given the context of the letter as a whole, this seems remarkable indeed, for Godwin's "long & interesting letter" apparently contained a lengthy and not very favorable discussion of Shelley's poetry, to which Shelley responds in both general and particular terms. I believe the show of enthusiasm over Godwin's response to his own praise of *Mandeville* with which Shelley began the letter was calculated to induce Godwin to soften his criticism of Shelley's work and both to rue and to revise his apparently harsh judgment of *Laon and Cythna*, a copy of which—in its original form—the poet had apparently sent him. As usual, Shelley professes a willingness to learn from criticism, but his overt determination in this instance to stand firm against Godwin's censures and even to question the older man's taste and judgment is unusual—an indication of Shelley's growing intellectual and critical self-assurance. Shelley argues that as "a genuine picture of my own mind" (*Letters*, I, 577), *Laon and Cythna* possesses an intellectual validity distinct from its poetic value, and he links his poetic efforts to the threat to his health posed by the English climate and his own constitutional eccentricities that had become more pronounced in 1817: "I felt the precariousness of my life, & I engaged in this task resolved to leave some record of myself. Much of what the volume contains was written with the same feeling, as real, though not so prophetic, as the communications of a dying man" (577). Shelley's ambiguous claim aims at effect, hedging on whether Shelley believed himself actually to be dying or whether imagining it was necessary to his process of composition: whether it is a statement of fact, in other words, or a highly loaded simile. In either case, the conviction of impending death is intriguing, for at moments of cultural crisis there is frequently a manifest connection between physical and psychic threat. When self-esteem is most threatened, both from without and from within, the presence of real or presumed illness seems greatest: "It is at this extreme that the vision comes—to an exceptional individual whose personal plight mirrors that of the society, in that he is himself usually ill, often beset by sorrows, recent deaths, deprivation, and feelings of hopelessness. Often he is himself at the point of death when the vision visits him, and his success in evangelizing his method gets its most powerful reinforcement from his own miraculous recovery."[30] So nearly does this explanation correspond to the details of Shelley's situation and career that Eleanor Wilner might almost be describing the poet.

Shelley's letter also reveals the intellectual carryover of his reprocessing of Wordsworthian poetics in the preface to *The Revolt of Islam*, with which he was also occupied at this time. The preface to *Lyrical Ballads*, for instance, informs Shelley's declaration that "in this have I long believed that my power consists: in sympathy & that part of imagination which relates to sentiment and contemplation.—I am formed,—if for any thing not in common with the herd of mankind—to apprehend minute & remote distinctions of feeling whether relative to external nature, or the living beings which surround us, & to communicate the conceptions which result from considering either the moral or the material universe as a whole" (577). This is Wordsworth's poet, the democratized artist who is nevertheless more sensitively attuned to the universe than his fellow men, in whom that superior responsiveness is as yet only virtual. Moreover, though Shelley emphasizes the extent to which his composition has been governed by the spontaneous overflow of powerful feeling, he still manages, for Godwin's benefit, an allusion to Wordsworth's qualifier, "recollected in tranquillity": "Yet after all, I cannot but be conscious in much of what I write of an absence of that tranquillity which is the attribute & the accompaniment of power. This feeling alone would make your most kind & wise admonitions on the subject of the economy of intellectual force, valuable to me. And if I live, or if I see any trust in coming years, doubt not but that I shall do something whatever it may be, which a serious & earnest es[ti]mate of my powers will suggest to me, & which will be in every respect accommodated to their utmost limits" (578).

His mention of tranquillity in this fashion is a nod to Godwin's sense of classical decorum, as is suggested by its connection here with "economy of intellectual force." This penultimate paragraph emulates a rededication of powers on Shelley's part largely for Godwin's benefit, even though the rest of the letter makes it clear that he is unlikely to shift course with respect to either subject matter or style. His declaration here would seem to be a rhetorical ploy designed to impress Godwin with both his earnestness and his willingness to act upon good advice. That Shelley considers the discussion closed is indicated by his brief conclusion, which follows immediately with an announcement of renewed health and vigor (the "miraculous recovery"?) and a pressing invitation to Godwin to visit the Shelleys.

Shelley's decision to add reviewing to his other literary activities during these months tells us something of his public plans. His *Proposal for Putting Reform to the Vote* had been published for general consumption, but he had also arranged for copies to be put directly into the hands of the public figures he regarded as best able to promote his proposal. These were not precisely the same readers at which *The Revolt of Islam* was aimed, nor was either audience exactly that for which the *Address to the People on the Death of the Princess Charlotte* was meant. Shelley envisioned several distinct and only partially overlapping audiences, as can be seen not only from the variety of modes and genres in which he composed during this period but also from the way he sought to disseminate his works.

It is tempting to conjure up an image of Shelley working in splendid isolation, trying single-handedly from his home at Marlow to initiate and coordinate a massive national movement for political, moral, and ethical reform: that is the stuff of which Romantic mythologies are constructed. The Regency produced a great many liberal reformers, however, many of whom were as devoted to their cause as was Shelley; even when they possessed neither his skill nor his notoriety they often commanded actual rather than invented audiences. Shelley's efforts were part of a national pattern; the *Examiner* was merely one of many liberal organs, many of which were both more liberal and more radical than it. To facilitate reform, one clear need was for a network of communication such as that which had emerged in the 1790s with the various Corresponding Societies,[31] a mechanism that would permit quick and efficient coordination among the efforts of the various reformers. Shelley had relatively little access to any such network. His alternative was to take his case directly to the people, through whatever means he could manage, and the periodical press was, for certain purposes, potentially as useful to his designs as the more formal medium of the printed book. Moreover, the note Mary Shelley appended to her selection of Shelley's "early poems" (i.e., pre-1816) makes a point Shelley must certainly have repeated to her more than once: "He had now begun to feel that the time for action was not ripe in England, and that the pen was the only instrument wherewith to prepare the way for better things" (*Works*, 528). To commit oneself to "the pen" is to dedicate oneself not only to one's immediate contemporaries but also to posterity. If he was indeed ahead of his time, as he believed himself to be, Shelley would simply have to allow time to catch up, leaving for those who would follow him, as he had written Godwin, "some record of myself."

Shelley's undiminished interest in practical contemporary issues is evident from a pair of essays, "On the Punishment of Death" and "A Future State," whose philosophical connections both with each other and with issues we have been pursuing dictate their consideration together here with other works of this middle period in Shelley's career.[32] The former essay, especially, may be related to the execution of the Derbyshire rebels, although the subject of capital punishment was being agitated in Parliament from about 1811 through 1817. These parliamentary discussions were reported widely in the press (the *Examiner*, for instance, both reported and commented on the debates with some frequency) and were the subject of much popular discussion.[33] In his essay Shelley risked offending his audience by criticizing the middle-class tradesmen who were the backbone of the urban reform movement.[34] He apparently considered drawing a semantic distinction between the middle-class supporters of capital punishment and the hereditary aristocracy ultimately responsible for its perpetuation, for the manuscript contains a direct reference to "the lords" as moral and ethical elitists, a reference Shelley canceled as soon as he wrote it.[35] The overall tone of Shelley's prose suggests that the essay is intended for a reasonably sophisticated audience capable of appreciating its philosophical nuances. Within the framework of measured, rational discourse, however, Shelley embeds several provocative propositions.

The philosophical center of the essay is the familiar theme of the renunciation of vengeance, though Shelley takes an interesting route to get there. He first asserts that since we cannot say with any certainty what follows (or precedes) our mortal life, we cannot know whether capital punishment confers upon its victim a curse or a blessing: "To compel a person to know all that can be known by the dead, concerning that which the living fear, *hope*, or forget; to plunge him into the *pleasure* or pain which there awaits him; to punish *or reward* him in a manner and in a degree incalculable and incomprehensible by us; to disrobe him at once from all that intertexture of good *and evil* with which Nature seems to have clothed every form of individual existence, is to inflict on him the doom of death" (I&P, VI, 186–87; my italics). Shelley originally included a reference to death as "that which the vulgar regard as the greatest of all evils or a good prodigiously great" (Bodleian MS Shelley adds. e. 8, ff. 28–29), but he apparently decided not to risk so blatantly categorizing what would be most of his audience. Shelley's insistence that executing the victims may in fact reward them effectively reduces the value of the "punishment" both as deterrent and as vengeance.

That supposed value stems from the collective ego reinforcement that capital punishment affords its advocates:

The spectators who feel no abhorrence at a public execution, but rather a self-applauding superiority, and a sense of gratified indignation, are surely excited to the most inauspicious emotions. The first reflection of such a one is the sense of his own internal and actual worth, as preferable to that of the victim, whom circumstances have led to destruction. The meanest wretch is impressed with a sense of his own comparative merit. He is one of those on whom the tower of Siloam fell not—he is such a one as Jesus Christ found not in all Samaria, who, in his own soul, throws the first stone at the woman taken in adultery. (I&P, VI, 190)

Public execution constitutes, in other words, the clearest and most dramatic public rejection of the principle of humanity. Capital punishment, in which act all of consenting society becomes the executioner's accomplices, encourages among its witnesses the most excessive self-righteous self-congratulation, achieved at the expense of the victim, whose essential brotherhood with them they deny by their consent to the execution.

Capital punishment is an act fraught with bizarre paradoxes, as Shelley attempts to demonstrate. This barbaric act supposedly undertaken to prevent crime in fact only perpetuates it. To institutionalize this form of punishment is officially to embrace violence and disorder even while claiming to condemn it. Individuals come in the process to view themselves not as a community of equals but rather as competitors: "Men feel that their revenge is gratified, and that their security is established by the extinction and the sufferings of beings, in most respects resembling themselves; and their daily occupations constraining them to a precise form in all their thoughts, they come to connect inseparably the idea of their own advantage with that of the death and torture of others" (I&P, VI, 188–89). The only way to correct this sociopolitical error—and Shelley intentionally associates the two components—is to abolish capital punishment and thereby renounce the revenge motive for which the government (and society generally) instituted the penalty in the first place. This is precisely why, as Shelley announces in his very first sentence, "the first law which it becomes a Reformer to propose and support, at the approach of a period of great political change, is the abolition of the punishment of death" (185).

The reference to the period of change works in several ways. It alludes to the impending death of George III and to the liberal hopes (however faint they had grown) for progress toward reform under the Prince Regent once he became king. But Shelley's notebook contains, only nine pages after the close of this essay, the first "fragment on reform," which begins by declaring "that our country is on the point of submitting to some [mighty] momentous change in its internal government, is a fact which few who observe & compare the progress of human society will dispute" (Bodleian MS Shelley adds. e. 8, p. 45). In this fragment Shelley predicts the fall of "those who are at present the depositories of" political power. The rest of this brief fragment is most insightful:

> It is a commonplace of political reformers to say, that it is the measures, not the men, they abhor; and it is a general practice, so soon as the party shall have gained the victory, to inflict the severest punishments upon their predecessors, and to pursue measures not less selfish and pernicious than those, a protest against which was the ladder that conducted them to power. The people sympathise with the passions of their liberators, without reflecting that these in turn may become their tyrants, and without perceiving that the same motives and excitements to act or to feel can never, except by a perverse imitation, belong to both. (I&P, VI, 295)

Shelley identifies here the familiar historical pattern: the replacement of old tyrannies with new. Power corrupts, in short. But the observation bears particular relevance to Shelley's thoughts about the direction his country might take. *Prometheus Unbound* documents one variety of "momentous change," but it is not the variety Shelley expects to witness in England in his lifetime. His view of the immediate future, despite the hope that informs both his spirit and his rhetoric, is darker. Hence his statements here, coupled with that reference in the essay on capital punishment to the impending period of great political change, undoubtedly reflect Shelley's often-voiced fears of a duplication in England of the bloodbath loosed in France after the Revolution, a disaster that might at least have been lessened—if not entirely prevented—by the renunciation of vengeance. France still presented most visibly the spectacle of national public self-immolation that follows inexorably from the repetition by the liberators of the sins of the oppressors.

According to Shelley, this lust for revenge is conditioned behavior, not instinct: it inheres in the existing class system and results at least in part from the contempt of the higher classes for the lower. Shelley observes that the richer and more powerful among the audiences at executions (whom he specifically identifies as "a numerous class of little tradesmen [who] are richer and more powerful than those who are employed by them") consider their own status to be reinforced by the penalties thus imposed upon others. This inhumane response produces ominous consequences for the society generally: "In those, therefore, whom this exhibition does not awaken to the sympathy which extenuates crime and discredits the law which restrains it, it produces feelings more directly at war with the genuine purposes of political society. It excites those emotions which it is the chief object of civilisation to extinguish for ever, and in the extinction of which alone there can be any hope of better institutions than those under which men now misgovern one another" (I&P, VI, 188). Shelley originally continued, "So long as the lords seem to believe, that they are each internally & spiritually better than" (Bodleian MS Shelley adds. e. 8, p. 34) but canceled the words in favor of more universal language. He recognized the tendency among the powerful (however defined) to regard their power as a validation of their ethical and moral standards. This self-congratulatory view, endemic to the emerging middle-class morality of capitalist society, reckons the social and economic failures of the less powerful as indicators of their moral inferiority.

I am not forgetting that the ostensible subject of Shelley's essay is the execution of *criminals*, nor did Shelley. But *criminals* is a word easily misused. Shelley appreciated that the term is at all times applied as a pejorative (like *deviant*) to those who resist or disturb the status quo defined and enforced by those in power. Indeed, Shelley makes the point explicitly here in defining a *traitor* as "a person who, from whatever motive, would abolish the government of the day" (187). It is a matter of perspective. But as the opening sections of *The Revolt of Islam* remind us, perspectives vary, and things are not always what they seem: actual and presumed values are often reversed. Opposition to an oppressive and immoral government is, for Shelley as for a whole tradition of radical dissenters, the most sincere form of patriotism. Treason was in Shelley's time, as in our own, one of the charges most commonly leveled against dissenters whom the official government wished to eliminate.

Shelley's sense of the inappropriately pejorative value of terms like these informs the definition of the word *atheist* he entered in a notebook probably dating from 1821.[36] He notes there that although the literal meaning of αθεος is not *atheist* but *godless*, "its accepted meaning among the Greeks was 'an impious person'—it was a mere term of reproach & revilement. Atheist on the contrary expresses a person who denies certain opinions concerning the cause of the Universe. It expresses neither blame nor praise but simply defines an opinion. . . . It is the last insolence in the advocates of an upstart & sanguinary superstition to use the word Atheist as a name of reproach" (Bodleian MS Shelley adds. c. 4, fol. 8 rev.). The "upstart & sanguinary superstition" is Christianity, and its "advocates" those who, like the authorities at Oxford, respond to inquiring dissenters with the mindless urge to stamp them out. Shelley sees church and state as both real and metaphorical mirror images of each other, as sanctimoniously intolerant bastions of vested interest. Hence his attempt to dissociate the imposed propagandistic connotations of *traitor* (state) and *atheist* (church) from the words' actual denotations reflects his desire to exclude irrational subjectivity from the forum of intellectual discourse. He knows how language can be used to misrepresent truth, how it can be turned both against itself and against rational thought by unscrupulous speakers and writers. Shelley's attempts both privately and publicly to defend himself against calumny consistently refer to his attackers' tendency to misuse language in just this fashion. Yet Shelley cannot entirely avoid "loading" his language either, in public or in private discourse, for he appreciates the advantages that accrue from the seduction of one's audience.

Finally, on the often counterproductive nature of public punishment, capital or otherwise, Shelley accurately observes that the government's plans often misfire, producing not an example but a martyr:

> The multitude, instead of departing with a panic-stricken approbation of the laws which exhibited such a spectacle, are inspired with pity, admiration and sympathy; and the most generous among them feel an emulation to be authors of such flattering emotions, as they experience stirring in their bosoms. Impressed by what they see and feel, they make no distinction between the motives which incited the criminals to the actions for which they suffer, or the heroic courage with which they turned into good that which their judges awarded to them as evil, or the purpose itself of those actions, though that purpose may happen to be entirely pernicious. (I&P, VI, 187)

Might Shelley have had in mind the example of Zastrozzi, with his compelling fortitude and dignity in meeting his fate in *Zastrozzi*? Was he thinking of the Derbyshire rebels, whose deaths he had more recently commemorated? Certainly he appreciated the enormous emotional impact of a public execution on the audience and the attendant possibility for unconsidered behavior.

In his important study of penal practice, Michel Foucault observes that in all the formal ceremonies of public execution before the advent of "modern" penal reform, "the main character was the people, whose real and immediate presence was required for the performance." But the audience's role was essentially ambiguous, Foucault claims, for while the spectacle of the execution process (itself a form of theater) enabled the people to share in the vengeance wrought upon the violator of the sovereign's laws, it also alerted them to the potential danger to themselves implicit in the process. Hence demonstrations and even interventions often accompanied executions, particularly if the conviction was seen as unjust, as in the case of a victim executed for a crime that would have brought a richer person a lighter sentence.[37] This un-predictability—this potential for misfire—was one of the principal reasons for the decline of public executions and the removal of punishment from public view generally during the later eighteenth and early nineteenth centuries. In a summary startlingly reminiscent of Shelley's argument, Foucault explains the change: "It was as if the punishment was thought to equal, if not to exceed, in savagery the crime itself, to accustom the spectators to a ferocity from which one wished to divert them, to show them the frequency of crime, to make the executioner resemble a criminal, judges murderers, to reverse roles at the last moment, to make the tortured criminal an object of pity or admiration. . . . The public execution is now seen as a hearth in which violence bursts again into flame."[38] Significantly, England was one of the countries least willing to give up its public executions, owing at least in part to the government's campaign to maintain law and order by whatever means might prove necessary during the period of social disturbances that had begun most notably with the Gordon riots of 1780 and that lasted through the entire Regency period.

Shelley's philosophical prose during the period following his relocation to Italy reveals a continuing concern with the nature of life and death, doubtless in part because of his own recurrent attacks of ill health. "A Future State" reflects his reading of Plato's *Phaedo*, though the essay is less a recapitulation than a repudiation of Plato's arguments.[39] Its relationship to "On the Punishment of Death" is interesting, for though it appears to undermine the first part of that essay by arguing against the existence of any empirically perceptible afterlife, this same argument reinforces the latter part, underscoring the barbarity of depriving another human being of his or her life and thus propelling that individual prematurely and unnaturally into what is to all outward signs and knowledge complete and perpetual oblivion.

Shelley's argument is both empirical and skeptical. His fundamental premise is that when we calmly separate the fact of mortal life from the apparent fiction imposed upon it by religion, by philosophy, and by the natural human fear of total extinction, we can discover no evidence to support our belief in an immortal afterlife: "All that we see or know perishes and is changed. Life and thought differ indeed from everything else. But that it survives that period [i.e., mortal life], beyond which we have no experience of its existence, such distinction and dissimilarity affords no shadow of proof, and nothing but our own desires could have led us to conjecture or imagine" (I&P, VI, 208). This is the position that informs "The Sensitive Plant" and serves as the starting point for *Adonais*.

Shelley composed more of this essay than Mary Shelley included when she published it in the *Essays* in 1840. The 1840 text concludes with Shelley's explicit declaration that humanity's instinctive desire "to be for ever as we are" and its corollary fear of violent and totally unexperienced change is "the secret persuasion which has given birth to the opinions of a future state" (I&P, VI, 209). But in an extended passage which he subsequently canceled, Shelley explains that the natural fear of the unknown may be countered by a philosophical understanding of both the necessity and the naturalness of death:

> The fear of death rather than love of life then renders the [period] grave terrible. If [the] the world were not disquieted by th[is]e fear & the hope of transvital existence [old] natural old age should sink down [slowly] calmly upon its couch of death. Youth it is true [more is able] braves violent death more willingly than age, not because it dreads it less, but because it is confident & rash & [cannot believe that] [takes] esteems the chance of security [for] as security itself. But let both be placed within the view of its certain & gradual advance and the fervour of its temperament. This reluctance [would] rather ably diminishes [as] as we approach towards dissolution, and such is yet the case with those who are yet in harmony with themselves. But[40]

Here the draft leaves off, Shelley apparently having found himself headed off in an unintended direction.

This canceled passage makes clear, first, that to the philosophic mind, death will be seen to be a natural part of the cycle of existence, whether or not it is perceived to be followed by any other state, different or like. This is the point toward which Shelley, pushing beyond Wordsworth, moves in his suggestions about the cycles of natural existence in poems ranging from "Mont Blanc" and "The Cloud" (with their water-cycle imagery) through *Adonais*, and on into the fragment jotted in a notebook probably in 1822:

> the spring rebels not against
> winter but it succeeds it—
> the dawn rebels not
> against night but it
> disperses it—
> (Bodleian MS Shelley adds. e. 18, front endpaper)

This philosophic perspective, it appears, is most commonly the gift of old age, when the rashness of self-confidence—which mistakes things as they are hoped to be for things as they are—is replaced by the wisdom of contemplation, and its advent significantly reduces the terror of the unknown inherent in death. Self-knowledge, or self-harmony, as the final sentence suggests, is the key to this reconciliation. Second—and particularly relevant to "On the Punishment of Death"—if any individual is cut off prematurely, he or she is denied the opportunity for the mature reflection that facilitates such self-knowledge. Hence execution works a double horror not only upon its victim but also upon its witnesses, creating the possibility that the crowd will sympathize with the victim, whose sufferings in the face of an unknowable ultimate fate become for them both more dramatic and more immediately personal.

Both these essays develop aspects of Shelley's doctrine of love, the keystone of his scheme for humanitarian reform not just of political systems per se but of all social relationships. Hence, though Shelley's use of the first-person plural in "A Future State" constitutes a conventional rhetorical device of philosophical prose, that device nonetheless imposes upon the reader a sense of unity and community with the author in a shared meditation on the one experience common to all human beings. Shelley employs *we* throughout "A Future State"; there are no occurrences of *I*. The reverse is true of "On the Punishment of Death." I think this no mere coincidence but rather a conscious stylistic decision intended—had the essays been printed in Shelley's lifetime—to define for rhetorical purposes the precise distance between author and audience in each case.

These two pronouns, which Shelley so carefully separates here, converge in "On Life," the essay from late 1819 that seems to have been a by-product of Shelley's draft of *A Philosophical View of Reform*[41] and which forms the logical culmination to his thoughts on these issues. Shelley now dismisses *both* pronouns, together with *they*, as mere "grammatical devices invented simply for arrangement, and totally devoid of the intense and exclusive sense usually attached to them" (I&P, VI, 196). These pronouns, all of which are nominatives, serve merely "to denote the different modifications of the one mind" (196). In other words, on the intellectual level of pure idea may be said to exist the most perfect and consistent state of community, Wordsworth's "one human heart" metamorphosing, as it were, into the "one universal mind" Shelley here implies. In such an ideal state pronouns (and all nominative terms) are rendered irrelevant because what is known is indistinguishable from the aggregate "one" who knows. This is why for Shelley poetry—and indeed all communication—resides finally not within the work itself, which is merely the medium or container, the outward form, but rather in the dynamic transaction between the minds of author and audience.[42]

"On Life" elaborates the skeptical view of the nature of reality and experience (or knowledge) explored in "A Future State." Shelley declares flatly that he is "unable to refuse my assent to the conclusions of those philosophers who assert that nothing exists but as it is perceived" and that "the difference is merely nominal between those two classes of thought, which are vulgarly distinguished by the names of ideas and of external objects" (I&P, VI, 194, 196). He recapitulates Wordsworth's explanation (most notably in the Intimations Ode) of the process of intellectual and imaginative desensitization by which humanity loses its proper appreciation of life. Like Wordsworth and Coleridge before him, Shelley suggests (as he had in the "Hymn to Intellectual Beauty") that "thoughts and feelings arise, with or without our will," but that "the mist of familiarity obscures from us the wonder of our being" (193–94). In Shelley's view, poetry "defamiliarizes existence to reveal its essential features,"[43] returning to the desensitized reader something of the natural spontaneity of response that characterizes the child or the savage (recall Wordsworth's ode and its epigraph, as well as "The World Is Too Much with Us").

Shelley's subsequent remark that "there are some persons who, in this respect, are always children" (195) is at least partially metaphorical. Such children are those who are perpetually struck with the full beauty and the inestimable mystery of life in all its forms, in whom

> The everlasting universe of things
> Flows through the mind, and rolls its rapid waves,
> . . . with a sound but half its own
> ("Mont Blanc," *Works*, 532)

They are the persons of superior sensitivity (if not intelligence) who have escaped the "shades of the prison-house," whose "natural piety" has not faded in "the light of common day." Speaking of the delights the universe offers to those who can apprehend them, Shelley observes, "But now these things are looked on with little wonder, and to be conscious of them with intense delight is esteemed to be the distinguishing mark of a refined and extraordinary person. The multitude of men care not for them" (I&P, VI, 193). Such individuals are the poets, as defined by both Shelley and Wordsworth, whose language and works the younger author again deliberately invokes in this essay as context and precedent for his own. Furthermore, the distinction drawn in that final sentence between the two types of sensibilities—the receptive and the deadened—is very important. For while Wordsworth, both in his poems and in the preface to *Lyrical Ballads*, keeps alive the impulse to democratize the arts in implying that every individual is potentially a poet, Shelley seems to back away from that notion, ruefully admitting that such imaginative vitality is the lot at best of a sacred few. There is an obvious connection between Shelley's comments here and those, for instance, in his preface to *Prometheus Unbound*, written at about this time, about the presumed ideal audience for that lyrical drama.

I have tried to stress Shelley's intentional verbal echoes of Wordsworth because the tendency in Shelley scholarship is so often to focus
on his many expressions of disapproval of the elder poet's gradual drift
into conservative orthodoxy. Whatever he may have thought of Wordsworth's retrogression, Shelley seems to acknowledge here late in 1819
that Wordsworth has been the leading spirit of an enormous shift in
the nature and direction of art as a social and political force. In thus
invoking Wordsworth, Shelley locates himself within a contemporary
impulse toward liberal social and humanitarian activism. Furthermore, both the recognizably Lockean underpinnings of Shelley's argument and the specific citation of Sir William Drummond's *Academ-
ical Questions* further legitimize his discussion as part of a mainstream
philosophical inquiry.

Finally, near the end of the fragment, Shelley adopts a typical posture of apparent humility: "Let it not be supposed that this doctrine
conducts to the monstrous presumption that I, the person who now
write and think, am that one mind. I am but a portion of it" (196).
Even taken out of context, Shelley's remark illustrates his determination to draw his readers into accepting a fair share (if not all) of the
responsibility for the message they extract from the text. For, returned
to its context in the essay, this passage implies that the author (who
writes and thinks) is coequal with the reader (who *reads* and thinks) in
partnership in that "one mind," and that, as Shelley implies in the
Essay on Christianity and elsewhere, the author is simply verbalizing
ideas and impressions that are as much the reader's as his own.

Although Shelley spoke and wrote much about imminent death, it
would be absurd to suggest that he planned to die young. His plan for
a long and productive career is indicated not only by the acceleration
of both the quantity and the scope of his works toward the end of his
life but also by the presence earlier on of so many anonymous or near-
anonymous pieces. Shelley's willingness to publish anonymously, despite his obvious craving for fame both as author and as reformer,
ought not to surprise us: anonymous publication had been a standard
part of the early careers of innumerable English authors. The tradition
continues, of course, though in our own time the device for anonymity
is more often the pseudonym. In either case, the scheme is the same:
once the author's skill has been acknowledged and his or her fame
secured, it is possible to accept responsibility for these literary orphans,
whose value is increased by the subsequent reputation of their author.
I have suggested above that Shelley may well have entertained just
such a notion in publishing his review of Hogg's *Prince Alexy*, for instance. A similar motivation might be suggested for most of those
works to which Shelley did not formally attach his name, and especially those in which he seems even to have attempted to disguise his

style. This strategy arose partly, of course, from plain frustration at having his work attacked when it bore his name (and occasionally even when it did not). But it stemmed also from Shelley's deep-seated sense of fun, which was remarked upon by many of those who knew him. Literary scholarship has a dismaying tendency to overlook humor and to regard its subjects' mouths as virtually incapable of shaping smiles. The pitfalls of such exaggerated sobriety become immediately apparent when we consider Shelley's friend Byron or notorious pranksters such as Charles Lamb. We need to keep in mind those images of Shelley sailing paper boats and playing at monsters for the entertainment of the children who so obviously loved him. We need always, I think, to entertain the possibility that Shelley is being less immediately serious than we customarily take him to be.

let the tyrant keep
His chains and tears, yea, let him weep
With rage to see thee freshly risen,
Like strength from slumber, from the prison,
In which he vainly hoped the soul to bind
Which on the chains must prey that fetter humankind.

SHELLEY, "To a Friend Released from Prison"

Chapter Five

HISTORY AND MYTH

Three Political Parables

The Cenci, Prometheus Unbound, and *Julian and Maddalo* reveal Shelley's increasing facility in, and mastery of, different styles, genres, and modes of composition. More than at any other period in his career, Shelley was determined from mid-1818 through mid-1820 (through the release of *Prometheus Unbound and Other Poems* in August) to find the appropriate means for addressing the different, frequently non-overlapping, and increasingly fictitious and "virtual" audiences to which he now sought to direct his works from his Italian self-exile. Although Shelley's early career prefigures this multifaceted literary activity, the often substantial accomplishments of those years pale beside the virtuosity of the works of this later period. In this chapter I shall discuss these three major works and, finally, the relationship with Byron they involve, reserving for the next chapter the overtly political writings of this period.

Particularly in the two dramas, Shelley attempts to link the relative authorial impersonality of dramatic works with the intensely personal voice of their prefaces.[1] One of the drama's unique features is its virtual elimination of the involved authorial narrator. The drama most nearly epitomizes that "virtual" art form in which the "work" itself is identical with neither the text per se nor its actualization in the reader's or viewer's consciousness, but rather exists somewhere between the two, in dynamic virtuality.[2] What transpires on the stage (or in the theater of the reader's mind) is both representation and interpretation, text and criticism, stasis and motion. The difficulties that such virtuality creates for author and audience alike are very evident in *The Cenci*.

The Cenci

Thinking he had completed *Prometheus Unbound* (in three acts) at Rome in April, Shelley took up the subject of the Cenci family, completing on 8 August at the Villa Valsovana, near Livorno, the first draft of the play that might have become "the focal point for the revival of a true poetic drama in the nineteenth century," had it been staged.[3] The only one of Shelley's works to see a second edition in the poet's lifetime, *The Cenci* commanded perhaps the most attentive readership of any of his productions. When it was printed in 1820 after being rejected by Covent Garden, Shelley's critics were forced to concede the author's power. Whatever their objections to Shelley or his subject, they could not ignore the skill of his composition. Nor could they fail to appreciate the play's revolutionary attack on the patriarchal system that formed the traditional structural basis of society. *The Cenci* dramatically illustrates how the sins of the fathers are visited upon the children. Whether those fathers be natural biological ones (Count Cenci), symbolic ones (the pope, and by analogy the king), or spiritual ones (God), their failures inhere in their oppressions.[4] Moreover, their dehumanizing humiliation of their victims engenders there a thirst for vengeance that consumes villain and victim alike. Shelley believed this tragic outcome might be averted, but only if both the oppressors and their victims could be educated into selfless benevolence.

Shelley had been thinking and writing for some time about the socially enforced degradation of women to the status of virtual slaves in the premodern world,[5] a point not without sociological consequence for *Rosalind and Helen*, whose women struggle against the repressive conventions of an unsympatheic patriarchal society. Even the ancient Greek society, according to Shelley, the "glorious generations" who "were, perhaps, the most perfect specimens of humanity of whom we have authentic record," had not been above enslaving not just the conquered citizens of other countries but also their own repressed countrywomen. This massive social and cultural error had undoubtedly produced a "diminution . . . in the delicacy, the strength, the comprehensiveness, and the accuracy of their conceptions, in moral, political, and metaphysical science, and perhaps in every other art and science" (I&P, VII, 223–27). Thus victimized, Shelley concludes, Greek women "became such as it was expected they would become," taking on "the habits and qualities of slaves" (I&P, VII, 228). As Mary Wollstonecraft and other pioneering feminists were beginning to demonstrate, the centuries of repression and domination had effectively deprived women not of the ability to choose their status and destinies but rather of any opportunity for doing so.[6] The impossibility of Beatrice Cenci's situation, caught between the Scylla of innate innocence and dignity and the Charybdis of societal pressure to submit to patriarchal domination, was shared by women generally in Shelley's time.

In composing a play specifically intended for the stage, Shelley was attempting to enter into a significantly different relationship with an audience based not on the solitary and tranquil act of reading but on the social and more subjective act of witnessing live theater. Furthermore, he determined to take an entirely new approach to language and style in an attempt to increase the play's accessibility for the theatergoer. He was undoubtedly responding both to Mary Shelley and to Hunt, who had also encouraged him to do more in the "popular style" of *Rosalind and Helen*. Over and over to his correspondents Shelley repeats his claim to have adopted this more popular idiom. To Peacock, he is most revealing and detailed:

> I have taken some pains to make my play fit for representation, & those who have already seen it judge favourably. It is written without any of the peculiar feelings & opinions which characterize my other compositions, I having attend[ed] simply to the impartial development of such characters as it is probable the persons represented really were, together with the greatest degree of popular effect to be produced by such a development. I send you a translation of the Italian Mss. on which my play is founded; the chief circumstance of which I have touched very delicately; for my principal doubt as to whether it would succeed as an acting play hangs entirely on the question as to whether any such a thing as incest in this shape however treated wd. be admitted on the stage—I think however it will form no objection, considering first that the facts are matter of history, & secondly the peculiar delicacy with which I have treated it—
>
> I am exceedingly interested in the question of whether this attempt of mine will succeed or no—I am strongly inclined to the affirmative at present, founding my hopes on this, that as a composition it is certainly not inferior to any of the modern plays that have been acted, with the exception of Remorse, that the interest of its plot is incredibly greater & more real, & that there is nothing beyond what the multitude are contented to believe that they can understand, either in imagery opinion or sentiment.—I wish to preserve a complete incognito, & can trust to you, that whatever else you do, you will at least favour

me on this point. Indeed this is essential, deeply essential to it's [sic] success. After it had been acted & successfully (could I hope such a thing) I would own it if I pleased, & use the celebrity it might acquire to my own purposes.—(*Letters*, II, 102; ca. 20 July 1819)

Shelley's concern about the incest theme anticipates the very point upon which many of the critics concentrated their attacks, even though Shelley had significantly modified and reduced the extent of the real Count Cenci's sexual depravity.[7] Ironically, sexual deviance, and incest in particular, were established conventions of Gothic fiction, to which tradition *The Cenci* is demonstrably indebted in both substance and effect. But Shelley insists—even to the point of providing Peacock with a translation of his source—that his story is not fiction but fact: history, however morally or intellectually horrifying, cannot with integrity be sanitized by author or critic, Thomas Bowdler notwithstanding. Shelley stresses the point to Peacock: "If my Play should be accepted don't you think it would excite some interest, & take off the unexpected horror of the story by shewing that the events are real, if it could appear in some Paper in some form.—" (*Letters*, II, 120; 21 September 1819). Such publication would yield a triple benefit: alerting the audience in advance to the nature and plot of the play, it would enable them better to understand its philosophical arguments. It would also insulate Shelley from charges that he had invented a morally outrageous fiction. Finally, it would provide free advertising.

Shelley's wish to remain anonymous initially is another indication of his craving for a fair and unbiased audience. Writing to Amelia Curran in September, Mary Shelley undoubtedly reflects her husband's feelings: "It is still *a deep secret* & only one person, Peacock who presents it, knows anything about it in England—with S's public & private enemies it would certainly fall if known to be his—his sister in law alone would hire enough people to damn it."[8] One suspects the delight Shelley would have taken in revealing his authorship had the play been performed at Covent Garden, hailed by the critics, and cheered by the public. What would have been the embarrassed perplexity of the reviewers had they acclaimed the play on its literary and dramatic merits, only to discover in its author the young radical they routinely vilified? How better could Shelley demonstrate to critics and general public alike the fallacy of failing to separate *ad hominem* attacks from objective literary criticism?

Shelley's letter to Peacock displays two other tendencies we have already glimpsed. First, his reference to the play's favorable reception by "those who have already seen it"—presumably Mary Shelley, Claire Clairmont, and John and Maria Gisborne—encourages Peacock to concur in this general approbation; Shelley is, after all, asking Peacock to carry the argument to Thomas Harris, manager of Covent Garden, and to use whatever influence he might command to procure its performance there. Second, he locates *The Cenci* within the mainstream of Regency drama, citing Coleridge's *Remorse* (which ran for twenty nights at Drury Lane in 1813) as its only serious modern rival, and undoubtedly thinking of Henry Hart Milman's tedious *Fazio* (in which Eliza O'Neill's portrayal of Bianca had fascinated him; *Letters*, II, 102n.).

Most interesting of all is Shelley's suggestion that *The Cenci* will not be perceived to be "beyond" the level of its audience "in imagery opinion or sentiment." His subversive intent hinges partly upon encouraging his audience to *believe* it understands what is going on, to empathize with Beatrice on the grounds of simple humanity. Such a gesture of solidarity would implicitly place the audience in opposition to the visible and implied patriarchs of the Regency establishment. It was this act of rebellious antipatriarchalism, engineered from within the play and practically without the audience's conscious consent, that constituted for many reviewers the play's real threat, not just to popular morality but to the entire social and political system.[9] In the aftermath of the "Peterloo massacre" of 16 August 1819, reviewers could scarcely have missed the play's inflammatory nature. Part of the difficulty modern critics have with *The Cenci* arises from Shelley's seeming attempt to have it both ways, philosophically, in a text in which he claims publicly in his preface to have renounced any desire to have it either way.

Writing to Hunt before completing his first draft, to tell him he would dedicate *The Cenci* to him, Shelley distinguishes the play from his previous works: "Those writings which I have hitherto published, have been little else than visions which impersonate my own apprehensions of the beautiful and the just. I can also perceive in them the literary defects incidental to youth and impatience; they are dreams of what ought to be, or may be. The drama which I now present to you is a sad reality. I lay aside the presumptuous attitude of an instructor, and am content to paint, with such colours as my own heart furnishes, that which has been." (*Letters*, II, 96; 29 May 1819). Shelley's notion of *The Cenci*'s realism suggests a link with his study in Italy of classical drama, one of whose principles Shelley reformulates in his comment in the preface to *Prometheus Unbound* that the poet is the voice of his age and therefore speaks only secondarily—if at all—in his own voice. In this sense the poet's works cannot be strictly personal reenactments of the experience of one individual alone.[10] Personal polemic must be rendered invisible by its diffusion through the texture of the work. As Shelley says in the preface to *The Cenci*: "There must also be nothing attempted to make the exhibition subservient to what is vulgarly termed a moral purpose. The highest moral purpose aimed at in the highest species of the drama, is the teaching the human heart, through its sympathies and antipathies, the knowledge of itself; in proportion to the possession of which knowledge, every human being is wise, just, sincere, tolerant and kind. If dogmas can do more, it is well; but a drama is no fit place for the enforcement of them" (*Works*, 276). In this Shelley follows Aristotle, who asserts that "it is the action in it, i.e., its Fable or Plot, that is the end and purpose of the tragedy," for "the most powerful elements of attraction in tragedy, the Peripeties and Discoveries, are parts of the Plot."[11] Shelley will appeal first to the heart, and through the heart to the rational, judging intellect. This emotional self-knowledge, whose benefits—wisdom, justice, sincerity, tolerance, and kindness—are the very qualities Beatrice Cenci gradually surrenders in her fatal commitment to vengeance and retribution, is the quality Shelley everywhere counsels.

Peacock remarks that the realism Shelley attempted in *The Cenci* (and in the unfinished *Charles the First*) was too alien for him to carry it through successfully: "He could not clip his wings to the littleness of the acting drama. . . . If his life had been prolonged, I still think he would have accomplished something worthy of the best days of theatrical literature. If the gorgeous scenery of his poetry could have been peopled from actual life, if the deep thoughts and strong feelings which he was so capable of expressing, had been accommodated to characters such as have been and may be, however exceptional in the greatness of passion, he would have added his own name to those of the masters of the art."[12] Why does Peacock ignore the fact that both the Cenci family and Charles I *were* "characters such as have been"? Did he want to see more "ordinary" characters and situations, or do his remarks, like Hogg's elsewhere, merely reflect the conservatism of retrospect? Or did he simply miss Shelley's point? Although Peacock and others judged Shelley's play unsatisfactory as theater, had *The Cenci* been merely the "domestic melodrama" devoid of "the least human warmth or moral richness," which Richard Holmes unsympathetically considers it,[13] Shelley would scarcely have invested in it the continuing concern he did during the final years of his life. Nor would he have made the effort in the first place to convey to a "popular" public audience a vital and powerfully committed political prophecy whose protagonist so clearly represented that very audience.

Shelley's tragedy posits a theater of participation, not of mere observation, geared to an illuminating and cathartic expansion of consciousness. George Bernard Shaw's view of the theater as a vehicle for propaganda is, I believe, despite its author's ironic tone, not far from Shelley's:

I am convinced that fine art is the subtlest, the most seductive, the most effective instrument of moral propaganda in the world, excepting only the example of personal conduct; and I waive even this exception in favor of the stage, because it works by exhibiting examples of personal conduct made intelligible and moving to crowds of unobserving unreflecting people to whom real life means nothing. . . . So effective do I find the dramatic method that I have no doubt I shall at last persuade even London to take its conscience and its brains when it goes to the theatre, instead of leaving them at home with its prayer-book as it does at present.[14]

Shelley likewise aims to exercise both the brains and the consciences of his audience. By showing things as they *were*, he intends by analogy to show things as they now *are* and thereby to issue a graphic warning about how things need not—indeed must not—be. In this intent, the play has clear links to Shelley's other dream-visions, including his earliest long poem, *Queen Mab*, and to later reformational dream-visions intended for popular audiences, perhaps most notably Charles Dickens's "A Christmas Carol."

Beatrice Cenci is more than just the protagonist in a proto-historical play; she is the central figure in a tragic prophecy that operates on several interrelated levels. At the level of surface narrative, her role is historical. At the level of moral and ethical significance, it is essentially allegorical. And at the level of actual human experience, the level most relevant to Shelley's private concerns and public intentions as he composed his play in 1819, her role is mythic. Shelley weaves these roles into the fabric of a tragedy that elevates history to the level and status of myth, creating a moral and political exemplum designed dramatically to reveal the inevitable destruction from within of even the noblest and best-intentioned society—epitomized in its most paradigmatically virtuous representative—when that society participates in the undermining of natural, humane love and the consequent embrace of brutality, domination, revenge, and retribution. To present in its most powerful and devastating fashion the terrible tragedy of such a misdirection of all that is noble and divine in humanity requires a compelling protagonist of tragic grandeur. Beatrice Cenci is just such a figure.

Beatrice is an exemplar both of social status (the Cenci are a powerful aristocratic family) and of moral character (she is, both by report and by initial behavior, extraordinarily virtuous), as was apparent to Shelley both from the historical account of her character and from her portrait (attributed at the time to Guido Reni[15]) at Rome: "There is a simplicity and dignity which, united with her exquisite loveliness and deep sorrow, are inexpressibly pathetic. Beatrice Cenci appears to have been one of those rare persons in whom energy and gentleness dwell together without destroying one another: her nature was simple and profound" (*Works*, 278). She is also intellectually acute. Shelley envisioned that her part should be acted at Covent Garden by the lovely and dynamic Eliza O'Neill (1791–1872), the Irish actress whom William Hazlitt admired and who from her first appearance at Covent Garden in 1814 as Juliet had increasingly been acclaimed the worthy successor to the great Sarah Siddons. Shelley wrote to Peacock that the part of Beatrice Cenci was "precisely fitted" for her, that "it might even seem to have been written for her," and that to see Miss O'Neill play the role would undoubtedly "tear my nerves to pieces" (*Letters*, II, 102).

Shelley considered it vital that Beatrice be represented by the actress who could most powerfully animate this complex character on the stage, an actress who specialized in scenes of madness and distracted grief.[16] Ironically, a week before he wrote to Peacock she had made her farewell appearance, on 13 July, before retiring from the stage to marry William Becher. Mary Shelley subsequently wrote Amelia Curran, "Now that Miss O'Neil [sic] is married I do not think it could be brought out [on the stage] with effect anywhere[.] I hope however that it will be liked in print."[17] Shelley envisioned as Count Cenci the immensely popular Romantic actor Edmund Kean, whose violent, passionate style would have effectively conveyed Cenci's vicious brutality. Kean was, however, under contract to Drury Lane; he could not act at Covent Garden, as Shelley seems to have acknowledged.[18] Still, that Shelley dreamed of enlisting O'Neill and Kean and considered at least the first a real possibility indicates his appreciation of the magnetism of the age's two most popular stars and his shrewd sense of both consumer appeal and marketing strategy.

Shelley's Beatrice bears out Aristotle's stipulation that the cause of the hero's reversal "must lie not in any depravity but in some great error on his part," some "error of judgement" (*Poetics*, 1467). Her "great error" lies—as Blake might have put it—in becoming what she beholds. Her reversal stems from a terrible error of judgment that occurs in a situation of enormous stress. Shelley makes her the victim, apparently, of more than simply incestuous rape. She is repeatedly unable to *name* her father's crime (e.g., III, i, 114–17, 154–55), and in his preface Shelley calls Cenci's "capital crimes of the most enormous and unspeakable kind" (*Works*, 275). The "unspeakable" crime may well be sodomy, of which offense the historical Francesco Cenci had in fact been convicted not once but three times, escaping the sentence of execution in each instance by bribing the pope, Clement VIII.[19] William Blackstone had echoed Pauline doctrine in his *Commentaries on the Laws of England*, deeming sodomy a "capital" crime "the very mention of which is a disgrace to human nature."[20] The general currency in the later eighteenth and early nineteenth centuries of this notion of sodomy as an unspeakable, unnamable act[21] would have enabled Shelley's audiences to identify the crime by virtue of the pointed references to its unnamability.

Convinced that the vicious and demeaning physical and psychological outrages to which she is subjected by her incestuous father have necessarily tainted her, Beatrice chooses to retaliate precisely as she has been wronged: by a physical attack upon the body of her oppressor. When she appears dazed and distracted in Act III immediately after she has been attacked, Beatrice understandably calls for the relief and comfort of vengeance. But later, when the immediate emotional shock has passed, she does not repudiate her bloody aims but instead reaffirms them. In carefully plotting her father's murder and in employing assassins to execute the deed, she adopts the behavior she has condemned in others. In effect, Beatrice appoints herself judge, jury, and executioner. In the *Essay on Christianity* Shelley had specifically attacked the principle of retributive "justice" associated with God the Father on the grounds of its singular injustice: "My neighbour or my servant or my child has done me an injury, and it is just that he should suffer an injury in return. Such is the doctrine which Jesus Christ summoned his whole resources of persuasion to oppose. 'Love your enemy, bless those who curse you[']" (I&P, VI, 233). Perhaps recalling the fate of Godwin's Falkland (*Caleb Williams*), Shelley writes: "Undoubtedly, no person can be truly dishonoured by the act of another; and the fit return to make to the most enormous injuries is kindness and forbearance, and a resolution to convert the injurer from his dark passions by peace and love. Revenge, retaliation, atonement, are pernicious mistakes" (*Works*, 276). Beatrice's error lies in promoting herself unilaterally to the role and status of God, specifically violating the injunction of Romans 12:19: "Dearly beloved, avenge not yourselves, but rather give place unto wrath: for it is written, Vengeance is mine; I will repay, saith the Lord." Beatrice Cenci's is the tragic flaw of hubris, the deadly sin of pride. That she is a Roman Catholic in a Catholic country, and, moreover, that her father is barely dead by her devices when the emissaries of the pope arrive to arrest him in the name of the church (and hence of God) adds the crushing weight of cosmic irony to the gravity of her crime. Guilty not just of parricide, she sins doubly in blaspheming as well.

The Cenci is a deeply skeptical play in which Shelley examines not the universal idealisms with which he had worked in the first three acts of *Prometheus Unbound* but the particularized psychology of innocence abused and corrupted by omnipresent and unbearable hypocrisy, depravity, and oppression. The particular focus of Shelley's skepticism is Beatrice Cenci, whose inherent innocence and calamitous failures are, and remain, both undeniable and irreconcilable.[22] Catharsis can be only partial and ultimately unsatisfying under these circumstances. The situation is so totally impossible morally, ethically, and politically that there can be neither victory nor vindication for any of the parties, and the audience is forced to share in this terrible impasse. The audience must recognize at last that the evil which must be repudiated is that of the entire degrading and misbegotten system which both produces and permits such crippling depravities, not merely the individual characters who are all its victims.

Yet Shelley's intended audience could only have reacted as the Italian people had reacted to the Cenci story, with an instinctive and entirely human outpouring of sympathy for Beatrice, whose plight is an appropriate emblem for the crisis that occurs in human affairs when coping—or simply surviving—appears to demand the sacrifice of one's ideals. Shelley is caught in a double bind between historical accuracy and artistic license. Aristotle distinguishes between poetry and history on the grounds that poetry's statements "are of the nature rather of universals, whereas those of history are singulars" (*Poetics*, 1464). Hence the author of a tragedy is advised to "first simplify [his story] and reduce [it] to a universal form, before proceeding to lengthen it out by the insertion of episodes" (*Poetics*, 1472). Shelley pursued this strategy, subsequently writing of the Cenci story in his preface that "anything like a dry exhibition of it on the stage would be insupportable. The person who would treat such a subject must increase the ideal, and diminish the actual horror of the events, so that the pleasure which arises from the poetry which exists in these tempestuous sufferings and crimes may mitigate the pain of the contemplation of the moral deformity from which they spring" (*Works*, 276). In short, history must be made into poetry: "the thing that *has* happened" must become also the "kind of thing that *might* happen" (*Poetics*, 1463; my italics). The history of the Cencis, pregnant with universal significance, assumes the nature and significance of myth.

Here, in fact, is where Shelley understood the immediate contemporary significance of his tragedy to lie: he saw in England an increasingly close analogy to the universally destructive collision of irreconcilable forces his play examines. England was ripe for revolution during these latter years of the Regency: crop failures and political repression had aggravated the already acute socioeconomic dilemma arising from a postwar economic recession, the mechanization of the trades and industries, and the return to the work force of war-weary soldiers who now had no jobs to which to return. Shelley appreciated that as its perceived injuries and oppressions become increasingly intolerable any oppressed group turns inevitably toward either the docile self-abnegation of compliance or the violent self-vindication of revolution. The moment of crisis is voiced in Beatrice's variation of a reverse definition in Act III:

> What have I done?
> Am I not innocent? Is it my crime
> That one with white hair, and imperious brow,
> Who tortured me from my forgotten years,
> As parents only dare, should call himself
> My father, yet should be!—Oh, what am I?
> What name, what place, what memory shall be mine?
> What retrospects, outliving even despair?
> ....
> —O blood, which art my father's blood,
> Circling through these contaminated veins,
> If thou, poured forth on the polluted earth,
> Could wash away the crime, and punishment
> By which I suffer . . . no, that cannot be!
> Many might doubt there were a God above
> Who sees and permits evil, and so die:
> That faith no agony shall obscure in me.
>
> (III, i, 69–76, 95–102; *Works*, 298)

Beatrice speaks for an English populace that was seeing with ever increasing clarity the indignities and oppression to which its ruling powers had subjected it and which was beginning now seriously to contemplate violent revolution.

From what the liberal periodicals he received in Italy told him about the growing crisis in England,[23] it is not unreasonable to see in *The Cenci* yet another attempt on Shelley's part to play an active part—even from the distance of several weeks' journey—in stabilizing, reforming, and reorienting English society and values. Shelley would have concurred entirely in Samuel Bamford's judgment in 1842 that at the time, "the people themselves wanted reforming,—that they were ignorant and corrupt; and that the source must be purified before a pure and free government could be maintained."[24] Like Shaw later, Shelley held that a direct relationship existed between the theater and any society's moral values.[25] Shelley's drama aims at producing in his audience a "creative moral insight," a "virtue-making discovery," and an increased self-knowledge achieved in the process of grappling with the moral dilemma posed through the sympathies and antipathies the play elicits.[26] Hence it is precisely in its community function as "live" theater that *The Cenci* might have held the greatest potential for instruction, for reforming and educating the public and providing the necessary brake to the speeding vehicle of public unrest that with every passing day increasingly threatened to become a runaway as had happened in France thirty years earlier.

Beatrice Cenci's "great error" consists in her conscious subscription to the cycle of abuse and vengeance that governs the world around her. Already in *Zastrozzi* and *St. Irvyne* Shelley had explored the poisonous nature of revenge in both male and female characters. The beautiful Matilda of *Zastrozzi* is an early (though far less complex or compelling) prototype of Beatrice Cenci, driven to the most hideous atrocities by a lust for revenge on her perceived enemies. Shelley had objected to Ariosto's poetry on the grounds that "he constantly vindicates & embellishes revenge in its grossest form, the most deadly superstition that ever infested the world" (*Letters*, II, 20; to the Gisbornes, 10 July 1818). More to the point is the *Address to the People on the Death of the Princess Charlotte*, in which the unnatural and extraordinary perversion of freedom and justice produced by the government's paranoia is viewed as part of the ultimately self-destructive institutional attack on individual and collective liberty. The funeral procession with which Shelley concludes his *Address* is relevant here:

> Mourn then People of England. Clothe yourselves in solemn black. Let the bells be tolled. Think of mortality and change. . . . A beautiful Princess is dead:—she who should have been the Queen of her beloved nation, and whose posterity should have ruled it for ever. . . . LIBERTY is dead. . . . But *man* has murdered Liberty, and whilst the life was ebbing from its wound, there descended on the heads and on the hearts of every human thing, the sympathy of an universal blast and curse. . . . Let us follow the corpse of British Liberty slowly and reverentially to its tomb: and if some glorious Phantom should appear, and make its throne of broken swords and sceptres and royal crowns trampled in the dust, let us say that the Spirit of Liberty has arisen from its grave and left all that was gross and mortal there, and kneel down and worship it as our Queen. (I&P, VI, 82)

Beatrice Cenci is the most important in a series of politically allegorical female figures in Shelley's works. Like the phantom of Liberty, she is a figurehead for the oppressed, for Liberty soiled and subjugated by irresponsible power and authority.

But unlike the figure in the funeral procession (who foreshadows a renascence of liberty), and unlike the rallying spirit that speaks in *The Mask of Anarchy* (who arises triumphant, even apocalyptic, from the carnage), and certainly unlike the spirit of Ianthe in *Queen Mab* (who is enjoined to "learn to make others happy"—*Works*, 767), Beatrice Cenci ultimately adds negative components to her character. Like Oedipus, she sentences herself by and to her own hand. But unlike Oedipus, hers is less a search for truth and justice than a vindictive quest for vengeance, a blood-lust that is no less vicious for its having arisen from the most despicable of persecutions. Shelley delineates her movement from a position of heroic potential to one of intellectual and ethical failure. The mythic pattern is that of the Fall. Beatrice succumbs to the temptation to commit an act—murder—that is expressly forbidden by God. But she is her own tempter within her personal psychodrama, and the nature of her fall is indicated in her announcement in Act III:

> I have prayed
> To God, and I have talked with my own heart,
> And have unravelled my entangled will,
> And have at last determined what is right.
> *(Works, 301)*

The entire play turns upon that final phrase, "what is right," with characters and audience alike drawn into the wrenching examination of the evidence. Beatrice's situation is in many ways similar to that of Christabel in the Coleridge poem Shelley undoubtedly knew. Convinced by the combined force of external circumstances and an insufficiently sound sense of innate self-worth that she is sullied and devalued by the brutality to which she has fallen victim ("these contaminated veins," III, i, 96), she responds in kind, returning injury for injury. In the process she proves herself to be not just Beatrice, but Beatrice Cenci: she is very much her father's daughter.

Yet since Shelley designed his play so that the audience would instinctively side with Beatrice from the start, he had to include some mechanism to prompt the audience to question that powerful emotional alliance. The clearest signal comes in the final act, in the fate of Marzio, one of the two assassins Beatrice had hired to kill Count Cenci. When Beatrice confronts him in Act V after he has named her to the authorities under torture, Marzio is so overwhelmed that he cannot repeat his accusation. In a speech of ironic self-deception, Beatrice swears a false oath as prelude to her crucial question to Marzio:

> . . . Think
> What 'tis to blot with infamy and blood
> All that which shows like innocence, and is,
> Hear me, great God! I swear, most innocent,
> So that the world lose all discrimination
> Between the sly, fierce, wild regard of guilt,

And that which now compels thee to reply
To what I ask: Am I, or am I not,
A parricide?

(*Works*, 326)

The audience is challenged to distinguish between appearance and reality—and between emotion and reason—and to see the facts of her case, lest it, too, "lose all discrimination" between truth and falsehood. She *is*, after all, a parricide.

Marzio dooms himself to an eternity in hell in responding with an outright lie which he never recants but bears to his death on the rack. His answer, like all of his final speech, indicates the extent to which he has been seduced by Beatrice's appearance and rhetoric, even as Eve had been deceived by the serpent. Overcome by emotion, Marzio denies that Beatrice is a parricide and concludes with misplaced pride:

I here declare those whom I did accuse
Are innocent. 'Tis I alone am guilty . . .
Torture me as ye will:
A keener pang has wrung a higher truth
From my last breath. She is most innocent!
Bloodhounds, not men, glut yourselves well with me;
I will not give you that fine piece of nature
To rend and ruin.

(*Works*, 326)

Marzio's denial of the truth and his self-castigation at having named the person the audience already knows to be guilty recall the grotesque and self-deluding irony with which Caleb Williams reviles himself after revealing the murderer Falkland in *Caleb Williams*. Both delude themselves in believing that those they accuse somehow do not deserve their just punishment, and both bitterly regret having revealed the truth to the respective authorities. Whatever we may feel about the calamity that engulfs Beatrice, we cannot back away from the horror of what she engineers in Marzio's final moments, for she ensures his eternal damnation by a cruel, self-serving, and presumably self-*preserving* bluff. Shelley demands that the audience see for itself the depth of callous inhumanity to which the beautiful Beatrice has sunk. That she is subsequently revealed by her own brother and mother makes even more poignant this needless sacrifice of Marzio's soul, a point Shelley underscores by insisting upon the play's Catholic framework. Moreover, Beatrice is so moved by her own situation and by the rhetorical maneuvering by which she repeatedly misstates facts in proclaiming her innocence that she convinces herself that she is blameless in her father's death.

As metaphor, then, *The Cenci* confronts its audience with the corruptibility of the prevailing model of family structure,[27] which is why this play about family relationships is also about ideology and about political struggle. Like Count Cenci, the English royal father figure (and the aristocracy that supports him) is an unprincipled disciplinarian who has seemingly arranged the deaths of his sons by subjecting them to protracted and often unpopular wars, to political entrapment, and to fatal domestic oppression. His cruelties against the "mother country" are manifest, from the destruction of her sons and daughters to the plundering of her national dowry. Like Beatrice Cenci, the later Regency English public could not but feel that the most heinous violence can sometimes seem justified when circumstances appear to offer no alternative. Finally, when we consider Beatrice Cenci on the allegorical level as Liberty—as *An Address to the People on the Death of the Princess Charlotte* gives us reason to do—we can appreciate that a liberal reformer like Shelley would see in England in 1819 a tale of brutality and incest not unlike that which had destroyed the Cenci family from within. The bloody lesson of the French Revolution was still fresh in the English mind. Like Beatrice, England stood in 1819 on the brink of committing the same sort of suicidal parricide. But unlike Beatrice—and the French—the English people had not yet taken the fatal step, and therein, finally, lies the real point of Shelley's political drama. There is nothing more authoritarian than revolution, but there is both virtue and nobility in revolution avoided. Shelley would have his country reclaim and preserve the grandeur of its greatest heroine—Liberty—before that grandeur becomes a tragic one.

What makes *The Cenci* such a "sad reality" is our recognition that Beatrice Cenci "dies" largely at her own hand: her moral and ethical wounds are ultimately self-inflicted. Shelley insists that we not permit the intensity of her suffering or the magnitude of the injuries done her to lead us to approve of her lust for revenge or to become accomplices in it by our approbation.[28]

> Revenge, retaliation, atonement are pernicious mistakes. If Beatrice had thought in this manner she would have been wiser and better; but she would never have been a tragic character: the few whom such an exhibition would have interested, could never have been sufficiently interested for a dramatic purpose, from the want of finding sympathy in their interest among the mass who surround them. It is in the restless and anatomizing casuistry with which men seek the justification of

Beatrice, yet feel that she has done what needs justification; it is in the superstitious horror with which they contemplate alike her wrongs and their revenge, that the dramatic character of what she did and suffered, consists. (*Works*, 276–77)

Like *The Revolt of Islam*, *The Cenci* is the record of a failed revolution. But unlike Laon and Cythna, who begin and end as principled, idealistic martyrs, Beatrice betrays the fundamental dignity which she—or any of the play's English spectators—might claim as inalienable birthright. The corruption of even the most saintly of humans is perhaps inevitable as long as the world is oppressed by the combined forces of inequality and social injustice and by the vindictive system of political and institutional tyranny that both promotes and enforces those ills.[29] Beatrice is merely the noblest character in a grossly flawed world: she is as "innocent" as it is possible for her to be, considering the corruption that surrounds her. Only in a radically transformed and purified world can there be hope for a genuine innocence that is not forced into fatal self-contradiction. Beatrice is not *necessarily* flawed, however, and this is Shelley's whole point. Her failure is not preordained: were it so, Shelley's play would be no tragedy but a mere deterministic farce.

Elise M. Gold argues that both in his play and specifically in the closing section of its preface Shelley "demonstrates . . . that art can ennoble man and his life by apparelling the real and the reprehensible in the beautiful and the ideal."[30] Gold is surely correct in claiming that Shelley endows *The Cenci*, and drama generally, with a moral purpose. But she seems to me also to misrepresent—or, perhaps more accurately, to oversimplify—the play's overall import. What ennobles the audience, whether of *The Cenci* or of *Oedipus Rex*, is the lesson it learns and applies about human nature, human dignity, and human resiliency by means of its interaction with the pathos of plot and character, an interaction that produces both catharsis and insight. Gold's suggestion would yield a Shelley apparently willing to close his eyes to the horrifying, destructive dualisms at work both in his play and in his audience's temporal world. But Shelley's is not a theater of escapism and distraction, any more than his art is a deliberate misrepresentation of reality. As I have already argued, Shelley's art seeks to alter sad realities by revealing them both actually and metaphorically and by offering—again actually and metaphorically—both ideal alternatives and practical means of attaining those ideals. This crucial distinction is one we need to keep before us in assessing both Shelley's poetics and his politics.

Shelley counted on several factors to effect *The Cenci*'s success. Having it acted at one of London's two licensed theaters, by at least one major star, was one of these. Another was the continuing interest in England in the cult of the Gothic sublime, an interest that, though it was waning in literature, remained vital in the passionate style of Romantic theater. Both the settings and the action of the play draw upon a tradition going back, on one hand, to *The Castle of Otranto* (and, of course, to *Zastrozzi* and *St. Irvyne*) and, on the other, to the Renaissance revenge tragedy. Furthermore, the descriptions of both the castle scenes and the ravine (III, i)—the latter in particular—are directly related to developments in the visual arts, where the Romantic landscape was shifting from a lush and golden Claudian paradigm to a dark, irregular, and often menacing Salvatoran one, as we can see in the works of Shelley's English contemporaries John Martin and John Constable.[31]

Shelley also (mistakenly) counted on the story's historical basis to help shield him from charges of both immorality and sensationalism. The opening of the preface, with its information about the "manuscript" from the Cenci archives, not only echoes a familiar device of the Gothic novel but also insists upon a Shelley who is less fictionalizer than historian.[32] Although he acknowledges making some alterations in the interest of art, he tries to legitimize his procedure by disclaiming any attempt at overt authorial interference with widely known historical fact: "I have endeavoured as nearly as possible to represent the characters as they probably were, and have sought to avoid the error of making them actuated by my own conceptions of right or wrong, false or true: thus under a thin veil converting names and actions of the sixteenth century into cold impersonations of my own mind" (*Works*, 277).

When Mary Shelley composed her concluding note to *The Cenci* years later, she remarked on the success with which Shelley had "inwoven the real incidents of the tragedy into his scenes" while at the same time obliterating "all that would otherwise have shown too harsh or hideous in the picture" (*Works*, 337). It is unfortunate that Shelley was apparently unaware of the degree to which critics of the play had recognized its real power. Some of Shelley's discouragement undoubtedly resulted, too, from the carelessness with which even those whose literary judgment he respected seemed unable to disentangle their estimate of the play as a work of art from their distaste for its subject matter. In this category we can place both Peacock and Byron, who declared to Richard Hoppner that "his tragedy is sad work—but the subject renders it so," even though in 1821 he wrote Shelley that the play "was a work of power, and poetry."[33] Mary Shelley and Hunt may have had a clearer vision of the general public audience than Shelley, after all. Certainly both appear to have understood what would sell, as it was indeed Hunt's business to know. Mary Shelley's final remarks on the play are revealing:

His success was a double triumph; and often after he was earnestly entreated to write again in a style that commanded popular favour, while it was not less instinct with truth and genius. But the bent of his mind went the other way; and, even when employed on subjects whose interest depended on character and incident, he would start off in another direction, and leave the delineations of human passion, which he could depict in so able a manner, for fantastic creations of his fancy, or the expression of those opinions and sentiments, with regard to human nature and its destiny, a desire to diffuse which was the master passion of his soul. (*Works*, 337)

Looking back in May 1820, in a letter to Hunt, Shelley put it differently: "Bessy [Marianne Hunt's sister Elizabeth] tells me that people reprobate the subject of my tragedy—let them abase Sophocles, Massinger, Voltaire & Alfieri in the same sentence, & I am content.—I maintain that my scenes are as delicate & free from offence as theirs. Good Heavens what wd. they have tragedy! But I fear no censure in comparison with your approbation—except that I wrote this thing partly to please those whom my other writings displeased, & it is provoking to have all sorts of pretences assumed against one—" (*Letters*, II, 200; 26 May 1820).

Shelley's chagrin was justified. He had responded to previous criticism of his works by composing a new work specifically crafted to take into account the particular linguistic (or idiomatic) and stylistic tastes of a public theater audience and even to adopt a style and format particularly suited to the English stage, only to have it rejected by Covent Garden and (so far as he knew) generally condemned once it was published. When his Irish expedition failed to achieve its immediate purposes, Shelley had suggested to Godwin that the Irish audience was perhaps simply too unfit—too ill-prepared and unsophisticated—and was therefore unready for either his message of liberation or the vehicles through which he sought to deliver that message. The same argument might be made here as well, although Shelley continued to experiment with the "popular" style in drama in his unfinished *Charles the First*. Even though Mary Shelley suggests that he encouraged her to compose a tragedy on this subject and that he told her he had already some notion of how some scenes might be conducted (*Works*, 335), Shelley continued to work on his unfinished play until nearly the end of his life, experimenting with a mixed style that occasionally rises to powerful rhetoric in expressing the pathos of another historical moment at which society appeared bent upon self-destruction.

When he finished *The Cenci*, Shelley returned to *Prometheus Unbound* to add the magnificent symphonic celebration with which his lyrical drama now closes. In doing so, he undoubtedly paid homage to his growing interest in the opera, with its dazzling combinations of voices and choruses in that most spectacular of theatrical forms. More important, he drew to some extent on the celestial celebration in Book III of *Paradise Lost*, in which all heaven celebrates the Son's offer to die for humanity in the consummate act of selfless community with mankind. The act parallels that of Prometheus, with the significant difference that in Milton's epic the Son's offer comes in response to another's demand, whereas Prometheus's renunciation of his curse addresses a purely internal imperative. Prometheus does not *have to* recant the curse; indeed most of the rest of creation—with the Earth as its spokesperson—misunderstands his recantation, thinking it surrender. Rather, he undergoes an expansion of consciousness that renders revenge and retribution not simply less desirable but rather entirely irrelevant and unworthy. In short, he chooses the moral high road that Beatrice Cenci ultimately rejects.

After lamenting the fate of *The Cenci* to Hunt on 26 May, Shelley inquires: "Have you read my Prometheus yet? but that will not sell— it is written only for the elect. I confess I am vain enough to like it" (*Letters*, II, 200). Shelley was acutely aware of the different styles and approaches he had employed in the two works, and he undoubtedly felt he was being truest to himself in *Prometheus Unbound*, composing in a form in which the "beautiful idealisms" of the poem's form and content mirror and reinforce each other. Certainly there is no question about Shelley's preference for the work, or about his sanguine estimate of its chances for general success or popularity: "'Prometheus Unbound', I must tell you, is my favourite poem; I charge you, therefore, specially to pet him and feed him with fine ink and good paper. 'Cenci' is written for the multitude, and ought to sell well. I think, if I may judge by its merits, the 'Prometheus' cannot sell beyond twenty copies" (*Letters*, II, 174; to Ollier, 6 March 1820).[34] This could scarcely have been reassuring to a publisher hoping to turn a profit. A Byron, whose works now sold almost automatically, might risk such a statement, but it is odd that Shelley would let his sense of personal irony so overrule the more common-sense persuasive approach to Ollier for which the situation so obviously called. Curiously, he makes few substantive comments about the poem to his other correspondents. Although he tells Byron, to whom he routinely deferred, that it is "a very imperfect poem" (*Letters*, II, 290; 4 May 1821), his remark to John Gisborne that "Prometheus was never intended for more than 5 or 6 persons" (*Letters*, II, 388; 26 January 1822) is more telling. That Shelley felt compelled, as a means of psychological self-preservation, to adopt any such attitude not just toward his lyrical drama but indeed toward the entire volume of poems in which it was contained—one of the finest collections in the history of English literature—suggests how seriously his self-confidence had been eroded by the series of private and public misfortunes that had overtaken him in Italy. That most of his projects in poetry and prose were apparent failures in their seeming lack of immediate impact colors to a significant degree what Shelley said about them afterward. But his attitude beforehand is nearly always positive. Only with *Prometheus Unbound* does he so frankly admit the slimness of its chances for success or acclaim.

Shelley's attitude indicates the change that was beginning to occur in his view of his audiences. The preface to *Prometheus Unbound* foreshadows his procedure in the preface to *Epipsychidion* (which poem he would also declare fit for only a select few readers), specifically limiting his audiences[35] and thereby seemingly insulating himself in advance from the attacks by those whom he categorized ahead of time as incompetent—and unintended—readers. His seeming overprotectiveness toward his favorite work reflects a natural impulse to shield it, and himself, from the negativism of the uninitiated. Shelley usually adopts the more positive attitude common among radical reformers that they speak for a majority whom social, political, spiritual, and intellectual deprivation and domination have rendered incapable of speaking for itself. Shelley shared with other messianic reformers the evangelical zeal that revolution typically evokes as a means of establishing the purity of its motives and the integrity of its actions. This view involved setting for himself ethical and intellectual standards higher than the norm, just as revolutionaries portray themselves—and their leaders particularly—as secular saints; Shelley heightens the comparison in so often equating himself as embattled radical reformer with Jesus Christ. Revolution—whether violent, as in France, or gradual, bloodless, and "perfect," as in Shelley's post-Godwinian model—tends to become a secular religion, with its leaders and spokespersons considering it part of their "religious" duty to serve as role models. Typically, such extraordinary dedication and apparent incorruptibility promote the public belief that the revolutionary cause has instilled in its disciples "a higher sense of responsibility than religion itself had achieved."[36] This sense of being a spokesperson for a particular interest group (which varies from work to work, as the Irish works, the Marlow pamphlets, and *The Cenci* demonstrate) prompted Shelley to adopt the literary forms he considered best suited both to his explicit moral or intellectual purposes and to the degree of political, literary, and intellectual sophistication he attributed to the audiences he defined as his particular targets. The problems stemming from his miscalculations about the nature and demographics of these virtual publics became more acute when Shelley deprived himself of the benefit of firsthand observation by leaving England. The secondhand information he received in Italy merely widened the gap between what Shelley understood to be the situation in England and what it actually was.

Although the idea of a writer's public is part of a fantasy both within a given literary work and within the process of its production, any author writing for the masses—as was increasingly the case after 1800—invents a particular *kind* of reader even while imagining a heterogeneous superclass of readers encompassing all psychological and social types. This tendency received perhaps its greatest stimulus in England during the period of Shelley's greatest productivity through the vast readership of radicals like William Cobbett, Richard Carlile, and Thomas Wooler.[37] The formerly undifferentiated crowd was becoming a public, an audience in its own right. This extraordinarily important development presumed some degree of literacy and thereby access to the printed word, hitherto the prerogative of the upper classes. Distinctions about the language of "the vulgar" mirrored distinctions about moral and social status that were being imposed upon that group from without, by the social, political, and intellectual power elite. Although he never entirely escaped his inherited aristocratic preconditioning, Shelley was too much a humanitarian to acquiesce in the oppression of the majority of his fellow human beings and too percipient a rationalist to believe there could be any inherent justification for maintaining such an unethical and inhumane oppression.

During the eighteenth century there had been little question among the literary elite that "the people" constituted a separate and distinctly inferior portion of society; the scornful treatment of common people, whether in the condescending treatment of the ubiquitous country bumpkin or in the would-be farcical handling of laborers of all sorts, was a staple of fashionable Western European art. Underlying the scorn is a perception that those who labor are by definition different from the titled leisure classes: from here it is but a small and unfortunately natural step to the materialistic notion that possessions (whether actual—like clothing, tools, or animals—or symbolic—like money) denote intrinsic superiority, generally interpreted as moral superiority. Coupled with the denial to "the people" of education, either by direct action or—more often—by the daily demands of their largely agrarian existence, this distinction had wide-ranging consequences. Perceived as both morally and intellectually deficient, "the people" seemed mindless slaves to superstition, insusceptible to discerning rationality, and craving the sensationalistic excitation of the wondrous, the spectacular, and the violent.[38] Shelley seems to take just such a view in characterizing "the multitude" in his review of Hogg's *Prince Alexy*: "The vulgar observe no resemblances or discrepancies, but such as are gross and glaring. The science of mind to which history, poetry, biography serve as the materials, consists in the discernment of shades and distinctions where the unenlightened discover nothing but a shapeless and unmeaning mass" (I&P, VI, 176).

What is surprising, though, and what has gone largely unnoticed, is the frequency with which Shelley attributes many of these same tendencies to the more elite and sophisticated classes. The appeal to such predilections figures not only in his Gothic romances but also in *The Cenci* and the *Address to the People on the Death of the Princess Charlotte*. When he observed that *The Cenci* was "written for the multitude" and "with a certain view to popularity" (*Letters*, II, 174, 190; 6 March, 1 May 1820) he was undoubtedly thinking in part of the perennial appeal of sensationalism. If in the eighteenth century "the people" were regarded as "the repository of the more overt forms of violence and passion,"[39] *The Cenci* rejects the attribution of such failings purely on the basis of class, for it is in the elite rather than in "the people" in Shelley's play in which such excess lies. In any event, a work like *The Cenci* is aimed at an audience significantly above what either the eighteenth century or the Regency meant by "the people." Only in the exoteric political poems, which I will examine in the next chapter, and in occasional pieces like "A Declaration of Rights" (1812) does Shelley make a concerted effort to descend beneath this essentially "middle" audience for his primary target. More often he chooses to move upward.

It is easier for the historian to learn about the reading habits of the upper classes than about those of the lower, whose "reading" was more often the secondhand experience of hearing something read. Besides, as I indicated in the introduction, there was great diversity among these various audiences. E. P. Thompson's assessment is still valid:

> It is a mistake to see . . . a single, undifferentiated "reading public." We may say that there were several different "publics" impinging upon and overlapping each other, but nevertheless organised according to different principles. Among the more important were the commercial public, pure and simple, which might be exploited at times of Radical excitement (the trials of Brandreth or of Thistlewood were as marketable as other "dying confessions"), but which was followed according to the simple criteria of profitability; the various more-or-less

organised publics, around the Churches or the Mechanic's Institutes; the passive public which the improving societies sought to get at and redeem; and the active, Radical public, which organised itself in the face of the Six Acts and the taxes on knowledge.[40]

For Shelley, the most practical course appeared to involve a coordinated assault on a variety of readerships, and in forms ranging from the carefully reasoned philosophical prose of *A Philosophical View of Reform* to the broad dramatic satire of *Swellfoot the Tyrant*, from sensational Gothic romance to powerful stage tragedy, from the highly charged polemic of the exoteric political poems to the sublime forms and "beautiful idealisms" of *Prometheus Unbound*, to which I will now turn.

Recognizing from the start that the style of *Prometheus Unbound* was anything but "popular," Shelley adopted the position he had taken toward such prose works as *A Refutation of Deism*, deliberately "excluding the multitude from the abuse of a mode of reasoning, liable to misconstruction on account of its novelty" (I&P, VI, 25). Shelley aims to address the few select minds capable of understanding the unconventional variety of civil disobedience advocated in Prometheus's history and in Demogorgon's concluding speech. He had chosen as his vehicle the extraordinarily difficult poetic form whose roots reach back through Dante to the Greeks and whose images are, as Shelley says in his preface, "drawn from the operations of the human mind, or from those external actions by which they are expressed" (*Works*, 205). Such imagery fuses the *process* of human thought with its *products* in an intensely reflexive variety of composition that explores language's "reciprocally generative relation to thought."[41] Shelley was striving for an imagery that was not only complete at the level of language but simultaneously prolific of meaning at other levels, including the political, social, moral, aesthetic, and mythic. Such a poetry would require a very special reader. Hence the claims and instructions Shelley sets forth in his preface, and the precedents he cites for his procedure, are neither apologies nor excuses but rather clear indications to the reader of the particular contexts in which he wants *Prometheus Unbound* understood and evaluated.

The preface's final paragraph underscores Shelley's immediate purpose:

> The having spoken of myself with unaffected freedom will need little apology with the candid; and let the uncandid consider that they injure me less than their own hearts and minds by misrepresentation. Whatever talents a person may possess to amuse and instruct others, be they ever so inconsiderable,

he is yet bound to exert them: if his attempt be ineffectual, let the punishment of an unaccomplished purpose have been sufficient; let none trouble themselves to heap the dust of oblivion upon his efforts; the pile they raise will betray his grave which might otherwise have been unknown. (*Works*, 207)

Shelley's last sentence recalls not only the note he had struck in his review of Hogg's *Prince Alexy* but also the unpleasant remark (about *The Revolt of Islam*) embedded in a note to the *Quarterly Review*'s January 1818 review of Leigh Hunt's *Foliage*. That review alludes to the unnamed composition as "the production of a man of some ability, and possessing itself some beauty" and then observes: "But we are in doubt, whether it would be morally right to lend it notoriety by any comments."[42] Shelley knew the review, of course, and specifically remarked on it in a letter to Peacock in July 1818 (*Letters*, II, 26; 25 July 1818). Moreover, we should remember Shelley's own dust-raising in connection with *Queen Mab*, which I discussed earlier.

The "candid" to whom Shelley refers in this final paragraph presumably identifies that select audience for whose eyes and minds he envisions *Prometheus Unbound*. But the notion that "the uncandid" injure themselves more than Shelley recalls as well the "unfruitful lives" the preface to *Alastor* forecasts for that work's critics, even as it echoes the appeal to the reader's charity in the preface to *The Revolt of Islam*. In his original notebook draft Shelley had written, "The having spoken of myself with unaffected freedom will need little apology in a candid mind & those who are uncandid may speak as they wish" (Bodleian MS Shelley e. 3, fol. 30r, inverted); having let the uncandid off too easily, he elaborated when he revised. This passage illustrates the increasing self-reflexivity of Shelley's works taken as a whole. And in any event it provides a particularly shrewd note upon which to end the preface to *Prometheus Unbound*, for it again renders Shelley's detractors unable to criticize him without also advertising their own uncharitable folly. To criticize will be to call public attention to what they would rather have consigned to oblivion, while to remain silent—their only viable alternative—is to give the impression of tacit sanction. Again he has maneuvered potentially hostile readers into a double bind that nullifies their opportunity for censure.

Most important here, though, is Shelley's formal statement of the prophetic artist's public imperative. His claim that the individual "is yet *bound* to exert" any talent he or she possesses "to amuse *and instruct* others" (my italics), reasserts his declaration to Elizabeth Hitchener some eight years earlier that "great responsibility is the consequence of high powers" (*Letters*, I, 196; 26 November 1811). The public figure's role in the renovation of the world is not an option but a duty: when Shelley refers in the preface to *Prometheus Unbound* to his "passion for reforming the world," his choice of "passion" reflects a deep-seated and thoroughly consistent attitude.[43] The line of reasoning that culminates in the images of poets as unacknowledged legislators of the world emerged early in Shelley's writings. Almost from the first he places both politics and poetry within a larger category of morals, viewed especially in terms of broad ethical and social philosophy. He rejects narrowly and overtly didactic poetry that substitutes a dogmatic monologue for the creative dialogue between author and reader, but he nevertheless places the instructive function of art at the heart of works even so esoteric as *Prometheus Unbound*. The Aristotelian point he made regarding *The Cenci* applies here as well: the instructional aspect of the work must be inherent in the material and in the formal aspects of its presentation in the text, not imposed artificially and forcibly by the author. "Meaning" must be a function of character, plot, and style, not a gratuitous intrusion.

Shelley may have been inspired to call *Prometheus Unbound* a lyrical drama by his reading in March 1818 of Augustus William Schlegel's *Lectures on Dramatic Art and Literature*. Schlegel distinguishes between the strictly theatrical and the poetic interest of dramatic literature, seeing in the former an essentially external, empirical mode of representation and in the latter a more internalized and sublime mode that centers less on external action than on transcendent and eternal ideas, thoughts, and feelings. By Schlegel's standard, *The Cenci* is theatrical, *Prometheus Unbound* poetic. But since the ideas in the latter constitute a manifesto for a radical change in the structure of society and in the belief system that governs it, Shelley's play proposes this revolutionary change in terms of the way the poet sees and externally figures the world.[44] The poem presents a model of completed, perfected egalitarian revolution which Shelley expects the sophisticated reader to internalize as a prototype, however ideal or idealistic it may initially appear, and to embody in substantive changes in the temporal world. To do so is to identify with the spirit of the age, to be in the vanguard of reform.

This is precisely why Shelley points, earlier in the preface, to the precedents of both the Renaissance and the age of Milton as examples of "fervid awakening[s] of the public mind": "The great writers of our own age are, we have reason to suppose, the companions and forerunners of some unimagined change in our social condition or the opinions which cement it. The cloud of mind is discharging its collected lightning, and the equilibrium between institutions and opinions is now restoring, or is about to be restored" (*Works*, 206). Shelley makes the "strength in numbers" argument to reassure the freethinking and progressive members of society of the collective propriety of their cause. But he has not idly linked "the great writers of our own age" with their English forerunners, as his discussion about poetry as a mimetic art indicates. In claiming that "one great poet is a masterpiece of *nature* which another not only ought to study but must study" (206; my italics), Shelley aligns himself and art generally with the cumulative and evolutionary processes of the entire natural universe rather than—as we might expect—merely with the institutions and artifacts of the human portion of that universe. This allows him to propose that thought and language (and, of course, poetry, the noblest manifestation of language) are endemic to nature. Rather than being mimetic in the customary sense of "mere" imitation of surfaces, poetry imitates by reflecting and embodying the very essence of the natural world, which is itself but a temporal manifestation of the intellectual world of pure idea. The poet, then, in his or her most exalted role, does not invent so much as convey what actually and eternally exists, which conforms precisely to Shelley's definition of the prophet. Shelley's argument is only partially self-serving; while it does in a sense set up a defense mechanism against criticism, it more importantly obviates the need for any such mechanism by asserting that the "great writers" by their very nature cannot do otherwise than represent the sublime truth inherent in the entire natural and intellectual universe.

This is an extraordinarily important claim, in view of the public forms which Shelley claims this universal poetry (or truth) may take:

> A poet is the combined product of such internal powers as modify the nature of others; and of such external influences as excite and sustain these powers; he is not one, but both. Every man's mind is, in this respect, modified by all the objects of nature and art; by every word and suggestion which he ever admitted to act upon his consciousness; it is the mirror upon which all forms are reflected, and in which they compose one form. Poets, not otherwise than philosophers, painters, sculptors, and musicians, are, in one sense, the creators, and, in another, the creations of their age. From this subjection the loftiest do not escape. (*Works*, 206)

Shelley originally included orators in this list as well but deleted the term when he added sculptors at some point.[45] In light of his pointed designation of Christ as orator in the *Essay on Christianity*, the deletion here is curious, though perhaps his point is that the orator's "artifact" is bound by temporal performance in a way that those of the other creators—even musicians—are not. More important are the opening words, which return to Wordsworth's notion that every individual is at least potentially a poet. But though this capacity is virtual in "every man's" mind, only in the mind of the true artist does the necessary development take place in conjunction with heightened sensorial and intellectual powers and the concomitant capacity for expressing the products of those powers in the artifacts of culture.

I have stressed this point because of the way Shelley proceeds immediately after these remarks to list pairs of writers from previous periods: "There is a similarity between Homer and Hesiod, between Aeschylus and Euripides, between Virgil and Horace, between Dante and Petrarch, between Shakespeare and Fletcher, between Dryden and Pope; each has a generic resemblance under which their specific distinctions are arranged. If this similarity be the result of imitation, I am willing to confess that I have imitated" (*Works*, 206–7). To some extent Shelley is responding to the *Quarterly Review*'s April 1819 review of *The Revolt of Islam*, which misrepresents his largely deliberate Wordsworthianism as virtual plagiarism, calling Shelley "an unsparing imitator" not just of Wordsworth but of Southey as well.[46] But I believe Shelley's response to the charges about imitation is less significant than his conspicuous pairing of authors. Can there be any doubt that Shelley is here inviting his reader to supply the pairings from "the great writers of our own age"? Despite his relatively lesser output, Coleridge would logically have been the counterpart of Wordsworth, though a less discriminating reader might have chosen to substitute Sir Walter Scott (who was already popular) or even (by stretching matters) Southey. More important, though, is the pair that most immediately belongs to "*our own* age": Byron and Shelley himself. Nowhere else in his formal public statements does Shelley advance so clear a claim to equality as he does here, even though his failure to name *either* of the two might suggest to the careless reader that the claim does not exist at all. Not only is there an immediate thematic parallel in the subject of *Prometheus Unbound* and Byron's "Prometheus" and the Promethean preoccupations of works like *Manfred* (and *Frankenstein*), there is a still more important connection between the differing world-views that inform the two poets' works.

I have said before that an important element of Shelley's later works is his attempt to engage Byron, within the public forum of the print media, in something of a skeptical debate. In the fullest discussion to date of the Shelley-Byron literary relationship, Charles E. Robinson has argued that each poet's influence on the other was more negative than positive; that is, their frequent disagreements over aesthetics, ethics, metaphysics, politics, and social considerations led each to embody in his works statements of his position meant to "correct" the other.[47] Although Shelley consistently adopts a deferential posture toward Byron, which he echoes in his comments to others about Byron, his growing distaste for the personal profligacy and the intellectual fatalism of his vastly popular counterpart had become increasingly apparent in his works already by 1819. Some of the immediate impetus for *Prometheus Unbound* seems to have been a desire on Shelley's part after meeting Byron on 23 August 1818 to respond particularly to "Prometheus" and *Manfred* "in order to liberate Byron from his vision of man's enslavement."[48] Had Shelley's purpose involved only an ongoing intellectual debate with Byron, he would not have gone to the extraordinary lengths of publication. There was much more at stake. When Byron renounced the Shelleyan Wordsworthianism he had seemed partially to adopt in Canto III of *Childe Harold's Pilgrimage* (completed when Shelley and Byron were first together, in Switzerland in 1816), Shelley was understandably disappointed. But disappointment turned to dismay when he read Canto IV in 1818; to Peacock he writes, "The spirit in which it is written is, if insane, the most wicked & mischievous insanity that ever was given forth. It is a kind of obstinate & selfwilled folly in which he hardens himself. I remonstrated with him in vain on the tone of mind from which such a view of things alone arises" (*Letters*, II, 58; 17 or 18 December). It appeared to Shelley that he had entirely failed in his attempts to encourage in Byron a more positive attitude, attempts marked by the hopes Shelley expressed to his other correspondents for Byron's conversion to something more akin to his own melioristic world-view.

Shelley's sense in 1818–19 of his failure to renovate Byron makes it clear why we must go beyond even Robinson's insightful view of Shelley's (and for that matter, Byron's) works as mere exercises in correction and public competition. They are that, of course, but why compose entire works and publish them when arguments and counterarguments might be exchanged in letters or in person? The answer surely lies in Shelley's unfailing social commitment. Shelley wanted to answer Byron on his own turf, *in the press*, taking his case to the reading audience. If Byron's isolationistic fatalism is "poison," then Shelley will offer his own works as antidote. Given Byron's immense popularity—and Shelley's conspicuous lack of it—the task is monumental. Shelley appreciated this, of course. But when Byron read him Canto V of *Don Juan* in 1821 he felt his efforts had borne fruit:

> He has read to me one of the unpublished cantos of Don Juan, which is astonishingly fine.—It sets him not above but far above all the poets of the day: every word has the stamp of immortality.—I despair of rivalling Lord Byron, as well I may: and there is no other with whom it is worth contending. . . . There is not a word which the most rigid assertor of the dignity of human nature could desire to be cancelled: it fulfills in a certain degree what I have long preached of producing something wholly new & relative to the age—and yet surpassingly

beautiful. It may be vanity, but I think I see the trace of my
earnest exhortations to him to create something wholly new.
(*Letters*, II, 323; to Mary Shelley, 10 August 1821)

Progress, apparently, was possible.

From the beginning, Byron's great popularity had struck Shelley
as an indication of the extent to which the reading public stood in
danger of being misled by Byron's (and his characters') misanthropic
fatalism, by the rejection of the creative world of community in favor
of withdrawal into a solitary state that was of no ultimate value to humanity, however splendidly that withdrawal might be clothed. Byron's
Prometheus is egocentric and vengeful, delighting in the discomfort
he is yet able to inflict upon his oppressor. Shelley's Prometheus, on
the other hand, rejects these impulses entirely once he recognizes the
folly of wishing to cause pain to anyone, whether friend or enemy.
Manfred finds human community intolerable, repairing to his isolated
tower for the play's conclusion. Earlier, Manfred is prevented from suicide only by the chamois hunter's unwillingness that Manfred's blood
should defile the natural environment. As is *Alastor*'s misguided solitary, Manfred is given to blackouts and negative alterations of consciousness when his visions are truncated and he is returned to the
ordinary world. Byron and his protagonists typically reject the impulse
toward human community that forms the foundation of the Shelleyan
ethic and aesthetic.

Although many of Shelley's later works contain clear verbal and
thematic echoes of Byron's, the tendency is particularly strong in *Prometheus Unbound*, in which Byron's works are deliberately subverted
within Shelley's portrayal of human nature. While "Prometheus" and
Manfred, like *Childe Harold's Pilgrimage*, explore the gulf that increasingly separates the protagonist from the rest of humanity (and from
"heaven," however defined), Shelley's works move in precisely the opposite direction. Shelley's Prometheus learns that the quality of life
depends on one's relationship with others: he courageously forgives his
enemy, recanting the curse in an act that is as natural an expression of
egalitarian community as his expressions of love for Asia. The lesson
that the young visionary in *Alastor* is incapable of learning is in *Prometheus Unbound* not just learned but internalized and passed on to
the rest of the world in the establishment of the utopia celebrated in
Act IV.

The extent of Shelley's frustration over his inability to command a
readership comparable to Byron's is apparent in his sonnet to Byron,
probably written after Byron's arrival in Pisa on 1 November 1821:

> [I am afraid these verses will not please you, but]
> If I esteemed you less, Envy would kill

Pleasure, and leave to Wonder and Despair
The ministration of the thoughts that fill
The mind which, like a worm whose life may share
A portion of the unapproachable,
Marks your creations rise as fast and fair
As perfect worlds at the Creator's will.
But such is my regard that nor your power
To soar above the heights where others [climb],
Nor fame, that shadow of the unborn hour
Cast from the envious future on the time,
Move one regret for his unhonoured name
Who dares these words:—the worm beneath the sod
May lift itself in homage of the God.

(Works, 658)

His self-confidence increasingly threatened, both personally and po-
etically, by Byron's success, Shelley yet manages this magnanimous
formal compliment to Byron, in the process repudiating envy of that
success. But as Keach notes, once Byron arrived at Pisa Shelley's own
poetic production dropped off considerably; what he did write took the
form of translations, fragments, and personal (rather than broadly
public) lyrics. *The Triumph of Life*, the seeming exception, was begun
only after Shelley left Pisa (and Byron) and resettled on the Bay of
Lerici.[49]

His claims to the contrary notwithstanding, Shelley obviously (and
naturally) did envy Byron's fame, particularly in relation to the psychological security which financial security could procure. He was caught
in a circular trap: to attain fame, he needed money, but he realized
that his best purely independent means of raising money lay with his
writing, which did not sell. Thus there is a keen irony in the terminology in which Shelley describes his inactivity to Claire Clairmont: "The
Exotic as you please to call me droops in this frost—a frost both moral
& physical—a solitude of the heart—. . . I cannot endure the company
of many persons, & the society of one is either great pleasure or great
pain. . . . I am employed in nothing—I read—but I have no spirits for
serious composition—I have no confidence and to write & [in] solitude
or put forth thoughts without sympathy is *unprofitable* vanity" (*Letters*,
II, 367–68; 11 December 1821; my italics). During these months of
proximity to Byron, who is unquestionably the "one" to whom he refers, Shelley was more than ever troubled by his lack of money, the
difficulty of his situation being a daily humiliation to him in his contact
with Byron.[50] Indeed, he wrote Hunt that even after the matter of financial assistance for Hunt had been somewhat resolved, he still
found that "particular dispositions in Lord B's character render the

close & exclusive intimacy with him in which I find myself, intolerable to me" (*Letters*, II, 393; 2 March 1822).

On 10 April Shelley spells out the problem of "this jealousy of my Lord Byron" more clearly still: "Certain it is, that Lord Byron has made me bitterly feel the inferiority which the world has presumed to place between us and which subsists nowhere in reality but in our own talents, which are not our own but Nature's—or in our rank, which is not our own but Fortune's" (*Letters*, II, 405; 10 April 1822). Shelley may (incorrectly but characteristically) acknowledge Byron's superior talent here, but he chafes at the *degree* of inferiority which an unfair and prejudicial public has assigned him relative to Byron, who has apparently been reminding Shelley of the fact. Byron's insensitivity to Shelley's frustration—like his insensitivity to others on a variety of matters—was clear to other members of their circle. Even before Shelley's death, for instance, Mary Shelley had confided to Claire Clairmont (who had good reason to understand) her own longing "to extricate all belonging to me from the hands of LB, whose hypocrisy & cruelty rouse one's soul from its depths."[51] The matter of financial relationships was, not surprisingly, particularly galling to the perennially strapped but nevertheless fiercely proud Shelley, and the economic game-playing in which Byron appeared to the Shelleys and the Hunts to be engaging was a continuing sore point. Shelley's attempts in late 1821 and 1822 to interest Ollier in *Charles the First* undoubtedly reflect his desire for some substantial sale that might improve his financial position and make this matter of relative wealth (or poverty) less an irritant in his relations with Byron.

The sonnet to Byron, then, offers an important late view of Shelley's attitude, and his revisions are especially revealing. As he composed, he revised the fourth through seventh lines heavily:

> The mind [that yearns in its witchcraft scarce]
>   [May]   [, as it beholds]   [can dare]
>   [To]   which [is] like a worm whose life may share
> A portion of the unapproachable,
> [It marks thy fan]
> [It marks thy] your
> Marks [thy] creations rise as fast & fair
> As [art the] perfect worlds [of the] at the Creator's will
>   presenting itself before
> [three words illegible] [worships] [to] the gilded throne.
>   (Bodleian MS Shelley adds. e. 17, p. 94 reversed)

The "yearns" (line 4) probably most nearly describes Shelley's actual sentiments. Was Shelley setting up a comparison here, his being the mind that "in its witchcraft" essays "to" (canceled line) do something—perhaps something as great? In context, the narrator is voicing the spectator's wonder at the rapid genesis of a succession of beautiful *and perfect* creations (the term Shelley chose halfway through writing what probably was "fantasies"). Furthermore, the cancellation at the end of this passage, involving worshiping at the gilded throne, likely refers to the public's response to Byron's works, in which context the monetary connotation of "gilded" supplies appropriate irony. There is, in other words, a sense here of Byron as doubly gilded idol, the object of paying public worshipers, a suggestion that could scarcely have been far from Shelley's thoughts late in 1821. Not surprisingly, Shelley suppressed and redirected these lines.

Shelley always wished to convince his readers to ally themselves with other dedicated liberals like himself, Hunt, Hazlitt, and even Byron behind the principles of love and community and against the prevailing dehumanizing tendencies of the Establishment. He believed—correctly, it turns out—that there were a considerable number of uncommitted readers who might be enlisted in his army of reform. These readers were largely liberals of the middle class and the aristocracy: Byron had already managed to address them with a less extreme radicalism couched in the figured rhetoric of the Byronic hero. That Shelley had decided by 1819—and particularly after again spending time with Byron in 1818—actively to go after Byron's own audience is further indicated by the matter and the nature of *Julian and Maddalo*, whose pairing of characters sheds further light upon Shelley's pairing of authors in the preface to *Prometheus Unbound*.

Julian and Maddalo

Shelley composed *Julian and Maddalo* at Este shortly after visiting Byron in Venice, completing the first draft before his return to Venice on 29 October 1818. It was not until 1819, however, as he worked on *The Cenci*, that Shelley finished the poem, weaving a good deal of autobiographical material and a complex skein of Byronic allusion into the Maniac's speeches and then assigning the poem a date of 1818, presumably to disguise from Hunt (to whom he sent the poem with instructions that it be passed on to Ollier for anonymous publication) and his other acquaintances just how nearly the poem reflected the facts of his life in 1818–19.[52] Although the poem may have stemmed from the events of 23 August, when Byron and Shelley rode along the Adriatic, it embodies the intellectual and philosophical debate they had been conducting since their first meeting and had continued during the late summer and early autumn of 1818.[53] Several important aspects of this poem have received insufficient attention, and considering them in the context of Shelley's running skeptical debate with Byron illuminates both his posture and strategy toward his fellow poet.

There is, for instance, the intriguing matter of the poem's form. The poem's urbane frame encloses the Maniac's ravings without really containing them. The powerful intellectual arguments advanced by Julian and Maddalo are so heavily overshadowed by the intense emotional effect of the madman's speech and behavior that at the conclusion of the asylum scene Maddalo in effect concedes that the madman has been partially responsible for his madness, and Julian, given this opportunity to claim triumph, omits to do so.[54] Richard Cronin draws a useful distinction about the sort of poetry Shelley set out to write in *Julian and Maddalo*, noting the difference between ethos and pathos, a difference of which both Byron and Shelley were demonstrably aware. Ethical poetry aims to teach virtue by persuading the reader to admire the virtues of a character who embodies the author's personal character. Ethos persuades the reader to judge and agree; pathos, which is more intense, enforces that agreement by appealing directly to the reader's imagination and thus more immediately and subjectively involving the reader. While the pathetic speaker dramatizes his subject, the ethical speaker dramatizes himself.[55] Shelley effectively combines the two, giving in the first part of the poem a pair of ethical speakers who become increasingly pathetic in their approaches to each other. But the madman, who is necessarily a pathetic speaker in his apparent obliviousness to the intrusive audience that observes him, overwhelms them both.

One explanation for this apparent collapse of philosophy in the face of distressing reality lies in the notion of the sublime, which for Shelley—particularly given his strong background in eighteenth-century philosophy—involved an essentially sense-grounded experience, which produces a temporary expansion of consciousness, a "going out" to the extremity not just of the external universe but also of the inner or psychological. For the Romantic, the experience of the sublime provided a means of resolving the disjunction between subject and object—or self and nature (or other)—through a physical and intellectual exploration *and temporary crossing* of horizons.[56] Shelley's speaker—who is very Shelleyan but is only part Shelley—and Maddalo are both strongly moved by the pathos of the scenes with the madman, and in this they share at least momentarily in the "one human heart" of community. This experience merges their normally separate characters into a single emotional and intellectual consciousness that stands opposite that of the madman. This is why Maddalo now becomes unnecessary to the poem's dramatic structure and disappears from the scene. In the retrospective passage in which Julian returns years later, Maddalo is kept offstage in the remote mountains of Armenia; indeed, he is symbolically killed in the form of his dog (line 588).

Within the poem's dramatic logic Julian is generally accounted a failure for choosing to return to friends and family rather than help the Maniac.[57] But the matter is more complicated, for Julian is a more sophisticated, less reclusive version of the character whose prototype is the Visionary of *Alastor*. Like the Visionary, Julian is unable to reconcile the disappointment of his ideals with the public life he must lead; consequently, he withdraws. Rather than choose the Visionary's slow, withering suicide, however, Julian achieves the qualified success (or failure) of his return to human community in the form of his familiar circle. In this, he is less a failure than the Visionary—and than Maddalo, off in the Armenian mountains. Yet when he returns at the end of the poem he is clearly changed and not a little hardened. His description of Maddalo's daughter, though appreciative of her beauty, is distant: his language lacks the vital images that characterize his descriptions early in the poem. Likewise, his unwillingness to share with his reader the story the young woman tells him marks an unfamiliar elitist attitude: indeed, lumping the reader into the generic category of "the cold world" is a measure of his distance. In this respect Julian leans in the direction of failure. Unable to internalize or to use what his obviously compelling experience with the madman had taught him about the recesses of the human personality, or to apply to his pristine theoretical idealism the opportunity thus afforded him for greater psychological insight and self-knowledge, Julian retreats into the safe, familiar world of convention, of custom, from which—like the narrator of *Alastor*—he subsequently narrates his tale without recognizing the degree to which he misunderstands his own story.

Another insufficiently considered point relates to Shelley's portrayal of Byron in *Julian and Maddalo*. In light of the poem's wealth of allusions both to Byron and to his works, Maddalo represents not just Byron but a quintessential Byronic hero. Moreover, however closely the Maniac's tale may reflect specific details of both Tasso's and Shelley's lives, his ultimate fate is "unquestionably Byronic."[58] That Maddalo adduces as proof of his own argument a tragically demented figure whose excesses mirror those which Shelley attributed increasingly to Byron in this period—isolationism, inflexible pride, a fatalistic view of human experience, "wilful ill"—is a daring irony on Shelley's part. And indeed Shelley's critics have generally undervalued the irony that informs the poem. Irony is not the device of the threatened artist: invective, Juvenalian satire, or farce are far more typical. But Shelley employs a subtle irony, working into the Maniac's speeches a succession of Byronic notions, all representative of great potential gone undeveloped, great talent misapplied. Above all, the madman increases his own suffering through self-delusion, the last line of defense for the egotistical but insecure personality. Was Shelley hinting at this point when he complained to Peacock in December 1818 about Byron's "obstinate & selfwilled folly"? I believe he was.

Part of the poem's ironic skepticism is that, apparently, no one entirely escapes censure. None of the three central figures is capable of coping with the real world: one escapes into self-delusion and madness, the second into casual misanthropy, the third into abstract idealizing. These escapes typify the way Romantic irony works. In a universe that is essentially "open"—neither benevolent nor malevolent but supremely indifferent—individuals construct their destinies within the limits of their perceptions and abilities. But all such personal constructions are relative and provisional.[59] Nor is the speaker in the preface entirely free of blame. Though he delineates the prejudices and aspirations of Julian and Maddalo, his reliance on ironic understatement ("Julian is rather serious") and equivocation ("How far this is possible the pious reader will determine"; *Works*, 190) render him both distant and potentially unreliable.[60]

That Shelley too must come in for part of the reader's criticism in *Julian and Maddalo* is inevitable, then, so long as we regard Julian *simply as Shelley*. But to read Shelley's poem in too narrowly autobiographical a fashion, or to see Julian as merely a stand-in for Shelley, is a mistake, for it renders a subtle psychological and philosophical poem too narrowly topical and biographical. If we know anything, we know that Shelley was well beyond such monodimensional simplicity. Julian and Maddalo represent conflicting world-views, and the poem constitutes an examination of what happens when these differing perspectives are brought to bear upon a particular problem. What happens in this instance, we learn, is surprisingly little. Disturbed, but not fundamentally altered, Julian and Maddalo leave the scene and, by the poem's end, it appears that life has gone on relatively unchanged for all three figures. The convergence of Julian and Maddalo in their response to the Maniac underscores an important affinity the two men share from the outset. Both are deeply interested in the relation of the individual to society and to the world generally. Both have thought long and hard on the problem, and though their conclusions differ greatly, they are anxious to convince others of their correctness. In each other they have encountered their most severe and penetrating critics: hence their willingness to consider the Maniac as an example, a sort of test case. Their separate hypotheses formed, they observe their experiment, gathering data upon which each expects to establish the irrefutability of his thesis. There is something of the callous social scientist in this procedure, proceeding even when the privacy and the human rights of the subject under study are violated, a point Shaw reiterates later in *Pygmalion* and *Major Barbara*. Ironically, the experiment so unnerves Julian and Maddalo that neither actually drives home his point and the question is left unresolved. This final irresolution is, of course, typical of the skeptical debate, which rhetorical form provides the vehicle for *Julian and Maddalo* and explains why Julian is necessarily at least partially a failure and why the poem's conclusion does not conclude the debate but merely clarifies the positions, leaving the matter in the reader's hands.[61]

Julian and Maddalo embody two varieties of liberal social and political philosophy. Maddalo's proud, Promethean resistance to real and perceived wrongs, however unsocial its underlying impulses, is nevertheless a reasonable posture in light of the inflexible stance of the Regency establishment. That Byron remained a partisan of revolution to the end is clear enough from his subsequent career; he simply concluded that revolution was unlikely (if not completely impossible) in England and that anything less subtle was not likely to arise either from the people or from even its most enlightened leaders. Hence his most prototypically Byronic heroes are motivated by self-interest in league with self-indulgence to indulge their passions with relative disregard for the consequences for anyone else. Julian's is the more radical position: he is the idealistic meliorist who envisions a grand social benevolence, a nondiscriminating community of individuals religiously devoted to the common good of all. But though he resembles him, Julian is not Shelley. Unlike Julian, whose theorizing has no place for exceptions, and whose humanity is insufficiently large to encompass the terrible case of the Maniac, Shelley was sufficiently committed to his general aim of the reform and perfection of humanity and its institutions to suffer the compromise of his Godwinian anarchist principles—as well, apparently, as the destruction of his own family—if that sacrifice would bring reform even an hour nearer.

Finally, if Julian and Maddalo embody quite different but nonetheless related liberal concerns, the Maniac is an apt Shelleyan analog for the English people, much as Beatrice Cenci is. It is entirely possible that as Shelley completed *The Cenci* he perceived the allegorical similarity of these two great works as political parables, as history functioning as myth. Like Beatrice, the Maniac is self-deluded; tormented by recriminations from without and an irrational obsession with guilt from within, he cracks under the pressure and destroys himself, becoming a pitiful, pathetic example of wasted greatness. Unlike Beatrice, he destroys no one else physically or spiritually; like Beatrice, he alludes to unnamable deeds as he movingly performs his egocentric part in a tragic public exhibition:

> *Me*—who am as a nerve o'er which do creep
> The else unfelt oppressions of this earth,

And was to thee the flame upon thy hearth,
When all beside was cold—that thou on me
Shouldst rain these plagues of blistering agony—
Such curses are from lips once eloquent
With love's too partial praise—let none relent
Who intend deeds too dreadful for a name
Henceforth, if an example for the same
They seek . . . for thou on me lookedst so, and so—
And didst speak thus . . . and thus . . . I live to show
How much men bear and die not!

(lines 449–60; *Works*, 199–200)

Both Beatrice and the Maniac may justifiably be regarded in part as personae for Shelley, but to see them exclusively so is to deny them the richness and complexity with which the poet endowed them. Particularly in the political and social context of the period, it is also to miss their significance as analogical representatives of the British public, reduced to desperate straits by a repressive establishment capitalizing at every turn upon the weaknesses and the gullibility of the populace to enforce its own tyranny and force upon the victims equally reprehensible and irresponsible alternatives.

Why, then, did Shelley not want his name attached to the poem? When he sent it to Hunt he was adamant on this point: "I dont particularly wish this Poem to be known as mine, but at all events I would not put my name to it—I leave you to judge whether it is best to throw it in the fire, or to publish it—So much for *self* [:] *self*, that burr that will stick to one. I cant get it off yet" (*SC*, VI, 852; 15 August 1819). Not for over a year did he bend on this point, and then only partially: "I believe you know that I do not wish my name to be printed on the title page, though I have no objection to being known as the author" (*Letters*, II, 246; 10 November 1820).

Shelley's motives here are quite unlike those that had led him to wish his authorship of *The Cenci* concealed at first. He apparently resisted allowing Julian a clear and obvious victory over Maddalo in the poem because he wished to avoid alienating the poet whose friendship he hoped for many reasons to maintain. But his dismissal of both the arguments and then the figure of Maddalo would almost certainly displease Byron. That Shelley never mentions the poem in any extant letter to Byron is itself a telling point. Shelley was obviously willing to sacrifice his identity as author in hopes of preserving a relationship while still publicly addressing the other party to that relationship in a poem meant for the popular periodical press. In this context it is interesting to consider Lee Erickson's point about the sacrifice of self in the poetry of one of Shelley's greatest Victorian admirers, Robert Browning: "If one supposes that one can sacrifice one's own private self-realization for the sake of the public's enlightenment and so as a prophet address the multitude instead of one's lover, one risks abandoning the ground of one's self in love and giving in to one's satanic desires to be raised above others and to become their tyrant."[62] If we substitute "friend" for "lover"—a substitution that for Shelley would have been one of only very slight degree—we can see the relevance of this comment to Shelley's view of his public role as prophet and patriot. He did not want to tyrannize, of course: his remarks about the fate of Christ in the notes to *Queen Mab* (*Works*, 819–25) and elsewhere prove that. But what the unwilling call tyranny, the willing often regard as inspired leadership: it is very much a matter of which side one is on. Moreover, Shelley intended all his audiences, public and private, to understand that he addressed them as both friend and lover.

Finally, there is the matter of *Julian and Maddalo*'s style. Knowing Hunt's preference for a less esoteric, less impressionistic style, he writes:

> You will find the little piece, I think in some degree consistent with your own ideas of the manner in which Poetry ought to be written. I have employed a certain familiar style of language to express the actual way in which people talk with each other whom education & a certain refinement of sentiment have placed above the use of vulgar idioms. I use the word *vulgar* in its' [sic] most extensive sense: the vulgarity of rank & fashion is as gross in its way, as that of Poverty, & its cant terms equally expressive of base conceptions & therefore equally unfit for Poetry. Not that the familiar style is to be admitted in the treatment of a subject wholly ideal, or in that part of any subject which relates to common life, where the passion exceeding a certain limit touches the boundaries of that which is ideal. Strong passion expresses itself in metaphor borrowed from objects alike remote or near, & casts over all the shadow of its own greatness—(*SC*, VI, 851–52; 15 August 1819)

Nine months later, writing to Ollier, he qualifies these remarks: "If I had even intended to publish 'Julian and Maddalo' with my name, yet I would not print it with 'Prometheus'. It would not harmonize. It is an attempt in a different style, in which I am not yet sure of myself, a *sermo pedestris* way of treating human nature quite opposed to the idealism of that drama" (*Letters*, II, 196; 14 May 1820). Taken together, these two statements shed a good deal of light on the manner in which Shelley had come to assess the audiences for his poetry.

First, he now appears to reject the notion of the "language really used by men" advocated in Wordsworth's preface to *Lyrical Ballads*, agreeing with Coleridge's position in the *Biographia Literaria* (which

Shelley had read soon after its appearance in 1817) that the *lingua communis* "is no more to be found in the phraseology of low and rustic life, than in that of any other class."[63] Wordsworth's attempt to democratize art by democratizing language in a literary style that might be understood by the literate but not classically trained reader of the middle and upper working class had been systematically attacked by both Coleridge and Francis Jeffrey, both relatively liberal critics.[64] Shelley had already announced his own more Coleridgean position in the preface to *The Cenci*, where he declared, "I have written . . . without an over-fastidious and learned choice of words. In this respect I entirely agree with those modern critics who assert that in order to move men to true sympathy we must use the familiar language of men. . . . But it must be the real language of men in general and not that of any particular class to whose society the writer happens to belong" (*Works*, 277–78). Shelley argues in effect that style is a factor of content and that the nearer the content of a work approaches the "wholly ideal" (as in *Prometheus Unbound*, for instance), the more the author must employ the highest style—the least ordinary, least "vulgar" idiom. Shelley had studied the theories of language advanced by Lord Monboddo, Horne Tooke, and Sir William Jones, and he surely appreciated Horne Tooke's contention in *The Diversions of Purley* (1798 and 1805) that though words like *vulgar* and *refined* that were immediately visible in Shelley's critical vocabulary in 1817–20 might continue to describe types of language, they could no longer claim scientifically to delineate the intellectual or moral capacities of different social classes.[65] Shelley's remarks to Hunt reveal that he was trying to collapse several audiences through his use of language. Hence *The Cenci*, which he had deliberately composed in the more "vulgar" style of which he speaks here, "ought to have been popular" (*Letters*, II, 263; to Ollier, 16 February 1821), presumably for this reason.

Shelley's comments also subtly reiterate his exclusion of the lowest classes of audience, for the idiom of people who possess "education and a certain refinement of sentiment" will not, even in the improving educational climate of the late Regency, be that of the masses. The target audience for *Julian and Maddalo* is Byron's readers, who will recognize not only the portrait of Byron but, more important, the many allusions to his poetry that delineate the Byronic hero represented in both Maddalo and the Maniac. Like Coleridge's *Biographia*, Shelley's *Julian and Maddalo* (and both *Prometheus Unbound* and *A Philosophical View of Reform*) is addressed in an hour of public peril to the educated, the intellectual elite, for the purpose of counteracting irresponsibility in "high places" and urging that privileged audience to fulfill its social responsibility,[66] first by private thought and then by public action.

Shelley's use of the term *sermo pedestris* reveals his conscious juxtaposition in his poem of a distinctly Horatian urbanity with the Maniac's passionate outbursts. Horace had applied this term to the language appropriate for tragic lament, but its connotation had come by 1800 to include any colloquial style that seemed to derive from Horace's manner in his satires or *sermones*. Shelley's more sophisticated readers might be expected to recognize this stylistic point and apply it to Byron, whose admiration for Pope's work was well known. Pope had himself linked the poetry of ethos with that of pathos in his *Moral Essays* and especially in his *Imitations of Horace*, composing poetry that dramatizes the character of the poet even as it renders moral judgments intended to teach virtue.[67] That Shelley adopts a form both familiar and attractive to Byron for a poem that subverts most of what Byron stands for is both audacious and shrewd. If Shelley's readers were paying attention, they could not fail to appreciate the subversion, nor could they escape the poem's publicly corrective function.

Although Shelley appears deliberately to invoke Byron in the preface to *Prometheus Unbound*, he reminds his reader of other points of comparison as well. Invoking not only the great poets of the English and Continental Renaissance, he begins his preface by citing as well "the Greek tragic writers" both as models and as precedents. The apparent original beginning of the preface suggests why Shelley chose for *The Cenci* a familiar story: "The Greek tragic writers were accustomed to choose a subject well known to their auditors & often treated by their [contemporaries & rivals]" (Bodleian MS Shelley adds. e. 11, p. 56). Shelley canceled these lines in favor of the present opening passage, in which he states that the Greek writers employed "a certain arbitrary discretion": "They by no means conceived themselves bound to adhere to the common interpretation or to imitate in story as in title their rivals and predecessors. Such a system would have amounted to a resignation of *those claims to preference over their competitors which incited the composition*" (*Works*, 204–5; my italics). This last phrase both anticipates the terms of the implied comparison (and competition) with Byron which Shelley introduces later and establishes Shelley's intention of relating *Prometheus Unbound* to the classical tradition that informs it. When he claims that "I have presumed to employ a similar licence" (*Works*, 205), Shelley affirms that his aim in composing entitles him to assume the same degree of "arbitrary discretion" accorded the great writers of the past.

Shelley's discussion of his lyrical drama's relation to Aeschylus's works reveals his intention not to compete with but to surpass his classical predecessor:

> Had I framed my story on this model, I should have done no
> more than have attempted to restore the lost drama of Aeschy-

lus; an ambition which, if my preference to this mode of treating the subject had incited me to cherish, the recollection of the high comparison such an attempt would challenge might well abate. But, in truth, I was averse from a catastrophe so feeble as that of reconciling the Champion with the Oppressor of mankind. The moral interest of the fable, which is so powerfully sustained by the sufferings and endurance of Prometheus, would be annihilated if we could conceive of him as unsaying his high language and quailing before his successful and perfidious adversary. (*Works*, 205)

Interestingly, in a draft of this passage Shelley indicated the danger of invoking too direct a comparison with Aeschylus, writing that such a comparison might prove "unfavorable" (Bodleian MS Shelley e. 11, p. 59); he suppressed the suggestion, though, apparently not wishing to supply his detractors with additional ammunition. More important, in declaring his express purpose of *not* attempting to complete or "restore" Aeschylus, Shelley opens the way for the alternative, which becomes clearer when he suggests the potential link between Prometheus and Milton's Satan, a link which he then explicitly disallows on the grounds that "Prometheus is, in my judgement, a more poetical character than Satan, because, in addition to courage, and majesty, and firm and patient opposition to omnipotent force, he is susceptible of being described as exempt from the taints of ambition, envy, revenge, and a desire for personal aggrandisement" (*Works*, 205).

That Shelley invokes Milton specifically here—regardless of his provocative designation of Satan as "the Hero of *Paradise Lost*"—further reveals his desire that the reader approach *Prometheus Unbound* mindful of the precedents established by his predecessors. In enlarging upon Aeschylus, and in reorienting the story of Prometheus's relationship with Jupiter, Shelley is not only doing what the Greeks had done with familiar stories, revising and embellishing them, he is also doing what Milton was perceived by Shelley's time to have done in his treatment of Scripture in the great epic and dramatic works of his maturity. Whereas in the eighteenth century Milton had been lauded as a religious poet and moralist, in the Romantic age he was viewed in political terms, with artists like Blake and Shelley discerning in his epics a revolutionary art that subverted the very systems of belief it ostensibly celebrated. Hence Shelley subsequently accounts Milton "a republican, and a bold inquirer into morals and religion,"[68] who was part of "that fervid awakening of the public mind which shook to dust the oldest and most oppressive form of the Christian religion" (*Works*, 206). Moreover, *Paradise Regained* provides an important precedent for *Prometheus Unbound* in the psychodrama of Jesus' discovery of himself. Like Jesus in Milton's internalized brief epic, who "Into himself descended" (*Paradise Regained*, II, 111), Shelley's Prometheus explores the recesses of his own psyche—his own personality—in a struggle for mastery of the self whose ultimate purpose is the recreation of Paradise.[69] Shelley's purpose is akin to what he believed Milton's to have been: to demonstrate that the "deeds above heroic" (*Paradise Regained*, I, 14–15) are deeds not of force and destruction but rather of self-realization and benevolent community. Shelley would not have missed the telling fact that once the fully individuated Jesus of *Paradise Regained* discovers that he is God he chooses not to return to heaven but instead to reassert his bond with humanity by going "Home to his Mother's house" (*Paradise Regained*, IV, 639), from which he will emerge to perform his redemptive public mission.

One final point Shelley raises in his preface requires comment: his suggestion that he hopes to live long enough to produce "a systematical history of what appear to me to be the genuine elements of human society" (*Works*, 207). Presumably he is thinking of a prose work here and in his earlier mention of the project to Peacock: "I consider Poetry very subordinate to moral & political science, & if I were well, certainly I should aspire to the latter; for I can conceive a great work, embodying the discoveries of all ages, & harmonizing the contending creeds by which mankind have been ruled" (*Letters*, II, 71; 23–24 January 1819). Ironically, *Prometheus Unbound* is itself such a work. Like *Queen Mab*, *Prometheus Unbound* is a philosophical poem whose narrative embodies the universal and synthesizing tendency of which Shelley speaks. But as visions of an ideal, which is what they are, each poem is precluded from being the sort of unified historical analysis Shelley seems to have in mind in these two comments. Both look forward to the philosophical prose of *A Philosophical View of Reform* and *A Defence of Poetry*, in which this comprehensive analysis is more directly undertaken.

I began this chapter with a brief discussion of Shelley's reading and translation of Plato, of his commentary on the nature of love in Greek society, and of the consequences of the failure of that society to extend genuine, egalitarian love to its women. The notion of love as a going out of the self—an idea that reappears in the *Defence*—is already present in "On Love," a draft of which appears in the same notebook with drafts of the opening of the preface to *Prometheus Unbound* and the essay "A Future State." The deletions and corrections in the manuscript's third paragraph are revealing: "*Thou* demandest [wh] what is *love*. [It is the sweet chalice of life whose dregs are bitterer than wormwood.] It is [all that] that powerful attraction toward all that we conceive or fear or hope [or] beyond ourselves when [the wings] [mind] We [feel that our] find within our own thoughts the chasm of an insufficient void [and the imagination /clings/ seeks the likeness of that which is most beautiful within itself that] and [seek] [feeling] seek to awaken in all things that are a [community] with [our own sen] what we experience within ourselves" (Bodleian MS Shelley adds. e. 11, pp. 2–3). The critical term here—*community*—is deleted in the manuscript, but it was restored when the essay was printed in the *Keepsake* in 1829.[70] The passage neatly isolates both the greatest hope for—and the greatest danger to—humanity in the search for "the likeness of that which is most beautiful within itself." Irresponsibly pursued and directed toward the discovery merely of oneself in others, this quest produces the alienation that kills the Visionary in *Alastor*, that cripples Julian, and that—in the works of Shelley's greatest "competitor"—renders the Byronic hero finally incapable of helping himself or his fellow creatures. It is potentially the most embittering experience of human life, as the canceled sentence about the "sweet chalice" indicates. Love is for Shelley not passive but active, not a bower of blissful indulgence but a battlefield of difficult and often painful choices.

The history of the world, Shelley's works everywhere argue, is the record of the failure to love—the substitution of self for other at the center of one's concerns and the fallacious creation of a myriad of isolated individual worlds in defiance of the grand interconnectedness that is the essence of the natural universe. In this, Shelley recognizes with Blake the pernicious influence of the Selfhood on the process of individuation. What Blake terms "Mental Fight" in *Milton*, Shelley dramatizes in *Prometheus Unbound*. At every turn Prometheus must resist the temptation to accept the answers with which the world—epitomized in the Earth—has too long been satisfied, answers that call for the elevation of self at the expense of other. Only when Prometheus successfully "into himself descends" in Act I, and only when he repeats that descent over and over throughout the remainder of the drama in conscious mental choices that are then actualized in physical phenomena, does Prometheus don the heroism in which Shelley sets out to clothe him. If *Prometheus Unbound* is the epitome of the transcendental literary form[71]—a structure that deliberately oversteps its traditionally accepted generic limits—then Prometheus is the transcendental hero par excellence, the fully realized symbol and embodiment of revolution perfected, internalized, and applied to the renovation of the universe. Should *Prometheus Unbound* succeed with even the few readers Shelley believed might actually understand it, its author's contribution might indeed both rival and surpass those not only of literary predecessors like Aeschylus, Milton, and Byron but also of symbolic predecessors like Prometheus and Jesus Christ. Despite his often calculatedly self-effacing rhetoric, Shelley never was given to modest expectations or modest aspirations.

the spring rebels not against winter but it succeeds it—
the dawn rebels not against night but it disperses it

SHELLEY, manuscript fragment

PUBLIC POLITICS ONCE AGAIN
1819 and After

The Exoteric Political Poems

Of all Shelley's works, the exoteric political poems of 1819 best demonstrate the validity of Marilyn Butler's observation that the arts "do
not exist faithfully to reproduce political realities or real-life political
arguments."[1] The artist routinely transforms both the external details
and the inner nature of temporal events for particular aesthetic, intellectual, or sociopolitical purposes. This point is especially relevant to
the overtly political poems Shelley composed after the Peterloo incident of 16 August 1819, when in Manchester a peaceable mass meeting for reform had been forcibly broken up by local yeomanry and
government troops, resulting in a number of deaths, many injuries,
and the arrest and imprisonment of both the main speaker (Henry
"Orator" Hunt) and several leaders of the reform movement.

English publishers had been made understandably fearful by the
government's subsequent passage in November and December 1819 of
the Six Acts, legislation specifically designed both to weaken the reform movement and to head off armed rebellion first by curtailing the
rights to public assembly and the bearing of arms, and second by
largely eliminating all printed opposition.[2] Coming in the wake of the
prosecution of the radical publisher Richard Carlile, which I will consider later in this chapter, the Six Acts sent a clear warning to the
liberal and radical press. The consequences for Shelley are obvious
from the refusal of the moderate Hunt to print the political poems—
The Mask of Anarchy, for example—Shelley sent him late in 1819.

From his removed position in Italy Shelley could not fully appreciate Hunt's very practical reasons for suppressing the poems. Hunt seems typically to have chosen silence rather than frankness when declining to publish any of Shelley's pieces, as is evident from Shelley's comment that "you do not tell me whether you have received my lines on the Manchester affair" (*SC*, VI, 1080; [16] November 1819).

Given the hesitancy of both Hunt and Ollier, it is curious that Shelley apparently never approached Carlile, Eaton, or any other notable radical publisher as a potential publisher for his own works, and especially for the exoteric poems. Perhaps Shelley felt morally bound to commit himself to a single publisher in each area (periodical and book). Probably, too, he retained hopes of convincing his regular publishers of the need for greater political commitment, as is clear from his effort to nudge Hunt in that direction:

> You will never write politics. I dont wonder; but I wish then that you would write a paper in the Examiner on the actual state of the country; & what under all the circumstances of the conflicting passions & interests of men, we are to expect;—Not what we ought to expect or what if so & so were to happen we might expect; but what as things are there is reason to believe will come; & send it me for my information. Every word a man has to say is valuable to the public now, & thus you will at once gratify your friend, nay instruct & either exhilarate [sic] him or force him to be resigned & awaken the minds of the people—(*SC*, VI, 1107; 23 December 1819)

Here are the familiar Shelleyan tactics: the appeal to Hunt both as private, personal friend and as public, liberal publisher, the posture of expecting to derive both satisfaction and instruction from Hunt's exertions, and the overt suggestion that it is Hunt's duty to "awaken the minds of the people."

The radical press had begun to play an increasingly important and highly visible role in English affairs, especially after the government's suspension of habeas corpus early in 1817. Shelley must have known, for instance, about the popularity of papers like Wooler's *Black Dwarf*, the circulation of which reached some twelve thousand in 1819.[3] The printed word, particularly as it appeared in the periodical press, had become by the time of the Manchester affair a vehicle for leading and inspiring the emerging lower- and lower-middle-class readership. Cobbett's *Political Register*, especially, had fostered a new journalism that overtly took to task the prevailing political, social, economic, and even religious status quo. That so much of the radical journalism of the period draws upon stylistic models as diverse as the Bible, popular songs, and folktales is little surprise; in deliberately adopting these familiar patterns the radical journalists mounted an effective subliminal appeal to their readers, preconditioning their assent by addressing them within familiar rhetorical and stylistic frameworks. Indeed, this new class of readers was coming to regard the printed word as "a new revelation" that was "infinitely more applicable to their immediate situation than the Scriptural precepts expounded in religious tracts."[4] Like all revolutionary art, radical journalism subverted the Establishment from within as well as from without, turning against it its own terminology and rhetorical models.

Shelley was not unaware of these developments, nor did he fail to appreciate the value at this juncture of yet another attempt to reach "the people" in a language and a style appropriate to what he regarded as both their limited sophistication and their potentially dangerous character. He writes Peacock eight days after the Manchester incident had occurred but before he had received word of it: "England seems to be in a very disturbed state, if we may judge by some Paris Papers. . . . But the change should commence among the higher orders, or anarchy will only be the last flash before despotism. I wonder & tremble" (*Letters*, II, 115; 24 August 1819). When he learns of Peterloo his response to his correspondents is revealing: "The torrent of my indignation has not yet done boiling in my veins. I wait anxiously [to] hear how the Country will express its sense of this bloody murderous oppression of its destroyers" (*Letters*, II, 117; 6 September 1819). Perhaps thinking of Cobbett, the political and economic shrewdness of whose work he had come to respect, Shelley again links the violence with its economic causes and consequences when he writes to Peacock: "These are, as it were, the distant thunders of the terrible storm which is approaching. The tyrants here as in the French Revolution have first shed blood[;] may their execrable lessons not be learnt with equal docility! I still think there will be no coming to close quarters until financial affairs decidedly bring the oppressors & the oppressed together" (*SC*, VI, 895–96; 9 September 1819). Although Shelley had been coming gradually to appreciate the purely economic issues involved in class oppression and class consciousness, he had likely read and approved much of Robert Owen's recent essay, "An Address to the Working Class," which had appeared in the *Examiner* on 25 April and which he would have received in Italy. Owen stresses that "the rich and the poor, the governors and the governed, have really but one interest,"[5] a point with which Shelley agreed entirely.

Widely acknowledged as Shelley's *annus mirabilis*, 1819 marked the confluence of his creative powers, his sociopolitical and artistic commitments, and his manipulation of genre and style in perhaps the greatest array of works and forms ever produced in a relatively short period by a single author in English literary history. Not only the two great dramatic works but also the exoteric political poems, the letter on Carlile's trial, and *A Philosophical View of Reform* explore closely related, often identical, issues from a variety of perspectives, in a variety of voices, and for a variety of audiences. Even as we attempt to consider these works individually, we must try to appreciate their relations to one another and to the coordinated literary program Shelley was pursuing at the time. Late 1819 marked a crucial moment for his hopes as author and activist. Both *Prometheus Unbound* and *The Cenci* had been sent off to England, attended by Shelley's high hopes particularly for the latter; if it succeeded, the former might gain by association. *Julian and Maddalo* was in Hunt's hands, and *The Mask of Anarchy* had been posted to him at the end of September. It does appear, however, that Shelley did not intend for his name to appear with *The Mask*, even had it been published, although at a later, "safer" time he would doubtless have been willing to acknowledge it as his own poem. What I have already said in this light about *Queen Mab*, his authorship of which Shelley had likewise initially attempted to shield if not conceal, might be applied to *The Mask* as well. Shelley was, at this time, already at work also on both the "popular songs" and *A Philosophical View of Reform*, and the long letter to Hunt (as editor of the *Examiner*) on Carlile's situation is dated 3 November 1819. Had *The Mask* appeared promptly and *The Cenci* been acted, they might have gained Shelley the visibility and credibility his public campaign required. That Hunt silently suppressed *The Mask* both puzzled and hurt Shelley, as is evident from the transparent nonchalance with which he subsequently writes to Hunt about his more political works. A telling example comes in an inquiry to Hunt in 1820: "I wish to ask you if you know of any bookseller who would like to publish a little volume of *popular songs* wholly political, & destined to awaken & direct the imagination of the reformers. I see you smile but answer my question" (*Letters*, II, 191; 1 May 1820).

Hunt had reacted to Shelley's political poems in December of 1819, when he warned him about the new associations Ollier seemed to be making: "I will write more speedily, & tell you about your political songs & pamphlets, which we must publish without Ollier, as he gets more timid & pale every day;—I hope I shall not have to add time serving; but they say he is getting intimate with strange people" (*SC*, VI, 1090). Hunt's suggestions about Ollier probably contributed to the suspicion with which Shelley subsequently regarded his publisher, who he felt lacked both courage and enthusiasm.[6] The "strange people" likely alludes to Ollier's growing connections with *Blackwood's Edinburgh Magazine*, which praised him as publisher and author and to which in 1821 he contributed at least two articles, one of which discusses *Epipsychidion* (*SC*, VI, 1090). Shelley had not abandoned the idea of a book of topical, politically committed "popular poems" like the one he had broached to Thomas Hookham in 1813 in connection with his Esdaile Notebook poems. This new effort would doubless have been a mixed bag: somehow "the reformers" suggests an audience different from that for "A New National Anthem" or "Song to the Men of England." Probably some of the poems (such as "Ode to the West Wind" and "Ode to Liberty") that eventually appeared in the *Prometheus Unbound* volume would have found a place in this collection, perhaps with poems as different stylistically and aesthetically as *The Mask of Anarchy*.

Poems of "the exoteric species" on "ordinary topics" Shelley intended for both his disciples and the general public.[7] *The Mask of Anarchy*, though distinguished by its greater length and complexity, shares with the other exoteric poems of late 1819 an immediate and overt topicality as well as a stylistic ruggedness that has often been mistaken for inartistry.[8] These poems are not comparable with Shelley's esoteric verses, of course, but they were never intended to be. To devalue them on the basis of their apparent roughness, though, is to misunderstand Shelley's vehicle and to judge the poems by the wrong standards. It is to deny the stylistic and rhetorical acuteness that is so evident in everything Shelley wrote. The criteria for comparison here are not Byron and Aeschylus but Wooler and Hone, not *Childe Harold's Pilgrimage*, "Prometheus," or *Prometheus Bound* but "The Political House That Jack Built" and "A Political Christmas Carol." Shelley's exoteric poems exhibit a surprising familiarity with both the texts and the iconography of the radical press and the pamphlet war of the latter stages of the Regency.[9]

Accurately characterized by Timothy Webb as "poems of exhortation, of vituperation and of fundamental political analysis, designed for the popular reader," [10] these poems employ a common and straightforward diction and syntax for the most part, as well as plain allegories and generally familiar, simple poetic structures. Like the radical journalists, Shelley drew upon familiar models ranging from the Bible through the colloquial ballad forms of popular culture. "A New National Anthem," for instance, draws power from its obvious parodic relationship to the conventional anthem. As he had done in his essay on the death of Princess Charlotte in 1817, Shelley invokes the figure of martyred Liberty:

> God prosper, speed, and save,
> God raise from England's grave
>   Her murdered Queen!
>   (*Works*, 574)

If the Bodleian manuscript (MS Shelley adds. e. 6) is the first draft, as it appears to be, Shelley apparently composed stanzas 1, 3, 4, and 5 first, revising the first heavily as he worked. Once under way, he must have composed more easily and more surely, for the next stanzas, written like the first in pencil, are only lightly revised (MS pp. 19–20). Apparently part of "The Cloud" was already in this notebook, for the next page of the manuscript contains a draft with revisions of "The Cloud," lines 60 through 66. It appears that Shelley stopped after what is now stanza 5 and then later returned to the anthem, making some revisions in ink, adding sideways on the page next to the first stanza what is now stanza 2, and then cross-writing in ink, over the lines from "The Cloud," the final stanza. When Mary Shelley later published the poem, she several times substituted in the final line of a stanza the phrase "*the* Queen" where Shelley had written "*our* Queen." A seemingly minor change, this substitution of the definite article for the inclusive personal pronoun makes a major difference in the distance it establishes between author and audience. Had she forgotten that throughout 1819 and on into 1820 Shelley had expressed to Hunt, Peacock, and others his hope to return to England? Perhaps she simply miscopied, or perhaps the printer erred. But such lapses (or deliberate alterations) contributed to the myth that Shelley renounced England and his countrymen. Indeed, in the first occurrence of the phrase in the original draft of line 16, he initially wrote "God save the Queen!" but canceled "the" and substituted "our," which revision clearly indicates his numbering himself among the English people in whose collective voice he is attempting to speak.[11]

The exoteric poems of 1819 are battle cries; they are calls not to mere contemplation but to action, filled with masterful manipulation of stock iconography. The bitter, devastating invective of "To S——th and C——gh," whose title Medwin and Mary Shelley subsequently sanitized and depersonalized as "Similies for Two Political Characters of 1819," exhibits a savagery not ordinarily associated with Shelley:

> . . . ye, two vultures sick for battle,
>   Two scorpions under one wet stone,
> Two bloodless wolves whose dry throats rattle,
> Two crows perched on the murrained cattle,
>   Two vipers tangled into one.
>
> *(Works,* 573)

These poems, in which Shelley asserts an empathic solidarity with the brutalized and maimed victims of Peterloo and all it stands for, attain a level of personal, passionate intensity found also in poems like "To the Lord Chancellor,"[12] which address the personal injuries to which Shelley felt he had been subjected. The formal posture of public suffering is, however, integral to poems of this sort; the outbursts against outrage and injustice underscore the undeserved nature of the outrage, imaging the persecutions of the public martyr. Although these heavily revised poems are, to some extent, exercises in therapeutic writing, Shelley's desire to publish them indicates a serious purpose: they are both models and examples of the community of shared suffering that unites all humanity when the most basic human rights—whether of political freedom or of possession of one's children—are violated by a seemingly mindless patriarchal tyranny.

These poems illustrate Shelley's penetrating understanding of economic and social issues. "Song to the Men of England," for instance, expresses the same rejection of economic vampirism we have already observed in his Irish writings of 1812. Most obviously of all the "popular songs," this one explicitly adopts the rhetorical features of working-class radicalism. Its central image of "Bees of England" is a trope that had been politicized and repopularized by Paine, Spence, and Wooler and that was used almost exclusively at this time by working-class socialists and radicals.[13]

> Men of England, wherefore plough
> For the lords who lay ye low?
> Wherefore weave with toil and care
> The rich robes your tyrants wear?
>
> Wherefore feed, and clothe, and save,
> From the cradle to the grave,
> Those ungrateful drones who would
> Drain your sweat—nay, drink your blood?
> *(Works, 572)*

Shelley concludes in a disturbing tone of bitter irony:

> Shrink to your cellars, holes, and cells;
> In halls ye deck another dwells.
> Why shake the chains ye wrought? Ye see
> The steel ye tempered glance on ye.
>
> With plough and spade, and hoe and loom,
> Trace your grave, and build your tomb,
> And weave your winding-sheet, till fair
> England be your sepulchre.
> *(Works, 573)*

Shelley's poem does not vacillate between exhortation and contemptuous satire nearly so much as it is often said to do. Shelley's strategy here must be seen in light of both his intended audience and his notion of how to arouse that audience from its self-induced torpor. Like the "Ode Written in October, 1819, Before the Spaniards Had Recovered Their Liberty," the "Song" adopts an "ardent missionary style"[14] in commemorating the committed patriots who have fought, suffered, and (temporarily) been defeated and in looking forward to the day when nations "arise" and "awaken" to shake their chains to dust (*Works*, 575–76). Like the "Ode," the "Song" is hortatory and declamatory: as a song it is both anthem and marching song in the manner of *La Marseillaise*. But its tone is ironic, its argument skeptical. To the questions that occupy the first four stanzas, the invented audience must necessarily respond, "Why, indeed?" Stanza five states the present dilemma, driving home the reality of labor's exploitation. Stanza six counsels continuing the same activities but for a different purpose: for the dignity that *self*-support provides. Further, it recommends taking up arms—"in your defence to bear." This is a difficult point; Shelley seems to imply that violence in self-defense is acceptable, which contradicts his position elsewhere. I would suggest that his sustained consideration of an analogous situation in *The Cenci* had made him more willing to countenance a united show of force against the oppressors, despite the terrible risks (and despite the idealistic response *Prometheus Unbound* proposes). This poem comes as close as Shelley ever comes to sanctioning violence as a last resort, and I believe that the reversal in both sense and tone in the final two stanzas suggests that he did not consider the "men of England" actually capable of so decisive an assertion. Even though subsequent poems such as "Ode to Liberty" support the cause of overt revolution in other countries, Shelley's position regarding change in England remains remarkably consistent: change must come gradually, through the joint exertions of enlightened leaders and an awakened populace capable of appreciating basic human dignity and seeking it not through violence and retribution but through reconciliation and community.

Hence though the conclusion of the "Song to the Men of England" ironically chastises its audience, it does so the more powerfully to alert them to the error they have already too long perpetuated. Like the ode on the Spanish situation, with which it is contemporaneous, the "Song" transcends purely national issues in its determined focus on the human issues that link all nations, all peoples. It shares with that ode, as it does with *Hellas*, written eighteen months later and under different circumstances, the conviction that the oppressed of all nations share a common cause even as they share in the "one human heart": they are participants in different scenes of the same drama.[15] The poem's conclusion is a variation on the reverse definition. Having presumably raised the audience's ire in the opening stanzas, and having stated the "sad reality" of their condition in the middle stanzas, Shelley concludes with a vision of the inevitable consequences of continued failure to alter the status quo. Neither a concession to the impracticality of his suggestions nor a contemptuous verbal gesture of despair over his inability to stimulate change, Shelley's final lines are a calculated challenge to the audience to reject their subhuman images as rats, moles, and bees ("your cellars, holes, and cells," line 25) and to assume their full status as human beings.

The fragmentary "To the People of England" affords another example of Shelley's approach both to his subject matter and to his working-class audience:

> People of England, ye who toil and groan,
> Who reap the harvests which are not your own,
> Who weave the clothes which your oppressors wear,
> And for your own take the inclement air;
> Who build houses . . .
> And are like gods who give them all they have,
> And nurse them from the cradle to the grave . . .
>
> *(Works, 573)*

As in "Song to the Men of England," of which this poem may have been an early version, Shelley makes the point that the oppressors are utterly dependent upon the victims' acquiescence in their own exploitation. If the people ever awaken, as the poems of this period repeatedly exhort them to do, they will not need to seize power for it is already theirs: it is in the people, not in the prevailing elitist minority, that true power resides.

Owen had made this same point:

> You [the working classes] now possess all the means which are necessary to relieve yourselves and your descendants to the latest period, from the sufferings which you have hitherto experienced, except the knowledge how to direct those means. . . . this knowledge is withheld from you only until the violence of your irritation against your fellow-men shall cease; that is, until you thoroughly understand and are influenced in all your conduct by the principle, "That it is the circumstances of birth, with subsequent surrounding circumstances, all formed *for* the individual (and over which society has now a complete controul) that have hitherto made the past generations of mankind into the irrational creatures exhibited in history, and fashioned them, up to the present hour, into those localized beings of country, sect, class and party, who now compose the population of the earth." [16]

Because individuals tend to be motivated by self-interest and to depend on others rather than on themselves, the oppressors exploit these propensities to subjugate their victims, cultivating among them the illusion that the welfare and security of all depends upon the unquestioned maintenance of the prevailing power structure, regardless of the cost to the suffering populace. Their insecurites thus nurtured and re-inforced, the deluded masses fall into the habit of nursing their op-pressors, literally "giving them all they have" rather than risk the de-stabilizing trauma of resisting this unjust arrangement.

As in *The Mask of Anarchy*, Shelley attempts in the unabashedly inflammatory "To the People of England" to awaken his readers to the extent of their own misery. And as in *The Mask*, the catalyst is a reverse definition designed to remind them of all that they are presently de-nied. Though the poem is only a fragment of what Shelley appears to have intended as a sonnet, it shares with the "Song to the Men of England" the familiar, generalized images of domestic labor and the emphasis on the disproportionate relationship between labor and re-ward. Although during the war years a journalism had appeared that was dedicated to mobilization over national issues, after the war radi-cal journalists in particular began more insistently to stress domestic issues and the actual condition of the people. The praxis of popular radicalism was rooted in tangible experience, in the realities of indi-vidual hardship, and in the alienation of the people from the political process.[17] Hence personal hardships like hunger, unemployment, and the frustration of petitions for industrial regulation contributed far more to the pressure for reform than did more abstract notions about liberty. Shelley's exoteric poems attempt to capitalize on the plain fact that ideological conversion is made easier when it is tied closely to the common people's direct experience of hardship.

Shelley's esoteric poems—*Prometheus Unbound*, for example—in-volve a rarefied intellectual atmosphere: their elevated diction and complex periodic syntax, their intricate symbolism, their wealth of so-phisticated and erudite background materials, and their broad "so-ciohistorical" sweep far outstrip anything we may classify as an exo-teric poem, even including *The Mask of Anarchy*.[18] Whereas the esoteric poems focus on fresh, even apocalyptic myths of the *new* man, the exoteric poems dwell with the righteous indignation of Jesus among the money changers on the dilemma of the *old* man crushed by the old, exploitive intellectual and sociopolitical system. The exo-teric poems aim to play a significant role in the repudiation of the old power structure by the oppressed Britons who are seemingly beginning at last to awaken and to assert themselves. Hence while Shelley in-structs the enlightened few who might comprehend the political pro-gram advocated in *Prometheus Unbound*, he also prepares the masses (or so he believes) for the institution of that new and benevolent sys-tem, beginning gradually to give them the "knowledge" of which Owen speaks in the passage quoted above.

The very real danger posed to all parties by the explosive situation, even well before Peterloo, is implicit in *The Cenci*, where everyone loses. John Farrell has written that violence is essential to revolution: "Revolution assaults a set of legitimizing norms, the prevailing paradigm. One of the distinguishing features of this paradigm is that it explicitly excludes whatever it is that the revolution wants. There is nothing in the paradigm to sanction its revolutionary replacement. Violence alone can alter this situation by enforcing the authority that revolution confers upon itself."[19] Shelley understood this, of course, which explains why he advocates for England not revolution but nonviolent *reform*, believing that both the hostile and the apathetic members of the working classes could be enlisted in reasonable courses of action, "if reason could once be got inside their defences."[20] Shelley counsels not violence but insubordination, not revenge but education, not retaliation but resistance. If history is "a roll call of iniquities" and "an unanswerable indictment of the present structure of society,"[21] its transformation cannot come by any of the methods that history has already proven ineffective: something new and daring is called for. Mary Shelley stated the case well in 1840: "His indignant detestation of political oppression did not prevent him from deprecating the smallest approach to similar crimes on the part of his own party, and he abjured revenge and retaliation, while he strenuously advocated reform. He felt assured that there would be a change for the better in our institutions; he feared bloodshed, he feared the ruin of many. . . . 'The thing to fear,' he observes, 'will be, that the change should proceed too fast—it must be gradual to be secure.'"[22] Here the "Scotch philosopher" Robert Forsyth, whose *Principles of Moral Science* (1805) discusses the "passion for reforming the world," is helpful. Forsyth, whom Peacock—and probably also Shelley—had read, deprecates as Godwin had done the inclination toward violent and precipitous social and political change:

> In times of public contention or alarm, . . . it is the duty of a virtuous man to recollect often, that human affairs are . . . so contrived, that their amelioration is slow and progressive, and that great good is never suddenly or violently accomplished. It is also his duty to render the passion [for immediate change in the world] . . . unnecessary in his own mind, by acquiring that self-command which . . . may enable him to do his duty to society, without suffering himself either to be so much inflamed by opposition, or so much blinded by attachment to particular projects or notions, as to forget that force is not reason, that the edge of the sword introduces no light into the human mind, and that the certain and immediate commission of sanguinary actions can seldom be balanced by the doubtful prospect of future good.[23]

Shelley shares Forsyth's estimate of the danger of allowing one's own political, social, moral, or intellectual program to blind him or her to society's best interests. Such a view is apparent, for instance, in Shelley's Aristotelian insistence that works like *The Cenci* and *Prometheus Unbound* not be burdened (or disfigured) by the superimposition upon them of the author's program, but rather that any ideological implications ought to inhere in and arise naturally from the materials of the works themselves.

The Mask of Anarchy, the longest and most complex of the exoteric poems, is also the most ambivalent. It is a poem of appearances, from its ambivalent descriptions of the characters—Murder, for example, who "had a mask like Castlereagh"—to the distracted "maniac maid," whose actual identity is uncertain ("her name was Hope, she said: / But she looked more like Despair") to the "Shape arrayed in mail" that appears between the maid and the hooves of the approaching horses. *The Mask* again addresses the problem of finding a viable way to resist an oppressive patriarchal establishment. Here the "maniac maid" lies down in the path of Murder, Fraud, and Anarchy and thus impedes their progress.[24] Her deliberate gesture of self-sacrifice offers a very different and very public alternative to Beatrice Cenci's method of dealing with a bad father. That the maid's course of action is inherently more correct is indicated first in that she is not simply trampled and, second, in that a sort of "miracle" occurs in the appearance and the subsequent speech of the inscrutable Shape.

That Shape constitutes another of the poem's ambiguities. When it apparently speaks, for instance, the speech—even though it is quoted as direct address—is presented within the framework of a simile: a transfiguration occurs, and, like the voice of God speaking to Moses from the burning bush,

> A sense awakening and yet tender
> Was heard and felt—and at its close
> These words of joy and fear arose
>
> *As if* their Own indignant Earth
> Which gave the sons of England birth
> Had felt their blood upon her brow,
> And shuddering with a mother's throe
>
> Had turned every drop of blood
> By which her face had been bedewed
> To an accent unwithstood,—
> *As if* her heart had cried aloud:
> (PP, 305; my italics)

We may infer that the words are the apparition's, but Shelley's equivocation permits us equally to infer that they are those of a universal spirit of England not unlike the elemental spirits who speak in *Prometheus Unbound*. This spirit's clear ties with the unseen and "awful shadow of some unseen Power," the Spirit of Intellectual Beauty, are indicated by the fact that while human beings cannot see it, they still know it is present.[25]

Even the poem's voices are ambivalent. The naive narratorial voice, whose rhetoric and figures are those of the popular ballad style, is countered by the more sophisticated authorial voice that, even when it intentionally mouths the balladeer's style, is often deliberately ironic and always reflective of Shelley's own isolation in Italy, where he, too, hears a disembodied "voice."[26] This doubling of voice reflects the poem's grounding in the skeptical debate. In an angry poem on a subject of pressing national concern, addressed principally to an audience of the aggrieved oppressed, this ambivalence of voice is potentially dangerous, for the poem implicitly condones a variety of the violence it explicitly condemns. Cautioning the people against retaliating against the soldiers who cut them down, the Voice nonetheless exonerates the multitude from guilt over "the blood that must ensue" (line 338).

Indeed, the vigorous actions the Voice recommends to the people in the "Rise like Lions" refrain and elsewhere contradict the notion of passive resistance. Hunt saw this and explained why he suppressed the poem until 1832:

> I did not insert it [in the *Examiner*], because I thought that the public at large had not become sufficiently discerning to do justice to the sincerity and kind-heartedness of the spirit that walked in this flaming robe of verse. His charity was avowedly more than proportionate to his indignation; yet I thought that even the suffering part of the people, judging, not unnaturally from their own feelings, and from the exasperation which suffering produces before it produces knowledge, would believe a hundred-fold in his anger, to what they would in his good intention; and this made me fear that the common enemy would take advantage of the mistake to do them both a disservice.

Hunt even had stanzas 81–83 set in italics, with a footnote informing the reader he had done so to stress "the sober, lawful, and charitable mode of proceeding advocated and anticipated by this supposed reckless innovator. '*Passive obedience*' he certainly had not; but here follows a picture and a recommendation of '*non-resistance*,' in all its glory."[27]

More lay behind Shelley's desire for *The Mask* to appear in the *Examiner* than his mere acquaintance with Hunt, though, for the poem invokes Hunt's own words on the Manchester incident in the *Examiner* for 22 August 1819. Stressing the speakers' and the crowd's peaceable intentions and demeanor, Hunt had attacked the official perpetrators of the violence, asking what would have been the consequences had "the military" succeeded in its apparent determination "to cut [Henry Hunt] in pieces": "Do we think that thousands and thousands of Englishmen would any longer have contented themselves with tamely looking on; or with execrations, or with brickbats and staves? No, most assuredly. *They would have risen in the irresistible might of their numbers*. . . . With what feelings can these *Men in the Brazen Masks* of power dare to speak lamentingly of the wounds or even the death received by a constable or soldier or any other person concerned against an assemblage of Englishmen irritated by every species of wrong and insult, public and private?" (my italics).[28] Shelley was attuned to both the tone and the substance of the popular press. Had *The Mask* appeared in the *Examiner*, a perceptive reader, noting the verbal echoes, might have been moved by the reminder.

Shelley appreciated that demonstrations of their unsuspected strength often tempt the impatient oppressed into employing that strength to avenge past wrongs, so the goad provided by *The Mask* was a calculated risk. Had Hunt published Shelley's poem in the *Examiner* or arranged for its publication elsewhere, it would certainly have attracted the notice of the aristocracy (liberal or otherwise) and of others outside the working classes. Shelley undoubtedly intended to address to these readers as well his warning of the clear and present danger of continued failure to enact real social, political, and economic reform. Technically not a part of the oppressed classes, the possessors of power and influence are nevertheless implicated by their own acts of omission in allowing injustice to continue. To this audience, as to the physical victims of Peterloo and to their sympathetic comrades throughout England, the brutality of the bullying yeomanry in Manchester was both an insult and a humiliation. As in *The Cenci*, Shelley wishes to instruct his audiences about present issues by exposing the terrible blunders of the past. Here, however, the example invoked is more immediate: the shed blood is English, not Italian, and the latter-day Beatrices—whose emblems Shelley found in press reports of the wounded Manchester women and who represent the entire populace—are nearer than ever to choosing a form of national patricide as a means of redressing their wrongs.

But if *The Mask* presents both a program (to one audience) and a warning (to another), it envisions an ultimately millennial transformation. Though Shelley never mentions the painting, he could scarcely have been unaware of Benjamin West's popular *Death on a Pale Horse* (1783), which had strongly impressed Hunt and for which

West had sketched revisions in 1787 and 1802.[29] Indeed, the subject became very popular during the French Revolutionary period among both liberal and conservative artists, each of whom viewed its applicability to contemporary events according to his personal political orientation. Shelley's poem invests this verbal and visual topos with the status of myth to suggest "how humanity may wrest the millennium out of God's hands" in an act of collective self-purification that reestablishes human community from the ruins of class warfare.[30] Like James Gillray, whose brilliant caricatures are characterized by a sophisticated intertextual allusiveness, Shelley understood that a central aspect of revolutionary art is its revisionist treatment of existing, traditional forms: outmoded, irrelevant, and ideologically unacceptable elements are cast off while what is retained forms the basis of a new work whose visible generic and thematic relationships to the old serve further to destabilize the old. In any such work of "redeployment," the old work is "harnessed," together with its characteristic effects, to an entirely new purpose.[31] This is precisely what Shelley is about in *The Mask*, inverting a conventional image of the Apocalypse so as more powerfully to suggest that both individual and collective destiny are the responsibility of each member of society and may not be surrendered to external agents without oppression as a certain result. Deliberately willed realignment of social values and behavior can generate the rise, Phoenix-like, of life from the present death-in-life state.

Shelley's reworking of genre points to another of the poem's striking ambivalences, the tension it embodies between masque and antimasque. Stuart Curran notes that Shelley's *Mask* stands together with Hunt's *The Descent of Liberty. A Mask* (1815) against the main historical tradition of the masque as the literary-theatrical property of the rich and powerful.[32] Shelley undoubtedly knew both Hunt's *Descent* and its prefatory essay treating "the Origin and Nature of Masks." Indeed, Shelley's title, though it sets up yet another ambivalence ("mask" versus "masque") pointedly aligns his poem with Hunt's. And though Hunt did not mention the tradition of the antimasque in his essay, Shelley would have found a striking discussion of it in Schlegel's *Lectures on Dramatic Art and Literature*. The antimasque had traditionally introduced into the pageantry "the grotesque, the vulgar, the chaotic,"[33] which were then superseded in the harmonious denouement. But Shelley reverses the traditional pattern, defining the prevailing status quo with which the poem opens as a grotesque perversion and introducing in contradistinction the millennial vision of social realignment that ought ideally to supersede the gross vulgarity of the existing state.[34] That the traditional antimasque is typically overcome by both the moral superiority and the sheer numbers of the figures in the masque proper lends added force to the Voice's repeated assertion of the righteousness of the cause it advocates and to its reminder that "Ye are many—they are few." The relevance of *The Mask* to *several* audiences is striking: to the oppressed it couples inspiration with instruction; to more sophisticated and enlightened leaders it laces its clear warning with instruction.

Shelley's physical and emotional distance from events in England, together with a certain characteristic naive rashness in all such matters, prevented him from understanding that Hunt would not publish the piece at the time. The danger to a publisher of Hunt's generally moderate nature was simply too great: a Carlile or a Hone might have taken the chance, but Hunt's memories of previous prosecution for a much lesser offense were understandably strong. In any event, Shelley may have opted for the wrong approach in his poem. If we compare the measurable public effect of the devastating visual treatments by James Gillray or George Woodward or George and Isaac Cruikshank of the activities of political figures (from Fox and Pitt through the royal family), we are quickly reminded that humor is frequently the sharpest sword and laughter the surest medicine. The propagandistic effect of Hone's *Political House That Jack Built* (1819), for instance, is enhanced by its ability to slip under the readers' guard so that they found themselves laughing and accepting a point about the rulers to which they might otherwise have objected.[35] It is a point well taken. Although the reader's political innocence is necessarily shaken, the laugh is salutary, both in clearing the vision and in dissolving tension (or anger, or anxiety). Shelley's remarks in the *Essay on Christianity* reveal his understanding of the successful orator's need to create a friendly audience, but in the fall of 1819 he was simply too angry, too inflamed, to see that the indignation and the bluntness of his exoteric poems would necessarily cut him off from the audiences he wanted to reach. Even a sympathetic publisher would think twice before risking imprisonment by publishing such radical works by an unpopular poet residing in the comfortable insulation (or isolation) of Italy.

Shelley applied this lesson elsewhere, however. *Peter Bell the Third*, for instance, reveals both his keen sense of humor and his ability to merge literary parody with political and philosophical satire. This generally underestimated work reformulates the essence of the first three acts of *Prometheus Unbound* in exposing humanity's lamentable state as nothing more than a mask that obscures its real nature.[36] Shelley seems to have thought his previous performances would preclude his audiences attributing to him anything like a sense of humor: "Perhaps no one will believe in anything in the shape of a joke from me" (*Letters*, II, 164; to Ollier, ?15 December 1819). Apparently Shelley was content to regard his poem as more or less a spontaneous overflow of effervescent feeling, for he consistently stresses the poem's slightness, both to Hunt and to Ollier.

Shelley sent his poem to Hunt with instructions to pass it to Ollier for publication, insisting that his identity as author be kept secret: "My Motive in this is solely not to prejudge myself in the present moment, as I have only expended a few days on this party squib & of course taken little pains. The verses & language, I have let come as they would, & I am about to publish more serious things this winter.— Afterwards, that is next year—if the thing should be remembered so long—I have no objection to the author being known but *not now*.—I should like well enough that it should both go to press & be printed very quickly; as more serious things are on the eve of engaging the public attention & mine" (*Letters*, II, 135; 2 November 1819).

These few lines to Hunt reveal much about Shelley's reasons for concealing his identity. For one thing, the underscored phrase "not now" indicates that timing is of the essence. At the beginning of November Shelley was not yet aware that *The Cenci* had been rejected.[37] He had already sent off *The Mask of Anarchy* and the three-act *Prometheus Unbound* and had begun *A Philosophical View of Reform* (which he first mentions four days later in a letter to the Gisbornes; *Letters*, II, 150). For all of these Shelley held the highest of hopes, and he understandably wished not to vitiate the effect of his more "serious" works by becoming known at this critical juncture as the author of the satire on Wordsworth. Later, when the collective effect of the great works of 1819 might (he hoped) have finally and indisputably established his literary credentials, he would be pleased to acknowledge his authorship of *Peter Bell the Third*. When "next year" arrived, the disappointed Shelley, who had witnessed the apparent failure of his public efforts on several literary fronts, reminded Ollier as late as 14 May 1820 of his wish that his authorship be concealed (*Letters*, II, 196). By this time, however, his motive may have been more like that which had originally governed his thoughts about *The Cenci*: he may have been hoping against hope for a public success to which he might then lay claim.

Shelley's theme in *Peter Bell the Third* is familiar: the determination with which individuals and whole societies typically shift responsibility for their circumstances away from themselves and onto others. Like Wordsworth, to whose reactionary attitudes Shelley had increasingly objected, English society of 1819—and the lower classes in particular—seemed to Shelley to have accepted the faulty notion that the artificial social hierarchy reflected an inhering moral one. Hence Wordsworth's zealous defense of God's ways in *Peter Bell* signaled to Shelley the degree to which "superstition" (the term he employs almost from the start for orthodox religion) had unbalanced even one of the subtlest and most humanitarian minds of the age.

Another consequence of such misguided and self-contemptuous thinking is apparent in Shelley's other notable late exercise in literary humor, *Swellfoot the Tyrant*, written at Pisa in August 1820. This Aristophanic satire makes pointed use of the familiar topos of the "swinish multitude" coined by Burke and turned against the conservatives by radicals like Eaton (in *Politics for the People, or, a Salmagundy for Swine*) and Spence (in *Pig's Meat; Lessons for the Swinish Multitude*).[38] Shelley deliberately returns to the figure much of the callousness with which Burke had originally invested it. His point is that in behaving like swine, rooting and grunting in the filth to which their oppressors have consigned them, the oppressed have come to *consider* themselves swine. Having conditioned their own subhuman behavior, they have grown accustomed to it and, like Byron's unfortunate prisoner of Chillon, have learned to prefer the security provided by their familiar degraded and dehumanized state to the physical and intellectual risks of attempting to reassert their natural state as full and equal members of the *human* community.

Though intellectual satire tends by definition to be condescending (at least intellectually, if not also politically, socially, and morally), conceived and delivered from a position of presumed superior insight and authority, Shelley avoids taking in *Swellfoot* the purely elitist position his choice of literary vehicle offers him. His harsh rendering of the porcine populace is a calculated gesture of apparent contempt intended, like the ending of the "Song to the Men of England," to force the oppressed overtly to choose their course: to continue in full consciousness to wear the yoke they have joined their oppressors in fashioning, or act to reassert their natural dignity. That the conclusion of *Swellfoot* presents a satirical Apocalypse of sorts is fully in keeping with the pattern that informs *The Mask of Anarchy*, Act IV of *Prometheus Unbound*, and "Ode to the West Wind." In poem after poem during this period Shelley presents millennia which are at least *potential* in nature. If the various members of the human community— whatever their present status—will act upon these presages, these potentialities, a social, political, and intellectual apocalypse is yet possible.

That *Swellfoot* incorporates not only a full range of satirical conventions from the radical press but also a set of allusions that only a classicist would fully appreciate[39] indicates that Shelley is experimenting with yet another conception of an audience. A general readership might enjoy the broad satirical sweep of the piece (though neither that reader nor Shelley could seriously have expected to see *Swellfoot* actually staged), but these readers would almost certainly be oblivious to the skein of classical allusions that would speak simultaneously to the more erudite reader. For this latter reader the "Chorus of the Swinish Multitude" would in some sense constitute a patronizing gesture, an apparent concession that the masses were indeed much as Burke had characterized them and that the author joined his upper-class readers in mutual ridicule. But then, in the final scene, the Minotaur invites Iona Taurina to mount him, so that they may

> . . . hunt these ugly badgers down,
> These stinking foxes, these devouring otters,
> These hares, these wolves, these anything but men.
> *(Works,* 409)

The self-satisfied readers who earlier had chuckled happily along with Shelley would doubtless find themselves discomfited at this stage, lumped in with the subhuman hordes of "anything but men" now pursued relentlessly by the Minotaur, Iona Taurina, and the army of "loyal Pigs." In this very violent imagery Shelley ominously projects the real consequences of revolution. Shocked to recognize the part Shelley has actually assigned them in the affair, these readers might be forced into considering more carefully the causes of the pigs' suffering, the unfeeling Malthusian system whose ministers Purganax, Dakry, and Laoctonos are only thinly masked versions of Castlereagh, Eldon, and Wellington, respectively.

Indeed the humor of *Swellfoot* grows steadily darker as the play proceeds. The scenes of exploitation to which the more reactionary reader might have given tacit approval at first become increasingly terrible, and the scheming with the poisoned Green Bag so despicable, that one is drawn practically against one's will into silent sympathy with the suffering swine. Finally, in a scene that echoes the Coleridge of the *Conciones ad populum,* Shelley's veiled figure of Liberty warns that in economic distress (here symbolized by the image of Famine attended by the fat priests in her temple) lies the greatest danger to society and the greatest threat of violent revolution.[40] By the time he composed *Swellfoot,* Shelley might have taken some comfort in the fact that revolution had been avoided during the months following Peterloo. But the disgraceful spectacle of the nation occupying itself with the Queen Caroline affair while the poor continued to go hungry and jobless struck Shelley as a tragedy in human affairs as great as Peterloo. His comment to the Gisbornes in June 1820 is indicative: "How can the English endure the mountains of cant which are cast upon them about this vulgar cook-maid they call a Queen? It is scarcely less disgusting than the tyranny of her husband, who, on his side, uses a battery of the same cant. It is really time for the English to wean themselves from this nonsense, for really their situation is too momentous to justify them in attending to Punch and his Wife" *(Letters,* II, 207; 30 June 1820). From his relative isolation in Italy Shelley seems not to have appreciated that the rigorous enforcement of the Six Acts had made the cause of Queen Caroline the only effective way to rally public demonstrations against the government. Nor was he fully aware that the bizarre trial that ensued actually produced a calculable reduction in the reactionary administration's excesses.

Though he remained generally optimistic about humanity's eventual progress, Shelley grew increasingly sanguine about the possibility for real progress under the circumstances that inhered in his own time. *Swellfoot's* facade of satire and burlesque only partially conceals dark and ominous shadows of tragedy. That Shelley himself never mentions *Swellfoot* in an extant letter is, I believe, a clear indication of his own ambivalent feelings about the piece and about the part it might have played in the public forum of print, even had the apparent call to overt revolution its indignant voice articulates not been almost immediately silenced by either the Society for the Suppression of Vice or Dr. Stoddart's Constitutional Association,[41] which saw to it that all but perhaps seven copies that had already been distributed were consigned to the flames.

The Case of Richard Carlile

In claiming puckishly in his preface for *Swellfoot the Tyrant* that the work was a translation from the antique, Shelley stated that his "translation" had taken no liberties with the original, "except the suppressing of a seditious and blasphemous Chorus of the Pigs and Bulls in the last Act" (*Works*, 390). The terminology is pointedly topical, for October 1819 marked the trial in England of the radical publisher Richard Carlile, accused of blasphemous and seditious libel in connection with his publication of Paine's *Age of Reason* and Elihu Palmer's *Principles of Nature*. The charges against Carlile, filed already in the spring, had been widely reported and discussed in the press, including the *Examiner*, which generally supported Carlile. In the space of five days at the beginning of November[42] Shelley composed the long letter, formally addressed to Hunt as editor of the *Examiner*, in which he examines Carlile's trial within the larger contexts of both English justice and freedom of the press. When he sent off his letter to Hunt on 6 November he did not know the court's verdict against Carlile, who was fined £1,500 and sentenced to three years' imprisonment—though he served not three but six years.[43] From the proceedings of the trial (as he was able to gather them in Italy), however, Shelley had little doubt that Carlile would be convicted.

Even though Hunt suppressed it, we need to consider Shelley's letter here as the formal document specifically aimed at the *Examiner's* liberal readership and which Shelley fully intended for publication. Ironically, it had been the similar prosecution of Daniel Isaac Eaton for publishing Paine's *Age of Reason* that had prompted Shelley in 1812 to compose his *Letter to Lord Ellenborough*. The central issues, and the lines of Shelley's defense of Carlile, are much the same as they had been then: the injustice of prosecuting Carlile apparently for his religious opinions, the failure to provide him with a legitimate jury of his peers, and the blatant hypocrisy of harassing this lower-class publisher when publishers more acceptable to the aristocracy (and the Crown) were permitted to publish Deistical writings with little fear of prosecution. But what was drastically different was the political climate in post-Peterloo England. The government could no longer use the war with France or the Luddite agitation either to justify or to distract attention from its employment of increasingly stiff censorship and repression. In the highly volatile circumstances of 1819, Carlile's prosecution constituted a far more blatant demonstration of class oppression than Eaton's had been seven years earlier. The similarity in Shelley's views about both cases indicates both the consistency of these views and, considered in retrospect, the early date at which he had arrived at a sophisticated conception of the public role of the courageous publisher in preserving the historical well-being of English liberty.

Several points about Shelley's letter need making because of their special relevance to the principal concerns of this study. First, whereas both the style and the author-audience relationship in the *Letter to Lord Ellenborough* are frequently inconsistent, the later letter largely resolves both these difficulties, balancing passages of rational, legal, and philosophical analysis against emotional, often personal outbursts. The style of the former passages turns on legal and philosophical arguments and distinctions by means of which Shelley carefully examines the prosecution's key terminology, revealing both the equivocation and the inadequacy of language to the perverse purposes to which it is being put by Carlile's accusers. These syntactically difficult passages of complex legal and philosophical discussion are regularly punctuated by emotional, personal interpolations voiced in short, direct statements cast in clear, assertive language. These stylistic and rhetorical alternations lend the letter something of the declamatory tone of oratory.

Shelley's handling of the distance between himself, his ostensible audience, and his actual, expanded audience is interesting. Shelley addresses the letter "To the Editor of *The Examiner*," yet his salutation is "My dear *Friend*" (*Letters*, II, 136; my italics). As he so often does, Shelley forces his correspondent to play more than one role. Furthermore, publishing the letter with the salutation intact would publicly reveal Hunt's close relationship with Shelley, which might redound to Shelley's advantage with Hunt's readership, since the extent of their personal relationship was not widely known.[44] Throughout most of his letter Shelley avoids addressing Hunt directly, but when he reaches the final four paragraphs he switches to the personal pronoun: "Views of the subject [of the letter] developed themselves as I wrote which determined me to address you through the press" (146). "I need not ask you to visit him in prison; you, to soothe whose captivity respect & admiration drew the best characters of the nation, as compassion will draw them to Mr. Carlisle's. I know the value of your occupation & the delicacy of your health, & I am sorry that in this winter time I cannot be with you to assist in the performance of this duty. But the great thing is to get him a good subscription. I will contribute to the proportion of my means; I hope you will do the same, & beat up among all our friends. Let everyone furnish something, no matter how little" (147).[45]

It is not unreasonable to see in each occurrence of "you" here an attempt on Shelley's part to address not just Hunt (as private friend and public publisher) but also the *Examiner* as public organ for the dissemination of facts and opinions, and, more important still, the readers themselves. This is the rhetorical force of Shelley's collective "you." Notice in the first instance that he writes of his wish to address "you" "*through*" the press, not "in" it: "through" is not the preposition to use if Shelley is addressing Hunt alone, nor need Shelley in that case involve "the press" at all. And though the reference in the second passage to "you . . . whose captivity" overtly refers to Hunt's own imprisonment in 1813–14 over still another issue of freedom of the press (and the occasion of Shelley's first letter to him, as we have seen), might we not reasonably see in the formerly imprisoned Hunt and the presently imprisoned Carlile the particular emblems of the English people, themselves imprisoned by their conditioned subscription to the custom and superstition which Shelley believes enslaves them and which persecutes dissenting publishers like Carlile, Eaton, and the Hunts? Certainly Shelley is instructing all of Hunt's readers—not just Hunt—to "visit him in prison" and to exert themselves both "in the performance of this duty" and in contributing to the subscription for Carlile's benefit.

Part of Shelley's reason for constructing what I see as this telescoped audience becomes evident in the penultimate paragraph, where Shelley merges himself with his readers: "*We* cannot hesitate which party to embrace; and whatever revolutions are to occur, though oppression should change names & names cease to be oppressions, our party will be that of liberty & of the oppressed. Whatever you may imagine to be our differences in political theory, I trust that I shall be able to prove that they are less than you imagine, by agreeing, as from my soul I do, with your principles of political practice" (148). Presumably Shelley will "prove" the moderation of his views by means of *A Philosophical View of Reform*, about which he was certainly already thinking when he wrote Hunt. Moreover, this passage ostensibly aligns him publicly with the more moderate program advocated by Hunt and the liberals, as opposed to the potentially revolutionary republican line he appears to take in the exoteric poems. In defining "our party" Shelley forces the reader to accept him as a fellow reformer. The passage becomes a public appeal to Hunt—and through Hunt to the *Examiner*'s liberal readership—for Shelley's reinstatement in the mainstream of the moderate reform movement. Given the nature of the several major works Shelley fully believed were about to appear in England, the appearance of the Carlile letter in the *Examiner* would provide an important lens through which the specifically political elements of those works might be recognized and appreciated. Though Shelley's letter comes late in the sequence of the 1819 works, it is not incidental to them—it is central.

At the same time Shelley's letter extends rhetorical gestures of political and intellectual solidarity toward the upper- and upper-middle-class liberals, it reaches out both to the lower classes and to all the socially, politically, or economically oppressed. The point is implicit in Shelley's argument that Carlile was motivated not by deliberate malice but by economic necessity: "As Mr. Carlisle had no other motive in publishing a book, containing certain abstract principles of opinion, which he held to be popular, than the creditable one of maintaining his wife & children, at a period when perhaps every other honest mode of doing so was preoccupied or exhausted, he is entitled to an indemnification from his country for whatever losses or sufferings he may have sustained in that innocent exercise of his vocation" (147). Invoking the suffering wife and children is a conventional—but invariably effective—means of arousing sympathy for the victim and indignation at the oppressor. It suggests the cruel ripple effect that penalizes the blameless dependents of any victim of oppression or ostracism, a phenomenon of which Shelley had good firsthand knowledge. Moreover, this suffering cuts across ideological distinctions and underscores the common bond of humanity. Before he suggests that Carlile's motive was simply the proper maintenance of his family's welfare by the publication of material for which he had determined that there was a popular market, Shelley lays out the general principle of which he intends Carlile's case to be seen as an illustration: "In every instance of the exercise of judicial intolerance towards speculative opinions which has occurred during the few late years, it is consolatory to reflect that the lower orders of the people, who at less enlightened epochs, have ever been the pronest instruments of religious tyranny, invariably have taken part with the victim. They rightly judge that he is suffering in their own cause. Common friendship springs from common enmity arising from a partnership in suffering" (146).

In his *Letter to Lord Ellenborough* Shelley drew an implicit connection among Socrates, Christ, Eaton, and himself as victims of persecution, which he there defines as "the only name applicable to punishment inflicted on an individual in consequence of his opinions" (I&P, V, 289). The same sentiment informs Shelley's line here about the "partnership in suffering" that convinces the common people that the martyr suffers on their behalf. In defining Carlile (or any other martyr to unconventional, that is, liberal, thinking) he was of course also defining himself. These real and implied linkages are apparent early in Shelley's letter in his description of the Unitarian: "He openly denies the divinity of Christ, or rather, if I understand his tenets, he asserts that every great moral teacher is divinely inspired in exact proportion to the excellence of the morality which he promulgates, & that Jesus Christ was a moral teacher of surpassing excellence. He considers whole passages of the Bible as interpolations & forgeries. He admires the book of Job & Solomons song as he admires Aeschylus or Anacreon, & considers those models of poetical sublimity & pathos as no more than the uninspired productions of distinguished genius" (140). That Shelley immediately introduces Sir Samuel Romilly, "a professed Unitarian," does little to disguise Shelley's accurate description of himself, right down to the admiration for Anacreon: the Harvard Shelley notebook contains a poem called "An Anacreontic," dated "Florence—January 1820" but already published as "Love's Philosophy" by Hunt in the *Indicator* of 22 December 1819 and hence obviously contemporary with the Carlile letter.[46]

Shelley again engages in name-dropping in his letter, ticking off the names of prominent upper-class figures including Romilly and William Smith and real or presumed Deistical authors Hume, Gibbon, Godwin, Bentham, and Sir William Drummond. This is at the very least a good bluff, given the authority and reliability readers instinctively attribute to information and opinions to which famous names are attached. Shelley increases the stakes, though, when he asserts that "even some of those very men who are the loudest to condemn & malign others for rejecting Christianity *I know to be Deists*. But that I disdain to violate the sanctity of private intercourse for good, as others have done for evil, I would state names" (142). Shelley achieves the effect of dropping names by *not* dropping them, drawing the readers into still greater involvement with the letter as they attempt to deduce the identities of these closet Deists.

Pressing the issue of defining a Deist enables Shelley so to broaden the range of possibility that many of his readers might reasonably find themselves enfolded by that definition. Shelley means, of course, to indicate that Carlile does not stand so alone and powerless as the government prosecutors might hope: his peers are more legion even than would at first appear from the more customary connotation of *Deist*. Shelley argues shrewdly that Carlile's trial is necessarily un-fair because the orthodox Christians who constitute the jury cannot reasonably be accounted his legitimate peers. Shelley makes it clear, however, practically from the outset that *he* is one of Carlile's peers: "For what was Mr. Carlisle prosecuted? For impugning the divinity of Jesus Christ? I impugn it. For denying that the whole mass of ancient Hebrew literature is of divine authority? I deny it" (137). Locating this verbal gesture of solidarity with Carlile immediately before his argu-ment that Carlile had not been tried by a jury of his peers explicitly declares Shelley more fit to try Carlile in the press than the jury had been to try him in court.

About Shelley's repeated attempts to overturn objections in ad-vance by verbalizing and then answering those objections in his letter, we need do no more than credit the aptness of this technique of per-suasive rhetoric, which serves always to anticipate the reader's misgiv-ings and reassure her or him of the reasonable and well-considered nature of the writer's position. The only other point we need note about Shelley's letter involves yet another echo: "I began this letter, animated by the indignation I conceived on the first news of the events to which it adverts. I had no idea of writing any thing more important than one of our ordinary letters. . . . But views of the subject developed them-selves as I wrote which determined me to address you through the press. I am convinced that it is every man's duty to obey an impulse so strong as mine is now" (146). As in the *Letter to Lord Ellenborough*, Shelley suggests that he regards his letter as at least partial fulfillment of his public duty to oppose the institutionalized injustice that resulted in Carlile's conviction, although he again hints that he would defer to other, more forceful and influential writers, were they to come forward in Carlile's defense. But his suggestion here of a public social con-science is an important reiteration of a commitment that had existed from the earliest stages of his career. Moreover, it underscores Shelley's determination that his readers should recognize both the great impor-tance of Carlile's trial and their consequent duty to involve themselves on his behalf. In this, as in so many of his public pronouncements, Shelley offers his own experience as paradigm.

Hunt did not publish the letter, of course, perhaps fearing that he would find himself keeping Carlile closer company than he cared to do. Unfortunately for Shelley, Hunt appears to have been characteris-tically silent about his reasons for suppressing the letter. When Shelley wrote Hunt the following April, he refers to the letter as a piece "in which I must tell you I was considerably interested" (*Letters*, II, 181; 5 April 1820). The past tense is telling. Of course, so topical a letter needed to appear at once, while its subject was current, or not at all, and the past tense reference indicates that Shelley realized the opportunity had been missed. Too, he had by this time written a more compelling political tract, one less immediately tied to matters of specific topical urgency.

A Philosophical View of Reform

Remarking upon the earnestness with which Romantic artists living in an age of revolutionary commitment tended to take their own world-views, Peter Thorslev reminds us that these world-views had ethical, social, and political implications as well as aesthetic ones, both for their own times and for the future.[47] Indeed, Shelley took precisely this view and committed himself and his art to preparing the world for the better times he fully expected would eventually arrive.[48] Hence, despite his discouraging experiences, he continued to contemplate and to write on the means by which reform might yet be accomplished and society moved forward into the utopian anarchy of which *Prometheus Unbound* is the idealized prototype. *A Philosophical View of Reform* was probably begun in November 1819 and largely completed in January of the following year, as Reiman suggests (*SC*, VI, 952–54). Hailed by Kenneth Cameron as "the most advanced work of political theory of the age," Shelley's manuscript draft constitutes a penetrating and sophisticated "plan for preventing a revolution which seemed inevitable."[49] Shelley's essay proceeds from an evolutionary view of historical development that applies the essential meliorism of Godwin and, to a lesser extent, of Owen and Bentham, to a practical program for social, economic, and political reform. Shelley's strong emphasis on the necessity of educating the leaders and the masses alike, both in self-awareness and in sociopolitical principles, reflects his conviction that oppression and injustice can best be overcome through education. On this point he agreed with Godwin that the impulse for change and the means of escaping the historically destructive dialectical nature of class conflict generally must be discovered at last within, rather than outside, the individual.

Shelley wrote Ollier in December that he was "preparing an octavo on reform," which he intended "to be an instructive and readable book, appealing from the passions to the reason of men" (*Letters*, II, 164; 15 December 1819). Later, when the draft had probably reached its present dimensions, he wrote more fully to Hunt: "Do you know any bookseller who wd. publish for me an octavo volume entitled 'A philosophical View of Reform'. It is boldly but temperately written—& I think readable—It is intended for a kind of standard book for the philosophical reformers politically considered, like Jeremy Bentham's something, but different & perhaps more systematic.—I wd. send it sheet by sheet. Will you ask & think for me?" (*Letters*, II, 201; 26 May 1820). "Bentham's something" was undoubtedly his *Plan of Parliamentary Reform*, published in 1817 and articulating a surprisingly radical approach. Shelley's emphasis on the readability of his essay and his "sheet by sheet" comment indicate that he was more than willing to revise the essay extensively and to complete what was then incomplete, if he could find a willing publisher. Indeed, even in its present state the essay shows signs of heavy revision during both the initial composition and subsequent rethinking. In the manuscript Shelley takes some false steps and tangential flights, which, since he never "finished" the essay, were not fully eliminated: often he seems to realize he has gone astray and simply starts in again, refocused on his intention. In other cases ideas are left as fragmentary and undeveloped as the sentences themselves. So we must proceed with caution: *A Philosophical View of Reform* is not a finished document like the Marlow pamphlets or the prefaces to the poems. Rather, it is a rich working draft whose contents reveal much about Shelley's ideas at this time, as well as a good deal about his designs for conveying those ideas to a projected audience.

Shelley's essay shares with the Carlile letter the impulse toward solidarity with its intended audience. What Ingpen and Peck designate the "foreword" pointedly employs the collective personal pronoun in its imperative statement about reform: "Let us believe not only that [it] is necessary because it is just and ought to be, but necessary because it is inevitable and must be" (I&P, VII, 4). The English audience is addressed immediately in the main text in terms of "we," "our own literature," and "[our own] intellectual existence" (6), an inclusive form of address that is repeated later in the question, "What is the Reform that we desire?" and in the list of specific proposals for reform ("We would . . ."; p. 34). This invented audience, among which Shelley deliberately numbers himself (or they with him), is an educated one, as his letter to Hunt indicates, capable of appreciating the arguments and proposals he offers as a result of their familiarity with literature (Dante, p. 5; Chaucer, p. 6), art (Raphael and "Michel Angelo", p. 6), and history generally, as well as with the most important aspects of contemporary events in all parts of the world. As in *A Proposal for Putting Reform to the Vote throughout the Kingdom* and in the pseudonymous correspondence of his earlier years, there is in the *View* an appeal for discussion and dialogue that both acknowledges and compliments the audience. For any would-be public communicator, this is an important point, for if one desires recognition (and approval) by others she or he must likewise recognize those others and appreciate that an audience worthy of addressing is also worthy of being heard.

But if this is the audience to and for which Shelley is writing, he occasionally loses sight of them and shifts focus. At one point, for instance, he injects a sensationalized account of the laborers' suffering under capitalism in the age of paper currency. Among his details is the description of children turned into "lifeless and bloodless machines at an age when otherwise they would be at play before the cottage doors of their parents" (27). Indeed, one of the essay's recurrent motifs is the destruction of the nuclear family (and the national and universal families of which it is the microcosmic type) by the unreformed status quo. In his draft, Shelley pursues his point in strident, lurid language for several sentences, then breaks off in midsentence and begins again in a more moderate and reasoned tone to develop the general train of the argument from which he had veered six sentences earlier (27; *SC*, VI, 1013–14). Within the next several pages he makes the same valid points about the exploitation of laborers and their children,[50] but he does so within the calmer, more objective language and syntax appropriate both to a philosophical discussion and to the audience to which that discussion is addressed.

A more curious swerve occurs near the end of the manuscript. Having declared that if Parliament "obstinately and perpetually" refuses to consent to reform he would then favor universal suffrage, Shelley inserts the objection he expects his audience to raise: how can this be done if the power establishment is unwilling? Here he interjects Peterloo, writing that the authorities and the forces they command "would shoot and hew down any multitude, without regard to sex or age, as the Jews did the Canaanites" (47), and would persecute the survivors, as they were doing in the cases of Henry Hunt, Samuel Bamford, and others (including Carlile). In a transitional sentence, Shelley proposes to answer his question with another: "Will *you* endure to pay half *your* earnings to maintain in luxury and idleness the confederation of *your* tyrants as the reward of a successful conspiracy to defraud and oppress *you*? Will *you* make *your* tame cowardice and the branding record of it the everlasting inheritance of *your* posterity?" (47; my italics). This passage seems patently to address a different social class—the working class—than the rest of the essay, even if we argue that Shelley is to some extent writing for middle-class as well as upper-class readers. Clearly, Shelley's continuing indignation over the particular outrage perpetrated at Manchester propelled him more than once into outbursts of this sort. Presumably these would have been altered or eliminated entirely had he found a publisher for the essay.

Like both the exoteric poems and the Carlile letter, the essay is marked by stylistic ambivalence. Shelley's professed intention is philosophical and educational, but his language and rhetoric frequently modulate from moderate to frankly revolutionary. As he had done in the Carlile letter, Shelley punctuates complex analytical sections with sharply imaged, almost epigrammatic, metaphorical constructions in the manner of Paine. Writing of the power of the rich, which attached itself to monarchy in the wake of the Glorious Revolution of 1688, for instance, Shelley caps a long analytical passage with an effective metaphor: "Monarchy is only the string which ties the robber's bundle" (25). This is precisely the sort of verbal technique the reactionary establishment had for years branded as "vulgar," as evidence of why the petitioners who employed it ought not to be heard. To a reader or a listener, however, such statements have remarkable sticking power, as political slogan-makers have known for generations. They are a staple of oratory as well as of persuasive rhetoric; coming in the midst of a difficult or complicated passage, they possess the riveting effect of seeming to clarify and simplify complex issues, an effect magnified by the complexity of the rhetoric that precedes or surrounds them.

Shelley's essay likewise displays another feature of popular oratory in its exploitation of vivid, sensationalistic language and imagery. His description of the torture of a single Spanish noblewoman as an example of the persecution of innocent victims by the savage Spanish power elite simultaneously understates and enhances facts by making her case both an example and an emblem. Shelley probably knew some of the antislavery and emancipist pamphlets of the period which paraded details of savagery and torture.[51] Like the crime reports in the popular press, albeit with a more directly propagandistic intent, these pamphlets aimed to generate reader sympathy with the victims. Shelley's account of the Spanish noblewoman's suffering recalls his description early in the Carlile letter of how the Manchester yeomanry proceeded to trample the people "& massacre without distinction of sex and age, & cut off women's breasts & dash the heads of infants against the stones" (*Letters*, II, 136).

In this same vein Shelley invokes also the nationalistic anti-Gallicism born of long-standing hatred and distilled especially through the popular vehicle of the political cartoon. His unflattering portrait of the French—"weak, superficial, vain, with little imagination, and with passions as well as judgements cleaving to the external form of things" (13–14)—reflects a historically ingrained attitude that appears likewise in Wordsworth's 1802 sonnets. But Shelley effectively capitalizes on the point by noting that the degraded state of the French people is a direct consequence of their own errors: "Their institutions made them what they were" (14). This argument is made in the other direction in the section devoted to America, in which the young republic is negatively defined and described in terms of the oppressive structures and institutions which, unlike England, it does *not* have. All the instances of sensationalist prose in this essay have in common Shelley's desire to generate a strong emotional response, which he hopes then to bring under control and direct by means of reason, as he indicates in his letter to Ollier.

But his discussion of France and the example of its revolution points to Shelley's real purpose in the essay:

> Blind in the possession of strength, drunken as with the intoxication of ancestral greatness, the rulers perceived not that increase of knowledge in their subjects which made its exercise insecure. They called soldiers to hew down the people when their power was already past. The tyrants were, as usual, the aggressors. Then the oppressed, having been rendered brutal, ignorant, servile and bloody by long slavery, having had the intellectual thirst, excited in them by the progress of civilization, satiated from fountains of literature poisoned by the spirit and the form of monarchy, arose and took a dreadful revenge on their oppressors. Their desire to wreak revenge, to this extent, in itself a mistake, a crime, a calamity, arose from the same source as their other miseries and errors. (13)

This passage, which almost perfectly glosses *The Cenci*, points up Shelley's use in the *View* of multiple negative examples or "presages" intended to alert his English readers to the grievous error of their ways. The attempts by monarchic (or aristocratic) power to suppress the necessary and inevitable progress of human development merely intensifies the tensions between oppressor and oppressed, making violent revolution the only option of the oppressed. That retaliation and brutality typically follow in the footsteps of revolution dramatizes how the thirst for revenge perpetuates inhumanity.

I stress this point because Shelley worries here as he does in his letters that events like Peterloo may be pushing affairs beyond salvaging, irrevocably polarizing the antipathies. The degree to which change can come without bloodshed depends largely on the disposition of the masses. If they are "enlightened, united, impelled by a uniform enthusiasm and animated by a distinct and powerful apprehension of their object,—and full confidence in their undoubted power —" (47), their cause will succeed because this peaceful and dedicated "united front" will convince the leaders (or "the minority," as Shelley calls them) of the futility of resisting such a popular groundswell. Since force is not turned against them, the leaders can concede while still saving face. If, however, the masses are what Carlyle would call a "mob," if they are "grossly oppressed and impotent to cast off the load," they will lack both unity and direction—as well as confidence and understanding—and will consequently "only imperfectly fulfill" the conditions for producing change (48). This is precisely why Shelley adduces the examples of the two revolutions—American and

French—both of which included conspicuous examples of the massacre of civilians by troops (the "Boston Massacre" and the repression of the Paris insurrection of 13 Vendémiaire 1795 by Napoleon), and both of which involved England in what English liberals and radicals alike regarded as "liberticide" wars.[52] Shelley enlists the examples of republican revolutions and insurrections not just in America and France but also in other countries of Europe, the Americas, and Asia to underscore his point that the revolutionary movement is both incendiary (loosing the purgative, purificatory fires that will purge the Old World of its oppressive structures) and infectious, a comprehensive and irresistible "spirit of the age" against which resistance is both futile and foolish.

Yet because tyrants are always the last to know their power has passed, their refusal to step aside so that affairs may take their natural course engenders in those who overthrow them the horrible—but entirely understandable—desire for revenge. Only Jupiter—and this is to his at least partial credit—is honest enough to submit without further sacrificing others (except Demogorgon, whom he designs to drag with him) when his "fall" occurs: faced with the reality of the end of his reign with which Demogorgon confronts him, he collapses in a series of truncated verbal gestures and sinks with Demogorgon into "the wide waves of ruin" (*Prometheus Unbound*, III, i, 61–83). In the mortal world of 1819–20, however, there were far more Cencis than Jupiters, and the responses of those they oppressed were more like Beatrice Cenci's than Prometheus's.

Early in the *View* Shelley remarks on the conclusions the utilitarian might reasonably draw from observing the status quo: "The various institutions regulating political society have been tried, and as the undigested growth of the private passions, errors, and interests of the barbarians and oppressors have been condemned" (10). Shelley implies that the nature of political and social error lies in the substitution of private for public interest, the elevation of self over other, the replacement of the fundamental reality of the "one human heart" by a fallacious concept of the disparate many. Like the enlightened leaders Shelley hopes to enlist and educate in his own program of humanitarian reform, Prometheus adopts a broader, universal perspective that enables him to locate the welfare of the many rather than the few at the center of his public mission. It is particularly appropriate that the last passages Shelley drafted in this essay emphatically define the need to repudiate revenge and retribution as a condition of civilization and intellectual refinement: "Men having been injured, desire to injure in return. This is falsely called an universal law of human nature; it is a law from which many are exempt, and all in proportion to their virtue and cultivation. The savage is more revengeful than the civilized man,

the ignorant and uneducated than the person of a refined and cultivated intellect; the generous and . . ." (55). Another running theme in
the *View* is the millennial vision of impending change. Shelley's works
in this period consistently echo the prescience of change that informs
the pages of liberal periodicals like the *Examiner* and radical ones like
Cobbett's *Political Register*. Perhaps nowhere in Shelley's work does
this pattern of imagery converge more powerfully than in the "Ode to
the West Wind," in which sociopolitical resurrection is made a part of
the great cycle of the natural universe that frames that remarkable
poem. Though the question mark with which the poem concludes
makes it possible to argue that Shelley may in fact be questioning the
applicability to the political universe of an analogy drawn from the
natural, I believe he fully intends a rhetorical question whose answer
is implied in works like *Prometheus Unbound* which accompanied it
when it was published in the volume of 1820. That Shelley specifically
identifies his own public role in the poem as provider of sparks (and
thus Promethean fire-bringer) to kindle the apocalyptic flames of pu-
rification and regeneration underscores the connections he draws here
among himself, Prometheus, and Christ.

The "thorns of life" Shelley falls upon in the fourth section allude
to the crown of thorns and thus to the Passion of Christ, but they suggest also the classical gesture of bonding with one's comrade by falling
upon one's sword. Both these associations involve public demonstrations of one's willingness to suffer and die for a cause. The point is
surely appropriate to Shelley, who employs the latter gesture in much
this sense in *Hellas* (lines 385–89; *Works*, 461). But its negative side is
revealed also in the myth of Narcissus, to which Shelley's works also
occasionally allude. There, as Photius records, Narcissus scorned the
devoted attentions of a young male lover, Ameinias, and finally sent
him a sword, with which Ameinias killed himself at Narcissus' own
door, begging the gods to avenge his death.[53] More important still, the
passage alludes to Canto IV of *Childe Harold's Pilgrimage*, for which
Shelley had expressed his distaste upon its publication. There Byron,
having temporarily dropped the distinction between Harold and his
own self-mythologizing presence, observes,

> . . . I seek no sympathies, nor need;
> The thorns which I have reap'd are of the tree
> I planted: they have torn me, and I bleed:
> I should have known what fruit would spring from such a
> seed.

(IV, x, 87–90)

Shelley's anguished cry about the thorns is not mere gratuitous
self-mythologizing in the Byronic manner, however, but considerably

more significant. It is the cry of self-doubt that occasionally bursts from even an exemplary figure like Jesus (in Gethsemene and on the cross) at moments when the terrible burden of one's mission calls that public commitment into question. The cry voices also the emotional crisis of the lover scorned (recall his accusatory cry, "have I not kept the vow?" in "Hymn to Intellectual Beauty"; *Works*, 531), though in the context of the ode Shelley's is an unrequited love directed toward country and humanity rather than to any particularized personal lover. The complex interweaving here of the myths of Narcissus, Prometheus, and Christ (and of the self-isolating Byron of *Childe Harold* IV) sheds light on Shelley's attitude toward the risks one takes in adopting a public mission: public self-sacrifice may occasionally be nothing more than needless self-destruction, somewhat in the manner both of the young Ameinias and the narcissistic Visionary of *Alastor*, when it is undertaken for incorrect and self-adulatory motives. The depth of one's anguish may be the measure of one's commitment, but it cannot finally determine the correctness of one's motives. Hence if there is a skeptical crux in the "Ode" it comes in these lines. What follows is an assertive recommitment to the humanitarian program of Prometheus and Jesus, from whose examples Shelley may be seen symbolically to draw strength.

Like the "Ode," the *View* assumes the irresistible nature of impending change. As usual, Shelley underscores his preference for gradual rather than abrupt change, although he no longer flatly rejects cataclysmic, violent change. After arguing initially that *"the will of the People to change their government is an acknowledged right in the Constitution of England"* (8), he subsequently declares that "a government that is founded on any other basis [than genuinely proportional representation] is a government of fraud or force and ought on the first convenient occasion to be overthrown" (42). This is neither a moderate nor a gradual position, despite the qualifying phrase "on the first convenient occasion." Shelley immediately asserts that "the broad principle of political reform is the natural equality of men, not with relation to their property but to their rights" (42), one of which is "the right of insurrection," which he regards as "the last resort of resistance" (53).

As in *The Mask of Anarchy*, Shelley argues that certain extreme circumstances justify the people in proceeding to the stage of active revolution. But though violence is an understandable response to unrelenting oppression, and though its inhumanity is attributable proportionately to the degree of oppression to which it is a response, it is finally a morally and ethically unacceptable course of action because it perpetuates rather than terminates the destructive cycle of violence in response to violence. It is not simply that the model offered by the previous history of human existence has produced unsatisfactory results; rather, the model is itself defective in its most fundamental assumptions about motivation for human behavior. Like Prometheus, both the reformers and the masses they propose to liberate must rethink their dualistic models and imagine a perfected and mutually acceptable model that does not require for its fulfillment either the oppression or the elimination of the adversary.[54] This is why Shelley here suggests disbanding the standing army. To redeploy the forces of power assumes that there is a necessary and inevitable linkage between power and force, whereas disbanding the standing army might remove the issue of force entirely, clearing the ground for "an *unwarlike* display of the *irresistible number and union* of the people" (53; my italics; note again the echoes of the *Examiner's* language).

Shelley also draws an important and easily overlooked distinction in his assertion that "no friend of mankind and of his country can desire that such a crisis should *suddenly* arrive; but still less, once having arrived, can he hesitate under what banner to array his person and his power" (45; my italics). The final phrases recall the conclusion of the Carlile letter, of course, but the conspicuous use of "suddenly" recalls a passage from Shelley's early *Proposals for an Association of Philanthropists* (1812): "Nothing would be farther from the views of associated philanthropists than attempting to subvert establishments forcibly, or even hastily" (I&P, V, 258). As I noted in Chapter 2, Shelley's statement disavows only forcible or hasty measures and not the subversion itself. Splitting an issue to permit him to advocate the real need (whether subversion or radical change) while deprecating the counterproductive measures that might accompany it is a technique Shelley had learned and employed early on. That it reappears in the later works is a reminder of the continuity both in Shelley's ideas and in the means he employed to convey them to his audiences.

Shelley's assessment of the consequences of the government's failure to act earlier is interesting: "Two years ago it might still have been possible to have commenced a system of gradual reform. The people were then insulted, tempted and betrayed, and *the petitions of a million* of men rejected with disdain. Now they are more miserable, more hopeless, more impatient of their misery. Above all, they have become more universally aware of the true sources of their misery. It is possible that the period of conciliation is past" (45–46). In addressing his exoteric works to the lower classes (the workers, the unemployed, and the poor), in adopting rhetorical and poetic forms familiar to them, in using reverse definitions to define their abject condition painfully in terms of what their oppressors deny them, Shelley has been attempting to stimulate among them a consciousness-raising activity. But the *View* is intended for the higher classes of readers, not the lower. Hence he explains to this audience—who he argues to himself are unlikely to have considered the situation from the perspective of the oppressed—the inevitable consequences of continued resistance to reform. Having established that the worldwide movement toward revolutionary change is a natural phenomenon not subject to human regulation, he now implies that personal or institutional resistance is an unnatural attempt to forestall the inevitable. In this position we perceive the direction Shelley's view of Godwinian necessity has taken.

That it will be harder now to accomplish gradual reform than it might have been in 1817 (that is, if there had been a response to Shelley's Marlow pamphlet on reform) makes it the more imperative that a start be made. But it also means the first step will need to be both smaller and more careful, lest the populace, perceiving the government to be moving at last, misinterpret the signal and force the issue or even seize power in a bloodbath of lawlessness. So Shelley says, "let us be contented with a limited *beginning*" (46). If the government was not ready for substantial reform it might at least be convinced to relax its restraints on progress.[55]

It is within this framework of calculated gradualism that we must regard Shelley's apparently curious view of suffrage. Part III of his draft, "Projected Means," suggests a Shelley unwilling to embrace the concept of universal *male* suffrage: "Any sudden attempt at universal suffrage would produce an immature attempt at a Republic" (43). Again, *sudden* is the key term. Shelley's program of reform is founded on a linkage between education and liberty: while the leaders are being educated both in enlightened and reformed leadership the people are to be educated in the responsibilities that attend upon liberty. Shelley envisions a system in which all components of the social framework earn their rights by demonstrating that they understand their responsibilities. Under the ideal system of benevolent anarchy, formal public leaders would be rendered unnecessary by the universal adoption of mutual benevolence and the substitution of general societal good for individual self-interest, as we see in metaphoric terms in Act IV of *Prometheus Unbound*.

I stress this point because Shelley's *View* is addressed to the audience most immediately threatened by the groundswell for reform. He needs to convince them not only that reform is inevitable but that their own interests are best served by beginning immediately to set in motion the wheels of reform. For them to take the initiative would be a good-faith gesture that might buy time and predispose the people to give peaceful reform a chance to work. Moreover, if Shelley can prod this readership into action by apparently aligning himself with *their* fundamental interests (by advocating a "limited beginning") he might presumably lessen unthinking initial resistance and gain a more favorable reception for his proposals. Finally, Shelley seems to offer the present possessors of power a means of retaining much of that power, of controlling both the rapidity and the extent of the enfranchisement of the general populace and thus defining for themselves the nature and the number of those whom they will admit to their exclusive circle. But he makes it clear that that circle must unquestionably be expanded. In short, if this audience is willing to take Shelley's frank discussion of the causes and consequences of revolution in the spirit in which they are ostensibly offered—in a spirit of sincere concern for the audience's own best interests—then they must concede the good sense of his proposals and thus accept him as one of their own number, albeit a more liberal one than they might wish.

This, I believe, explains why Shelley says that only "if the Houses of Parliament obstinately and perpetually refuse to concede any reform to the people" is he prepared to cast his vote "for universal suffrage and equal representation" (47), and why he remarks that Bentham's proposal for female suffrage seems "somewhat immature" (44). The audience for which Shelley constructs the *View* is predominantly, even exclusively, male. Shelley understood the virulence of the attacks on Mary Wollstonecraft's feminist proposals and would have appreciated that advocating female suffrage to this particular audience could only prejudice them hopelessly against him and preclude any rational consideration of the issues he discusses. Like the repeated reassurances about gradualism, the explicit elimination of women from consideration for suffrage is a tactical concession to the audience, an attempt to reassure them, even to patronize them. Shelley had decided to argue in the *View* less for ideal than for practical reform.[56] Because the possessors of power have shown no movement at all toward reform, and because Shelley is arguing for a "gradual beginning," any suggestion of female suffrage is far too extreme, far too ambitious, for an essay that recommends at the start merely a partial extension of male suffrage.

Finally, it is worth considering Shelley's discussion here of the public role of the artists and thinkers—the poets and philosophers whom he here first calls "the unacknowledged legislators of the world." Shelley's remarks in part I of the *View* on the state of English literature develop the ideas in the preface to *Prometheus Unbound*, but they add an interesting twist, particularly in Shelley's view of Byron. Of poets and poetry, the latter of which he defines as "an intense and impassioned power of communicating intense and impassioned impressions respecting man and nature," he remarks:

> The persons in whom this power takes its abode may often, as far as regards many portions of their nature, have little ten-

dency [to] the spirit of good of which it is the minister. But although they may deny and abjure, they are yet compelled to serve that which is seated on the throne of their own soul. And whatever systems they may [have] professed by support, they actually advance the interests of Liberty. It is impossible to read the productions of our most celebrated writers, whatever may be their system relating to thought or expression, without being startled by the electric life which there is in their words. (19–20)

One sees in Shelley's reference poets like Wordsworth and Coleridge, as well as philosophers like Godwin and Bentham, of course, but there is little question that the most "celebrated" writer at the end of 1819 was Byron,[57] whose contribution to that expansion of social, political, and personal consciousness which he regards as the leading accomplishment of the age he covertly acknowledges here. Previous writers such as George Puttenham and Samuel Johnson had also designated poets as legislators, but it was Shelley's innovation to suggest that they might be unacknowledged both by the external public and by themselves, that they might not even be aware of the extent of their formative influence on the "spirit of the age."[58]

It appears that Shelley had reservations about the nature of Byron's contribution to "the interests of Liberty," though, for when near the end of the draft he began to list the "poets, philosophers and artists" (he originally wrote "Literary men artists &"; SC, VI, 1059) who might compose petitions for reform, he originally included Byron's name with Godwin's and Hazlitt's but subsequently canceled Byron's name and added those of Bentham and Hunt (SC, VI, 1060). Although this may be simply a judgment about Byron's politics, it is also possible that Shelley did not wish explicitly to name the poet he felt had so far eclipsed him and to whom he customarily adopted such a deferential attitude. It is, after all, the same procedure he followed in the pairing of names in the preface to Prometheus Unbound, where both his own name and Byron's are made perhaps the more visible by their conspicuous absence.

Shelley had no idea as he drafted this section of the essay that The Cenci had been rejected, that Hunt would suppress the Carlile letter and stymie his efforts to publish the exoteric poems, and that Prometheus Unbound would be slow to appear. Had all these projects gone forward as Shelley still had reason to hope they might, his would have been the new star to have burst upon the national horizon in early 1820, and the comet image of the View, which would have made its appearance probably in the spring (Shelley might have guessed as he composed) might reasonably be understood to refer not to Byron but to this *new* republican poet. I believe this possibility must be considered, particularly in light of the relationship (or rivalry) that existed between Shelley and Byron.

Shelley had no doubts about his own contribution to "the interests of Liberty," though. The most important autobiographical references in the *View* appear near the end in Shelley's description of the committed prophet and patriot:

> The true patriot will endeavor to enlighten and to unite the nation and animate it with enthusiasm and confidence. For this purpose he will be indefatigable in promulgating political truth. He will endeavor to rally round one standard the divided friends of liberty, and make them forget the subordinate objects with regard to which they differ by appealing to that respecting which they are all agreed. He will promote such open confederations among men of principle and spirit as may tend to make their intentions and their efforts converge to a common centre. He will discourage all secret associations. . . . He will urge the necessity of exciting the people frequently to exercise their right of assembling. . . . Lastly, if circumstances had collected a more considerable number as at Manchester on the memorable 16th of August, if the tyrants command their troops to fire upon them or cut them down unless they disperse, he will exhort them peaceably to risque the danger, and to expect without resistance the onset of the cavalry, and wait with folded arms the event of the fire of the artillery and receive with unshrinking bosoms the bayonets of the charging battalions . . . because in this instance temperance and courage would produce greater advantage than the most decisive [violent] victory. (48–49)

Here in capsule form is the program Shelley had been evolving for years, linked now with the same policy of disregarding minor differences and uniting behind the common goal he had voiced at the end of the Carlile letter.

Of course Shelley was writing about himself here. In a very real sense this passage of this particular manuscript marks Shelley's final effort to persuade himself that he might yet play an active role in his country's reform, physically distant though he was. But for publishers like Hunt and Ollier, to whom he sent his manuscripts, the consequences of the measures Shelley advocated were immeasurably greater and more dangerous, as the example of Carlile had dramatically demonstrated. That Hunt apparently neither made inquiries about a potential publisher for the *View* nor responded to Shelley's request was rude, of course, but understandable. That the essay was subsequently laid aside and left unpublished until its appearance in 1920 is a shame. For both in its sophisticated and humane view of the political process as it is and as it ought to be, and in its unreserved embrace of moderation and flexibility as central features of reform, it is the sort of reformer's guide of which the nation was most in need. That it mediates among issues and alternatives with as much skill as it mediates among frequently disparate audiences and their particular concerns, even in its incomplete and unpolished state, is a testament to Shelley's skill as writer and visionary, as patriot and prophet.

There is thus another man gone, about whom
the world was ill-naturedly, and ignorantly,
and brutally mistaken. It will, perhaps,
do him justice *now*, when he can be no better for it.

BYRON to Thomas Moore, on Shelley's death

Chapter Seven
AUDIENCES AND THE
LATER WORKS

In her "note" to the poems of 1819, Mary Shelley wrote:

> Shelley loved the People; and respected them as often more
> virtuous, as always more suffering, and therefore more deserv-
> ing of sympathy, than the great. He believed that a clash be-
> tween the two classes of society was inevitable, and he eagerly
> ranged himself on the people's side. He had an idea of pub-
> lishing a series of poems adapted expressly to commemorate
> their circumstances and wrongs. He wrote a few; but, in those
> days of prosecution for libel, they could not be printed. They
> are not among the best of his productions, a writer being al-
> ways shackled when he endeavours to write down to the com-
> prehension of those who could not understand or feel a highly
> imaginative style; but they show his earnestness, and with
> what heartfelt compassion he went home to the direct point of
> injury—that oppression is detestable as being the parent of
> starvation, nakedness, and ignorance. Besides these outpour-
> ings of compassion and indignation, he had meant to adorn
> the cause he loved with loftier poetry of glory and triumph:
> such is the scope of the *Ode to the Assertors of Liberty*. (*Works*,
> 588)

She is propagandizing here, to be sure, to some extent inventing and
mythologizing both Shelley and his relation to "the People." For the

poet to have ranged himself "on the people's side" would have been to profess an alliance rather than to affirm any inhering egalitarian relationship, for Shelley never was "one of the people." Born into an aristocratic family and afforded a privileged—though truncated—education, Shelley ended by publishing poems not for "the People" but for a deliberately narrowed audience of cognoscenti, an audience neither broad nor populist.

But even in 1839, nearly two decades after her husband's death, Mary Shelley had to be careful. Sir Timothy Shelley, upon whom her income largely depended, had forced the suppression of the *Posthumous Poems* (1824), which she had edited, and had only grudgingly consented to the editions of 1839 and 1840 when she had promised not to include a biographical memoir of the poet.[1] Like her husband, Mary Shelley had to consider her audiences, and Sir Timothy was a hostile audience of one who had to be mollified by painful concessions if she was to publish Shelley's works. Seen in their proper context, her occasionally disparaging remarks in many ways resemble devices Shelley employed in his works and his statements about those works: they are devices of exigency, tactical concessions. If we put together her annual "Notes" in the 1839 and 1840 volumes, we find in them—as any perceptive reader must have—the general outline of the biographical memoir against which Sir Timothy had specifically warned her. It is singularly appropriate that such strategic manipulations should have been a part of the first "official" edition of Shelley's writings.

Mary Shelley's comments, here and elsewhere, about Shelley's ability (or inability) to capitalize on a popular style accord with the opinions of Hunt and Peacock. They also echo the sentiments of the reviewer for Gold's *London Magazine*, who spoke for those of his colleagues inclined to view Shelley at all favorably: in a generally positive and laudatory essay "On the Philosophy and Poetry of Shelley" published in 1821 the reviewer nevertheless observes that "with all the combined attractions of mind and verse, we feel that Mr. Shelley can never become a popular poet. He does not sufficiently link himself with man; he is too visionary for the intellect of the generality of his readers, and is ever immersed in the clouds of religious and metaphysical speculations. His opinions are but skeletons, and he does not sufficiently embody them to render them intelligible. They are magnificent abstractions of mind,—the outpourings of a spirit 'steeped to the very full' in humanity and religious enthusiasm."[2] The comments seem at first self-contradictory: the reviewer's assertion that Shelley's works are steeped in humanity scarcely accords with his subsequent claim that the poet "does not sufficiently link himself with man." But the reviewer had not seen the suppressed exoteric writings and does not mention

The Cenci, although the same journal had reviewed Shelley's tragedy (negatively) in April 1820. In distinguishing between the broadly humanistic intent or sentiment of Shelley's work and the forbidding aesthetic and semantic vehicles by which the poet chose to convey that intent or sentiment, though, these remarks are not far from the judgments rendered by Shelley's own circle.

The *London Magazine*'s reviewer insightfully assesses the "religious enthusiasm" of Shelley's writing, although Shelley would probably have regretted his choice of that particular adjective. This reviewer recognized the missionary zeal that energizes all of Shelley's works. That this aspect of his work should be acknowledged would doubtless have pleased Shelley, had he ever seen the review, as would the reviewer's observations on his relation to Byron: "In intensity of description, depth of feeling, and richness of language, Mr. Shelley is infinitely superior to Lord Byron. He has less versatility of talent, but a purer and loftier imagination."[3]

The accusation that he insufficiently linked himself with humanity would have disheartened Shelley, although the reviewer's observations are not unjust. Although Shelley's writings reveal that he had moved from the general liberal Whig position of his early works toward the more distinctively radical stance of the later ones, he came increasingly to feel that his energy was largely wasted on a contemporary audience. When he was disappointed by Covent Garden's rejection of *The Cenci* and the suppression of the exoteric poems and the Carlile letter, he not surprisingly reassessed his position and opted realistically to reaffirm the opinion he had angrily voiced to Godwin in 1812: he would devote himself to becoming the cause of effects that would not become apparent until long after his own death. What changed increasingly with the passage of time was not the nature of his ideas but the manner and direction of their expression in his poetry and prose as he began to see that the directness he had termed "virtue and truth" in 1812 (*Letters*, I, 259) had apparently cut him off from his intended audiences. His comment to the Gisbornes upon learning of the death of Elena Adelaide Shelley in Naples (on 9 June 1820) epitomizes his state of mind in the summer of 1820: "It seems as if the destruction that is consuming me were as an atmosphere which wrapt & infected everything connected with me" (*Letters*, II, 211; ?7 July 1820).

Trelawny reports that when a reviewer characterized *Epipsychidion* as "the rhapsody of a madman," Shelley responded that "all the mass of mankind consider everyone eccentric or insane who utters sentiments they do not comprehend."[4] But his reviewers' repeated accusations both of insanity and of moral and aesthetic infamy, coupled with their complaints about unintelligibility, took a toll on Shelley, and his work after 1819 reflects a change of heart. The self-preserving declaration Trelawny reports is telling: "I have the vanity to write only for poetical minds, and must be satisfied with few readers. Byron is ambitious; he writes for all, and all read his works."[5] Inevitably, Shelley sees himself in relation to Byron, and if Trelawny's recollection of Shelley's words is at all accurate, Shelley's candid comparison suggests that he regards Byron's universal appeal as in some respects almost a point against that poet, an indication of questionable sincerity and commitment. Shelley is engaging in self-justification, of course, but not without reason.

Even if Shelley was writing "only for poetical minds" now, though, the major works he undertook in his final years exhibit great range and diversity. *Epipsychidion* may well be addressed to the SUNETOI, or cognoscenti, as Shelley claimed to John Gisborne (*Letters*, II, 363; 22 October 1821) and to Ollier, whom he instructed to print the poem in a limited run of only one hundred copies, "for the esoteric few" who "are capable of judging and feeling rightly with respect to a composition of so abstruse a nature" and who "certainly do not arrive at that number" (*Letters*, II, 263; 16 February 1821). Such an invented audience of ideal readers, which at least partially overlaps the envisioned audience for *A Philosophical View of Reform*, would also appreciate that *Adonais* was a complex manipulation of the Adonis myth and the scriptural concept of the Adonai; that *The Triumph of Life* directly invoked not only its Italian Renaissance predecessors (Dante's *Divine Comedy* and Petrarch's *Triumphs*) but also Plato, Milton, and Rousseau (particularly *Julie*) as keys to its meaning; that *A Defence of Poetry* demanded of its reader a sophisticated understanding of literary and cultural history; and that *Hellas* was a serious "imitation of the Persae of Aeschylus, full of lyrical poetry" and not the "lyrical, dramatic, nondescript piece of business" he later offhandedly termed it to Horace Smith (*Letters*, II, 364; 22 October 1821, to John Gisborne; II, 411; 11 April 1822). Given Hunt's inability or unwillingness to assist him in publishing his more overtly political poetry and prose and Ollier's real or assumed unreliability, Shelley cannot be faulted for deciding to write for a distinctly elite audience, particularly as it became clear to him that he would not return to England, where he might have taken matters into his own hands and secured new publishers. Nor can he be faulted for building into his prefaces the rhetorical and semantic gestures that explicitly limit this range of readers and exclude both hostile and inept readers, as Elise Gold has claimed.[6] In these considerations the particular case of *Hellas* dramatizes Shelley's dilemma.

Some six months after he had completed *Hellas*, Shelley asked John Gisborne's reaction to the poem, adding that "it was written without much care, in one of those few moments of enthusiasm which now seldom visit me, & which make me pay dear for their visits" (*Letters*,

II, 406; 10 April 1822). If his work on *Hellas* (or any creative project) now made him "pay dear," it may have been because of the mixed emotions that attended composition: his enthusiasm for his work, and for the creative process itself, was necessarily tempered by the sober realization that his efforts were likely to meet once again with public rebuffs. So he struck the familiar pose of nonchalance as a defensive and self-preserving measure. Shelley was always enthusiastic about seeing his works into print quickly: indeed, his occasional rashness in this respect cost him more than once. With *Hellas* he likewise sought immediate publication, giving Ollier very particular instructions: "I send you the Drama of Hellas, relying on your assurance that you will be good enough to pay immediate attention to my *literary* requests.— What little interest this Poem may ever excite, depends upon it's [sic] *immediate* publication; I entreat you therefore to have the goodness to send the Ms. instantly to a Printer, & the moment you get a proof, dispatch it to me by the Post. . . . If any passages should alarm you in the notes, you are at liberty to suppress them; . . . the *Poem* contains nothing of a tendency to danger" (*Letters*, II, 365; 11 November 1821). Shelley's offer to let Ollier suppress any of the manuscript is both a compliment and a concession. Given Shelley's increasing dissatisfaction with Ollier, the offer is clearly a calculated attempt to press him into action.

Like Shelley's letter on Carlile's trial or *The Mask of Anarchy*, *Hellas* seemed to him to require immediate circulation because the events it commemorated were, for Shelley, of immediate concern to English readers, to whom the poem's particular relevance would have been underscored by its preface. Significantly, while he gives Ollier the option of suppressing passages from the notes to the poem, he attempts to preserve poem and preface alike by declaring the poem (and, by extension, presumably its preface as well) free of dangerous (that is, seditious or blasphemous) material. Not only did Ollier proceed slowly, however—the poem was not yet printed late in February of 1822, and a copy reached Shelley only in early April—but he also suppressed passages not only from the notes but from poem and preface alike, including the entire penultimate paragraph of the latter. This deletion, coupled with the long delay in publishing the poem, seriously undermined Shelley's attempt to define the poem's specific relevance to English affairs.

Shelley intended his poem as "a political action" that would promote the cause of both Greek independence and English liberty by rallying public opinion in England around the Greek cause.[7] This intention is borne out by the Shelleys' earlier involvement with Prince Alexander Mavrocordato, the exiled Greek patriot they had met at Pisa in December 1820 and who joined their circle until June 1821, when he returned to Greece to play a leading role in the revolution. As Charles Robinson has revealed, the Shelleys—apparently working together as they had done when they translated Spinoza in June 1820—prepared a translation of Alexander Ypsilanti's rousing proclamation of Greek liberation, a copy of which (in Mary's hand with corrections by Shelley) exists among the Bodleian Shelley manuscripts.[8] Shelley (or perhaps his wife) subsequently sent a copy to Hunt, together with a cover letter, for insertion in the *Examiner* (though Hunt printed only the letter, having already on 15 April printed another translation). Shelley meantime sent another copy of the translation—and another cover letter—to the Whiggish *Morning Chronicle* (which had also already published the translated proclamation and so printed only Shelley's letter). Both letters call attention to the rise of the Greek national liberation movement and explicitly link the Greek cause with the interests of all lovers of national independence and personal liberty.

In *Hellas*, as in these letters, Shelley's increasingly ardent Hellenism (he had originally taken a much more negative view of the Greek contribution to Western culture) converges with his own resilient patriotism. In dramatically commemorating the momentous struggle of present-day Greece to liberate itself from "alien" occupation and oppression and thus, by reanimating it, to recapture the glory of its historical contributions to Western society, Shelley offers his perceptive readers yet another analogy. England had long congratulated itself on what it considered its position as the bastion of all that was accounted great and good in the modern world, as illustrated, for instance, in the self-congratulatory manner in which England, particularly in 1788–89, regarded its "glorious" bloodless revolution of 1688, or in Wordsworth's 1802 sonnets, or in the countless expressions of nationalistic pride published after Waterloo. In rallying his English audience around the Greek cause, Shelley meant to rally them also around their own analogous English cause. The restoration of independence to Greece might commemorate past glory but it could not reinstate it: in the modern world that glory could only belong to the most fitting inheritors of the Greek legacy, the English nation. Furthermore, Shelley's stress in *Hellas* and in his letters upon the Christian orientation of the revolutionary Greeks of 1821 (as opposed to their barbarous Turkish oppressors), and upon their position as the descendants of the founders of Western civilization, further underscores the parallel with the would-be reformers of late Regency England (and perhaps specifically with victims of political violence, like the victims of Peterloo, whose historic rights and freedom as English citizens have been violated by a repressive Tory "occupation"). But as in *The Cenci* and the never-completed *Charles the First*, Shelley elevates history to mythic status, as may be seen in part in his choice for title of *Hellas* rather than the modern *Greece*.⁹ In each case Shelley's intention is to reveal the importance to the overall welfare of his English audiences of studying the parallels between their present situation—and the options available to them—and particular events of past and contemporary history.

Hellas shares with many of Shelley's later works the multistability inherent in productions that simultaneously address different messages to their audiences. On one hand, it counsels moderation: a sort of wait-and-see attitude for which the poem offers one precedent and the preface several others. On the other, it may be seen to advocate active intervention by the people, as in the case of the revolutionary Greeks, to speed up the process by which oppression is cast off. Both messages are viable instructions to members of the same sophisticated audience, which differs only in its preference for one alternative or the other as the best means of achieving reform. Properly speaking, if both these factions were to set things in motion, even simultaneously, the two groups might recognize their natural affinity and join together in service to the cause of reform that presumably motivated both: this is the point Shelley makes at the end of his letter on Carlile's trial.

One cannot be much surprised that Ollier deleted a paragraph beginning with the phrase "should the English people ever become free" and referring to "the privileged gangs of murderers and swindlers, called Sovereigns." Given their already troubled relations, it is in many ways surprising that Ollier published Shelley's poem at all. Did Ollier, whose connection with *Blackwood's Edinburgh Magazine* had already begun, and whose profession may have lent him a better perspective on the book trade than Hunt had as a periodical journalist, perceive that Shelley's reputation was rising and that the association that had to date been unprofitable might yet prove quite the reverse? Shelley's relative ignorance of his own reputation in England appears to have been as profound as his ignorance of English political and social affairs. Cautious friends like Hunt kept him in silence or, perhaps worse, misinformed, while others like Peacock sought to persuade him to redirect his efforts into channels more in keeping with their own opinions. It is tempting to consider what might have happened had Shelley's ties been with publishers like Carlile or, earlier, Eaton—or even John Murray—and had he earlier on acquired Horace Smith and John Gisborne as agents to represent his interests in England.

I have stressed this point because *Hellas* marks the end of Shelley's overt public attempts on behalf of immediate and practical reform. Rather than merely lapsing into bitter (or suicidal) silence because of the apparent unpopularity of his public writings, however, in his final years Shelley devoted himself more consciously to writing primarily for an audience of posterity, for virtual readers of the future who might yet prove to be ideal readers. Embarking upon so ambitious a poem as *The Triumph of Life*, once he was away from Byron, suggests anything but the terminal despondency some have attributed to him.

In looking at Shelley's final years, we should also consider, briefly, his unfinished drama, *Charles the First*. He had originally encouraged his wife to take up the subject in a tragedy, according to Mary Shelley's note to the poems of 1822 (*Works*, 676). In September 1818 he twice prodded her to "remember *Charles the 1st*" (*Letters*, II, 39), but she never took up the assignment. Shelley wrote Medwin in 1820 that he had taken up the gauntlet and would write the play himself, "in the spirit of human nature, without prejudice or passion" (*Letters*, II, 219–20; 20 July 1820). He seems to have worked at it sporadically, expressing his doubts about the project to Ollier twice in 1820 and in greater detail in 1821: "*Charles the First* is conceived, but not born. Unless I am sure of making something good, the play will not be written. Pride, that ruined Satan, will kill *Charles the First*, for his midwife would be only *less than him whom thunder has made greater*" (*Letters*, II, 354; 25 September 1821).[10] Even though he told Ollier that "the Historical Tragedy of 'Charles the First' will be ready by the Spring" (*Letters*, II, 372; 11 January 1822) and offered to sell him the work's copyright, he told Peacock at about the same time that "a devil of a nut it is to crack" (*Letters*, II, 373; ?11 January 1822).

The nut never did get cracked, though Shelley had good reason to persist in his efforts. Horace Smith had informed him in April 1821 of Brooks and Co.'s failure to pay the spring quarter of his annuity and freezing of his account pending a suit brought by Dr. Thomas Hume, guardian of Shelley's children by his first wife. Though Smith proved invaluable to Shelley in resolving the crisis, Shelley was painfully reminded of the pressing need for additional income. The play was, he thought, a potential moneymaker worth pursuing, but on 19 February 1822 Gisborne wrote that the Olliers "decline paying any price whatever for 'Charles Ist'." Even though Gisborne sensibly tried to persuade Shelley to allow him to seek out other potential publishers for this and his future works, Shelley seems to have lost interest in the drama.

Shelley wrote Hunt in the spring of 1822 that work on *Charles the First* had come to a virtual standstill. His explanation is interesting: "What motives have I to write.—I *had* motives—and I thank the god of my own heart they were totally different from those of the other apes of humanity who make mouths in the glass of time—but what are *those* motives now? The only inspiration of an ordinary kind I could descend to acknowledge would be the earning of £100 for *you*—& that it seems I cannot" (*Letters*, II, 394; 2 March 1822). Shelley's remarks make greater sense when we recall his comment less than four months previously to Claire Clairmont about the "*unprofitable*" nature of writing in solitude and without sympathy (*Letters*, II, 368), that is, without a buyer in sight. But Shelley's original motives seem to have been other than merely economic. Trelawny reports that Shelley's intentions for *Charles the First* were like those for *The Cenci*: "I am now writing a play *for the stage. It is affectation to say we write a play for any other purpose.* The subject is from English history; in style and manner I shall approach as near our great dramatist as my feeble powers will permit. 'King Lear' is my model, for that is nearly perfect."[11] Perhaps Shelley recalled that in refusing *The Cenci* Covent Garden had invited him to submit another play and felt that the opportunity to influence affairs at home through the vehicle of the theater might not yet have slipped away.

But the fragments of Shelley's play suggest that it would have met with little enthusiasm at Covent Garden or Drury Lane, for even in its uncharacteristically austere form it contained a rather too overt attack on the English power structure. Like *The Cenci*, it aimed to educate by reminding the audience of the nearness with which the present appeared mistakenly to be repeating the errors of the past. Presumably the play would have developed the antirevenge line his other works consistently take, perhaps treating the insulted and degraded aristocrats, and the people generally, much as *The Cenci* had treated Beatrice Cenci. But Shelley found himself in an impossible position. Beatrice had been beautiful and virtuous: a theatre audience would warm to her immediately. But how could he make *Charles*'s aristocrats—Leighton, Bastwick, Bishop Williams of Lincoln, even branded and tortured as they are—attractive, when for most of his adult life he had portrayed aristocracy's unattractive nature? Although the several scenes in which Charles I figures are relatively well developed, those with the oppressed aristocrats and the rebels-to-be are fragmentary and undeveloped. Mary Shelley's speculation that Shelley abandoned the project because "he could not bend his mind away from the broodings and wanderings of thought, divested from human interest, which he best loved" (*Works*, 676) surely underestimates the practical side of Shelley's character that hoped yet to discover not only an avenue to real public influence but also one that would produce some measurable financial security. The seventeen years following Shelley's death, taken together with her stated preference for Shelley's less esoteric works, influenced Mary Shelley's misremembering (or her misrepresentation) of the practical exigencies of the Italian years, as did her understandable desire to create for a new generation a more distinctly ethereal Shelley than history reveals.

Of all Shelley's formal essays *A Defence of Poetry* involves perhaps the least overt rhetorical manipulation of its audience. Although it might be argued that this is a consequence of the essay's nature as a philosophical and aesthetic discourse, the fact remains that the essay is also intensely political and social. Nor are its political and social implications masked by indirectness or by abstraction: Shelley reiterates clearly and explicitly his cardinal principles of "community before self," the "one human heart," and the role and function of the poet as prophet, patriot, teacher, and example. Rather than anatomizing particular temporal manifestations of human behavior and misbehavior, however, Shelley addresses the fundamental human characteristics that have typically produced the misbehavior and likewise hold the key to perfectible (if not perfected) behavior. Although the essay addresses an audience of virtual readers possessing a sophisticated appreciation of the history and the literature of the Western tradition, it manages nevertheless to enfranchise *all* humanity, variously defined (with the era's customary gender specificity) as "men," "man in society," and "every man" (*PP*, 481 [12]).

Furthermore, Shelley instructs his readers to enfranchise those who may not presently be among the initial primary audience. This is to be accomplished by means of love, which in the *Defence* is repeatedly aligned with creativity and the imagination. Nowhere does Shelley more clearly demonstrate why he so often links poetry and morals: "The great secret of morals is Love; or a going out of our own nature, and an identification of ourselves with the beautiful which exists in thought, action, or person, not our own. A man, to be greatly good, must imagine intensely and comprehensively; he must put himself in the place of another and of many others; *the pains and pleasures of his species must become his own*. The great instrument of moral good is the imagination" (*PP*, 487–88; my italics). It is in the pains of others that Shelley instructs his readers humbly to discover their own other selves among the poor, the suffering, and the oppressed, as Christ had done in choosing the society of fishermen, prostitutes, and tax collectors and in kneeling to bathe the feet of his disciples. Ironically, this merger with others provides the surest means of promoting one's own self-interest, for it engenders oneness where faction and disparity had prevailed. The imagination, motivated by the Promethean principle of love, enables the individual to imagine the harmony of human community rather than merely "knowing" the present destructive chaos.

Shelley carries Wordsworth's view that every individual is at least potentially a poet to its logical conclusion in terms of a profound social commitment, claiming that the perception of the divine potential of the individual is experienced principally—but not exclusively—by "the most delicate sensibility and the most enlarged imagination": by the poet and by all who, cultivating their imaginative capabilities, become poets. Furthermore, "the state of mind produced by them is at war with every base desire. The enthusiasm of virtue, love, patriotism, and friendship is essentially linked with these emotions; and whilst they last, self appears as what it is, an atom to a Universe" (*PP*, 504–5). The presence of patriotism among the poet's attributes is crucial to the way Shelley styled himself from the very first. Indeed, all four terms—virtue, love, patriotism, and friendship—turn upon a directing outward rather than inward of human impulses, in a process resembling what Carl Jung terms individuation. These are the reverse of the concerns of, for instance, the self-destructive, superfluous Visionary of *Alastor*, whose narcissistic yearning for a self-reflecting ideal ironically demonstrates his lack of genuine "self-possession."[13] The poet, above all others, defines himself or herself in terms of society rather than merely of self. That the poet's integrative impulses should be rejected by the very society he or she would serve and educate is, of course, the most stinging rebuff of all. But this rejection in no way frees the poet from the socializing obligation to maintain the commitment to community, to "fear himself, and love all human kind."

There is more. Shelley implicitly attempts to rescue his own reputation, both as poet and as person, by appealing to the tests both of poetic genius and of time. In a much-quoted section, Shelley claims that

> a Poet, as he is the author to others of the highest wisdom, pleasure, virtue and glory, so he ought personally to be the happiest, the best, the wisest, and the most illustrious of men. As to his glory, let Time be challenged to declare whether the fame of any other institutor of human life be comparable to that of a poet. That he is the wisest, the happiest, and the best, inasmuch as he is a poet, is equally incontrovertible: the greatest poets have been men of the most spotless virtue, of the most consummate prudence, and, if we could look into the interior of their lives, the most fortunate of men: and the exceptions, as they regard those who possessed the poetic faculty in a high yet inferior degree, will be found on consideration to confirm rather than destroy the rule. (*PP*, 506)

Shelley's model is Milton, and beyond him Plato. In the "Apology for Smectymnuus" Milton had written that "he who would not be frustrate of his hope to write well hereafter in laudable things, ought himself to be a true Poem, that is, a composition and pattern of the best and honorablest things—not presuming to sing high praises of heroic men or famous cities, unless he have in himself the experience and the practice of all that which is praiseworthy."[14] Given the contemporary estimate of Shelley, his admission into the sanctified circle would seem precluded, if only on the criterion of "spotless virtue."

Shelley, however, turns the point about virtue and prudence to his own advantage (though he names neither himself nor Byron) in what follows. Asking his audience to suppose Homer a drunkard, Tasso a madman, and Raphael a libertine (to cite three of his suggestions of what are historically correct "suppositions"), he declares that given the long view which time affords, "their errors have been weighed and found to have been dust in the balance; if their sins 'were as scarlet, they are now white as snow'; they have been washed in the blood of the mediator and redeemer Time" (*PP*, 506). In a calculated gesture of apparent decorum Shelley declines to name living poets, knowing full well that calling attention to this polite omission makes the invisible names all the more conspicuous to the reader: "It is inconsistent with this division of our subject to cite living poets, but Posterity has done ample justice to the great names now referred to. . . . Observe in what a ludicrous chaos the imputations of real or ficticious crime have been confused in the contemporary calumnies against poetry and poets; consider how little is, as it appears—or appears, as it is; look to your own motives, and judge not, lest ye be judged" (*PP*, 506). Nowhere else in the heavily revised *Defence* does Shelley so directly address his audience as on this, perhaps the essay's most immediately personal point. Moreover, his significant melding of the prophetic contexts of Isaiah 1:18 and Revelation 7:14 in the first of these passages underscores his belief in the prophet's eventual vindication. Indeed, in invoking the Book of Revelation Shelley specifically adds creative artists to that multitude of sealed servants of God who appear in white robes as "they which came out of great tribulation" and who shall neither hunger nor thirst any more, for the Lamb shall feed them "and God shall wipe away all tears from their eyes" (Rev. 7:14–17). Time, which Shelley substitutes for the traditional Christian mediator and redeemer, Christ, will function as both healer and vindicator when the millennium arrives, compensating the ostracized and persecuted artists for the "great tribulation" to which their temporal lives subjected them.

Shelley's comment, above, about those who possess the poetic faculty "in a high yet inferior degree" should give us pause. Shelley would certainly have been conscious that he was using this terminology in telling fashion, as would, presumably, readers like Peacock, Hunt, and of course Mary Shelley, to all of whom he had repeatedly expressed himself vis-à-vis Byron in similar terms. The term would also have sent a signal to other readers who knew that Shelley's works had been branded as inferior by most English reviewers through 1820. Moreover, the audacious warning to the reader to "judge not, lest ye be judged" marks Shelley's desire to retaliate for the blows he had so long endured. His remarks indicate that he is willing to entrust himself and his works to "the mediator and the redeemer Time" for vindication, but they reveal as well the proud, feisty zealot sure of his own cause even in the face of almost insurmountable opposition. To this matter of striking back, I shall return shortly.

Shelley had written his *Defence* as a studiously earnest response to Peacock's lighthearted "The Four Ages of Poetry," which had appeared in 1820, in the one and only issue of *Ollier's Literary Miscellany*. The story is well known and needs no reiteration here. But it is instructive to remember that Peacock had anticipated Dickens's Thomas Grad-grind in urging individuals to stop wasting time writing poetry and to direct their energies toward "facts" and "practical matters" (like the sciences), which Peacock claimed were the real mechanisms destined to improve the world. Shelley's response is the response of all artists who regard their critics as myopically mired in custom and pragma-tism. He argues that poetry and art are in fact the shapers, not the artifacts, of civilization, and that as such they subsume within them all other categories of human endeavor, just as his own works deliberately incorporate science (e.g., "The Cloud"), history (*The Cenci*), geogra-phy/travel (*History of a Six-Weeks Tour*), art criticism (*Notes on Sculp-tures in Rome and Florence*), and political theory (his reform essays). Art is no mere peripheral luxury, as post–Industrial Revolution culture has often impercipiently regarded it: it is in and of the very mainstream of human existence. Blake had written in his epigrammatic fashion that "Empire follows Art & Not Vice Versa as Englishmen suppose." [15] Writing in the *Defence* some thirty-three years later, Shelley agreed enthusiastically.

Since Peacock's "Four Ages of Poetry" had appeared in Ollier's journal, Shelley not surprisingly wished his "antidote" to appear there as well. [16] He wrote Ollier on 22 February 1821 that he would dispatch "my paper" "in a very few days" (*Letters*, II, 268). On 4 March, how-ever, he warned Ollier that more time would be required, although by 20 March he had finished "Part I," his wife's transcription of which he sent to Ollier (*Letters*, II, 271, 275). Busy with other matters, Ollier seems not even to have acknowledged receipt of Shelley's essay (*Let-ters*, II, 297; 8 June 1821). In September Shelley inquires when Ollier wishes to receive the second part of *A Defence*, for which Shelley asks, he reminds Ollier, no payment: "I give you this Defence, and you may do what you will with it" (*Letters*, II, 355; 25 September 1821). That Shelley apparently did no more with the *Defence* (although several manuscript notes and fragments may have been intended for it) sug-gests that he was waiting for word from Ollier before proceeding. Yet in February of 1822 John Gisborne met with the Olliers on Shelley's behalf and reported that they appeared "inclined to try another num-ber" of the *Literary Miscellany*, even though they had lost money on the first, and that they apparently proposed to use the *Defence* in this second number (*Letters*, II, 378n.; 19 February 1822).

Gisborne had undoubtedly already posted his letter when he received Shelley's of 26 January, instructing him that, should the Olliers not publish the *Defence*, he might take the initiative and "do what you will with it—Publish it as a pamphlet" (*Letters*, II, 387). Clearly, the "do what you will" statement, made first to Ollier and then to Gisborne, indicates that Shelley wanted the essay published in some form. Although it may not have been as essential to answer Peacock immediately as it had been to publish the Carlile letter, *The Mask of Anarchy*, and *Hellas*, there is no question that Shelley intended that Peacock be answered, as he had desired that Byron be answered, *in print*. Shelley's annoyance at the delays is apparent in a final reference to his essay: in the letter in which he calls Ollier "this infinite thief," Shelley tells Gisborne, "The Defence of Poetry was not given to him to keep two years by him—If he chooses to publish it in a pamphlet (the likeliest form for success) he is welcome; if not I wish it to be sent to me" (*Letters*, II, 396; 7 March 1822). Since he had only sent Ollier the manuscript of "Part I" in March 1821, what does Shelley mean by "two years"? Had Ollier suggested waiting yet another year before trying a second number of the *Literary Miscellany*? Or was he simply dragging his feet, perhaps feeling he owed little courtesy or consideration to the poet who owed him so much cash? Annoyed though he was, Shelley continued to press for publication, even suggesting the appropriate vehicle (a pamphlet—the form of his Marlow essays) for an independently published version of the *Defence*.

After her husband's death Mary Shelley wished the still unpublished *Defence* to appear in the *Liberal*. Both Leigh Hunt and his brother John, who was seeing to the actual publication in London of the *Liberal*, appear to have been willing, but plans miscarried and the essay lay hidden until 1840, when Mary published it from the transcript that had originally been sent to Ollier and had subsequently been lent to Peacock so that John Hunt might edit it according to instructions from Leigh Hunt and Mary Shelley.[17]

Of quite a different nature, and perhaps the most ambitious of Shelley's late publishing enterprises, was the *Liberal*, which set itself the formidable task of uniting the efforts of Shelley, Byron, and Hunt in a journal that Hunt would edit in Italy and his brother John would publish in England. It is not clear who originally got the idea for such a journal, although Byron is most often given credit.[18] One of his earliest biographers, John Watkins, who called the journal a product of Byron's brain, an "academy of blasphemy," and a "poetical school of immorality and profaneness" that included in its company "the proprietor and editor of the most seditious paper in England," predicted with alarm that the *Liberal* was likely to "make a considerable noise in the world." Leigh Hunt was probably nearer the truth, however, in suspecting that Shelley was the moving spirit behind the enterprise.[19]

I believe Shelley was sincere in claiming, on 26 August 1821 when he wrote Hunt to convey Byron's suggestion about establishing a journal, that he sought no greater role than that of facilitator: "As to myself, I am, for the present, only a sort of link between you and him, until you can know each other and effectuate the arrangement; since (to entrust you with a secret which, for your sake, I withhold from Lord Byron), nothing would induce me to share in the profits, and still less in the borrowed splendour, of such a partnership. . . . I am, and I desire to be, nothing" (*Letters*, II, 344). Mary Shelley repeats the claim in her notes to Shelley's 1821 poems, arguing that Shelley's reasons were twofold: he was too proud to wish to seem to be "acquiring readers for his poetry by associating it with the compositions of more popular writers" (that is, Byron), and he did not wish to undermine the *Liberal*'s chances of financial success (which he desired, for Hunt's benefit) by appearing in its pages (*Works*, 664).

Both Shelley's letter and Mary Shelley's subsequent comments seem to me to have concealed ulterior motives, and both aimed at particular objectives with their respective audiences. Shelley wanted to persuade his friend Hunt to come to Italy; the *Liberal* seemed to offer an appealing reason for doing so as well as a potential means of alleviating Hunt's own financial difficulties. Although Byron's apparent wealth was painful to Shelley, it appears that he hoped to enlist some of that wealth in his friend's assistance, though he could scarcely say so openly, either to Byron or to Hunt. Moreover, in claiming that he had no desire *"for the present"* to participate actively—that is, to contribute his own writings—he relieved Hunt of any possible anxiety about the humiliation of placing a "distant third" in an implicit literary competition while opening the way for Hunt (and presumably also for Byron, at some point) to invite him, and even to press him, to contribute.

An analogous impulse governs Mary Shelley's note. Given her desire to enhance Shelley's reputation by underscoring his humanitarian idealism—a constant theme in her notes to his poems—she would naturally stress how considerate of others and how generously self-sacrificing were Shelley's attempts to establish the *Liberal* on a firm footing. Yet one cannot help but feel that Shelley would finally have participated—even if pseudonymously—in the venture, had it in fact become firmly established. The opportunity it would have afforded him would have been irresistible. He intended, for instance, that his translations of passages from *Faust*, like those from Calderon's *Magico Prodigioso*, should serve "as the basis of a paper" in the journal. He apparently planned also to contribute his translation of Plato's *Symposium*,[20] to which he might have appended his *Discourse on the Manners of the Ancient Greeks*.

Since Murray had by the summer of 1821 become somewhat restive about publishing Byron's works, Byron may have been casting about for another publishing outlet and might well have suggested a joint venture. Shelley, who had already made a similar suggestion to Peacock early in 1819,[21] would have agreed eagerly and would have encouraged Byron for reasons of his own. Mary Shelley's comments notwithstanding, Shelley would surely have appreciated that in such a publication his work would appear for the first time together with Byron's: not only would he benefit from the attention that Byron's work would assure the journal, but he might yet have the chance more profitably to press his ongoing public skeptical debate with Byron. At the risk of oversimplification, we may consider the *Liberal* to have rested upon a variously motivated triumvirate: Shelley (who would presumably supply much of the philosophical and intellectual impetus even as he claimed to act as moderating link between Byron and Hunt), Hunt (who possessed demonstrated journalistic, editorial, and publishing experience—and a ready press manned by brother John), and Byron (who had money and who appeared to Hunt to be in the venture more for immediate personal gain than for any philosophical devotion to the cause of liberal reform).

Shelley's involvement in this project is not unrelated to his activities as pamphleteer at Marlow in 1817. The *Liberal* would be different, however, in the way it advocated reform. Rather than addressing temporal political concerns as the Marlow pamphlets had, the *Liberal* would address the "spirit" of liberalism as manifested in "the general progress of opinion (we do not mean in a political so much as in a general sense) throughout Europe."[22] So wrote the *Examiner* in advertising the new journal in language that directly reflects Shelley's own views.

Interestingly, the anxiety over the *Liberal*'s potentially "considerable noise" voiced by Watkins in 1822 mirrored the sentiment of the conservative Tory press, as well as of Byron's friends, who were not at all pleased to hear of him publicly associating himself with Shelley and particularly with Hunt, who had long been the target of such Tory organs as *Blackwood's Edinburgh Magazine*.[23] The conservative establishment appears to have recognized that the *Liberal* intended to present its political and social program through the vehicle of popular literature by important, albeit controversial, authors and to have feared the subversive effect of the journal's intended advocacy of intellectual and aesthetic freedom generally. Had Shelley survived, rather than drowning only six days after welcoming Hunt to Italy, and had he been able to hold together the uneasy coalition behind it, the *Liberal* might somehow have beaten the odds and fulfilled the destiny which Shelley and Hunt, at least, envisioned for it. The journal, which has been called the "periodical of the highest literary quality of the first quarter of the nineteenth century," [24] might indeed have stood a chance of significantly shaping the intellectual climate of England in the ten years that preceded the passage of the First Reform Bill in 1832. Certainly the unmistakable collective sigh of relief heaved by its critics at the *Examiner*'s announcement on 31 August 1823 of the *Liberal*'s demise indicates the seriousness with which the short-lived *Liberal* had been taken by even its severest critics.

His participation in the scheme for the *Liberal* again underscores Shelley's commitment to publication. Though his conception of the nature of his real and assumed audiences was much altered from its earliest form, and though he had reached the sanguine conclusion by 1822 that his actual public audience must necessarily include only a very few of his contemporaries and must, instead, consist primarily of generations who would come perhaps much later, Shelley clearly believed that his works would eventually find an enlightened and responsive audience. But there existed yet another audience, and it was a decidedly private one, as we see in the series of lyrics addressed or conveyed late in his life to Jane Williams.

The Williamses, friends of Medwin, had arrived in Italy on 13 January 1821, becoming almost daily companions of the Shelleys until 8 July 1822. Shelley apparently liked Williams from the first, perhaps because he was an aspiring author, but found his wife less immediately attractive, writing to Claire Clairmont that "I have got reconciled to Jane" and only later calling her (also to Claire) "pretty and amicable" but "selfish" (*Letters*, II, 292, 427; ?14 May 1821, 28 May 1822). Nevertheless, the two couples apparently became close, even intimate friends.

William Keach suggests that the physical presence at Pisa of Byron, with whom his relations had become increasingly strained, proved debilitating for Shelley. With Byron installed as the celebrity of the Pisan circle, the succession of major and minor works—which had included *Epipsychidion*, *Adonais*, *Hellas*, and the *Defence*, as well as some thirty lyrics—ground to a halt, the cessation marked by the pained (and painful) "Sonnet to Byron" I considered in Chapter 5. Until he left Pisa (and Byron) to relocate at the Bay of Lerici, where he began *The Triumph of Life*, Shelley produced only some ten lyrics and a number of fragments, a remarkable and telling falling off.[25] The majority of these lyrics are either explicitly or implicitly related to Jane Williams. These are intensely personal poems—not the public works with which Shelley was so often occupied. Moreover, they are ambivalent in simultaneously suggesting and concealing aspects of their author's personal relationship with Jane Williams. In these lyrics Shelley returns to that tone of urbanity that governs *Julian and Maddalo*, exploring the theme of romantic familiarity within the context of a private moment shared by the poet and the woman he addresses, a point particularly evident in the two-part lyric "To Jane. The Invitation" and "To Jane. The Recollection."[26]

When Shelley transmits these poems to their intended audiences, he reverts to some of the same fictions he had employed earlier in his career. Sending Williams "The serpent is shut out from Paradise," for instance, he includes this note: "Looking over the portfolio in which my friend used to keep his verses, & in which those I sent you the other day were found,—I have lit upon these; which as they are too dismal for *me* to keep I send them you. . . . If any one of the stanzas should please you, you may read them to Jane, but to no one else,—and yet on second thought I had rather you would not [some six words scratched out]" (*Letters*, II, 384; 26 January 1822). Shelley had more than once hidden his works behind the transparent guise of an imaginary friend, or had adopted the old Gothic fiction ruse of "discovering" a manuscript, as he had done both with the *Posthumous Fragments of Margaret Nicholson* and, more recently, with *Epipsychidion*. Furthermore, his apparent vacillation about whether Williams is to share the poem with his wife seems like a calculated rhetorical and psychological maneuver designed more to ensure than to prevent any such sharing. At about the same time Shelley sent his lyric "Swifter far than summer's flight" to her, with these instructions: "If this melancholy old song suits any of your tunes, or any that humour of the moment may dictate, you are welcome to it. Do not say it is mine to any one, even if you think so; indeed it is from the torn leaf of a book out of date" (*Letters*, II, 386–87; date uncertain). The manipulative devices are much the same, and the reference to the torn leaf and the out-of-date book are tantalizing autobiographical suggestions, taken in the context of Shelley's implicit reference to his own publications (and to himself) in the image of the "withered leaves" in the conclusion of his "Ode to the West Wind."

There is also "The Magnetic Lady to Her Patient." At the top of the page Shelley wrote "For Jane & Williams alone to see," and on the outer wrapping he added the more explicit warning, "To Jane. Not to be opened unless you are alone, or with Williams." Shelley appears specifically to warn her against opening the poem in Mary Shelley's presence, for obvious reasons.[27] Finally, there is the note Shelley scrawled across the page of the copy of "The keen stars were twinkling" he sent her: "I sat down to write some words for an ariette which might be profane; but it was in vain to struggle with the ruling spirit, who compelled me to speak of things sacred to yours and to Wilhelm Meister's indulgence. I commit them to your secresy [sic] and your mercy, and will try to do better another time" (*Letters*, II, 437; ca. 18 June 1822).[28]

What is so striking about these poems is that Shelley converts them, through comments such as these, to very private *gifts* bestowed not upon a general and faceless public but upon intimate private friends. The requests for secrecy undoubtedly reflect Shelley's anxiety that his wife, with whom his relations had grown increasingly problematic, might understandably misinterpret the gestures—if the gestures were in fact merely an urbane posturing and not something more intimate, more physical. But these requests also reinforce the value of the gesture itself: the tendering of the gift—whether a guitar or a poem—becomes at least as valuable as the item being given, so that the poet engages his small, intimate audience in the purest sort of community. It is an idealized, platonic sort of reciprocal relationship, and perhaps little more than a dalliance on Shelley's part. But that compulsion to *give*—to objectify an idea or an impulse in temporal, verbal form and then pass it on to another, or to others—is the compulsion of the committed social being we have observed in Shelley from the very first. Furthermore, his suggestions that, like the poems, his identity be concealed hint at the delightful sensation associated with sharing a secret, with indulging in private knowledge in the midst of public experience. Even in his apparent disavowals and disguising of the Jane Williams lyrics, Shelley never ceased to cultivate and manipulate his audience. But in this case it was a known and highly particularized private audience, strictly limited in number and largely reliable, rather than amorphously public, numerous, and capricious. In many ways, it was also his last.

Adonais

Adonais is an appropriate work with which to conclude this study, for it epitomizes the way the more mature Shelley combined the conventions of genres and literary traditions with identifiably personal materials to create poetry in which the medium is transformed, the personal elements fused with an exalted universal mythology. Moreover, the poem and its preface examine with particular relevance the nature of the life to which Shelley had from the first committed himself. Hence it is also very much a temporal poem, a work both occasioned by and, at least indirectly, addressed to the professional critics of the leading reviews. Yet it directs its universal aesthetic and philosophical message toward a sophisticated and enlightened readership including Byron,

Peacock, Medwin, and Smith, to whom he sent copies, and the Gisbornes, whom he called "some of the very few persons who will be interested in it and understand it" (*Letters*, II, 294; 5 June 1821). *Adonais* illustrates in almost paradigmatic fashion the relevance of Jerome McGann's recent observation that any poetic work is "a nexus of reciprocating expectations and interactions between the various persons engaged over and within the poetic event."[29] It is a poem of remarkable continuities, an expression of the timeless nature of art and the artistic life. Like all of Shelley's prefaces, its preface is mediatory: it connects the poem's universal, mythological implications with the world of actual men and women, suggesting both implicitly and explicitly the manner in which Keats's career and untimely death are of central significance not only to other poets, who like Shelley might justifiably see in his fate the shadows of their own, but also to every individual who has undertaken the risky business of public action. The shaping myths of Adonis (in the poem) and of Jesus Christ (in the preface) powerfully define the risks and consequences inherent in all such public endeavor.

Stuart Curran observes that in *Adonais* Shelley redeems past and present for the future, creating a poem that is "both echo and light," that illuminates its contemporary milieu even as it revitalizes the seemingly dated tradition of the pastoral elegy.[30] Shelley's poem capitalizes on the irony that lies at the center of this tradition: such poems are typically less concerned with speculating on the nature (or existence) of a postmortal existence than with demonstrating "the ultimate invulnerability of this world to mortal threat."[31] In placing Keats within a mental or intellectual frame of reference in which questions of temporal fame and temporal suffering are rendered irrelevant, Shelley elaborates upon the eternal and social aspects of art (and its makers) he had examined little more than two months earlier in *A Defence of Poetry*. The relationship of the dead Keats and the living Shelley who commemorates him traces the most obvious and immediate temporal consideration. But the complex skein of deliberate references to his own elegiac predecessors defines and underscores Shelley's relationship to an undying literary heritage and to a roster of poets whose individual identities and universal value are preserved in their works and into whose company Shelley overtly introduces himself through his obvious allusions to their works.

This is one reason why Shelley painstakingly insisted to his correspondents upon the formal qualities of his poem. Telling the Gisbornes that *Adonais* was "a highly wrought *piece of art*" (Shelley's pointed emphasis), he remarks that the poem is "perhaps better in point of composition than any thing I have written" (*Letters*, II, 294). He repeated the claim in the weeks that followed, telling Ollier, for instance, that though it was "little adapted for popularity" it was nonetheless "perhaps the least imperfect of my compositions" (*Letters*, II, 299; 11 June 1821). As a "piece of art," *Adonais* is first and foremost a "made" thing, a consciously crafted artifact whose overt invocations of its predecessors serve to emphasize both the poem's place within the continuum of literary tradition and the claims to originality and fame that rest on its innovations. Cronin claims that *Adonais* reveals the characteristic "equipoise" of the later Shelley who has rediscovered his own harmony with literary tradition and who now works *with* the conventions and requirements of the various genres rather than *against* them. This Shelley, we are told, finds his own freedom from literary history "in asserting his ability to write the literary history within which he places his poem." [32] But this is not quite accurate. The *Defence* shows that Shelley was less interested in writing (or rewriting) literary history than in defining the relation of literary history to the broader history of society and culture. To write or rewrite literary history as though it could be detached from the history of civilization as a whole would have struck Shelley as a shortsighted enterprise that incorrectly relegated poetry to the periphery of cultural history rather than placing it—as Shelley does in both *A Philosophical View of Reform* and the *Defence*—in a central and encompassing position. Such a detached, compartmentalized view simply does not square with Shelley's moral and intellectual commitment to art and its place in human affairs.

Shelley set out in *Adonais* deliberately to highlight the apparent discontinuities in literary tradition to demonstrate their ultimate irrelevance to what emerges as the greatest continuity: the shared human experiences of death, dying, grief, and reaffirmation that provide both the occasion and the theme of his great elegy. *Adonais* bears greater moral and social implications than is generally recognized. Just as the poet has a social obligation, so too does the audience generally and the critic particularly. Reduced to its most elemental form, that obligation, which author, critic, and audience alike share, *is to love*. Upon this foundation all human relationships, whether private or public, are to be based.

In Shelley's view, readers must, ideally, extend this love first to the authors they read, in a gesture of charity and friendship that reciprocates the author's own gesture of giving, of sharing. Among professional literary critics the obligation is greater because they are presumed to have a duty not only to both truth and beauty but also to the enlightenment of their readers. The failure to "love" the authors whose works they assess—the failure to proceed with charity and without what Shelley would call "prepossessions"—is hence a failure less of reason than of love. It is a frustration of community, an *unfeeling* rejection of the author's invitation to the mutually creative interpersonal activity implied by the acts of writing and reading. Hence even if Shelley indeed entertained the idea that the critic of the *Quarterly Review* who attacked Keats's works had actually brought on the poet's death, it is foolish to become so enamored of this notion that we miss the appropriateness of the idea as metaphor.

That Shelley has in mind an attack not just on the body is apparent in his early description of the poem to Ollier: "It is a lament on the death of poor Keats, with some interposed stabs on the assassins of his peace and of his fame. . . . If you have interest enough in the subject, I could wish that you inquired of some of the friends and relations of Keats respecting the circumstances of his death, and could transmit me any information you may be able to collect, and especially as to the degree in which, as I am assured, the brutal attack in the *Quarterly Review* excited the disease by which he perished" (*Letters*, II, 297; 8 June 1821). Shelley says the "stabs" at the critics are "interposed" and that what the critics have assassinated is not Keats's mortal body but his peace and his fame. Shelley is of course referring to the passages on "the herded wolves," the "many reptiles," and "these carrion kites" (the reviewers; lines 244, 253, 335) and to the "fond wretch" (line 416), who is both the *Quarterly Review*'s critic and an amalgam of the entire critical industry. That this latter "wretch" is not one of the procession of mourners but is rather the invisible critic further emphasizes the multiplicity of functions Shelley has built into his poem and the diversity of levels upon which he intends it to operate.[33]

Owing to the temporal specificity the preface invokes, the poem begins ostensibly as a personal lament for Keats, which, because of the force of the elegy tradition, rapidly assumes a formal, ceremonial aspect in which the act of composition repeats the similar acts of previous elegists. Moreover, as a "piece of art," the poem is by definition a formal, public act that postulates a primary listener or reader who, like the mourners within the poem, is present because he or she shares for the dead person a prior love which death has turned to grief. This, too, is part of the fiction of the elegy. But as soon as the poem is published (or performed) its ceremonial aspect is enhanced, for the public ritual is extended now to involve many to whom the elegy's subject may have been entirely unknown. By stimulating the imagination of such readers (or listeners) to go out of their own natures and to identify with others (that is, with the poem's subject, its speaker, and the other mourners), the poet generates in them feelings of love for a fellow being on the basis not of personal acquaintance but rather of shared human experience. At this point the process of loss, grieving, and consolation that, ostensibly for the poet and some few mourners, had been a private affair becomes a public and social affair. In attacking Keats (and by extension any author, including Shelley) the reviewer exhibits disregard for human decency and either a lack of—or an outright rejection of—that essential love upon which human relationships must stand. Furthermore, to attack *Adonais*, an expression of this very activity of loving human community, as Shelley undoubtedly expected his hostile reviewers to do, would necessarily be again paradoxically to demonstrate their own misanthropy.

But to address simultaneously in his elegy the primary mourners (Keats's acquaintances), the secondary mourners (those who may have known him only through his writings), a tertiary group of mourners (those with no knowledge of Keats whatsoever but who respond to the human appeal in Shelley's poem), and the reprobate critical wretch is to be ambitious indeed. And yet, despite the difficulty, Shelley succeeds. For this latter wretched figure, however, as stanzas 47–51 make clear, there is no refuge but in the grave, for in the mortal world both the physical grave of Keats in Rome and the equally physical published elegy that addresses him will remain perpetual public reminders of his callousness, his inhumanity. This harsh treatment of the critic is a departure from Shelley's customary practice. Earlier, in other circumstances, he might have forgiven the critic; indeed his direct allusion in the preface to Christ's forgiveness of his persecutors ("Father, forgive them; for they know not what they do," Luke 23:34) seems almost a tentative gesture in this direction. Yet Shelley's own bitterness prevents his entirely emulating Christ; hence both the poem and its preface cast the critic more as Judas than as forgiven sinner. This, I think, together perhaps with the image of the Wandering Jew that so fascinated Shelley, explains the image of the wandering wretch of stanzas 47–51. And in this image of the self-tormenting Judas, driven finally to suicide by the despair arising from his recognition of his role in destroying (mortally, at least) "one of the noblest specimens of the workmanship of God" (*PP*, 391), we have also an echo of the self-torment Shelley had forecast in *The Mask of Anarchy* and *A Philosophical View of Reform* for those who, like the Manchester yeomanry, brutalize innocent and well-intentioned individuals who respond only with passive resistance. The point also directly echoes his claim in the preface to *Alastor* that "those who love not their fellow-beings live unfruitful lives, and prepare for their old age a miserable grave" (*Works*, 15). Shelley was aware, of course, of the formal difficulties posed by the disparity between the "critic" passages and the "Keats-Adonais" passages, both of which he was determined to have in the poem for the reciprocal light and emphasis they shed on each other. Writing to Claire Clairmont, he claimed, "I have dipped my pen in consuming fire to chastise his destroyers; otherwise the tone of the poem is solemn & exalted"; writing to John Gisborne (apparently on the same day), he used practically the same words (*Letters*, II, 302, 300; 16 June 1821).

His request that Ollier send him additional details of the circumstances of Keats's death reflects Shelley's characteristic attention to historical detail. Although Shelley's poem overtly advertises his familiarity with the minute particulars of the pastoral elegy tradition, his request indicates that he envisioned tying it also in more particular detail to the facts of Keats's life and death. Had he done so to the degree his request suggests he considered doing, he might in *Adonais* have realized more fully his apparent intention of again elevating history to the status of myth. At the same time, the parallels Shelley both exploits and imposes between Keats's fate and his own serve to introduce himself into the mythology he is creating, for a number of important reasons.

As he does in other prefaces, Shelley pairs authors in the preface to *Adonais*, though to a somewhat different effect: "It may be well said, that these wretched men know not what they do. They scatter their insults and their slanders without heed as to whether the poisoned shaft lights on a heart made callous by many blows, or one, like Keats's composed of more penetrable stuff. One of their associates, is, to my knowledge, a most base and unprincipled calumniator" (*PP*, 391). The dualistic either-or structure, with Keats named as the vulnerable poet, invites the reader to supply Shelley's name as the hardened heart, which is of course how he read his own situation in 1821. In a sense his language serves notice that he will require more killing than Keats had. But this passage carries interesting echoes of Shelley's comments elsewhere, and a brief consideration of these resonances sheds additional light on Shelley's poem and its preface.

Shelley had, of course, been attacked repeatedly by the conservative voice of the *Quarterly Review*. He had in November 1820 drafted a letter to William Gifford in his capacity as editor of the *Quarterly* to defend not himself but Keats. Recounting the story of Keats's supposed extreme physical reaction to John Wilson Croker's review of *Endymion*, published in the April 1818 issue, Shelley chastises both Gifford and his reviewer for focusing on the poem's deficiencies while ignoring its attributes: "Why it should have been reviewed at all, excepting for the purpose of bringing its excellencies into notice I cannot conceive" (*Letters*, II, 252). Although the letter apparently was never sent,[34] Shelley's defense of Keats on the grounds of both human decency and objective critical judgment (he says he has instructed his bookseller to send Gifford a copy of the *Lamia* volume of 1820, that he might judge of Keats's progress), recalls the criteria he wished applied to himself, even as it reflects his characteristic sympathy for the maligned and the persecuted. Probably he did see in Keats a less resilient, more vulnerable reflection of himself, although there is no mistaking from this letter and from his recorded comments elsewhere his considerable aesthetic and intellectual differences with Keats. And probably, too, he was deliberately channeling a measure of his own self-pity through the figure of the unfortunate Keats, which strategy might enable him to deflect charges of public self-pity away from himself and to some extent onto Keats, his ostensible subject.

Shelley began his letter in an interesting fashion:

> Sir,
>
> Should you cast your eye on the signature of this letter before you read the contents you might imagine that they related to a slanderous paper which appeared in your review some time since. I never notice anonymous attacks. The *wretch* who wrote it has doubtless the additional reward of a consciousness of his motives, besides the *30 guineas* a sheet or whatever it is that you pay him. Of course you cannot be answerable for all the writings which you edit, & *I* [Shelley's emphasis] certainly bear you no ill will for having edited the abuse to which I allude—indeed I was too much amused by being compared to Pharoah [sic] not readily to forgive editor printer publisher stitcher or any one, *except the despicable writer*, connected with something so exquisitely entertaining. Seriously speaking, I am not in the habit of permitting myself to be disturbed by what is said or written of me, though I dare say I may be condemned sometimes justly enough.—But I feel in respect to the writer in question, that 'I am there sitting where he durst not soar—' (*Letters*, II, 251; my italics)

Shelley's attempts to manipulate Gifford by acknowledging his pressing responsibilities as editor, by excusing him from blame—even forgiving him—and by adopting a posture of amusement rather than injury (exaggerating the effect by forgiving even the stitcher) are consistent with practices he employed throughout his career. But why did Shelley hit on "30 guineas a sheet" as a guess at the reviewer's payment? Since he indicates he does not know what the rate actually is, it seems more than mere coincidence that he suggests exactly the number of pieces of silver paid Judas for betraying Christ. The emphasized language in the paragraph prefigures the preface to *Adonais*, as does the subsequent discussion of the review of *Endymion* and its effects on Keats. Shelley must have kept this draft at hand, drawing on it when he came to compose his preface.

Among the Bodleian manuscripts is a draft of an earlier—and presumably also unsent—letter to Gifford,[35] written after Shelley had read the journal's attack on *The Revolt of Islam*, which had appeared in April 1819 and which he had specifically asked Ollier to send him (*Letters*, II, 119; 6 September 1819). This review is undoubtedly the "slanderous paper" to which Shelley refers in the letter quoted above and which Shelley suspected Southey had written.[36] In the concluding paragraph the reviewer returns to his *ad hominem* attack on Shelley, threatening publicly to "unmask" him: "—if we might withdraw the veil of private life, and tell what we *now* know about him, it would be indeed a disgusting picture that we should exhibit."[37] Responding, Shelley demands that the reviewer produce the evidence that "what he *now* knows to the disadvantage of [Shelley's] personal character affords 'an unanswerable comment' on the text, either of his review or [Shelley's] poem" (*Letters*, II, 130). Though he did not send this letter, he remembered both the review and, more particularly, his response, for his comment in the preface to *Adonais* that "to my knowledge" one of the *Quarterly*'s reviewers is a base calumniator adopts the reviewer's terminology, turning the point of *ad hominem* attacks against that reviewer and, by extension, against all journals that, like the *Quarterly Review*, make critical objectivity subservient to ideology.

Shelley normally resisted the temptation to retaliate, to answer injury with injury in responding to his critics: to do so, he believed, would be to repeat the errors of history and to surrender to the destructive cycle of revenge against which he always argued. But his draft to Gifford in Keats's defense foreshadows the tactic he adopts in *Adonais*. There the indisputable fact of Keats's death and the supposed "fact" of the reviewers' complicity in that death affords Shelley both a reason for publicly rising to Keats's defense and a means of doing so. In composing his memorial for Keats he effectively composes one also for himself. The figure of stanza 34 whose "ensanguined brow" is "like Cain's or Christ's" is to some extent Shelley, yet it is a composite of all artists, all thinkers, all reformers, who, like Adonais, are both the authors and the victims of their own well-intentioned efforts. It has been argued that, from a Jungian perspective, Christ represents both self and ego, both sacrificing priest and sacrificial victim: "He is the agent who extracts from himself the redeeming blood."[38] In this context the figure of stanza 34 recalls the "Ode to the West Wind," whose image of the speaker falling upon the thorns of life implicitly links Shelley both with Christ and with the outcast Cain who is in so many ways the antinomian prototype for protagonists in both Shelley's and Byron's works.[39]

This composite mythological nature informs the "one frail Form" whose thoughts, "Like raging hounds, their father and their prey," pursue him "o'er the world's wilderness" (stanza 31). Shelley overtly links this figure with Actaeon, but his cypress-cone thyrsus with its ivy tresses tie him also to Dionysus. Interestingly, one Orphic interpretation of the Dionysus myth connects Dionysus with Narcissus. According to Proclus the infant Dionysus (or Zagreus—"torn to pieces"—as he is known in this variant) was torn to pieces by the Titans as he was playing with a mirror. Infatuated with his own image, Dionysus fell victim to a yearning for self-realization that resulted in his being "confined in matter (incarnated)" and thus made susceptible to dismemberment.[40] The incarnation and symbolic dismemberment by crucifixion and side-piercing undergone by Christ provide an obvious parallel, with the significant difference that Christ's sufferings and death are deliberately chosen in a fully informed act of love and self-sacrifice rather than endured as a consequence of blundering into mistaken self-adulation. Of course, Shelley regarded his own treatment by critics and public alike as a dismemberment of sorts and would have argued that his motives for public action were more akin to Christ's than to Actaeon's or Dionysus's.

The account of the conflict between Dionysus and King Pentheus offers another significant foreshadowing of the final phase of Christ's life. When Pentheus dispatched a servant in charge of an armed guard to seize Dionysus, the servant returned bewildered, for Dionysus had held out his hands and submitted to the shackles with a smile. Though he was struck by the radiant beauty of Dionysus, Pentheus nevertheless treated him as a vagabond and an adventurer feigning to be a god and had him chained and imprisoned. But at a word from the god the earth shook, walls crumbled, and Dionysus's bonds dissolved, enabling him to appear, transfigured into even greater loveliness, among his worshipers.[41] The obvious parallels with the passion, death, and resurrection of Christ would not have escaped Shelley, nor would he have failed to derive from them further reinforcement for his belief that his work (and he) would outlive those who had castigated and persecuted him during his lifetime.

Finally, the myth of Dionysus adds two other elements to the complex mythological parallels at work in *Adonais*. Dionysus is linked to the release of mass emotion, in which context he was associated with the communal rites that gave birth to the Athenian theater. The release of powerful irrational impulses through controlled ritual was, according to Aristotle, an essential catharsis that facilitated relaxation, relief, and restoration.[42] The calming effect associated with the figure in Shelley's poem facilitates the progress of narrator and fellow mourners alike to the next stage of reconciliation and reaffirmation. Furthermore, when we recall that the death of vegetation was regarded as marking Dionysus's flight to avoid the sentence of his enemies—even his extinction[43]—we discover yet another level of significance in Shelley's brilliant manipulation of images of vegetation and the seasons in his poem.[44]

The rich texture of pre-Christian and Christian associations makes all the more curious the insistence of some critics upon seeing the "one frail Form" narrowly as merely an embarrassingly self-indulgent Shelleyan self-portrait. The poem's deliberate exaggerations are a part of the conventional heightening of effect inherent in the pastoral elegiac tradition, in which grief is diffused through the physical body and manifested in external phenomena. The Shelley of the Pisan circle was not the "companionless" "phantom among men" fleeing "with feeble steps" which stanza 31 describes. That many of the descriptive details reflect Shelley's own attitude and appearance is inevitable, but this Dionysiac figure is, as stanza 32 tells us, not any particular poet but rather the spirit of poetry:

> A pardlike Spirit beautiful and swift—
> A Love in desolation masked;—a Power
> Girt round with weakness;—it can scarce uplift
> The weight of the superincumbent hour;
> It is a dying lamp, a falling shower,
> A breaking billow . . .

This "herd-abandoned deer struck by the hunter's dart" (line 297) is Poetry in the dark hour of the summer of 1821, pushed aside by a nation—indeed a civilization—so mired in custom, so blinded by superstition, and so incapacitated by self-paralysis that it has lost sight of what the ancient Greeks had understood, that "poets are the unacknowledged legislators of the World" and that poetry provides the vehicle for the catharsis of which the nation—indeed the world—has such pressing need.

That Shelley is personifying Poetry in the "one frail Form," and not merely engaging in public self-indulgence, is further indicated by his pointed use in stanza 32 of neuter rather than masculine pronouns, which have the effect of deflecting our attention from the masculine figure that precedes and follows this stanza and focusing it instead on the essence rather than the form of that figure. That Shelley specifically wishes to minimize—even if he does not wish entirely to eliminate—the self-vindication associated with this figure is indicated also by his accession to John Taaffe's apparent suggestion that he remove from the preface an intensely personal passage on his own relation to the critics, though he rejected Taaffe's suggestions about similarly altering the poem itself. Since no fair copy of the preface is known, the passage Shelley deleted has to be reconstructed—or perhaps more correctly, intuited—from his notebook drafts.[45] We may gather the sense of the comments Shelley deleted, however, from this remark on literary critics, which occurred early in the draft material: "Reviewers, [are generally] with some rare exceptions are in general a most stupid & malignant race; and as a bankrupt thief turns thief taker in despair, so an unsuccessful author turns critic & [?eats?] punishes others of that [—]" (MS fol. 5r). Presumably Shelley numbers himself among the exceptions.

Among the draft passages that do not appear in any form in the preface as finally published is a description of Shelley's motives, as he saw them, both for writing generally and for voicing his personal complaints at this time in particular:

> [This expression of my indignation & sympathy] [extracted] wrested from my sore [?some?] indignation & [sympathy] my pity I will allow myself a [brief] first & a last word on public calumny the subject [of calumny] as it relates to m[e]y own person [and] then all further *public* discussions as must be closed.—As an author I have dared & invited censure; [my opinions] if I understand myself I have written neither for profit nor for fame. I [have sought to erect] have employed a sympathy between my species & myself [publication] poetical [other] my compositions & publications simply as the instruments of that sympathy between myself & [my species] others. which the ardent & unbounded love I [felt] cherished for my kind, [sought] [demanded as its] [demanded that][46] incited me to acquire I [expected all sort of stupidity [?&?] unsocial[47] contempt from those] (Bodleian MS Shelley adds. e. 20, fol. 11r)

Shelley pointedly renounces as motives both fame and fortune, though during this period he had hoped desperately to acquire at least enough of the latter to enable him to meet his many financial obligations. Fame, of course, would have much facilitated his ability to advance his programs of reform and renovation by gaining him a receptive audience, but after the earliest works it was less and less a primary objective. Shelley's adoption of the present perfect verb tense ("I have written") is thus interesting in that it denotes a process that has ended. "Until now," in other words, Shelley's motives have been philanthropic and social, proceeding from his shared status (or "sympathy") as a human being. The implication of Shelley's words is that this bond has been significantly weakened or even broken, that he has reached a turning point, and that he is now redirecting his efforts.

This change of course is marked also by his declaration that after this single outburst he plans to refrain from any further "*public* discussions." Although a cursory, careless reading might suggest that Shelley plans now to keep his silence, a more careful reading reveals that he intends only to cease raising his voice publicly: the campaign will now proceed on a private scale, in the fashion of the guerrilla warfare by which the Creature attempts to undermine and to destroy Victor Frankenstein. The end of the passage raises the unpleasant suggestion that Shelley now habitually expected his efforts to be attacked and that, moreover, he was building into his works a more consciously self-serving martyr's defense. This is, however, the Shelley of 1821. As late as the end of 1819, Shelley did not anticipate rejection and abuse as his only responses; he expected to win over both hostile and indifferent audiences.

Another passage, following close upon the first, is similarly revealing: "As a man, I shrink from notice & regard; the ceaseless ebb & flow of the world [?vexes?][48] me; [My habits are simple] [I have] [I desire to have] [I wa] [am] I desire to be left in peace. [I have been the victim of] [It was natural to expect that an oppression] [that the tyranny that] a monstrous and unheard of [the number of] [that] I am the victim of [oppression] a [tyranny] despotic power which has violated in my home the rights of nature & has" (fol. 13r). Shelley's great agitation is evident from the repeated false starts and cancellations in the manuscript. Startlingly moving, however, among the many crossouts is the stark and telling sentence, clear and uncanceled "I desire to be left in peace," which predates by less than three months his statement to Hunt that "I am, and I desire to be, nothing" (*Letters*, II, 344). This passage again underscores Shelley's indignation at the *ad hominem* attacks to which he has been subjected, since he considers all such personal matters irrelevant to judgments about his work *as poet*. His point is that to attack his poetry on the basis of a stated or unstated objection to his personal life is not only unprofessional but uncharitable and unethical. His first sentence implies the parallel assertion he had made earlier: while he shrinks from notice and regard as a private individual, he has been willing to face the consequences of his public activity as poet and patriot. The distinction was important to Shelley, even if it was not to his detractors.

The final, incomplete sentence of this last passage alludes to the Chancery decision depriving him of his children by Harriet Shelley, to which injury he returns repeatedly in both explicit and implicit references in his poetry and prose alike. Soon after, he tries again to express his resentment: "[I have been made the victim of a tyranny] domestic conspiracy [of] and legal oppression combined have violated in my person the most sacred rights of Nature & of humanity; [My health is] [my health is—] [I am] [my health is] [my]" (fol. 14r). The final three lines on this page of the notebook are nearly indecipherable. Anthony Knerr posits a tentative reading that includes a possible reference to the "chastising" of Shelley's health and spirits, presumably as a result of both the Chancery action and the hostile criticism. Were this reading accurate, as it may well be, it would supply further evidence of the striking parallels between the situations of Keats and himself that Shelley was consciously exploiting. But the "hardened" heart passage of the published preface indicates a crucial difference. Earlier in his drafts Shelley writes: "The offence of this poor victim seems to have consisted solely in his intimacy with Leigh Hunt Mr. Hazlitt & some other [friends] of the enemies of despotism & superstition. My friend Hunt has a very hard skull to crack & should take a great deal of killing" (fol. 9r). Left unspoken but implied is Shelley's conviction of the hardness of his own skull.

It seemed to Shelley that Keats was not sufficiently hardened to the slings and arrows of outrageous reviews. Perhaps his humble origins, his less sophisticated education, and his somewhat closeted life struck Shelley as factors contributing nearly as much as his delicate constitution to Keats's inability to withstand the criticism leveled at him. He writes later in the canceled section: "[But a young mind /is seldom armed/] panting after fame is the most vulnerable thing:[49] he is armed neither with philosophy] [But let it be considered that an animat] [But] [It is] But a young spirit panting for fame, doubtful of its powers & certain only of its aspirations is [ill qualified] not fitted to assign its true value to the [?shouts?] [?clapping?] the success of this deceitful world" (fol. 15r). Since this passage comes after that in which Shelley has disavowed any real interest in fame on his own part, it marks what seems to have struck Shelley as Keats's greatest weakness: his lack of self-confidence. Did Shelley's opinion stem from Keats's graceful but honest rejection of his overtures toward greater familiarity? Keats had been concerned about being overly influenced by the strong-willed Shelley. Certainly Shelley would have attempted, given the opportunity, to "convert" and direct Keats, as he had tried to do with Byron. Despite Shelley's apparently increasing regard for Keats (Shelley was not much impressed with his early poetry but found especially in *Hyperion* the signs of emerging poetic genius), and despite his well-intentioned invitation to Keats to join the Shelleys in Italy (a proposal whose execution would have imposed even greater pressures upon the Shelleys' limited space and finances), Shelley and Keats held significantly different views of the poet as public, political leader. This, in itself, undoubtedly served as a considerable check on any inclination on Keats's part for greater intimacy.

Shelley finally saw the sense of Taaffe's objections to his intensely personal comments:

> Accept also my thanks for your strictures on Adonais. The first I have adopted, by cancelling in the preface the whole passage relating to my private wrongs.—You are right: I ought not to shew my teeth before I can bite, or when I cannot bite. I am afraid that I must allow the obnoxious expressions if such they are, to which you so kindly advert, in the Poem itself, to stand as they are. . . . if you are not discouraged by my liberty in

accepting & rejecting your valuable advice, I would pray you to favour me still further with it,—as I consider myself to have been essentially benefited by the adoption of the cancel in the preface. (*Letters*, II, 306; 4 July 1821)

Shelley's comments suggest that he would bide his time until he might take on his detractors from a position of strength. The image of teeth-baring and biting is particularly intriguing in light of a draft in a note-book apparently dating from this period of a poem about a serpent and a mastiff.[50] In that fragmentary poem the poisonous serpent (Shelley first wrote "snake" but canceled it for the more powerfully charged associations of the Edenic serpent) visits a mastiff (traditional symbol for the shepherd/priest who guides and protects his human flock[51] and a friendly—Shelley says "good"—inversion of the grim mastiff that guards Pluto's stronghold in the myth of Proserpine). The serpent wears "a certain alluring grin," smiling beneath his crimson hood "as shily and sweetly as sin / To the welcoming growl of the mastiff good."[52] There are undoubtedly autobiographical elements at play in Shelley's poem (Byron had jocosely dubbed him the "snake," after all), even as there are certainly echoes of Coleridge's "Christabel." It may not be amiss to see in this curious half-echo of imagery some connection between Shelley's letter to Taaffe and the poems he was writing at the time.

Of more substantive use in understanding Shelley's intentions and performance in *Adonais* and its preface is a letter he wrote Byron in July when he sent him a copy of *Adonais*:

I need not be told that I have been carried too far by the enthusiasm of the moment; by my piety, and my indignation, in panegyric. But if I have erred, I console myself by reflecting that it is in defence of the weak—not in conjunction with the powerful. And perhaps I have erred from the narrow view of considering Keats rather as he surpassed *me* in particular, than as he was inferior to others: so subtle is the principle of self! I have been unwillingly, and in spite of myself, induced to notice the attack of the *Quarterly* upon me; it would have been affectation to have omitted the few words in which I allude to it. I have sought *not* to qualify the contempt from which my silence has hitherto sprung—and at the same time to prevent any paper war, as it regards my case; which, averse as I am from all wars, is the only one which I should unconditionally avoid. (*Letters*, II, 308–9; 16 July 1821)

Since Shelley had by now removed from the preface the passage that had bothered Taaffe, the allusions he mentions to Byron are probably those to the "base and unprincipled calumniator" and the "heart made callous."[53] The fury reflected in the manuscript drafts of the preface largely bears out Shelley's contention that he wrote almost in spite of himself; they appear to constitute a flood of therapeutic self-expression which Shelley felt was nevertheless relevant to his argument vis-à-vis Keats. Shelley may have wished to avoid a "paper war," but his two letters to Southey regarding the review reveal an angry and intemperate spirit so poorly held in check that the offended Southey refused further correspondence with Shelley.[54] But though Shelley voices his anger in his private correspondence, he had decided that his public posture would be as coolly unflappable as he could manage. It is never easy to be Promethean in public, but in print it is always necessary.

Naturally, in sending the copy of *Adonais* to Byron Shelley felt compelled to assume his customary posture of self-deprecation: "As to the Poem I send you, I fear it is worth little. Heaven knows what makes me persevere (after the severe reproof of public neglect) in writing verses; and Heaven alone, whose will I execute so awkwardly, is responsible for my presumption" (*Letters*, II, 309). Shelley's letters to his other correspondents reveal that, for the most part, he was sincere in flatteries of this sort, even if he was essentially incorrect in rating his own abilities beneath Byron's. He saw in Byron not only the greatest poet of the age. If such a surpassing poetic genius as Shelley considered him to be—regardless of what Shelley or anyone else may have thought about Byron's personal life—could be enlisted in the cause of humanitarian reform, what advances might not yet be possible? This had been Shelley's objective from the first: to enlist and redirect that massive talent in support of reform, both political and social. Indeed the next paragraph of Shelley's letter again encourages Byron to "write a great and connected poem, which shall bear the same relation to this age as the 'Iliad', the 'Divina Commedia', and 'Paradise Lost' did to theirs." This is one reason why I have stressed Shelley's repeated efforts to find in the vehicle of print a forum for what he appears to have regarded as the public skeptical debate with Byron. Shelley saw clearly the immense influence Byron was capable of exerting, and he felt that influence must be either answered or redirected. Significantly, Shelley increasingly stresses the option of redirection, the option of answering directly having been rendered impracticable by the "reproof" administered to his own efforts by public neglect.

The second paragraph of this letter to Byron in many ways epitomizes Shelley's paradoxical view of his public career as a writer. His comments, written only eight days short of a year before he drowned in the Bay of Lerici, underscore the extent to which Shelley's life seems almost to have approached the nature of self-fulfilling prophecy. From his exile in Pisa he offers one of his own works to Byron—"as Diomed gave Glaucus his brazen arms for those of gold"—as an exchange in advance for the recent poems he had asked Byron to send him, poems he both overtly and by analogy concludes will outstrip his own efforts. Then he traces his relation with Keats, as he viewed it as fact and as he had mythologized it in the preface and verse of *Adonais*. He dwells on the injuries his critics have done him, implying their large responsibility for the lack of an audience he goes on to lament. "There for the present it rests," he writes. Then comes the remarkable passage quoted just above, in which Shelley echoes the platonic view of the inspired artist whose activities and productions are only partly under his or her control. His remarks suggest Shelley's view of the artist as messenger and instrument of the divine power (perhaps of pure idea, as suggested elsewhere) that shapes and moves the universe. "Heaven" has been his motivation and his inspiration, even as he has called upon the west wind to inspire (to blow into—and through) him in his great ode. Driven by divine inspiration, Shelley has, like Adonais, composed his works and played his public role at times almost against his own will. But if the speaker in the "Ode to the West Wind" is inspired—played—by the wind, he comes at last to assume an active role, supplying the wind to sound the trumpet. If the artist is at times an eolian harp—or even a trumpet—sounded initially by an external force of inspiration, he or she is also a trumpeter, objectifying and publicizing that inspired vision through conscious, calculated volitional acts. And in sounding that trumpet the artist implicitly accepts both the opportunities and the risks, the potential rewards and the potential dangers to self and to psyche.

Edwin Edinger regards the conscious acceptance of the psychological trials inherent in this risk-taking as an expression of "the ego attitude needed in the face of an individuation crisis." In Edinger's view, when an individual is able to achieve and sustain this attitude of psychological self-sufficiency—this willingness to accept potential reversals as a necessary but endurable component of one's private and public role and identity—"support from the archetypal psyche is usually forthcoming."[55] Under such circumstances the anxiety that accompanies the perception of one's vulnerability as an individual is superseded by the inner peace that proceeds from the recognition that one is not "alone" but is rather a participant in a universal design that encompasses the entire community of humankind. With this recognition comes the awareness that in accepting one's suffering in an informed manner one joins the company of the many others who have gone the same way before.

Writing in *The Poet and His Audience*, Ian Jack remarks that Dryden never wrote a line without considering its effect on his readers, adding that much the same was surely true of Chaucer, Pope, and Byron. But, Jack continues, "Shelley never came to terms with the elementary fact that it is part of a poet's task to be constantly aware of the likely reactions of his audience."[56] Jack's position echoes those of Peacock (whom he quotes), Hunt, and Mary Shelley. It is a view stunning in its disregard of the facts of Shelley's writings. When Shelley remarks of a work, as he does to Horace Smith about *Adonais*, that he has written "as usual, with a total ignorance of the effect that I should produce" (*Letters*, II, 349; 14 September 1821), he is engaging in rhetorical posturing. One does not write such a poem, nor introduce it with the sort of preface Shelley composed, in "total ignorance" of its potential effect. Although Shelley sometimes misconceived the nature of the readerships for which he specifically designed various works, he never worked in the critical and cultural vacuum to which Jack—and others who share his position—would relegate him.

It is impossible definitively to document Shelley's relations with his audiences. Even if we could somehow account for all the formative influences that coalesced in Shelley's printed works, we could never hope fully to trace the infinite number of ways in which those works were read in his own time. Nor can we entirely account for how they are read today, when not only the language itself but also its entire social, political, intellectual, and aesthetic framework—indeed the entire framework of culture that surrounds, permeates, and absorbs text and readers alike—has evolved into something quite unlike what it was when those words first appeared. But we need to bear these concerns in mind if we are more fully to appreciate how Shelley viewed both his works and himself as their author and if we are more accurately to see him as a man *of* his times who was very much involved *in* his times. For *involved* is the word that perhaps best characterizes Shelley's relationship to his world and to the various audiences he sought repeatedly to address.

That Shelley fully appreciated the difficulty of rendering passionately held ideas in words that might do full justice to those ideas is amply illustrated by his painstakingly revised manuscripts. It is a familiar difficulty for which his simile of the fading coal is extraordinarily appropriate:

> Poetry is not like reasoning, a power to be exerted according to the determination of the will. A man cannot say, "I will compose poetry." The greatest poet even cannot say it: for the mind in creation is as a fading coal, which some invisible influence, like an inconstant wind, awakens to transitory brightness: this power arises from within, like the colour of a flower which fades and changes as it is developed, and the conscious

portions of our natures are unprophetic either of its approach or its departure. Could this influence be durable in its original purity and force, it is impossible to predict the greatness of the results; but when composition begins, inspiration is already on the decline, and the most glorious poetry that has ever been communicated to the world is probably a feeble shadow of the original conception of the Poet. (I&P, VII, 135)

Is Shelley not expressing something here that each of us has experienced? Why else would we typically regard our writing as labor, even when we call it a labor of love? Why else would we revise—sometimes endlessly—if not to blow life back into a conception we have seemingly devitalized in the process of composition? Shelley, I am convinced, not only was singularly devoted to the proposition that language can and does communicate effectively and forcefully but also was acutely conscious of the extent to which an author can enhance the potential for effective communication by skillful manipulation of both text and audience. Shelley wrote not for a single, undifferentiated audience but for what he perceived as a variety of definable virtual audiences, attempting to address each through what he considered the vehicle most likely to ensure clear, effective communication.

Throughout this study my intention has been to delineate some of the rhetorical and stylistic manipulations that constitute a fabric of continuity in Shelley's works, a fabric that connects without precisely uniting both the discrete works in prose and poetry (both private and public) and the various and often distinct and nonoverlapping audiences to which those works were addressed. Just as the preface to *Adonais* has, surprisingly, received little critical attention in Shelley studies, owing perhaps to the surpassing loveliness of the poetry that follows it, so have most of the other prefaces received insufficient notice, as have also some of the essays I have considered here. Hence my focus in this study has been primarily, though not exclusively, upon Shelley's prose. Central to all of Shelley's writing is a determined focus on imagined or invented audiences. These audiences, which in many cases were something of a fiction for the author whose firsthand knowledge of them was often sketchy and inaccurate, constituted audiences nevertheless, both in an actual and in a rhetorical sense. They were entities to be addressed, manipulated, and seduced within the context of the author's powerful impulse to shape them, to mold them into an army of inspired and animated reformers who might carry out the resurrection, Phoenix-like, of a strong new England from the ashes of the post-Napoleonic welter of superstition, custom, and factionalism.

Shelley's deliberate appropriation to himself of the precedents provided by mythic and mythological figures like Prometheus, Socrates, and Jesus Christ is much more than the grandiose self-mythologizing for which some of his impercipient detractors have mistaken it or— more perversely—misrepresented it. The parallels were not drawn hastily or superficially but were evolved out of careful study and long thought. These parallels, along with the other clear indicators of the depth and breadth of Shelley's knowledge and appreciation of the works of a stunning diversity of predecessors and contemporaries in all fields of human endeavor, reveal an encyclopedic mind continuously thirsting for new knowledge, new materials for a revolutionary poetic and philosophical production whose diversity is equally stunning. Indeed, parallels of this sort signal the fervency with which Shelley regarded his publicly committed role as artist, as prophet, and finally as patriot and liberator within a much broader, universal scheme of things that transcended—even as his own works have at last done— the limits of time and place. It was a noble and humanitarian commitment, activated by love and self-sacrifice, and pursued with the resolution of one who, even as he had told Trelawny, was never to be stopped.

NOTES

Introduction

1. Richard Cronin, *Shelley's Poetic Thoughts* (New York: St. Martin's, 1981); William Keach, *Shelley's Style* (New York: Methuen, 1984). See also, especially, J. Hillis Miller, "The Critic as Host," in *Deconstruction and Criticism*, ed. Harold Bloom (New Haven: Yale University Press, 1978); Paul de Man, "Shelley Disfigured," in *The Rhetoric of Romanticism* (New York: Columbia University Press, 1984); and Tilottama Rajan, *Dark Interpreter: The Discourse of Romanticism* (Ithaca: Cornell University Press, 1980).

2. See Stephen C. Behrendt, "Art as Deceptive Intruder: Audience Entrapment in Eighteenth-Century Verbal and Visual Art," *Papers on Language and Literature* 19 (1983): 37–52.

3. Shelley employs the term specifically with regard to *Epipsychidion* in a letter to John Gisborne on 22 October 1821 (*Letters*, II, 363). William Keach explored Shelley's ideas about the SUNETOI in a paper presented at a Special Session on the Shelley circle and its audiences at the 1985 meeting of the Modern Language Association of America.

4. J. F. C. Harrison, *The Second Coming: Popular Millenarianism, 1780–1850* (New Brunswick: Rutgers University Press, 1979), pp. 4–8.

5. This struggle for a sustaining self-knowledge, complete with a temptation on a geographical or architectural "pinnacle," figures prominently in both Byron's *Manfred* and Shelley's *Prometheus Unbound*.

6. Walter J. Ong, S.J., "The Writer's Audience Is Always a Fiction," *PMLA* 90 (1975): 9–21.

7. Gerald Prince, "Introduction to the Study of the Narratee" (1973), rpt.

in *Reader-Response Criticism: From Formalism to Post-Structuralism*, ed. Jane P. Tompkins (Baltimore: Johns Hopkins University Press, 1980), p. 9. Prince's view is partially indebted to Walker Gibson's concept of the "mock reader" and to Wayne Booth's "unreliable narrator."

8. Marilyn Butler, *Romantics, Rebels and Reactionaries: English Literature and Its Background, 1760–1830* (Oxford: Oxford University Press, 1981), p. 154.

9. Jane P. Tompkins, "The Reader in History: The Changing Shape of Literary Response," in *Reader-Response Criticism*, ed. Tompkins, p. 214.

10. Jerome J. McGann, *Social Values and Poetic Acts: The Historical Judgment of Literary Work* (Cambridge, Mass.: Harvard University Press, 1988), p. 29.

11. Tompkins, "Reader in History," p. 204.

12. Louise M. Rosenblatt, *The Reader, the Text, the Poem: The Transactional Theory of the Literary Work* (Carbondale: Southern Illinois University Press, 1978), p. 88.

13. Umberto Eco, *The Role of the Reader: Explorations in the Semiotics of Texts* (Bloomington: Indiana University Press, 1979), pp. 22, 49; Wolfgang Iser, "The Reading Process: A Phenomenological Approach," in *Reader-Response Criticism*, ed. Tompkins, pp. 50–69.

14. Edward John Trelawny, *Records of Shelley, Byron, and the Author*, 2 vols. (London: Basil Montagu Pickering, 1878), 1, 100.

15. See Thomas Jefferson Hogg, *The Life of Percy Bysshe Shelley*, 2 vols. (London: Edward Moxon, 1858).

16. Kenneth Neill Cameron, *The Young Shelley: Genesis of a Radical* (1950; rpt. New York: Collier Books, 1962), pp. 125–26.

17. Ong, "Writer's Audience," p. 9.

Chapter One

1. Calling it so, rather than *Laon and Cythna*, its original title, is purely a convenience, albeit one that reminds us that Shelley was forced to revise his poem, not by choice but owing to the demands of Charles Ollier, his publisher, which Shelley had to meet if he was to reach any audience at all.

2. Michael Henry Scrivener, *Radical Shelley: The Philosophical Anarchism and Utopian Thought of Percy Bysshe Shelley* (Princeton: Princeton University Press, 1982), p. 122.

3. Charles E. Robinson, *Shelley and Byron: The Snake and Eagle Wreathed in Fight* (Baltimore: Johns Hopkins University Press, 1976), pp. 61–62.

4. William Wordsworth, *Lyrical Ballads*, ed. R. L. Brett and A. R. Jones (London: Methuen, 1965), p. 7.

5. Richard D. Altick, *The English Common Reader: A Social History of the Mass Reading Public, 1800–1900* (Chicago: University of Chicago Press, 1957), p. 5. See also Jon P. Klancher, *The Making of English Reading Audiences, 1790–1832* (Madison: University of Wisconsin Press, 1987).

6. Elise M. Gold, "Touring the Inventions: Shelley's Prefatory Writing," *Keats-Shelley Journal* 36 (1987): 85. Gold's brief discussion of Shelley's pref-

aces is the most insightful treatment to date of these carefully crafted and closely reasoned essays to which Shelley scholarship has been remarkably inattentive.

7. P. M. S. Dawson, *The Unacknowledged Legislator: Shelley and Politics* (Oxford: Clarendon Press, 1980), pp. 68–75. Dawson reads "out of" as "something like 'without', or as a slip for 'not of'" (p. 69).

8. Eleanor Wilner, *Gathering the Winds: Visionary Imagination and Radical Transformation of Self and Society* (Baltimore: Johns Hopkins University Press, 1975), p. 5. See also Robert F. Pack, "Shelley and History: The Poet as Historian" (Ph.D. dissertation, University of Pittsburgh, 1970); and Harrison, *Second Coming*, esp. chap. 1.

9. Scrivener, *Radical Shelley*, pp. 124–25.

10. *Letters*, I, 563n.

11. Gold, "Touring the Inventions," p. 79.

12. Keach, *Shelley's Style*, p. 97. For a more modern instance of this same idea of consenting self-enslavement, see Antonio Gramsci's views on the manner in which people may be both seduced and coerced into becoming accomplices in their own oppression: *Selections from the Prison Notebooks of Antonio Gramsci*, ed. and trans. Quintin Hoare and Geoffrey Nowell Smith (London: Laurence and Wishart, 1971).

13. See Moira Ferguson, *Subject to Others: British Women Writers and Colonial Slavery, 1678–1836*, forthcoming; and David Brion Davis, *The Problem of Slavery in Western Culture* (Ithaca: Cornell University Press, 1966).

14. See Scrivener, *Radical Shelley*, p. 118.

15. William Godwin, *Enquiry Concerning Political Justice and its Influence on Morals and Happiness*, ed. F. E. L. Preistley, 3 vols. (Toronto: University of Toronto Press, 1946), I, 104.

16. See Kenneth Neill Cameron, "Shelley vs. Southey: New Light on an Old Quarrel," *PMLA* 57 (1942): 489–512.

17. Samuel Taylor Coleridge, *Conciones ad Populum. Or Addresses to the People* (Bristol, 1795), in *The Collected Works of Samuel Taylor Coleridge*, I: *Lectures 1795: On Politics and Religion*, ed. Lewis Patton and Peter Mann (London and Princeton: Routledge and Kegan Paul/Princeton University Press, 1971), p. 43. See also Kenneth Neill Cameron, "Shelley and the *Conciones ad Populum*," *MLN* 57 (1942): 673–74.

18. *The Journals of Mary Shelley, 1814–1844*, ed. Paula R. Feldman and Diana Scott-Kilvert, 2 vols. (Oxford: Clarendon Press, 1987), I, 98. *The Statesman's Manual* in *The Collected Works*, VI: *Lay Sermons*, ed. R. J. White (1972), p. 36. In fairness to Coleridge, he claimed that the strict class elitism of the published title page of *The Statesman's Manual* misrepresented his intentions; writing to George Frere in December 1816, Coleridge asserted that "the Title ... ought to have been, and I had so directed it—addressed to the Learned and Reflecting of all Ranks and Professions, especially among the Higher Class" (*Statesman's Manual*, p. 3n.).

19. "Shelley finishes his Pamphlet" (*Journals of Mary Shelley*, I, 184; entry for 12 November 1817). A later entry for this day: "walk to Mr. Ollier's"; did she deliver the completed manuscript? Frederick L. Jones notes that no copy of the "original edition" is known (*Letters*, I, 566n.), but as Reiman has shown

(*SC*, V, 125n.), printed copies existed by 1833 and presumably earlier. Thomas Rodd's "fac-simile reprint" of the essay, dating from around 1843, includes a claim that Shelley had had printed some twenty copies of the original (*Letters*, I, 566n.), one of which Rodd must have reprinted. No conclusive evidence is presently known to exist, however, that Shelley's pamphlet was in fact printed soon after its completion.

Ingpen and Peck noted that Ollier may well have declined to publish the essay and that the manuscript may have fallen into Rodd's hands eventually. They further speculated that in printing it for what they believed was the first (not the second) time Rodd may have invented the "twenty copies" as a means of protecting himself by enabling him to claim that his edition was simply a "reprint" (I&P, VI, 355n.). Yet the existence at the Pforzheimer Library of a copy bearing the inscription "Given to me by Mr. T. Rodd, July 31, 1830" (*SC*, V, 125n.) lends credence to Rodd's claim that he was in fact actually reprinting Shelley's pamphlet.

20. David Hume, *A Treatise of Human Nature*, ed. L. A. Selby-Bigge (Oxford: Clarendon Press, 1888), p. 398.

21. Scrivener, *Radical Shelley*, p. 137.

22. Altick, *English Common Reader*, p. 326.

23. Dawson, *Unacknowledged Legislator*, p. 283.

Chapter Two

1. The note to "Even love is sold" (*Works*, 806–8) is a good example of Shelley's early thoughts on the stifling effect upon individuals, and upon human relationships, of the legalistic, emotionless moral code. Shelley was undoubtedly thinking in personal as well as general, social terms, for his relationship with Harriet Grove had foundered on her family's moral objections. See also John Pollard Guinn, *Shelley's Political Thought* (The Hague: Mouton, 1969), pp. 41–43.

I have discussed Shelley's novels at some length in my introduction to *Zastrozzi and St. Irvyne* (Oxford: Oxford University Press, 1986), pp. vii–xxiii. See A. D. D. Hughes, "Shelley's *Zastrozzi* and *St. Irvyne*," *Modern Language Review* 7 (1912): 54–63; David G. Halliburton, "Shelley's 'Gothic' Novels," *Keats-Shelley Journal* 16 (1967): 39–49; John V. Murphy, *The Dark Angel: Gothic Elements in Shelley's Works* (Lewisburg, Pa.: Bucknell University Press, 1975); Frederick S. Frank, "Introduction" to *Zastrozzi and St. Irvyne* (New York: Arno Press, 1977), pp. ix–xxii; and David Seed, "Shelley's 'Gothick' in *St. Irvyne* and After," in *Essays on Shelley*, ed. Miriam Allott (Liverpool: Liverpool University Press, 1982), pp. 39–70.

2. *Letters*, I, 2; Cameron, *The Young Shelley*, p. 51. Although Shelley's letter is dated 1808, the continuity between its subject matter and that of his letter to Tisdall of 1 January 1809 (*Letters*, I, 3) suggests that he had forgotten it was a new year.

3. Thomas Medwin, *The Life of Percy Bysshe Shelley*, ed. H. Buxton Forman (London: Oxford University Press, 1913), p. 25. Swinburne reportedly

contended that "in style throughout, and occasionally in incident, *Zofloya* was the immediate model of *Zastrozzi*" (Forman, in ibid., p. 26n.).

4. See Peter L. Thorslev, Jr., *Romantic Contraries: Freedom versus Destiny* (New Haven: Yale University Press), esp. pp. 126–41.

5. Frederick L. Jones, in *Letters*, I, 4n. Jones implies that several novels were in progress at this time, one of which might have been *The Nightmare*, a horror tale that Shelley may have intended for illustration by Henry Fuseli (Richard Holmes, *Shelley: The Pursuit* [New York: E. P. Dutton, 1975], p. 31). Or had Shelley seen an original or a print of one of Fuseli's famous *Nightmare* pictures and composed a tale based on it?

6. Holmes, *Shelley*, p. 36.

7. Schiller's popular *Die Räuber* (*The Robbers*, 1781) had been translated into English and published by the Robinsons of London as early as 1792. By 1809 it was available in at least fourteen different English editions.

8. Frank, "Introduction," p. xiv.

9. Cameron, *The Young Shelley*, p. 43; Newman Ivey White, *Shelley*, 2 vols. (New York: Knopf, 1940), I, 54.

10. Observing that at this point Shelley appears to regard "philosophical prose" as "a medium superior to 'wild Romance & Poetry'" (p. 84), Timothy Webb locates *Hubert Cauvin* within the philosophical category (*Shelley: A Voice Not Understood* [Atlantic Highlands, N.J.: Humanities Press, 1977]).

11. Shelley subsequently discovered that Stockdale had acted as Sir Timothy's agent in investigating and disparaging Hogg. His indignation is apparent in his frosty letter to Stockdale of 28 January 1811 (*Letters*, I, 49), but he may have become suspicious of Stockdale earlier: on 23 December 1810 Timothy Shelley had thanked Stockdale for his efforts in the investigation (*Letters*, I, 26n.).

12. Shelley ultimately took Hogg's manuscript to his own Oxford publishers, Munday and Slatter, after Stockdale had turned it down, presumably because it contained "heretical principles." Upon discovering the novel's contents, Slatter's printer refused to complete the typesetting. The task passed next to the Abingdon printer, King, who nearly finished the job but stopped when Shelley and Hogg were expelled from Oxford. See *Letters*, I, 27n. and ff.

13. See also John Freeman's comments on this letter as a mirror of Shelley's mind in "Shelley's Early Letters," in *Shelley Revalued: Essays from the Gregynog Conference*, ed. Kelvin Everest (Leicester: Leicester University Press, 1983), pp. 115–16.

14. Shelley had published *St. Irvyne* at his own expense, but Stockdale subsequently claimed that Shelley never paid him.

15. Holmes, *Shelley*, p. 26.

16. Shelley expected Hunt to publicize his works, whether he published them or not. In the letter accompanying "England in 1819," he tells Hunt in a P.S., "I do not expect you to publish it, but you may show it to whom you please" (*Letters*, II, 167; 23 December 1819).

17. *Letters*, I, 23n.

18. Holmes, *Shelley*, p. 51. Holmes suggests that this unknown work may lie behind the Esdaile Notebook poem "a Tale of Society as it is." Cameron,

however, argues that Shelley had probably only just written this latter poem before sending its first seventy-eight lines to Elizabeth Hitchener in a letter of 7 January 1812; see *The Esdaile Notebook: A Volume of Early Poems*, ed. Kenneth Neill Cameron (New York: Knopf, 1964), p. 198. See also Cameron's speculations about the poem in *The Young Shelley*, p. 66.

19. Shelley had appended to *The Wandering Jew* a glowing dedication to Burdett when the poem was published in Edinburgh in the summer of 1810, shortly after Burdett had been imprisoned for publicly attacking the House of Commons' decision to imprison John Gale Jones, a London radical who had chastised Commons for conducting a secret rather than a public inquiry into the failed Walcheren expedition. See Cameron, *The Young Shelley*, pp. 64ff.

20. See *Letters*, I, 54; and Holmes, *Shelley*, pp. 52–53.

21. Cameron, *Esdaile Notebook*, p. 6.

22. The term occurs in the letter to Hunt which accompanied the manuscript of *The Mask of Anarchy* (*Letters*, II, 152; 14–18 November 1819).

23. *Milton*, in *The Complete Poetry and Prose of William Blake*, ed. David V. Erdman (Garden City, N.Y.: Doubleday, 1982), p. 96, plate 1; Harrison, *The Second Coming*, pp. 6–7.

24. Webb, *Shelley*, p. 89. Although Webb is describing the political poems of 1819, his description also fits these youthful political poems.

25. Cameron, *Esdaile Notebook*, p. 180. Cameron (ibid., pp. 194–95) suggests that "To Liberty," like "The Crisis," dates from the later period, noting that its final stanza is "a kind of summary of the first half of the final canto of *Queen Mab*."

26. Wolfgang Iser, "Interaction between Text and Reader," in *The Reader in the Text: Essays on Audience and Interpretation*, ed. Susan R. Suleiman and Inge Crosman (Princeton: Princeton University Press, 1980), pp. 110–11.

27. As the French Revolution had attempted to mandate an egalitarian society, so by 1800 the Western European family had begun to develop significantly away from the strictly patriarchal model of an often brutal, father-dominated family and toward a relatively more egalitarian model in the companionate marriage. See Lawrence Stone, "The Rise of the Nuclear Family in Early Modern England," in *The Family in History*, ed. Charles E. Rosenberg (Philadelphia: University of Pennsylvania Press, 1975), and *The Family, Sex and Marriage in England, 1500–1800* (New York: Harper & Row, 1977). Stone's conclusions, which are controversial, should properly be regarded as relative rather than absolute. See also Max Horkheimer, "Authoritarianism and the Family," in *The Family: Its Function and Destiny*, ed. Ruth Nanda Anshen, rev. ed. (New York: Harper & Row, 1959); and Stephen C. Behrendt, "'This Accursed Family': Blake's *America* and the American Revolution," *The Eighteenth Century: Theory and Interpretation* 27 (1986): 26–51.

28. Based on Shelley's having assigned the poem a date of 1810, and on the onset of George III's serious illness after the death of his favorite daughter, Amelia, on 2 November 1810, Cameron suggests that the poem was composed late in 1810.

29. See Cameron, *Esdaile Notebook*, esp. pp. 21–29.

30. A very useful perspective on this matter of art as "gift" is provided by Lewis Hyde in *The Gift: Imagination and the Erotic Life of Property* (New York:

Random House/Vintage, 1983). Hyde's main point is that the value of a gift is both determined and increased by the gift's being passed on to others, a point exactly apropos of Shelley's view of his public mission. See also Ronald A. Sharp, *Friendship and Literature: Spirit and Form* (Durham: Duke University Press, 1986).

31. Freeman, "Shelley's Early Letters," p. 110.

32. Olivia Smith, *The Politics of Language, 1791–1819* (Oxford: Clarendon Press, 1984), p. 2.

33. Keach discusses this matter in detail; see *Shelley's Style*, esp. chap. 1.

34. Unlike Byron, whose admiration for the American Revolution and for Washington as "the Cincinnatus of the West" is readily apparent, Shelley seems not generally to have turned to America as paradigm, perhaps reckoning that in Europe the struggle was against a much more localized and long-entrenched status quo.

35. Cameron, *The Young Shelley*, p. 161.

36. Dawson, *Unacknowledged Legislator*, p. 136.

37. Shelley's full title, which I have abbreviated in the fashion of most editors, reads: *Proposals for an Association of those Philanthropists, Who Convinced of the Inadequacy of the Moral and Political State of Ireland to Produce Benefits which are nevertheless Attainable are Willing to Unite to Accomplish its Regeneration.*

38. Cameron, *The Young Shelley*, p. 169. Dawson (*Unacknowledged Legislator*, pp. 140–41) also suggests that Shelley may have concluded that he might be more successful working with existing structures than trying to "create them to order."

39. Jean-Paul Sartre, *What Is Literature?* trans. Bernard Frechtman (1949; rpt. New York: Washington Square Press, 1966), p. 32.

40. See Dawson, *Unacknowledged Legislator*, pp. 152–54.

41. Cameron, *The Young Shelley*, pp. 203–10, discusses the trial and Shelley's reactions.

42. T. B. Howell, *A Complete Collection of State Trials*, 34 vols. (London, 1832), XXXI, 938–47.

43. *John Stuart Mill: A Selection of His Works*, ed. John M. Robson (New York: Odyssey Press, 1966), pp. 85, 90.

44. Ibid., pp. 81–82.

45. Freeman, "Shelley's Early Letters," p. 117.

46. Cameron, *The Young Shelley*, p. 209. Cameron calls the *Letter* "Shelley's first important work of literature" (p. 210).

47. Scrivener, *Radical Shelley*, pp. 65–66.

48. Ibid., p. 66.

49. *John Milton: Complete Poems and Major Prose*, ed. Merritt Y. Hughes (New York: Odyssey Press, 1957), p. 745.

50. See also Jacques Ellul's powerful analysis of this phenomenon in *Propaganda: The Formation of Men's Attitudes* (New York: Vintage, 1973).

Chapter Three

1. Cameron, *The Young Shelley*, p. 266.

2. Donald Reiman has noted in correspondence that these mutilated copies are very rare, as opposed to the more common, uncut copies that must have been part of the remainder Richard Carlile subsequently purchased in 1822.

3. Webb, *Shelley*, p. 87, likewise expresses this salutary caution.

4. *Letters*, II, 567n. Little is known of Mr. Waller. Indeed, White even puzzles over the gender of "Mr. [or Mrs.?] Waller"; see *Shelley*, II, 614. Cameron suggests that Mr. Waller may have been William Waller, a Drury Lane bookseller (*SC*, IV, 488n.). Another possibility is Nicholas Waller (née Proctor), the brother of "Barry Cornwall"; see Charles N. Taylor, *The Early Collected Editions of Shelley's Poems: A Study in the History and Transmission of the Printed Text* (New Haven: Yale University Press, 1958), p. 3n.

5. Cameron discusses these various manuscripts and copies in *SC*, IV, 487ff.

6. Carl Woodring, *Politics in English Romantic Poetry* (Cambridge, Mass.: Harvard University Press, 1970), p. 252.

7. See also Cameron, *The Young Shelley*, pp. 266–67; and Scrivener, *Radical Shelley*, pp. 67–68.

8. Donald H. Reiman discusses the circumstances of this review in *The Romantics Reviewed: Contemporary Reviews of British Romantic Writers*, ed. Donald H. Reiman, 3 vols. in 9 parts (New York: Garland, 1972), pt. C, II, 849. Louise Schutz Boas demonstrated that Shelley's connection with the *Theological Inquirer* was probably his acquaintance in 1815 with its radical editor, George Cannon; see "Erasmus Perkins and Shelley," *MLN* 70 (1955): 408–13.

9. Newman Ivey White, *The Unextinguished Hearth: Shelley and His Contemporary Critics* (Durham: Duke University Press, 1938), p. 454.

10. Donald H. Reiman, *Percy Bysshe Shelley* (Boston: Twayne, 1969), pp. 27–28.

11. Hogg, *Life of Shelley*, II, 484–85.

12. The Pforzheimer Library has Mary Shelley's copy, in which the printer's errors are also corrected.

13. The format may have been chosen because, like that of Godwin's *Political Justice*, it helped forestall prosecution by making the work too expensive for the masses.

14. Scrivener, *Radical Shelley*, p. 79. On the rhetoric of the *Refutation* and on Shelley's interest in the skeptical debate, see also C. E. Pulos, *The Deep Truth: A Study of Shelley's Skepticism* (Lincoln: University of Nebraska Press, 1954).

15. White, *Unextinguished Hearth*, p. 45.

16. Cameron, *Esdaile Notebook*, p. 89.

17. Cameron, *The Young Shelley*, pp. 221–22.

18. Trelawny, *Records*, I, 100.

19. *Journals of Mary Shelley*, I, 45, 58.

20. White, *Unextinguished Hearth*, p. 35.

21. The title page of this pseudo-autobiography stated only that the prince's memoirs had been translated by "John Brown, Esq."

22. *Journals of Mary Shelley*, I, 58.

23. This was, of course, the point at which the projected liaison between Hogg and Mary—to which Shelley was full party—was being discussed most seriously, despite the advanced stage of Mary's pregnancy at the beginning of 1815.

24. White, *Shelley*, I, 421.

25. See Neil Fraistat, "Poetic Quests and Questioning in Shelley's *Alastor* Collection," *Keats-Shelley Journal* 33 (1984): 161–81.

26. Ibid., p. 173.

27. See Mary Shelley's note to *Peter Bell the Third (Works*, 362–63) which is not unrelated to the point of the *Alastor* volume.

28. Hutchinson attributes the view to Bertram Dobell, William Michael Rossetti, and Edward Dowden (*Works*, 902).

29. Charles E. Robinson speculates that a recently discovered note may indicate that Shelley sent Byron a copy of the *Alastor* volume. See "Shelley to Byron in 1814: A New Letter," *Keats-Shelley Journal* 35 (1986): 104–10.

30. Of course, Shelley would not have known Coleridge's poem, which did not appear until 1816.

31. Elise M. Gold agrees, suggesting that the preface furnishes Shelley with "the critical distance" necessary for him as poet to sacrifice some of his personal vision in the interest of his ties with his fellow men ("Touring the Inventions," pp. 78–79). I am less certain than Gold is that the voice in the preface is authentically Shelleyan, however, or that the vision articulated in the preface "goes beyond the poem's two limited visions" (ibid., p. 78n.). Rather, as the following discussion suggests, I see there yet another incomplete vision.

32. See the preface to Jacques Derrida, *Of Grammatology*, trans. Gayatri Chakravorty Spivak (Baltimore: Johns Hopkins University Press, 1976).

33. Jerrold E. Hogle discusses Shelley's use of metaphors of transformation generally in "Shelley's Poetics: The Power as Metaphor," *Keats-Shelley Journal* 31 (1982): 159–97.

34. Scrivener, *Radical Shelley*, p. 84.

35. Keach, *Shelley's Style*, p. 87.

36. Earl R. Wasserman, *Shelley: A Critical Reading* (Baltimore: Johns Hopkins University Press, 1971), p. 12.

37. William Wordsworth and Samuel Taylor Coleridge, *Lyrical Ballads*, ed. R. L. Brett and A. R. Jones (London: Methuen, 1968), p. 7.

38. Judith Chernaik, *The Lyrics of Shelley* (Cleveland: Press of Case Western Reserve University, 1972), p. 9.

39. Ian Jack, *English Literature: 1815–1832* (Oxford: Clarendon Press, 1963), p. 78.

40. Ingpen and Peck bear out the claim (I&P, VI, 355). For more on Shelley's role in this journal, see also Reiman, *SC*, VII, 41–45.

41. Robinson, *Shelley and Byron*, p. 61.

Chapter Four

1. Cronin, *Shelley's Poetic Thoughts*, p. 245.
2. Kenneth Neill Cameron, *Shelley: The Golden Years* (Cambridge, Mass.: Harvard University Press, 1974), pp. 253–54. See also Reiman, *SC*, VI, 659–60; Webb, *Shelley*, p. 44; and Holmes, *Shelley*, p. 379.
3. He terms it thus in letters to Ollier and Peacock (*Letters*, II, 29, 31; both 16 August 1818).
4. *William Wordsworth: The Poems*, ed. John O. Hayden, 2 vols. (New Haven: Yale University Press, 1981), II, 54.
5. In this matter, the insightful discussions of Shelley's views on the relation of language and thought by Cronin (*Shelley's Poetic Thoughts*) and Keach (*Shelley's Style*) are very helpful.
6. Stuart Curran, *Poetic Form and British Romanticism* (New York: Oxford University Press, 1986), pp. 118–19.
7. Holmes, *Shelley*, p. 380.
8. Cameron, *Shelley*, p. 163; Dawson, *Unacknowledged Legislator*, p. 283.
9. I have, of course, made certain assumptions about the order in which Shelley did things, based on firsthand study of the manuscripts, where considerations like color of ink, condition of pen points, lineation and pagination, and distinguishing characteristics of handwriting (not to mention watermarks, paper type and size, and the like) provide evidence about Shelley's process that cannot be represented in conventional typography. The series of facsimiles *The Manuscripts of the Younger Romantics* and *The Bodleian Shelley Manuscripts*, now being issued by Garland Press under the general editorship of Donald H. Reiman, will make more generally available these manuscript materials.
10. Mary Shelley published her edited version of the *Defence*, which Shelley had intended for the *Liberal*, in *Essays, Letters from Abroad, etc.* in 1840.
11. See Keach, *Shelley's Style*, esp. pp. 154–59.
12. Scrivener's excellent analysis of the essay (*Radical Shelley*, pp. 87–106) also addresses some of these issues.
13. Cameron, *Shelley*, p. 163.
14. Dawson, *Unacknowledged Legislator*, p. 182n.
15. If Scrivener's dating of the *Essay* (1816–March 1817) is correct (*Radical Shelley*, pp. 89–93), then its composition both precedes and partly coincides with the other works we associate with Shelley's Marlow period.
16. Both are in Bodleian MS Shelley adds. c. 4, the first on ff. 276–79, the latter on ff. 295r–296r, with the second fragment on reform (I&P, VI, 295–96) and "On the Jews" (from Tacitus) appearing between them. This dating is still unclear to me. Cameron (*Shelley*, p. 163) places *The Moral Teaching* in 1819, whereas Dawson considers it "certainly" to be from 1822 (*Unacknowledged Legislator*, p. 284). Since both the Shelleys were reading Tacitus in 1817–18, the presence of "On the Jews" with these two fragments may link them with 1817, along with the first part of the *Essay on Christianity*. Since Bodleian MS adds. c. 4 is not a bound notebook but a collection of loose leaves, however, precise dating of these fragments is yet to be satisfactorily established.

17. Immanuel Kant, "What Is Enlightenment?" (1784), trans. Ernst Cassirer, in *The Philosophy of Kant: Immanuel Kant's Moral and Philosophical Writings*, ed. Carl J. Friedrich (New York: Modern Library, 1949).

18. Webb, *Shelley*, p. 159.

19. M. Roxana Klapper, *The German Literary Influence on Shelley*, Salzburg Studies in English Literature, 43 (Salzburg: University of Salzburg, 1975), p. 50. Shelley includes a derogatory reference to F. G. Born's Latin translation of Kant's works in *Peter Bell the Third* (1819; *PP*, 340, lines 518–27). In September 1821 he was reported to be reading Kant (*Journals of Mary Shelley*, I, 378), who is subsequently numbered among "those spoilers spoiled" in *The Triumph of Life* (*PP*, 461; lines 235–38).

20. Kant, "What Is Enlightenment?" pp. 132–34.

21. *A Vision of the Last Judgment*, in *Complete Poetry and Prose*, p. 565.

22. Webb cites the Sermon on the Mount as a good example of Christ's manner of "reassuring his audience that he has come not to destroy but to fulfill, easing himself into the confidence of the multitudes" (*Shelley*, p. 161). See also Cameron, *Shelley*, p. 168; and Scrivener, *Radical Shelley*, p. 98.

23. See Harry White, "Relative Means and Ends in Shelley's Social-Political Thought," *SEL* 22 (1982): 613–31.

24. Wilner, *Gathering the Winds*, p. 21.

25. Alexander Pope, *An Essay on Criticism*, in *The Poems of Alexander Pope*, ed. John Butt (New Haven: Yale University Press, 1963), p. 153, line 298.

26. See Anne Mellor, *Mary Shelley: Her Life, Her Fiction, Her Monsters* (New York: Methuen, 1988). Like Betty T. Bennett, Mellor refutes the view of contemporary critics like Sir Walter Scott and modern ones like E. B. Murray that Shelley was so heavily involved in the novel's composition as to be almost its co-author. See *The Letters of Mary Wollstonecraft Shelley*, ed. Betty T. Bennett, 3 vols. (Baltimore: Johns Hopkins University Press, 1980–87), I, xvi; and Murray, "Shelley's Contribution to Mary's *Frankenstein*," *Keats-Shelley Memorial Bulletin* 29 (1978): 50–68. Mellor rejects, for reasons I detail here, Murray's claim that Shelley's extensive revisions "were always in keeping with Mary's conception" (p. 67), while Bennett credits Shelley in the endeavor with "the judgment and suggestions of an astute and committed editor" (p. xvi).

27. See Bennett, in *Letters of Mary Shelley*, I, xvi.

28. *Frankenstein*, ed. James Rieger (Chicago: University of Chicago Press, 1982), presents the 1818 text together with a collation of those of 1818 and 1831.

29. See *Letters*, I, 569n., and I&P, VI, 371.

30. Wilner, *Gathering the Winds*, p. 25.

31. Edward Royle and James Walvin, *English Radicals and Reformers, 1760–1848* (Lexington: University Press of Kentucky, 1982).

32. Their dating is problematic. Ingpen and Peck followed William Michael Rossetti in dating "On the Punishment of Death" at 1814–15 (I&P, VI, 360), which is certainly too early. Cameron dates it 1816–17 (*Shelley*, p. 157), while Dawson assigns it to mid- to late 1820 (*Unacknowledged Legislator*, p. 283). Dawson suggests (ibid., p. 183) that Shelley may have considered incorporating the essay into *A Philosophical View of Reform*, where it might have

provided an appropriate illustration to Shelley's attack on revenge. Indeed, a blank page of that essay contains the inscription, "On the punishment of death."

There is general agreement that "A Future State" "cannot be dismissed as a juvenile effort" (Reiman, *SC*, VI, 639n.): Dawson attributes the essay to September–December 1818 (*Unacknowledged Legislator*, p. 283), but Cameron (*Shelley*, p. 160) opts for 1820–21.

33. For a helpful discussion of the eighteenth-century background to the issue, see Douglas Hay, "Property, Authority and the Criminal Law," in *Albion's Fateful Tree: Crime and Society in Eighteenth-Century England*, ed. Douglas Hay et al. (New York: Pantheon, 1975), pp. 17–64.

34. See Dawson, *Unacknowledged Legislator*, p. 183.

35. Bodleian MS Shelley adds. e. 8, p. 34.

36. The notebook contains a draft of the fourth note to *Hellas* as well as a draft of the "serpent and mastiff" poem.

37. Michel Foucault, *Discipline and Punish: The Birth of the Prison*, trans. Alan Sheridan (New York: Vintage Books, 1979), pp. 57–62.

38. Ibid., p. 9.

39. See James A. Notopoulos, "The Dating of Shelley's Prose," *PMLA* 57 (1943): 477–98; and Cameron, *Shelley*, pp. 160–63.

40. Bodleian MS Shelley adds. e. 11, pp. 128–30 rev. Preceding this passage is an only partially coherent and legible transition sentence: "And as [the wh] the [substance] unorginagized [sic: unorganized? ed.] substance[s] that approaches toward that period of its decay retains, [lives and] as a [mas] whole less of that principle of resistance to change, thro which it has hitherto subsisted; so a [? ?] is trusted by superstition feels the [desire] res which man being valuable detach themselves from [his] around it."

41. See Reiman, *SC*, VI, 971n. Despite both stylistic evidence and its presence in the Italian notebooks, the essay is still occasionally assigned a considerably earlier date.

42. See Cronin, *Shelley's Poetic Thoughts*, pp. 28, 162. Cronin's first chapter provides a useful background to the Lockean view of language as Shelley inherited it, both from poets like Wordsworth and Coleridge and from philosophers like Hume, Bentham, and Godwin. Keach (*Shelley's Style*), carries the discussion further, especially in his first two chapters.

43. Scrivener, *Radical Shelley*, p. 250.

Chapter Five

1. Marilyn Butler claims that *The Revolt* and *Prometheus Unbound* adopt a wholly impersonal mode (*Peacock Displayed: A Satirist in His Context* [London: Routledge & Kegan Paul, 1979], p. 301). This is an example of the skewed readings that can result when we fail adequately to consider Shelley's prefaces.

2. See Iser, "Interaction between Text and Reader," p. 111. On the dynamics of reading and/or performance, see also Jonas Barish, "Shakespeare in the Study: Shakespeare on the Stage," *Theatre Journal* 40 (1988): 33–47.

3. Stuart Curran, *Shelley's "Cenci": Scorpions Ringed with Fire* (Princeton: Princeton University Press, 1970), p. 33. On *The Cenci*, see also my essay "Beatrice Cenci and the Tragic Myth of History," in *History and Myth: Essays on English Romantic Literature*, ed. Stephen C. Behrendt (Detroit: Wayne State University Press, 1989).

4. See Eugene R. Hammond, "Beatrice's Three Fathers: Successive Betrayal in Shelley's *The Cenci*," *Essays in Literature* 8 (Spring 1981): 25–32; and Wasserman, *Shelley*, chap. 3.

5. See "A Discourse on the Manners of the Ancients, relative to the Subject of Love," which Dawson attributes to the summer of 1818, when Shelley was translating Plato's *Symposium*, for which he may have intended it as a commentary.

6. See Nathaniel Brown, *Sexuality and Feminism in Shelley* (Cambridge, Mass.: Harvard University Press, 1979). Brown's detailed discussion of Shelley's *Discourse* forms the basis for his analysis of the poet's handling of psychosexuality in his poetry. Brown argues ambitiously, though incorrectly, that Shelley was the first major writer to engage in literary consciousness-raising. More useful is his perception that Shelley's sexual philosophy presupposes an erotic psychology based on equality between the sexes (p. 3).

7. See Curran's detailed discussion in *Shelley's "Cenci."*

8. *Letters of Mary Wollstonecraft Shelley*, I, 106; 18 September 1819.

9. See Curran, *Shelley's "Cenci,"* chap. 1.

10. See Butler, *Peacock Displayed*, p. 305.

11. Aristotle, *Poetics*, in *The Basic Works of Aristotle*, ed. Richard McKeon (New York: Random House, 1941), p. 1461; subsequent references, inserted parenthetically, are to this edition.

12. Thomas Love Peacock, *Memoirs of Shelley and Other Essays and Reviews*, ed. Howard Mills (London: Rupert Hart-Davis, 1970), p. 73.

13. Holmes, *Shelley*, pp. 514, 524.

14. George Bernard Shaw, "The Author's Apology," in *Mrs. Warren's Profession*; *The Bodley Head Bernard Shaw: Collected Plays with Their Prefaces*, 7 vols. (London: Max Reinhardt/The Bodley Head, 1970–74), I, 236.

15. It appears that the portrait is not by Guido Reni, although its creator's identity is still unestablished. The Shelleys in any event apparently saw two different pictures in Rome. See Barbara Groseclose, "A Portrait Not by Guido Reni of a Girl Who Is Not Beatrice Cenci," in *Studies in Eighteenth-Century Culture*, vol. 11, ed. Harry C. Payne (Madison: University of Wisconsin Press, 1982), pp. 107–32.

16. Curran, *Shelley's "Cenci,"* p. 170.

17. *Letters of Mary Wollstonecraft Shelley*, I, 127; 19 January 1820.

18. "The chief male character I confess I should be very unwilling that any one but Kean shd. play—that is impossible, & I must be contented with an inferior actor" (*Letters*, II, 102–3).

19. George Yost, *Pieracci and Shelley: An Italian "Ur-Cenci"* (Potomac, Md.: Scripta Humanistica, 1986), p. 11.

20. William Blackstone, *Commentaries on the Laws of England*, 4 vols. (Oxford: Clarendon Press, 1769), IV, 215–16.

21. See Louis Crompton, *Byron and Greek Love: Homophobia in 19th-*

Century England (Berkeley and Los Angeles: University of California Press, 1985).

22. See Wasserman, *Shelley*, pp. 125, 127–28.

23. In addition to the *Examiner*, he was also receiving Cobbett's *Political Register*, both of which regularly sought to produce change by predicting it. He subscribed in Pisa to *Galignani's Messenger*, a weekly Parisian English-language paper that excerpted and reprinted materials from English papers of a variety of persuasions, many of which—like the *Courier*, whose pages were frequently represented—were strongly conservative. See *Letters of Mary Wollstonecraft Shelley*, I, 139n. and 140–41.

24. Samuel Bamford, *Passages in the Life of a Radical* (1842), ed. Tim Hilton (Oxford: Oxford University Press, 1984), p. 116.

25. See James Brazell, *Shelley and the Concept of Humanity: A Study of His Moral Vision*, Salzburg Studies in English Literature: Romantic Reassessment, no. 7 (Salzburg: University of Salzburg, 1972), p. 82.

26. See Wasserman, *Shelley*, p. 102; and Michael Worton, "Speech and Silence in *The Cenci*," in *Essays on Shelley*, ed. Allott, p. 119.

27. John Raymond Greenfield, "Populous Solitude: The Poet, His Audience, and the Social Context in Selected Works of Shelley" (Ph.D. dissertation, Indiana University, 1980), p. 191. I have discussed a related instance of the use of the metaphor of the family in "'This Accursed Family.'"

28. See Webb, *Shelley*, pp. 165–66.

29. Carlos Baker, *Shelley's Major Poetry: The Fabric of a Vision* (Princeton: Princeton University Press, 1948), pp. 147–48.

30. Gold, "Touring the Inventions," p. 83.

31. Though its concern is with other aspects of the sublime, James B. Twitchell's *Romantic Horizons: Aspects of the Sublime in English Poetry and Painting, 1770–1850* (Columbia: University of Missouri Press, 1983) is useful in this context, as are Ronald Paulson's *Representations of Revolution, 1789–1820* (New Haven: Yale University Press, 1983) and Morton D. Paley's *The Apocalyptic Sublime* (New Haven: Yale University Press, 1986).

32. Mary Shelley substantiates Shelley's claim about the manuscript in her note to the play (*Works*, 335). Reiman discusses her translation of an Italian manuscript entitled "Relation of the Death of the Family of the Cenci" in *SC*, VI, pp. 897–98, and suggests that Shelley may at one point have intended that this translation should be printed between the preface and the text of the drama. See also Yost, *Pieracci and Shelley*, on the various manuscript records of the Cencis.

33. *Byron's Letters and Journals*, ed. Leslie A. Marchand, vol. 7: *Between Two Worlds* (London: John Murray, 1977), p. 174; to Richard Belgrave Hoppner, 10 September 1820; vol. 8: *Born for Opposition* (Cambridge, Mass.: Harvard University Press, 1978), p. 103.

34. See also his letters to Ollier of 15 October and 15 December 1819 (*SC*, VI, 926, and *Letters*, II, 163–64), which express similar sentiments.

35. Thinking of Shelley's conception of the limited audiences for which he claimed that poems like *Epipsychidion* were intended, Gold regards such prefaces as "screening devices not only for defining but for reducing his readership" ("Touring the Inventions," p. 73).

36. John P. Farrell, *Revolution as Tragedy: The Dilemma of the Moderate from Scott to Arnold* (Ithaca: Cornell University Press, 1980), p. 48.

37. Jon P. Klancher, "From 'Crowd' to 'Audience': The Making of an English Mass Readership in the Nineteenth Century," *ELH* 50 (1983): 156, and *The Making of English Reading Audiences.*

38. See Harry C. Payne, "Elite versus Popular Mentality in the Eighteenth Century," in *Studies in Eighteenth-Century Culture*, vol. 8, ed. Roseann Runte (Madison: University of Wisconsin Press, 1979), pp. 3–32.

39. Ibid., p. 23.

40. E. P. Thompson, *The Making of the English Working Class* (1963; rpt. New York: Vintage, 1966), p. 719.

41. Keach, *Shelley's Style*, p. 47; see his detailed discussion in chaps. 2 and 3, and Wasserman's in part III of *Shelley.*

42. *The Romantics Reviewed*, ed. Reiman, pt. C, II, 759.

43. Shelley ironically turns against Peacock the phrase from *Nightmare Abbey* (1818) in which the Shelleyan idealist, Scythrop, is described as being "troubled with" this passion. Peacock attributes the phrase to Robert Forsyth's *Principles of Moral Science* (1805), a book Shelley may have known, judging from the language of his preface. In a chapter devoted to "the passion for reforming the world," Forsyth opposes revolutionary extremism as counterproductive, counseling instead moderation, self-discipline, and self-knowledge.

44. Angela Leighton, *Shelley and the Sublime: An Interpretation of the Major Poems* (Cambridge: Cambridge University Press, 1984), pp. 76–77.

45. Bodleian MS Shelley e. 2, fol. 35r inverted.

46. See *The Romantics Reviewed*, ed. Reiman, pt. C, II, 771.

47. Robinson, *Shelley and Byron*, p. 2. See also Robinson's analysis of Shelley's later responses, pp. 204–21.

48. Ibid., pp. 113–14.

49. See Keach, *Shelley's Style*, pp. 205–6.

50. Robinson, *Shelley and Byron*, pp. 211–12. Robinson recalls (p. 216) the poets' agreement that whichever first received his full estate would settle a thousand pounds on the other. When Byron subsequently inherited after Lady Noel's death in January 1822, he reneged on the agreement, to the dismay of Shelley, who thereafter found it painful to discuss money matters with Byron.

51. *Letters of Mary Wollstonecraft Shelley*, I, 226; 20 March 1822.

52. See especially Cameron's detailed explanation (*Shelley*, pp. 255–56) of the relation of the Maniac's words to the actual events of the Shelleys' troubled relationship during this period.

53. See Robinson, *Shelley and Byron*, p. 82.

54. Ibid., p. 103.

55. Cronin, *Shelley's Poetic Thoughts*, pp. 110–11.

56. Twitchell, *Romantic Horizons*, p. 11. Interesting in this light is Vincent Newey's remark that Shelley's poem invites us to take (with Julian) the role of psychologist rather than moralist ("The Shelleyan Psycho-Drama: 'Julian and Maddalo,'" in *Essays on Shelley*, p. 100).

57. Scrivener, *Radical Shelley*, p. 186, for example, takes this line of interpretation.

58. Robinson, *Shelley and Byron*, p. 101.

59. Thorslev, *Romantic Contraries*, p. 168.

60. Gold regards the voice in the preface as entirely reliable, a "detached," "cultivated interpreter of the human heart," who underscores the poem's "universal applicability" ("Touring the Inventions," pp. 68–69). Here and elsewhere, however, Gold appears unwilling to entertain the possibility—indeed the likelihood—that Shelley's prefaces present us with rhetorical personae whom we ought not without a good deal of care to assume are Shelley himself.

61. See Robinson, *Shelley and Byron*, p. 103.

62. Lee Erickson, *Robert Browning: His Poetry and His Audiences* (Ithaca: Cornell University Press, 1984), p. 18.

63. Samuel Taylor Coleridge, *Biographia Literaria*, 2 vols., in *The Collected Works*, VII, ed. James Engell and W. Jackson Bate. (Princeton: Princeton University Press, 1983), II, 56. In her journal Mary Shelley lists the *Biographia* among works Shelley read in 1817.

64. *Burke, Paine, Godwin, and the Revolution Controversy*, ed. Marilyn Butler, (Cambridge: Cambridge University Press, 1984), p. 14.

65. *Letters*, I, 344–45; Smith, *Politics of Language*, pp. 150–51. Keach explores Shelley's familiarity with these theorists in *Shelley's Style*, esp. chap. 1.

66. See Butler, *Romantics, Rebels, and Reactionaries*, pp. 62–63.

67. Cronin, *Shelley's Poetic Thoughts*, pp. 109–10.

68. In a draft of the passage, Shelley wrote simply "and a bold enquirer into faith" but subsequently replaced "faith" with the more specific "morals & religion" (Bodleian MS Shelley e. 3, fol. 206)

69. Stuart Curran, "The Mental Pinnacle: *Paradise Regained* and the Romantic Four-Book Epic," in *Calm of Mind: Tercentenary Essays on "Paradise Regained" and "Samson Agonistes" in Honor of John S. Diekhoff*, ed. Joseph Anthony Wittreich, Jr. (Cleveland: Press of Case Western Reserve University, 1971), p. 136.

70. See I&P, VI, pp. 201, 361.

71. Stuart Curran, *Shelley's Annus Mirabilis: The Maturing of an Epic Vision* (San Marino, Calif.: Huntington Library, 1975), p. 112. The term is Angus Fletcher's, from *The Transcendental Masque: An Essay on Milton's "Comus"* (Ithaca: Cornell University Press, 1971).

Chapter Six

1. Butler, *Romantics, Rebels and Reactionaries*, p. 15.

2. Altick, *English Common Reader*, pp. 327ff.

3. Ibid., p. 326.

4. Ibid., pp. 326–27.

5. *Examiner*, 25 April 1819, p. 259. The *Examiner* gave prominent notice to Owen, whose speeches it also printed on 29 March, 5 April, and 4 July 1819.

6. Mary Shelley's letters likewise record the growing estrangement from Ollier, whom on 7 July 1820 she calls "a ninny or worse." By 7 March 1822 she is even more emphatic in her judgment that "he is a very bad bookseller to publish with" (*Letters of Mary Wollstonecraft Shelley*, I, 153, 222).

7. I have discussed this matter in greater detail in "The Exoteric Species: The Popular Idiom in Shelley's Poetry," *Genre* 14 (Winter 1981): 473–92.

8. Webb, for instance, regards these poems as vastly inferior, even crude (*Shelley*, p. 93).

9. See Curran, *Shelley's Annus Mirabilis*, chap. 6; and Scrivener, *Radical Shelley*, pp. 196–210.

10. Webb, *Shelley*, p. 89.

11. Bodleian MS Shelley adds. e. 6, p. 19. Scrivener, *Radical Shelley*, pp. 227–28, rightly laments the distortions of the texts of these poems by their various editors.

12. In Bodleian MS Shelley adds. e. 9, pp. 180ff. the poem is titled "To the C.——." The subsequent revised transcription in the Harvard Shelley notebook bears the title "To the Lord Chancellor," though "Lord Chancellor" has been line-canceled. The table of contents at the back of this incomplete notebook refers to the poem as "To Lxxd Cxxxr."

13. Dawson, *Unacknowledged Legislator*, p. 51.

14. Brazell, *Shelley and the Concept of Humanity*, p. 76.

15. Ibid., p. 138.

16. *Examiner*, no. 591, 25 April 1819, p. 259.

17. John Bohstedt, *Riots and Community Politics in England and Wales, 1790–1810* (Cambridge, Mass.: Harvard University Press, 1983), p. 219.

18. See also Cameron, *Shelley*, chap. 9, on this distinction.

19. Farrell, *Revolution as Tragedy*, pp. 51–52.

20. R. K. Webb, *The British Working-Class Reader, 1790–1848: Literacy and Social Tension* (London: George Allen & Unwin, 1955), p. 35.

21. See Brazell, *Shelley and the Concept of Humanity*, p. 129. Butler notes (*Burke, Paine, Godwin, and the Revolution Controversy*, p. 5) that insubordination was the leading message by the 1780s and early 1790s, in the rhetoric of liberty evolved by Priestley and other Dissenting intellectuals who were developing a rhetoric that addressed *individual*—rather than class—consciousness, a rhetoric that "has no class accent" (p. 5).

22. Percy Bysshe Shelley, *Essays, Letters from Abroad, Translations and Fragments*, ed. Mary Shelley, 2 vols. (London: Edward Moxon, 1840), I, xxv–xxvi.

23. Robert Forsyth, *Principles of Moral Science* (Edinburgh, 1805), pp. 291–93.

24. Scrivener claims that her act instigated the revolution (*Radical Shelley*, p. 207), but especially in view of her "maniac" nature this seems to me to overstate the case. On *The Mask*, see also the Garland Press facsimile in *The Manuscripts of the Younger Romantics* (Shelley, vol. II, 1985).

25. See Paul Foot, *Red Shelley* (London: Bookmarks, 1984), p. 176.

26. See also Cronin, *Shelley's Poetic Thoughts*, pp. 42–43; and Reiman, "Shelley as Agrarian Reactionary," *Keats-Shelley Memorial Bulletin* 30 (1979): 12–13.

27. *The Masque of Anarchy*, preface by Leigh Hunt (1832; London: J. Watson, 1842), pp. 3, 21–22.

28. *Examiner*, no. 608, 22 August 1819, pp. 530–31.

29. See *SC*, VI, 894n.; Robert C. Alberts, *Benjamin West: A Biography* (Boston: Houghton Mifflin, 1978), pp. 223–24; and Paley, *Apocalyptic Sublime*, pp. 18–31.

30. Curran, *Shelley's Annus Mirabilis*, p. 185.

31. Butler, *Romantics, Rebels and Reactionaries*, p. 54.

32. Curran, *Shelley's Annus Mirabilis*, pp. 187–92.

33. Ibid., p. 190.

34. Dawson, *Unacknowledged Legislator*, pp. 207–8, discusses Shelley's apparently "condescending" presentation of his program for political action in the poem's final section, which Dawson regards as "Shelley's own address to his readers" (p. 207). Given Shelley's sophisticated handling of voices in his poems, I am not at all sure we should equate this voice with Shelley's own quite so quickly and so certainly.

35. *Radical Squibs and Royal Ripostes: Satirical Pamphlets of the Regency Period, 1819–1821, Illustrated by George Cruikshank and Others*, ed. Edgell Rickword (Somerset: Adams and Dart, 1971), p. 24.

36. See Dawson, *Unacknowledged Legislator*, p. 203. Dawson's perceptive analysis directly addresses Shelley's penetrating critique in *Peter Bell the Third* of a society that "has become alienated from itself" (p. 199).

37. On 15 December he asked Ollier to write or call on Peacock to "ask *if my tragedy is accepted*" (*Letters*, II, 163).

38. Olivia Smith discusses this aspect of popular piggism in *Politics of Language*, pp. 79–86.

39. Scrivener, *Radical Shelley*, p. 262. See also Newman Ivey White, "Shelley's *Swellfoot the Tyrant* in Relation to Contemporary Political Satire," *PMLA* 36 (1921): 332–46. Cameron also discusses the play's historical context in *Shelley*, pp. 354–62.

40. See Cameron, *Shelley*, pp. 361–62.

41. Dawson, *Unacknowledged Legislator*, pp. 179–80.

42. Shelley's letter is dated 6 November, the day it was dispatched. Mary Shelley's journal indicates it was begun on 1 or 2 November and completed on the fifth or sixth (*Journals of Mary Shelley*, I, 301).

43. Because Carlile was required to remain in jail until he paid his fines, and because he was further required to post a security bond of £1,200 against his future acceptable behavior, he was saddled with what Scrivener correctly calls "an indeterminate life sentence" because he could scarcely hope to raise the money. His release on 18 November 1825 came as a result of popular pressure, not because his fines had been paid (Scrivener, *Radical Shelley*, p. 225). See also *SC*, VI, 1084n.

44. Hunt knew that Shelley had dedicated *The Cenci* to him, but the public did not because the play was not published until 1820.

45. I have silently followed Jones in supplying here and elsewhere some letters that have been obscured or lost in the manuscript of Shelley's letter. I have preserved Shelley's incorrect spelling of Carlile's name.

46. *Works*, 583. See *The Shelley Notebook in the Harvard College Library*, ed. George Edward Woodberry (Cambridge, Mass.: John Barnard Associates, 1929), facsimile p. 71.

47. Thorslev, *Romantic Contraries*, p. 81.

48. Indeed, he wore a ring bearing on the inside of the band the Italian for "Better times will come."

49. Cameron, *Shelley*, p. 149; Guinn, *Shelley's Political Thought*, p. 66.

50. Among the many who attempted to publicize the horrific factory con-

ditions had been even Southey, whose pseudonymous *Letters from England* (1807) several times (e.g., Letters 26 and 36) detail these matters.

51. Two early, very popular, and widely known indictments of the slave trade are A. Benezet, *Some Historical Account of Guinea, Its Situation, Produce, and the General Disposition of its Inhabitants, with an Inquiry into the Rise and Progress of the Slave Trade, Its Nature and Lamentable Effects* (1771), and James Ramsey, *An Essay on the Treatment and Conversion of African Slaves in the Sugar Colonies* (1784). Samuel Romilly, whom Shelley mentions by name in the Carlile letter, had in 1818 introduced in discussions in Parliament specific instances of cruelty toward slaves, which the periodical press, including the *Examiner*, mentioned in their reports on parliamentary sessions. Romilly had referred to abolition already in 1807, in a letter to William Smith, as "that great act of natural justice"; see Roger Anstey, *The Atlantic Slave Trade and British Abolition, 1760–1810* (Atlantic Highlands, N.J.: Humanities Press, 1975), p. 401. See also Frank J. Klingberg, *The Anti-Slavery Movement in England* (New Haven: Yale University Press, 1926).

52. Even Wordsworth had lamented the unhappy paradox of England's leaguing itself against the forces of liberty, arguing as Blake had and as Shelley would that in both the American and the French revolutions England had been on the wrong side. See "Concerning the Relations of Great Britain, Spain, and Portugal, to Each Other, and to the Common Enemy, at this Crisis; and Specifically as Affected by the Convention of Cintra" (late 1808, published 1809), in *The Prose Works of William Wordsworth*, ed. Alexander B. Grosart, 3 vols. (London: Edward Moxon and Son, 1876), I, 135.

53. Grace Stuart, *Narcissus: A Psychological Study of Self-Love* (London: George Allen & Unwin, 1956), p. 17. The source of this aspect of the Narcissus story would seem to be the twenty-fourth of the historico-mythic narratives by the classical Greek mythographer, Conon. The tale was repeated by [St.] Photius I, Patriarch of Constantiople (ca. 820–ca. 891 A.D.), who compiled a great descriptive encyclopedia of Greek mythology. This variant on the Narcissus myth is detailed by William Smith, *Dictionary of Greek and Roman Biography and Mythology*, 3 vols. (Boston: Little, Brown, 1867), II, 1138, where Narcissus's own self-destruction is attributed as much to the torments of repentance as to those of self-love.

54. As Dawson remarks, the achievement of any total transformation of social life "depends on the ability to imagine an alternative" (*Unacknowledged Legislator*, p. 3).

55. Gerald McNiece, *Shelley and the Revolutionary Idea* (Cambridge, Mass.: Harvard University Press, 1969), p. 93. In his critical biography of Godwin, Peter H. Marshall likewise notes Shelley's adoption of the Godwinian notion of "piecemeal reform of existing institutions through gradual education and enlightenment"; see *William Godwin* (New Haven: Yale University Press, 1984), p. 334.

56. Foot, *Red Shelley*, p. 186; Cameron, *Shelley*, p. 142.

57. Robinson, *Shelley and Byron*, pp. 150–51, notes the similarity of Shelley's language and phrasing in this passage to that which he later employed in discussing Byron in his letters.

58. Holmes, *Shelley*, p. 585.

Chapter Seven

1. White, *Shelley*, II, 401.

2. Theodore Redpath, *The Young Romantics and Critical Opinion, 1807–1824* (London: Harrap, 1973), p. 361. For the sensitive, favorable review of *Prometheus Unbound and Other Poems* (published in September and October 1820), see *The Romantics Reviewed*, pt. C, II, 627–38.

3. Ibid., p. 361.

4. Trelawny, *Records*, I, 116.

5. Ibid., p. 118.

6. Gold, "Touring the Inventions," pp. 72ff. and passim.

7. See Scrivener, *Radical Shelley*, p. 287; and Cameron, *Shelley*, p. 381.

8. See Charles E. Robinson, "The Shelleys to Leigh Hunt: A New Letter of 5 April 1821," and "Shelley to the Editor of the *Morning Chronicle*: A Second New Letter of 5 April 1821," *Keats-Shelley Memorial Bulletin* 31 (1980): 52–56, and 32 (1981), 55–58. The translation is the "Cry of War to the Greeks" (Bodleian MS Shelley adds. c. 5).

9. See Wasserman, *Shelley*, p. 374.

10. The italics are Shelley's, an allusion to Satan's reference to God the Father, *Paradise Lost*, I, 257–58.

11. Trelawny, *Records*, I, 117; my italics.

12. In discussing the *Defence*, I have followed Reiman and Powers's corrected text, the most accurate presently available. Among recent discussions of the *Defence*, see especially that of Keach, *Shelley's Style*, chap. 1.

13. See the helpful discussion of the Jungian aspects of the Narcissus myth in Edward F. Edinger, *Ego and Archetype: Individuation and the Religious Function of the Psyche* (Baltimore: Penguin Books, 1973), esp. pp. 161–64.

14. *Complete Poems and Major Prose*, p. 694. The claim derives from Plato's *Republic* and *Laws* and from Renaissance commentaries by Italians like Tasso and Englishmen like Sidney.

15. *Complete Poetry and Prose*, p. 636; annotations to Reynolds's *Discourses on Art*.

16. The word is Shelley's (*Letters*, II, 275; 21 March 1821, to Peacock). Shelley had used analogous terminology to Peacock in December 1818 regarding *Childe Harold's Pilgrimage*, Canto IV.

17. See William H. Marshall, *Byron, Shelley, Hunt, and "The Liberal"* (Philadelphia: University of Pennsylvania Press, 1960), pp. 140–42.

18. Byron had made such a suggestion in December 1820, in a letter to Thomas Moore, and he apparently revived the idea in conversations with Shelley at Ravenna in August 1821, though he seems never to have had a great deal of enthusiasm for the project. See *British Literary Magazines: The Romantic Age, 1789–1836*, ed. Alvin Sullivan (Westport, Conn.: Greenwood Press, 1983), p. 221. Mary Shelley, too, attributes the idea to Byron (*Works*, 664).

19. Marshall, *Byron, Shelley, Hunt, and "The Liberal,"* pp. 48–49, 22.

20. Ibid., p. 74. See *Letters*, II, 407; 10 April 1822, to John Gisborne.

21. Marshall, *Byron, Shelley, Hunt, and "The Liberal,"* p. 23; *Letters*, II, 81; 25 February 1819.

22. *Examiner*, no. 767, 6 October 1822, p. 633.

23. As Marshall demonstrates, Byron's friends and acquaintances, including Thomas Moore, John Cam Hobhouse, Douglas Kinnaird, and John Murray, worked actively to undermine the *Liberal* and to ensure its failure; see Marshall, *Byron, Shelley, Hunt, and "The Liberal,"* pp. 39–68.

24. Walter Graham, *English Literary Periodicals* (New York: Thomas Nelson and Sons, 1930), p. 286.

25. Keach, *Shelley's Style*, pp. 205–6.

26. Keach's discussion of these lyrics casts valuable new light on Shelley's rhetorical maneuvering in the poems. As witty, complimentary poems, these lyrics have much in common with their Renaissance and post-Renaissance ancestors, though they focus on the characteristically Romantic (and Shelleyan) theme of the instability of happiness and of human relationships. See Keach, *Shelley's Style*, pp. 202–34.

27. Chernaik, *Lyrics of Shelley*, p. 257.

28. Jones sees in "Wilhelm Meister" a pun on Williams's name (*Letters*, II, 437n.).

29. McGann, *Social Values and Poetic Acts*, p. 85.

30. Stuart Curran, *"Adonais* in Context," in *Shelley Revalued*, ed. Everest, p. 170.

31. Ibid., p. 168.

32. Cronin, *Shelley's Poetic Thoughts*, pp. 38, 201, 223.

33. Cameron, *Shelley*, pp. 440, 422, identifies three levels: Urania's lament for Adonais, Shelley's elegy on Keats and his attack on the *Quarterly's* reviewer, and the "partly conscious and partly unconscious" projection of Shelley's own career and treatment by the reviewers into the myth he is himself constructing in his poem. Though my own division and descriptions of the poem's levels differ in their details from Cameron's, I agree in principle with his suggestions.

34. A note in Mary Shelley's hand at the end of the unfinished, unsigned draft, reads "This letter, I believe, was never sent" (*Letters*, II, 253).

35. Bodleian MS Shelley adds. e. 12, pp. 150–51a.

36. See, for instance, Cameron, *Shelley*, pp. 428–30, and "Shelley *vs.* Southey," as well as the biographies by White and Holmes. Shelley also suspected Henry Hart Milman, author of *Fazio* (1815) and an Eton and Oxford contemporary. The review was actually written by John Taylor Coleridge.

37. *Quarterly Review*, no. 21, April 1819, p. 471.

38. Edinger, *Ego and Archetype*, pp. 241–42.

39. Had Shelley and Byron discussed Cain before Byron composed his play, *Cain*, in the summer of 1821? Given their mutual interest in *Paradise Lost* and in both orthodox and radical views of the Fall and its consequences, it seems likely. Shelley must certainly have approved of the attack on orthodox religious doctrines articulated in Byron's play by Cain and Lucifer. When he read the play in manuscript, he pronounced it "second to nothing of the kind" (*Maria Gisborne and Edward E. Williams, Shelley's Friends: Their Journals and Letters*, ed. Frederick L. Jones [Norman: University of Oklahoma Press, 1951],

p. 109). To John Gisborne, Shelley wrote, "Cain is apocalyptic—it is a revelation not before communicated to man" (*Letters*, II, 388; 26 January 1822).

40. Edinger, *Ego and Archetype*, p. 162. See also Joseph Raben, "Shelley the Dionysian," in *Shelley Revalued*, ed. Everest, pp. 21–36.

41. Gustav Schwab, *Gods and Heroes: Myths and Epics of Ancient Greece*, trans. Olga Marx and Ernst Morwitz (1946; rpt. New York: Random House, 1974), p. 64. See also *Harper's Dictionary of Classical Literature and Antiquities*, ed. Harry Thurston Peck (New York: Cooper Square Publishers, 1965), pp. 524–25.

42. See Betty Radice, *Who's Who in the Ancient World* (Harmondsworth: Penguin Books, 1971), pp. 105–6.

43. *Harper's Dictionary*, p. 524.

44. The "Ode to the West Wind," with which *Adonais* shares a number of imagistic, mythological, and rhetorical associations, points toward this same Dionysian context in its treatment of images of defoliation.

45. As Anthony D. Knerr observes, apparently there was a great deal more draft material for this heavily revised poem (and its preface) than has survived; see Knerr, *Shelley's "Adonais": A Critical Edition* (New York: Columbia University Press, 1984), esp. pp. 11–19. Knerr explains that he has been assisted in completing his transcriptions of manuscript materials by technological aids such as ultraviolet and infrared light, as well as by previous transcriptions including Ingpen's in *Shelley in England* (1917), Garnett's in *Relics of Shelley* (1862), and the Ingpen-Peck version for the Julian edition (1926–30). Knerr is apparently occasionally misled by previous faulty readings to see what others have seen rather than what Shelley actually wrote, though, both in the drafts of the poem (where the sad state of the much reworked manuscripts make such errors understandable) and in those for the preface (where Shelley's writing is in most cases both clearer and less torturously revised). A new transcription and facsimile is in preparation for the Garland Press series supervised by Donald H. Reiman.

46. Knerr reads "demanded as its reward" (*Shelley's "Adonais"*, p. 195), which makes good sense; the manuscript suggests, however, that Shelley is still trying to construct a verb phrase beginning with "demanded."

47. Knerr reads "insolent" (*Shelley's "Adonais"*, p. 195).

48. An uncertain reading; I adopt Knerr's "vexes" as a contextually sensible reading, though the word in the manuscript looks very much like "urges."

49. Knerr reads "vulnerable being" (*Shelley's "Adonais"*, p. 201).

50. Bodleian MS Shelley adds. c. 4, ff. 179r–v. An altered and presumably later version of the poem is transcribed in Mary Shelley's hand in MS Shelley adds. d. 7, pp. 100–101. Curiously, the poem seems not to have been published. The presence of draft material for Shelley's fourth note to *Hellas* in the notebook containing the draft of the serpent and mastiff poem suggests that it dates from 1821.

51. Gertrude Grace Sill, *A Handbook of Symbols in Christian Art* (New York: Collier Books, 1975), p. 19.

52. Bodleian MS Shelley adds. d. 7, p. 101.

53. Jones, *Letters*, II, 309n., suggests that either Shelley sent Byron a ver-

sion that still contained some subsequently removed passages or he was referring to the "calumniator" passage.

54. See *Letters*, II, 203–5, 230–33; 26 June, 17 August 1820); and *SC*, VI, 931–33.

55. Edinger, *Ego and Archetype*, p. 150.

56. Ian Jack, *The Poet and His Audience* (Cambridge: Cambridge University Press, 1984), p. 113.

INDEX

—Works: *Cain*, 285–86 n.53; *Childe Harold's Pilgrimage*, 17, 100, 107, 170–71, 191, 218–19, 284 n.16; *Don Juan*, 170; *Manfred*, 17, 42, 169–71, 265 n.5; "The Prisoner of Chillon," 19, 204; "Prometheus," 169–71, 191

Cameron, Kenneth Neill, 53, 59, 212, 270 n.18, 25, 28, 271 n.41, 46, 272 n.4, 5, 274 n.16, 275 n.32, 276 n.32, 279 n.52, 282 n.39, 285 n.33, 36
Carlile, Richard, 50, 84, 89, 163, 187–90, 202, 206–15, 233, 272 n.2, 282 n.43
Carlyle, Thomas, 71, 216
Caroline, Queen, 205–6
Carpenter and Son (publishers), 101
Cartwright, John, 119
Castlereagh, Lord, 198, 205
Charles I, 148
Charlotte, Princess, 33–37
Chaucer, Geoffrey, 213, 261
Cicero, 66, 125
Clairmont, Claire, 11, 94, 146, 172–73, 234, 243, 249
Clarke, William, 81–86
Clement VIII, Pope, 150
Cobbett, William, 25, 28, 36, 65, 77, 163, 188–89
Coleridge, John Taylor, 285 n.36
Coleridge, Samuel Taylor, 11, 22, 33, 44, 56, 93, 101–2, 115, 118, 140, 169, 180–81, 205, 223, 276 n.42
—Works: *Biographia Literaria*, 180–81, 280 n.63; "Christabel," 155, 258; *Conciones ad Populum*, 33, 36, 205; "Kubla Khan," 3, 101, 273 n.30; *Remorse*, 145, 147; *The Statesman's Manual*, 33, 267 n.18
Constable, John, 159
Critical Review and Annals of Literature, 94, 97–98
Croker, John Wilson, 250
Cronin, Richard, 1, 175, 247, 274 n.5, 276 n.42
Cruikshank, George, 202
Cruikshank, Isaac, 202
Curran, Amelia, 146, 150
Curran, Stuart, 113, 201, 246, 277 n.7

Dante Alighieri, 105, 165, 169, 213, 230, 259
Darwin, Erasmus, 88

Davies, Scrope, 107
Dawson, P. M. S., 24, 267 n.7, 271 n.38, 274 n.16, 275 n.32, 276 n.32, 277 n.5, 282 n.34, 283 n.54
Defoe, Daniel: *Moll Flanders*, 42
Dickens, Charles, 149, 239
Dionysus, 252–54, 286 n.44
Drake, Henry, 93
Drummond, Sir William, 141, 210
Dryden, John, 169, 260

Eaton, Daniel Isaac, 54, 60, 65, 74–80, 84, 112, 188, 204, 206–10, 233, 271 n.41
Eco, Umberto, 6
Edinger, Edwin, 260, 284 n.13
Eldon, Lord, 85, 205
Ellenborough, Lord, 74
Ellul, Jacques, 271 n.50
Erickson, Lee, 179
Euripides, 169
Examiner, 30, 34–36, 51, 60, 81–86, 127–28, 131–32, 188–90, 199–200, 206–9, 218, 220, 232, 242, 278 n.23, 280 n.5, 283 n.51

Farrell, John, 197
Finnerty, Peter, 51–53
Fletcher, John, 169
Forsyth, Robert: *Principles of Moral Science*, 197–98, 279 n.43
Foucault, Michel, 136–37
Fox, Charles James, 30, 202
Freeman, John, 269 n.13
Freistat, Neil, 273 n.25
Fuseli, Henry, 269 n.5

Galignani's Messenger, 278 n.23
George III, 133, 270 n.28
Gibbon, Edward, 210
Gifford, William, 107, 250–52
Gillray, James, 201–2
Gisborne, John, 9, 11, 85–86, 146, 162, 203, 205, 229–30, 233–34, 239–40, 246, 249, 265 n.3, 286 n.39
Gisborne, Maria, 146, 203, 205, 229, 246
Godwin, William, 20, 30–32, 48, 51, 60–64, 69, 74–80, 88, 119, 127–31, 160, 197, 210, 212, 223, 229, 276 n.42, 283 n.55
—Works: *Caleb Williams*, 40, 51, 127–29, 151, 156; *Essay on Sepulchres*, 34,